I0112926

LHA YUDIT'IH

WE ALWAYS FIND A WAY

Bringing the Tŝilhqot'in Title Case Home

LORRAINE WEIR

with

CHIEF ROGER WILLIAM

and contributions by

Elders Mabel Solomon xinli, Cecile William xinli,
Martin Quilt xinli, Ivor Deneway Myers xinli,
and forty-one Xeni Gwet'ins, Tŝilhqot'ins, and Allies

All royalties from this book will be donated to
Lha Yudit'ih Seniya Tŝilhqot'in Ch'ish Yats'elhtig Qa
The Lha Yudit'ih Fund for Tŝilhqot'in Language,
Xeni Gwet'in First Nation.

Talonbooks

T
J

© 2023 Xeni Gwet'in First Nation
Text by Lorraine Weir © 2023

All royalties from this book will be donated to Lha Yudit'ih Seniya Tŝilhqot'in Ch'ish Yats'elhtig Qa The Lha Yudit'ih Fund for Tŝilhqot'in Language, Xeni Gwet'in First Nation.

All rights reserved. No part of this book may be reproduced, stored in a retrieval system, or transmitted, in any form or by any means, without the prior written consent of the publisher or a licence from Access Copyright (the Canadian Copyright Licensing Agency). For a copyright licence, visit accesscopyright.ca or call toll-free 1-800-893-5777.

Talonbooks
9259 Shaughnessy Street, Vancouver, British Columbia, Canada V6P 6R4
talonbooks.com

Talonbooks is located on xʷməθkʷəy̓əm, Sḵwx̱wú7mesh, and səlilwətaɬ Lands.

First printing: 2023

Typeset in Minion
Printed and bound in Canada on 100% post-consumer recycled paper

Interior and cover design by Leslie Smith
Cover photograph by Chief Roger William

Talonbooks acknowledges the financial support of the Canada Council for the Arts, the Government of Canada through the Canada Book Fund, and the Province of British Columbia through the British Columbia Arts Council and the Book Publishing Tax Credit.

Canada   Canada Council   Conseil des arts   BRITISH   BRITISH COLUMBIA
          for the Arts   du Canada   COLUMBIA   ARTS COUNCIL
                                                              An agency of the Province of British Columbia

Library and Archives Canada Cataloguing in Publication

Title: Lha yudit'ih = We always find a way : bringing the Tŝilhqot'in title case home / Lorraine Weir with Chief Roger William ; & contributions by Elders Mabel Solomon xinli, Cecile William xinli, Martin Quilt xinli, Ivor Deneway Myers xinli, and forty-one Xeni Gwet'ins, Tŝilhqot'ins, and allies.

Other titles: Lha yudit'ih we always find a way | We always find a way | Bringing the Tŝilhqot'in title case home

Names: Weir, Lorraine, author. | William, Roger, author.

Description: Includes bibliographical references and index. | Text in English. Some text in Tŝilhqot'in with English translation.

Identifiers: Canadiana 20230483461 | ISBN 9781772013825 (softcover)

Subjects: LCSH: Tsilhqot'in National Government. | CSH: First Nations—British Columbia—History. | CSH: First Nations—British Columbia—Land claims. | CSH: First Nations—British Columbia—Social conditions. | CSH: First Nations—British Columbia—Social life and customs.

Classification: LCC E99.T78 W45 2023 | DDC 971.1/75—dc23

Ivor Deneway Myers xinli binaghilni

We remember the late Ivor Deneway Myers

You know, you could probably write a book
of stories – stories that you live in.

—Chief Roger William (Xeni Gwet'in)

What happens to people and what happens
to the land is the same thing.

—Linda Hogan (Chickasaw)

We do not speak for the Tŝilhqot'in National Government (TNG) or the Chiefs of the other five Tŝilhqot'in communities. As Plaintiff in the Title case and as a member of the Xeni Gwet'in community, Chief Roger William tells the story he was part of until victory in the Supreme Court of Canada (2014) and the negotiation of the Nenqay Deni Accord (2016–2018). The opinions expressed in this book are those of each of the contributors.

Contents

Chapter 9: Nen gagunlhchugh deni nidlin We live all over this land

Protecting the Nen

Nen the Land

Nenqayni deni The People

Baskets Are ʔEsggidam Ancestors

Chapter 10: Teẑtan Biny Fish Lake and the (New) Prosperity Mine

Nenqay gagunlhchugh
All the beings of the earth:

Raising our hands

Chief Roger William and Lorraine Weir

Roger: What's a "land acknowledgment"?

Lorraine: Is it what ʔInkwel Eileen your mom says when she opens a community event?

Roger: She does prayers that acknowledge Creator, Land, water, and so on. One of our prayers and drumsongs talks about Nenqay gagunlhchugh, meaning the earth and all its resources, like water, wildlife, fish, people – all the beings of the earth. We burn sage and juniper back into the Land and cremate the body back into the Land. We begin many events with a prayer and sometimes with a drumsong.

Lorraine: The way Gilbert Solomon did when he spoke at the beginning of the thirtieth anniversary celebration of the roadblock at Henry's Crossing?

Roger: Yup.

Lorraine: Okay, then we should start our book with Gilbert's prayer.

Roger: Yup.

Lorraine: I also want to acknowledge that I've been an uninvited guest on the Land of the hǝn̓q̓ǝmin̓ǝm̓-speaking xʷmǝθkʷǝy̓ǝm People for all of my years teaching at the University of British Columbia in Vancouver. I raise my hands in respect and honour to all of my hǝn̓q̓ǝmin̓ǝm̓ language teachers at xʷmǝθkʷǝy̓ǝm and I especially want to thank sʔǝy̓ǝɬǝq Elder Larry Grant, sχɬemtǝna:t Audrey

Siegl, and the late Terry Point. seʔcsəm cən niʔ ʔə tə ɬwələp. c̓əy̓ətala si:y̓ém̓. hay ce:p q̓ə, si:y̓ém̓. You prepared me well for this journey.

Lha yudit'ih was written near qʷeyaʔχʷ, at the delta of stal̓əw̓, known in Tŝilhqot'in as ʔElhdaqox, Sturgeon River, where c̓əc̓iʔq̓ən̓ Mink made his way upstream and Lhuy diyenẑ Salmon Boy swam out to salt water.

Born in Tiohtià:ke Montréal, Lorraine Weir is a settler scholar and oral historian, descendant of displaced Celts from An Gorta Mór the Irish Famine and the Highland Clearances. She grew up on unceded Kanien'kehá:ka Territory at the gathering place known as Tiohtià:ke Montréal, and on the Ancestral Homelands of the Beothuk on the island known as Ktaqmkuk Newfoundland, in St. John's, on the Traditional Territories of the Mi'kmaq and Beothuk. Weir is Emeritus Professor of Indigenous Studies in the Department of English Language and Literatures at the University of British Columbia, Vancouver, on the unceded, Ancestral, and Traditional Territory of the hən̓q̓əmin̓əm̓-speaking xʷməθkʷəy̓əm People.

The Last Green Place

Gilbert Solomon, Xeni Gwet'in [*]

A while ago we start seeing more moose coming in and more mosquitoes, more animals showing up at our area. We finally realized they were refugees from out there, you know. They were coming in.

We had the last green part of BC here. That's why, if you go up to the satellite and look down on the earth, you'll see this spot. Green. So that's how we knew that they were refugees. All of a sudden, lots of moose.

I used to tease the people that these animals roadblock me over here, going back to Nemiah from here, that way. I'd tell 'em that they were talking to me, saying that this was the last place, and don't wreck it. We're refugees from over there, you know.

Anyways, we start calling in, how do you say, outside help, help from the other side.

We start singin'. We were being taught by our aunties and uncles. They knew, they still knew these songs, these sacred songs for what we have.

So I wanna honour you all and everything here on Mother Earth and sing a song.

---

[*] Gilbert Solomon testified at trial for seven days and prepared two affidavits. He worked as an interpreter for the Elders during interviews with the lawyers and transcribed taped interviews. He is one of the founders of Ts'utanchuny Dadabeni Medicine Camp, with Edmund Faubert, David Faubert, and Juanita Cervantes, and testified about the Medicine Camp in court. "The Last Green Place" is from a speech made by Gilbert at the thirtieth anniversary, on August 23, 2019, of Nenduwh jid guẑit'in the Declaration, Brittany Gathering, Henry's Crossing. Weaving humour through ancient and contemporary teachings about the Nen Land and the responsibility of Nenqayni deni the People not to "wreck it," Gilbert calls on all the "aunties and uncles" in the spirit world for help in this prayer.

K'etsish Sheep Creek, crossing ʔElhdaqox the Fraser River to the Tŝilhqot'in Plateau. Photo by Chief Roger William

"Lha yudit'ih": On the Title

People say that the Tŝilhqot'in have always had it hard in a way, and even the saying "Lha yudit'ih," the need to persevere, it's something that keeps coming back. I heard from an Elder whose grandmother told her, "No matter what, Nenqayni [Tŝilhqot'in People] always find a way." So I see that as another layer of hard work or determination – all the things that you need to do to keep living by. We're inspired by our values, and that challenges us to express them and to fight for them. All the stuff that could've happened should've happened, but you have to be in the fight for the long haul, no matter what.

—NITS'ILʔIN RUSSELL MYERS ROSS (Yuneŝit'in) *

"Lha yudit'ih": literally, "We don't give up." There's all the sacrifices.

—CHIEF ROGER WILLIAM (Xeni Gwet'in)

---

*   Throughout this book, the name of each Tŝilhqot'in contributor is followed by the name of their Tŝilhqot'in community in parentheses. Thus Nits'ilʔin [Chief] Myers's surname is followed by "Yuneŝit'in," his community. The only exception to this practice is the name of Chief Roger William, whose community, Xeni Gwet'in, is specified on this page but not elsewhere in this book, given his role as collaborator and as Plaintiff in the Title case.

Note on Pronunciation and Orthography

for non-Tŝilhqot'in speakers

Tŝilhqot'in orthography is largely phonemic. Readers familiar with the American Phonetic Alphabet (APA) will recognize the digraph *lh* in the first word of this book's title as the voiceless alveolar lateral fricative [ɬ] (noted [ɬ] in the International Phonetic Alphabet, or IPA, and sometimes called the "slurpy-*l* sound"). The word *yudit* is pronounced "YOO-dit," as spelled, but the following suffix *-ih* sounds a bit like the German pronoun *ich*, where *-ch* represents the voiceless palatal fricative [ç] (sometimes called the "soft *ch*"). In addition, Tŝilhqot'in is a tonal language using two tones, high and low. The first and last syllables of the phrase ***lha yudit'ih*** are both heavily stressed, and there's a rising tone on the final *-ih*. It's simpler than it looks if you practise a bit!

More information on the Tŝilhqot'in language can be found on the Tŝilhqot'in (Xeni Gwet'in) home page of the First Voices website (www.firstvoices.com) and in the free Xeni Gwet'in language app, a media-rich bilingual dictionary and phrase book produced by the First Peoples' Heritage Language and Culture Council. The Tŝilhqot'in language is more properly called Nenqayni Ch'ih, in which *Nen* means "land, earth," *qay* "surface," *[de]ni* "people," and *ch'ih* "way": the People of the surface of the earth's way. See also chapter 9 in this book.

Lha yudit'ih We Always Find a Way

Introduction

Lorraine Weir

This book is a cross-cultural conversation. It began in August 2012 when then-Councillor Roger William and I first met and has continued for the past ten years as a collaboration for which we both take responsibility, though our contributions have been very different. The way we summarize it is that without Chief Roger's work over a quarter-century, there would be no Title case, and without mine over the past decade, there would be no book. Our division of labour for the book was simple: I did all the interviews, transcriptions, editing and writing, book preparation, and working with our publisher. Chief Roger recorded sixteen lengthy interviews, which are the core of this book, was fully involved as a reader and fact-checker of his own portion of the book, and, when all of the work on the other contributors' excerpts had been completed, read the whole draft and commented again. Through the months I have worked with our publisher, Chief Roger and I have continued our conversation about the process and have discussed revisions and questions as they have arisen. Most of the editorial work and manuscript preparation have taken place with me in Vancouver and Chief Roger in Xeni, but nisdẑun night-owl conversations on Messenger have kept us in touch throughout the process. Every effort has been made to ensure accuracy and proper attribution of material throughout this book. If any errors have inadvertently been made, we apologize and request that we be contacted so corrections can be made in future printings of this book.

Several months after we first met, Chief Roger was elected to his fifth term as Chief.[1] On May 30, 2013, he presented the book project for the first time at a Xeni Gwet'in General Assembly, and on September 26, 2013, he formally introduced me at a second Assembly during which I gave an initial presentation. He followed up with introductions at a couple of annual Brittany Gatherings at Henry's Crossing, as well as during Canadian Environmental Assessment Agency (CEAA) panel hearing sessions in each community during June 2013. By invitation, I also presented on this and related projects[2] at a meeting of the Chiefs of the Tŝilhqot'in National Government (TNG) in Vancouver on September 25, 2015, and maintained contact with TNG Counsel Jay Nelson throughout the years of my work with Chief Roger. When we sent the completed manuscript to our publisher, we also made it available to then-Chief Jimmy Lulua and Council of Xeni Gwet'in First Nations Government for their comments. During the final stages of production of *Lha yudit'ih*, Roger was elected Chief for a sixth term.

Early in our interviews, I asked Chief Roger for a "job description" for myself so expectations and responsibilities would be clear from the beginning. In a nutshell, Chief Roger understood the Title case in terms of his role as Plaintiff. Many Elders and other Tŝilhqot'in witnesses went to court in Victoria, BC, to tell their story and keep their Land from being clearcut and mined. They sought a decision from the settler court which would affirm Tŝilhqot'in control of their own Land, which had never been ceded to anyone and for which they and their Ancestors had fought the Tŝilhqot'in War (1864). What Chief Roger wanted was to have the story of the Title case brought back home by a midugh, a settler, as an act of restorative justice demonstrating that their stories had been heard and understood. He didn't want a settler legal analysis – there was no lack of lawyers and legal scholars to do that work. He wanted to tell his own story of the Title case and the reasons for it, reaching back to the first illegal incursions by settlers onto Tŝilhqot'in Land and the colonial genocide of smallpox, the Tŝilhqot'in War, residential schools, and the ceaseless violations of the Land by clearcut logging and the threat of open-pit mining. Later in our project, Chief Roger wanted his community members, Xeni Gwet'ins and other Tŝilhqot'ins and allies involved in the case, to have the opportunity to record their words if they chose to do so. As far as we know, everyone in Xeni who wished to contribute did so. We apologize to anyone who was inadvertently left out.

That was the task I undertook, and I proposed to fund it as best I could with academic grants. We had no other funding, and my only remuneration was my University of British Columbia (UBC) salary until I retired to complete the book during the last two years of our project. The impact of this challenge on a project of such scope and scale was considerable, including the fact that our primary focus on Xeni Gwet'in became a practical necessity. Since none of the contributors received any remuneration for recording their stories, they truly spoke from the heart with no thought of any payment as this was explained to them from the beginning. We also explained that any royalties that Chief Roger and I may earn from the book will be donated to Lha Yudit'ih Seniya Tŝilhqot'in Ch'ish Yats'elhtig Qa – The Lha Yudit'ih Fund for Tŝilhqot'in Language, Xeni Gwet'in First Nation.

Chief Roger was clear from the beginning of the project that he wanted our book to communicate with everyone, whether Indigenous or non-Indigenous, who was interested in hearing the story of Xeni Gwet'ins and Tŝilhqot'ins who had fought to protect their Land and their way of life through the Title case. He wanted to share the story of how he and his community had undertaken this monumental task so that others could learn from it and draw inspiration from their victory. When I asked why he hadn't chosen a Tŝilhqot'in person for the book, Chief Roger answered that few had time or resources to undertake such a task and that it required skills which, given my interest in and knowledge of the case, together with my academic background, I probably had. There was also an element of a test associated with inviting a midugh woman to take on the task of putting together the Title case book, and this was particularly evident when after a year of training me in the details of the story via a rigourous schedule of interviews, Roger announced that it was now time for me to interview in the community. I was completely on my own to choose interviewees and make arrangements for recording. As a result, the selection of interviewees in *Lha yudit'ih* reflects my choices, people's availability and consent, and the vagaries of the moment. There was no political interference whatsoever by Chief Roger during that process, and he was scrupulously respectful of people's contributions when he read them for the first time during manuscript preparation.

Chief Roger's choice of an academic outsider also was, and is, an expression of his deeply held belief in the transformative power of education, both in the sense of my capacity to learn and of the importance of sharing these stories widely by sending them out with a messenger from outside, working mainly in English, and working with a publisher which has national and international distribution. Throughout the years of this project, my teachers have been generous, knowledgeable, and kind, and I have done my best to take good care of their words, holding them up to the highest honour and respect which they deserve. Many of the great knowledge holders and storytellers who recorded for this book have now gone to the spirit world, and I am privileged not only to have interviewed them, but also to have lived with their voices and their words for all the years of this project.

How This Book Is Organized

Lha yudit'ih is structured in a loosely chronological way following the trajectory of the Title case from its beginnings to victory in the Supreme Court of Canada and the first agreement emerging from that victory, the 2016 Nenqay Deni

Accord. The main through-line of the narrative is by the Plaintiff, Chief Roger William, who has devoted twenty-five years of his life to the case. To give some sense of how that came to be, we recorded Chief Roger's stories of growing up Xeni Gwet'in and of his years as a champion mountainracer and bullrider. In the analogy I used to describe the book to contributors, Chief Roger's narrative is like the spine of a salmon, while the narratives by all other contributors are like its lateral bones and fins. For the most part, these narratives are organized thematically in relation to the overall structure of the book. Together, all of these stories comprise this community history of the Title case, though very few of the community members who recorded chose to discuss the case in terms of settler law. Their contributions are rich in knowledge of Dechen ts'edilhtan Tŝilhqot'in law and Tŝilhqot'in ways of living and being that are at the heart of the case.

Tŝilhqot'in and English

Where a contributor recorded in the Tŝilhqot'in[3] language or included words in that language in their narrative, Tŝilhqot'in is presented first wherever possible, and is followed by an English translation. I have not adhered to the convention of separating one language from the other with parentheses or of italicizing words in Tŝilhqot'in, preferring to stand both languages up as equals in a book which is written mostly in English but priorizes Tŝilhqot'in history, culture, and language. Each transcriber and translator who contributed to this book relied on the Tŝilhqot'in orthography that was familiar to them, representing sounds as they heard them, registering dialect variations and individual speaker preferences, and reflecting different approaches to the printed representation of the Tŝilhqot'in language, which remains primarily an oral medium for many fluent speakers, especially Elders. We are grateful to all of the translators who contributed to *Lha yudit'ih* and to community interviews: Dinah Lulua, Dorrine Lulua, Margaret Lulua, Maria Myers, Linda R. Smith, Maryann Solomon, June Williams, and Lois Williams. This book would have been impossible without their work.

Many writers working with the translation of materials from Dene languages like Tŝilhqot'in into English have discussed the challenges of rendering very different strategies for expressing time as well as for sequencing narrative elements. A glance at Elder Henry Solomon's story Seʔintsu My Grandmother will give some idea of the challenge when comparing the morphological translation (which preserves the storyteller's Tŝilhqot'in syntax) with the English version. Linguist Eung-Do Cook writes in his authoritative *Tsilhqút'ín Grammar* that in comparison with the ways verbs function in English, "there is no tense in Tsilhqút'ín and probably in other Athabaskan languages as well," but there is a "rich inventory of aspects," which "enable complex expressions of time."[4] Like the rich inventory of spatial indicators, the complexity of expressions of time poses challenges for modern English which has lost most of its repertoire of such indicators. In her classic 1991 study, *Life Lived like a Story: Life Stories of Three Yukon Native Elders*, ethnographer Julie Cruikshank addressed questions of sequencing in terms of syntactic challenges by "reorder[ing] the sequence if it clarifies the meaning [and] standardiz[ing] subject–verb agreement where there is ambiguity." I've followed her methodology wherever required for clarity in editing our contributors' excerpts in this book. As mentioned earlier in relation to Chief Roger's story, I've also followed Cruikshank's practice of bringing "together materials recorded in ... different sessions and [in some cases] over ... [several] years as one continuous narrative."[5]

Cruikshank notes also that "speakers of Athapaskan [Dene] languages frequently remark that their language and English are 'backwards'"[6] in relation to each other, a concern not uncommon among Tŝilhqot'ins who grew up in their own language. The first time I heard that "English is a 'backwards' language" was from one of the Tŝilhqot'in translators who had assisted the court during the Title case trial, and it wasn't the last. Not surprisingly, the sense of English being backwards also contributes to a perception of the trickiness of English-speakers, as well as to syntactic complexity in the colloquial English of many Tŝilhqot'in speakers. As Roger says, "English is a very strange language." An additional challenge is posed by the fact that Tŝilhqot'in is a polysynthetic language. One of our translators, Lois Williams, explains that this "means the words are very long. There's a story within the sentence, so [it will make more sense] once it's broken down and you start to understand the words and the larger pieces." Although James Joyce played with the polysynthetic past and potential of English in *Finnegans Wake*, few translators would see it as an option now and other strategies must be used to convey such compressed meaning. Summarizing many of these issues, Roger notes that when he translates from one language to the other, "I'm not gonna worry about word for word, because it's impossible." However, every effort has been made in this book to convey the cadence and nuance of each contributor's speech and to reject colonization by so-called standard English.

Stats and Methodology

Of the forty-eight people whose words were recorded, forty-three were Tŝilhqot'ins, five were Allies, and a total of sixty-one interviews were logged. Between August 11, 2013, and February 2, 2017, Chief Roger recorded sixteen interviews, plus three recordings at public events. Community interviews usually happened on the fly at gatherings, though most of the interviews with Elders were made by prior arrangement with translators or helpers. Between September 21 and 24, 2016, fifteen Elders and community members made the trip from Xeni to Vancouver to be with their Tŝilhqot'in belongings at the Museum of Anthropology at UBC (MOA) and to record their knowledge as part of our project. Between May 14 and 20, 2017, Maria Myers came to the BC Breath of Life Archival Institute for First Nations Language at UBC to work with me and student assistant Ben Chung on Elder Henry Solomon xinli's story Seʔintsu My Grandmother and to teach us about all things Tŝilhqot'in.

Transcripts of Chief Roger's interviews comprise some five thousand pages. Transcripts of interviews with all the other contributors run to almost the same length. I did all of the transcribing except for the extract from Roger's talk in the Musqueam 101 speaker series which begins the book. Transcribing, editing and excerpting took almost five years, interspersed with more visits and recordings, and reduced the amount of material by roughly half. As I worked with thematic groupings, subtitles, and timelines taken from Chief Roger's interviews, the basic structure of his contribution to *Lha yudit'ih* began to emerge. Using the same process with all of the other interviews expanded the number of categories and produced a parallel draft. Cross-referencing from Chief Roger's draft to the parallel draft created the beginnings of a chronological structure which would provide a clear path for the reader, while allowing related stories and types of knowledge to be grouped together. Grouping most of the teachings on Dechen ts'edilhtan Tŝilhqot'in law in one chapter served to ground the whole book in those teachings, which are the foundation of the Title case in terms of Tŝilhqot'in Traditional Knowledge, and also enabled the inclusion of a wide range of contributions which would not otherwise have fitted the storyline of the book, while also creating the only chapter in which Chief Roger's narrative doesn't serve as the anchor.

For readers interested in the details of our process for this book, it may be helpful to provide a snapshot focused on Chief Roger's interviews. We were in catch-up mode at the beginning of the project in June 2013, and our first interview lasted almost five hours, during which Chief Roger rushed to provide a lot of information covering many years of the Title case. We began in Xeni during the CEAA panel hearing's visits to the six Tŝilhqot'in communities and followed up first in Yuneŝit'in, and then in Tl'esqox the day after CEAA's site visit to Teẑtan Biny Fish Lake. Before any transcript was available from CEAA, I asked Chief Roger to tell me about that day, and we were fortunate to be recording at night when it was possible for him to tell me the great creation story known as Lhin Desch'osh. Chief Roger's story of his childhood and his involvement in mountainracing was told much later in the sequence of interviews, on an evening when we were less rushed to record the political developments of that day. Five months later, the Supreme Court of Canada hearing took place in Ottawa, and we recorded during the lead-up and afterward, at a time when the decision hadn't been handed down and speculation about the outcome was rife. I had attended the hearing and asked Chief Roger about his experience. He responded with a description of his preparation for the big day and his feelings when it was all happening. Then, in June 2014, the decision came down, and the story took another leap forward. Since Chief Roger's meeting and travelling schedule provided our interview schedule, we seized opportunities whenever he was in the Vancouver area to meet, regardless of where we were in the Title case story. When the xʷməθkʷəy̓əm and UBC organizers of the Musqueam 101 speaker series invited Roger to come and talk about the Title case, I recorded his introduction, and that became the beginning of this book. By the time we'd completed most of Chief Roger's interviews, I had assembled thousands of pages of transcripts, producing a narrative which, in order to be comprehensible, was in need of a timeline and sequencing. The process of sequencing by topic and chronology lifted materials out of individual interviews and began to create access points in the narrative so the reader could gain a foothold. Sequencing also addressed the challenges of the chaotic timeline and simultaneous reflections on events past and present which characterized many of the interviews. As most interviews included a good deal of conversational back and forth which took a lot of space and would have tried the patience of many readers, the editing process also involved the removal of most signs of those interchanges, reducing the volume of material from thousands of pages to hundreds. Editing thus served to focus each contribution and to reveal stories in their power and elegance on the page.

The consent and corrections process happened in two stages, beginning with Chief Roger's materials going to him for a careful read and flagging of changes needed. Because the same topics looped through interviews recorded months or years apart, I had to make decisions about how to sequence topics which were evolving across the time of the project, and this often required intricate work with verb tenses in order to create a comprehensible narrative. Working this through together was a complicated process, and overall the creation of Chief Roger's part of the book took almost a year. Then it was time to work with excerpts from other contributors' edited interviews, organized by topic so that some materials could be collated into Chief Roger's draft. Other excerpts took the narrative in different directions, and chapters needed to be reorganized many times in order to produce a fairly seamless sequence. After another year, I had a complete draft of the book without what was to become the "Nen" chapter. After that chapter was put together, the last half of the book was completely reorganized around it. Finally, we had a complete draft, which Chief Roger carefully reviewed, reading other contributors' materials for the first time.

Then it was time for the rest of our contributors to engage the consent process. This was complicated by the COVID-19 pandemic and the resulting community lockdowns. Each contributor's excerpts were gathered into a digital file ready to be sent as an attachment via Messenger or email, often preceded by a Facebook exchange. Facebook is still part of everyday life in many rural rez communities and is widely used to connect distant family members. It served our purpose well. Family members also put the word out for others who were less likely to go online, and in some cases, Chief Roger went visiting with printed copies of excerpts so they could be reviewed in person with the interviewees. Where Elders had recorded with a family member as translator, that person reviewed their contribution. In a couple of cases, translators who had not been present for the recording, but were family members and served as that Elder's representatives, were the ones who reviewed that material. The same process was used for photographs included in this book, and it should be noted that, in Tŝilhqot'in protocol, there is no prohibition against publishing photographs of the deceased.

As for corrections, I had phone and video-chat conversations with some contributors, and Chief Roger made corrections on printouts and sent them to me as photos. Several people scheduled detailed conversations with me in order to make sure I had understood what they'd said in their excerpts. One person added more information to their contribution, while another included an update. Several people found their spoken English too colloquial and wanted to "fix" it, which we did. Three people were so happy with their materials that they wanted to record a lot more but were encouraged to wait for another opportunity. One person scheduled a FaceTime meeting and proceeded to record a new story, while commenting on the one already recorded. I sent corrected excerpts back for approval and consent, and Chief Roger went visiting with a couple of them. Slowly, the process was done, and we did another complete review. I added photographs, and Chief Roger and I spent hours on Messenger crafting captions. Maryann Solomon helped with last-minute translation requests as we fact-checked and prepared to send the draft off to our patient publisher, who had hoped to receive it two years earlier. Of the forty-eight people who had recorded, five Tŝilhqot'ins chose not to give consent, one interview wasn't used (as it was judged to be off topic in relation to the book as it came to be), and one interviewee chose not to record at length due to a health concern. While *Lha yudit'ih* records the story of the Title case from the point of view of the Plaintiff and of the community where it originated, the story has continued to evolve since 2016–2017, when our narrative ends, and some contributors may have found in 2022 that they no longer supported the views which they'd recorded years earlier. We are grateful for their contributions to the project nonetheless.

Recording Gwenig Stories

Lha yudit'ih is not only a book of gwenig stories but of teachings about them and their classification, particularly in terms of time. For example, Chief Roger teaches that sadanx gwenig are stories "of long, long ago," the time when the Land was created. Yedanx gwenig are stories of a more recent past, and digudanx gwenig are stories told during the time when midugh settlers started coming in. Elder Minnie Charleyboy speaks of yedanx denilin, "long-time-ago people." Further back are ʔEsggidam yedanx denilin, from even longer ago than the gwenig stories of yedanx denilin. For Minnie Charleyboy, sadanx refers to a time "when our Ancestors were like animals." Ivor Deneway Myers xinli taught that sadanx gwenig are stories from "before" (-danx) the beginning of the "sun" (sa), when Datsan chugh Raven spoke in darkness. Gwenig is a participle in need of a pronoun to tell the story. Gwenig stories come to life as they are told by a storyteller. Gwenig are true. As Chief Roger says, "I really believe it happened." In Elder Henry Solomon's story Seʔintsu My Grandmother, the stylistic characteristics, language, and tone of a sadanx gwenig are mobilized to tell of more recent events like the smallpox genocide and the survival of Galín and ʔImili. To use an analogy from Shakespeare, this is like telling the story of the War in Ukraine through the cadences and rhetoric of *King Lear*. Thus gwenig are not static. As Tŝilhqot'in scholar Linda R. Smith (Yuneŝit'in) writes, "storytellers rearrange scenes, delete and shorten some, others they elaborate on as they tell their stories. Storytellers use voice and expressions to effectively validate the authenticity of their stories and also to give their stories meaning."[7]

Oral history may be understood in similar ways. The Italian oral historian Alessandro Portelli maintains that "the interview is, ultimately, a form of dialogue," and that "the root meaning of the word *dialogue* is 'to speak across,' 'to speak beyond.'" Echoing the terms of Chief Roger's job description for me and for this project, Portelli stresses that "the reason we are seeking the interview is because we are different," though it "couldn't happen without some common ground, if only a common language, or the mutual willingness to meet and talk. But what the interview is about is the distance we have to cross in order to speak to each other."[8] Bringing the Title case home is about attempting to cross that distance between worlds, one story after another, so we, non-Indigenous and Indigenous Peoples in this country called Canada, might communicate with each other.

So I prefer the term recording to interviewing, and I understand recording as a shared process rather than, as often understood by social scientists, a set of scripted questions with goals predetermined by the interviewer and preauthorized by anonymous adjudicators of grant applications. This latter approach, which Portelli classifies as positivist, not only restricts what can be asked but also much of what can be said in response. It precludes any element of personal connection between the two people involved and, by stipulating anonymity, seeks to inhibit or even prevent the proud sharing of their own experiences characteristic of the contributors to this book. The positivist approach also seeks to inhibit or prevent the dialogue that Portelli sees as fundamental to the interview as a process of sharing. While we are together creating a digital sound file, we are recording our interchange, perhaps recording a moment when the interview subject asks about the interviewer's own experiences and responds to what they share. Stories are told to listeners, sometimes reflecting the listener's capacity to hear or be with the emotion expressed, and perhaps shared.[9] Perhaps the storyteller senses that the listener needs a particular story as medicine at that time. Sometimes the midugh recorder becomes a vehicle for the expression of rage against midugh residential school teachers, as in Gilbert Solomon's "Working with the Negative." Sometimes they are a messenger, honoured to write down a poet's words during his last year, as for Ivor Deneway Myers's "Nendidah gatŝ'i gan, gu deni helin han Everything is like a spirit"). Sometimes the recorder is working with a politician who stays on script and needs to be challenged to switch gears and speak from the heart.

Stó:lō scholar Q'um Q'um Xiiem Jo-ann Archibald outlines the principles of what she calls "storywork" as "respect, responsibility, reciprocity, reverence, holism, inter-relatedness, and synergy." She writes that stories can "take on their own life" and "become the teacher" if these principles are engaged. "[T]hese storywork principles are like strands of a cedar basket. They have distinct shape in themselves, but when they are combined to create story meaning, they are transformed into new designs and also create the background."[10] Referring to this process as making a "storybasket," Dr. Archibald articulates a "Stó:lō and Coast Salish theoretical framework for making meaning from stories," which is close to its Tŝilhqot'in analogue in *Lha yudit'ih*. Engaged in these ways, all of the stories in this book are alive.

In the service of "storywork," recording is itself an organic and reciprocal process which honours the teachings shared by holding them up. By using the resources of writing and of the English language, and, whenever possible, the Tŝilhqot'in language in order to convey the cadence, nuance, and intent of speech, I have sought in this book to make available to the reader what was revealed when all of the recordings were transcribed, edited, and excerpted and the pattern of *Lha yudit'ih* gradually became clear. My teachers took me to a river of stories reaching back to the beginning of time, and to a love of Tŝilhqot'in ways of being and knowing which are at the heart of the Title case, alongside a passionate, indomitable commitment to freedom and self-determination. All of the stories in *Lha yudit'ih* have the power to change the world. May you experience that power of transformation as you read this book.

Nits'ilʔin and Other Titles

Since the Title case victory, the term Nits'ilʔin has returned to frequent usage as part of a larger process, initiated by the 2016 Nenqay Deni Accord, of engaging the six Tŝilhqot'in communities in dialogue about the development of Tŝilhqot'in forms of governance together with cultural and linguistic revitalization. Before the arrival of midugh settlers, Nits'ilʔin was the word used for the respected leader of a community. It is used in the phrase Gudi Nits'ilʔin, literally "the leader up above or on high," and translated as Creator or God. In everyday usage, Nits'ilʔin is now sometimes used interchangeably with Chief and I have followed the usage of each of our contributors in their interviews.

The word Chief comes from the Indian Act and is part of the colonial regime of reserves, Bands, and elections of Chief and Council under settler law. This term was commonly used during Chief Roger's many years in elected office and as Plaintiff in the Title case. He was "Chief Roger" when I first met him and during all of the interviews for this book. Although *Lha yudit'ih* concludes with the end of Chief Roger's fifth term as Chief, which coincided with the initial stage of the Nenqay Deni Accord (2017–2018), his election in February 2023 to a sixth term as Chief (or Nits'ilʔin) has enabled us to identify him here once again as Chief. However, our decade-long collaboration on this project is also reflected in the informality of "Roger" and "Lorraine" and the conversational tone which we've retained where appropriate throughout this oral history.

As for academic titles, an honorary Doctor of Laws degree (LL.D.) was conferred in 2015 on Chief Roger by the University of Northern British Columbia, in recognition of his service as Plaintiff in the Title case. Weir holds a Ph.D. from Ollscoil na hÉireann The National University of Ireland and is an Emeritus Professor of Indigenous Studies in the Department of English Language and Literatures at the University of British Columbia, Vancouver.

"xinli"

It is Tŝilhqot'in custom to honour a deceased person by adding xinli (literally, "they were" – one who has passed on) to their name. Many of the Elders and community members who recorded for *Lha yudit'ih* have now gone to the spirit world so we have respectfully designated them as "xinli" throughout the book.

"Indigenous Issues 101"

There is a vast literature, from many different perspectives and locations, on the history of specific Indigenous nations before colonization, and on settler colonial history in the place which came to be called "Canada." Readers in search of introductions from Indigenous perspectives may consult Métis writer and lawyer Chelsea Vowel's blog *âpihtawikosisân* (apihtawikosisan.com/aboriginal -issue-primers/) at the "Indigenous Issues 101" tab; Gwawaʼenux̱w Hereditary Chief Bob Joseph's book *21 Things You May Not Know about the Indian Act: Helping Canadians Make Reconciliation with Indigenous Peoples a Reality* (Indigenous Relations Press, 2018), and its follow-up, *Indigenous Relations: Insights, Tips & Suggestions to Make Reconciliation a Reality* (with Cynthia F. Joseph, Indigenous Relations Press, 2019). For more comprehensive histories, see the fourth edition of Olive Patricia Dickason and William Newbigging's *Indigenous Peoples within Canada: A Concise History* (Oxford University Press, 2018) and Roxanne Dunbar-Ortiz's *An Indigenous Peoples' History of the United States* (Beacon Press, 2014). For a critical introduction to the Indian Act, see Mary-Ellen Kelm and Keith D. Smith, *Talking Back to the Indian Act: Critical Readings in Settler Colonial Histories* (University of Toronto Press, 2018).

Dasiqox from Dasiqox Nadiltil the Davidson Bridge. Photo by Chief Roger William

INTRODUCTION ENDNOTES

1   Chief Roger William served five terms as Chief (Xeni Gwet'in), three as Councillor, and is now (2023) serving his sixth term as Chief (Xeni Gwet'in). His five completed terms as Chief were as follows: 1991–1993, 1993–1998, 1998–2003, 2003–2008, and 2013–2018. His terms as Councillor were: 1988–1989, 1989–1991, and 2010–2013. As Plaintiff in the Title case, he testified for forty-seven days in total: twenty-eight days as Chief and nineteen days in cross-examination. Examination for discovery in 2003 required thirty days.

2   After the Supreme Court of Canada hearing in November 2013, I began to work on two additional projects related to the Title case: placing the Tŝilhqot'in Trial Archive at the University of British Columbia, Vancouver; and accessing and digitizing the Court Reporter's cassette tapes of the Elders' evidence (mostly in Tŝilhqot'in) at trial. A site visit to the Registry Office in Victoria revealed that mould had damaged paper files left in a storage room for many years after the trial and, sadly, that discovery was sufficient to make the archive unattractive to the UBC Library. However, I discovered that through a fortunate error, the Court Reporter's tapes had not been destroyed (which is the usual procedure five years after the end of a trial) and, with the TNG Chiefs' approval, I began to work with counsel Jay Nelson on accessing and digitizing these crucial resources for Tŝilhqot'in language revitalization. Several years later, it became clear that there was little momentum on this project and I withdrew.

3   Following current Tŝilhqot'in National Government (TNG) practice, we use in this book the spelling Tŝilhqot'in for the language, People, and Nation, only retaining the anglicized form Chilcotin for the Cariboo Chilcotin region of British Columbia and for speakers who distinguish between the two forms in their pronunciation. Spelling conventions vary in Tŝilhqot'in, reflecting the principle that, as Tŝilhqot'in linguist Susie Lulua instructed me, "You spell it the way you hear it." The first orthography for the language was developed in the 1970s by Eung-Do Cook with Bella Alphonse, Maria Myers, Stanley Stump, and Quindel King. See Eung-Do Cook, *A Tsilhqút'ín Grammar*, First Nations Languages series (Vancouver: UBC Press, 2013), 1–3. For the spelling of place names, we rely, wherever possible, on *Nexwenen: Lands and Waters of the Tŝilhqot'in People*. See "Tŝilhqot'in Place Names / Tŝilhqot'in Ch'ih Gudzish," www.tsilhqotin.ca/tsilhqotin-place-names/.

4   Eung-Do Cook, *A Tsilhqút'ín Grammar*, First Nations Languages series (Vancouver: UBC Press, 2013), 137.

5   Julie Cruikshank, *Life Lived like a Story: Life Stories of Three Yukon Native Elders* (Vancouver: UBC Press, 1990), 17–18. For another example of a similar approach, see Gaadgas Nora Bellis with Jenny Nelson, *So You Girls Remember That: Memories of a Haida Elder* (Madeira Park, BC: Harbour Publishing, 2022).

6   Cruikshank, *Life Lived like a Story*, 17–18.

7   Linda R. Smith, "*Súwh-tŝʼéghèdúdính: The Tsìnlhqút'ín Nímính* Spiritual Path" (M.A. thesis, University of Victoria, 2008), 33, hdl.handle.net/1828/934.

8   Alessandro Portelli, "Living Voices: The Oral History Interview as Dialogue and Experience," *Oral History Review* 45, no. 2 (2018): 241–242, doi.org/10.1093/ohr/ohy030.

9　　Thanks to filmmaker and storyteller Vitellina Torres (Yup'ik) for conversation about this point.

10　　Q'um Q'um Xiiem Jo-ann Archibald, *Indigenous Storywork: Educating the Heart, Mind, Body, and Spirit* (Vancouver: UBC Press, 2008), ix. See also Greg Sarris (Federated Indians of Graton Rancheria / Coast Miwok and Southern Pomo), *Keeping Slug Woman Alive: A Holistic Approach to American Indian Texts* (Oakland: University of California Press, 1993) and Craig Womack (Este Mvskokvlke Muskogee Creek and Aniyvwiyaʔi DhBΘᏦᎢ Cherokee), *Red on Red: Native American Literary Separatism* (Minneapolis: University of Minnesota Press, 1999).

Sunrise, Tŝilhqox Biny Chilko Lake.
Photo by Maryann Solomon

CHAPTER 1

Where I Come From[1]

Chief Roger William

Where I come from is a place called Nemiah Valley. Nemaya is the name of a Chief that the Europeans met back in the day. They named my community Nemiah Valley Indian Band, but we changed it back to our original Tŝilhqot'in name. Xeni is the place, and Xeni Gwet'in is us. Nemiah Valley is near Tŝilhqox Biny, Chilko Lake. That lake is five miles wide and fifty miles long. There's a river called Dasiqox, Taseko River, and there's Taseko Lake, which is about twenty miles long. Xeni is where the rivers meet between Tŝilhqox Biny and Dasiqox Biny at Tŝilhqot'in Yeqox, Tŝilhqot'in River. That's where Tŝilhqox Biny, Chilko River, starts.

There's a story about Chief Nemaya. The authorities were trying to catch him, and they were asking our Tŝilhqot'in people if they knew where Nemaya was because he'd done this and that. And they're like, "No, we don't know Nemaya." The authorities didn't know where he was and couldn't find him, so they just gave up. After a while, they didn't even think he existed! In the court case, BC and Canada said that there are Tŝilhqot'ins in the Chilcotin, but in Nemiah there are outlaws.[2] According to them, Nemaya and his bandits moved to Nemiah, and he killed somebody and threw them in the river, so he's an outlaw! So I guess I'm an outlaw too.

The Tŝilhqot'in Nation is comprised of six communities, and we're all Tŝilhqot'ins. We have different dialects because we have neighbours. In Xeni, we're in the Cascade Mountains. If you go further out, there's the Northern Secwépemc. If you go further north, there's the Southern Carriers. There's Carriers on the north side of the Tŝilhqot'in near Bella Coola as well. Then there are the Xwémalhkwu (Homalco) and the Kwakiutl. Those are the neighbours where we come from, and we've got stories about those connections. In Xeni and in the Tŝilhqot'in, there are a lot of Elders who are more comfortable speaking in their language, and they can speak some English. In Xeni, we've got some Elders who don't speak English at all. I was born speaking Tŝilhqot'in. I learned the English language in residential school – in our area, St. Joseph's Mission, Sugarcane,[3] where I went for two years, and then my third year at Kamloops Mission.[4] Three Nations were in those residential schools together – the Southern Dakelh Carrier, the Northern Secwépemc Shuswap, and us. We had history long before that, and now we have history from those residential schools.

We don't have BC Hydro in Xeni – there's no power lines in our community.[5] Before 2000, the only communication system in place was the radio phone. Until the 1970s, we had trails to get to the other communities. There was no road. Now if you're gonna go to Nemiah from Williams Lake, you gotta travel a hundred kilometres of pavement and another hundred kilometres of gravel. I remember when I was little going to Williams Lake in a wagon with teamhorses. I've ridden horses all my life, starting on my mom's back when she was riding. We used to put up our hay with teamhorses. We had family routes, family trails that we used to move through the Territory. Each season we would move to different places. Tŝilhqot'ins being river people, the salmon was really important to us, and we were good at catching it and other fish. We were good at hunting, too, and used rock blinds. We were well trained in terms of knowing the game around us, like mountain sheep and mountain goats, when they'd come around, when to hide behind the rock blind, and when to get meat.

When ranching came in, we started cutting hay at Naghataneqed, at one end of Xeni Biny Konni Lake, and slowly made our way to Lhizbay. Naghataneqed and Lhizbay are about twenty-five kilometres apart. In the winter, we crossed Tŝilhqox Biny Chilko Lake and lived on the other side, hunting and trapping. Chilko Lake is five miles wide, and we used dugout canoes and rafts to get across. We used to raft horses across the lake, and we still have pictures of that. In spring, we'd come back and feed our cattle at the Lhizbay end, and when we ran out of hay, we chased all our cattle and moved to the Naghataneqed end, finishing off in the spring. In the summer, we'd come back to Xeni Biny, and then move down the Chilcotin River, and up to Chilko Lake for salmon fishing. We went up in the mountains to hunt.

When I was young, only a handful of people owned a vehicle. Today, there's probably a handful of vehicles outside one home! For a while, the connection with horses was getting lost. In 2000, my community got a microwave phone system, and that was the first time we had phones in our homes. Before that, we rode our horses and visited each other. If you wanted to phone out, you had to go to the Band office radio phone and wait in line. In 2000, all that changed. You had a phone in your home, and people visited each other less. Then we started getting into computers, the internet, Facebook, and all that. It's not that long ago that we preserved big game, salmon, and other fish in the traditional way and had no fridges or freezers. It's always good and bad when technology comes in. Things change.

Growing Up

Chief Roger William

I went to the residential school in my area, Saint Joseph's Mission, for two years. Then, because it was full in the third year, when I was eight, all of us younger Xeni Gwet'ins ended up going to Kamloops Mission, while grade five and up remained at Saint Joseph's Mission. We were there in Kamloops for one year, and then our former Chief, late Marvin Baptiste, got the school going out here in Xeni. I went to school here and graduated in grade nine, and then I graduated from high school in Williams Lake. I also went to Chilliwack Senior High to finish off one course that I was lacking. Then I took a one-year correspondence course in business. In school I learned English, but I clearly understood about our Land, resources, and who we are through our legends. For years our people have been passing down how you're taught the Tŝilhqot'in language, the Tŝilhqot'in way, the traditions, the legends, the ritual beliefs, while you're inside the mother's womb. When you're born, you're born into that understanding and belief and feeling. And then, as you go forward, you're working to be an adult and there's a process for that. That's my understanding. When I was growing up, the Tŝilhqot'in language was the dominant language. Everybody knew it. I never knew a word of English. Me and my cousins would pretend that we were speaking English.

I was born and raised here in Nemiah at the east end of Konni Lake at a place called Naghataneqed. My mother, Eileen Sammy William, was haying with teamhorses, raking, when she went into labour. My auntie, late Madeline Setah, delivered me with our grandfather Sambulyan, the late Sammy William, overseeing and helping out. He was known to deliver babies since way back, but when I was born, he was at an age where he couldn't do those things, but he was able to guide his daughter through that. I'm so honoured, so privileged, to be able to be born into my culture, who I am, in my own community, in the Tŝilhqot'in.

When I was born, our transportation was horses, teamhorses and wagons. I was born into a ranching way of life. Ranching complemented the Tŝilhqot'in

Xeni Gwet'in way. Where I'm sitting now is a place called Tl'ebayi, on the west end of Konni Lake. My grandfather Sambulyan cultivated, ditched, and cut some willow to enlarge some of the meadows on this end at Tl'ebayi, and when he was younger, he gave it to his youngest son, late Danny Sammy William, who is a former Chief. Where I was born is where we start doing our haying. People fish and hunt and do haying. Our family is a big family, and my mom is the youngest of thirteen siblings. She's a single parent. My father is Walter Stobie. He's a member of the Toosey Indian Band, and he's passed on now. He had six daughters and one son. I've got half-sisters and -brothers there, and nieces and nephews there, but he never was part of my life. But former Chief, late Marvin Baptiste, always talked to me about him and would tell me his skills. He worked for ranchers and was a very skilled cowboy, a good horse trainer, and a saddlebronc rider in his day, and he hunted and fished. He was known for his skills, and people had a lotta respect for him, but I never really met him. We were starting to communicate when he passed on.

My mom is where I really come from. She went to residential school longer than me – six years – and her parents, my grandparents, never did go to residential school. But they ranched, hunted, trapped, and they travelled the Tŝilhqot'in. My mom, still today [2013], tans hide and scrapes hide. She's seventy-four, and she tans about thirteen to sixteen hides a year and she makes briefcases, gloves, moccasins, coats, pants, vests. You name it, she can do it. My mom used to hunt and fish. She used to put nets in the water. She built fences and houses. Because of her, I have so much respect for women, because she can do anything. She owned horses that a lot of men in this community wouldn't want to use. She was out on the land, haying, fencing, hunting, getting wood, and her teamhorses were so wild that sometimes we'd have a runaway and would have to dive out of the way, or she'd have to save me because I was too scared to jump off! There's a lotta stories about that. She was and she still is an amazing woman. She's more comfortable in Tŝilhqot'in, but she can speak English, and she's very quiet. The way she raised us was by showing us, by actually doing it on the land. I was probably in a packhorse box going into the mountains from the time I was a baby, and then when I could hold onto a string on the saddle, I'd be sitting on her back, going into the mountains and chasing cattle, horses. So I've been on a horse all my life. I know Xeni and the surrounding areas from that.

Elder Eileen Sammy William. Photo by Shannon Stump

Moose

Elder Eileen Sammy William and
April William xinli, Xeni Gwet'in

Elder Eileen Sammy William: You know, old Eddie [Quilt, husband of Eileen's older sister Eliza], he came up with it – "Try some moose!" It taste really good, and then we ate all the meat. And then he said, "Does that bear taste good?" [laughs] Maybe that's why sometimes he's [Roger] mean! [laughs]

April William: Ses [bear].

Elder Eileen: He has bees sting him. And then dogs, they don' like him. They bark at him.

April: He gets frightened of dogs sometimes. They have a Rottweiler, our neighbour. Came to visit us. Jumped down the stairs, so scared. We're like –

Elder Eileen: The dog's okay, he don't mind him [Roger].

Thinking and Feeling

Chief Roger William

Your brain has two parts. Thinking is back here [pointing]. You blink, you breathe, that's all. You don't think about it, that's all. It just happens. And when you get scared, hurt, or angry, it goes back here, and when you're thinking, it's up here. Think about being in your vehicle and driving to town. You don't smell, you don't think, you're driving fast. You're numb. You probably play music, or you're talking. But when you're on horseback or on foot, you smell, you hear, you feel the cold air, warm air, you're aware of all that's actually moving along. If something changes, you start looking around, you start feeling something back here, you start to be like a dog when its hair stands up. That's how our people were back before contact, and even not too long ago when I was younger. There'd be maybe a handful of people that went in vehicles, and the rest of us were on horseback or with teamhorse and wagon. It's the same thing when I'm riding out in the mountains. You smell, you hear, you feel cold, warm, and if you're out there long enough, you're just like how an animal is still. They feel fear right away. If you're riding, your horse will notice and smell something or feel something, and they start to get fidgety. Then you're looking around. You feel it in your horse, and then you start. It's all about that.

I remember when I was young, I came out in the field, and my grandma came out, and she stood outside, and she said, "Yeah, somebody's coming." We were little kids, and we're like, "Ha!!" We were looking around, and we couldn't see anybody, but we were aware of it, and we kept playing. Then we saw somebody riding over about an hour later. The place we were at was at Naghataneqed, where I was born. Our uncle was coming over Elkins Creek, coming down, and she already felt it, our grandma.

To get to Xeni – we're at Chilko Lake and Xeni is sort of in the centre. It's twenty-five miles north to one end of the lake and twenty-five miles south to the other end. The lake is five miles wide. Taseko Lake is right alongside Chilko Lake, and Tatlayoko's on the other side of Chilko. Chilko Lake is fifty miles long, and Taseko is further south and about twenty, twenty-five miles long. Tatlayoko is more northwest, and it's about fifteen, twenty miles long. I've gotten to know those three lakes because we always travel between those and I've heard stories from my mom, my grandparents, uncles, and aunts. In my lifetime, different Elders would talk about that whole area. The main big lakes in there are Tsuniah, Konni Lake, and Fish Lake. They've all got Tŝilhqot'in names. Konni Lake, Xeni Biny, is where our ranch is. We started at Naghataneqed. We cut hay there and then we went to Lhizbay. We finished haying at Chilko Lake – we call it Tŝilh-qox Biny – and then we started feeding our cattle, and winter started coming. Then my grandfather and uncles would go and live across the lake in trapping cabins, and they trapped in the winter. The rest of the family fed the cattle and there was trapping in the valley, too. So trapping and hunting are to me one and the same, because what we trap and hunt we also eat, and we also use the hide.

When I was growing up, we were done feeding when the hay ran out on the Lhizbay end, the Chilko end, and by that time, our grandpa, uncles, and aunts would be coming back from trapping. Then we moved down to Naghataneqed, to the east end of Nemiah, east end of Konni Lake – Xeni Biny, we call it – and then from there we chased our cattle into the Spring range and Summer range. It's all in the valley. We used to also go out of the valley to Taseko, and then we'd move to a place called Tl'ets'inged. Tl'ets'inged is halfway between Naghataneqed, the east end of Konni Lake, and Lhizbay, the west end. We used to camp there at a cabin my mom was involved in building. I remember being a little child and camping there and watching the cabin being built. That was where we stayed all summer, a rest from ranching. Then we used to go in a wagon and start camping out where we fished.

One year we'd probably go towards Stoney, Yuneŝit'in. My oldest aunt, Helena Myers, was married into Yuneŝit'in, Stone community, and we used to stay there. She passed on when she was ninety-five. And then from there we used to go fishing at a place called ʔElhghatish, or along Chilcotin River for salmon and for berry picking, 'cause the berries would ripen there quicker than here in the valley, and we'd be picking berries later here in August, early September, here in the valley. As time went on, Williams Lake Stampede was another event that our people used to go to with teamhorses, and you'd see a lotta Tŝilhqot'ins going there, camping out. A lotta them participated in the rodeo, the mountainrace. We'd also go up north to a place called Henry's Crossing, where you'd go gaffing. So you could go fishing earlier in August around the Stone Toosey area, Farwell Canyon, Alexis Creek area, all in that area. Then by the end of August, early September, you'd go to Henry's Crossing. So, with teamhorse and wagon, you would alternate your years. Some families would always go to Henry's Crossing, but we used to go back and forth, depending, because some families go both ways. This year was the fifth year we had our Xeni Gwet'in youth wagon trip, which one of my younger cousins, Jimmy Lulua, and his wife, June Cahoose Lulua, got started, and we kept it going. That's how we used to get to Williams Lake Stampede, by teamhorse and wagon.

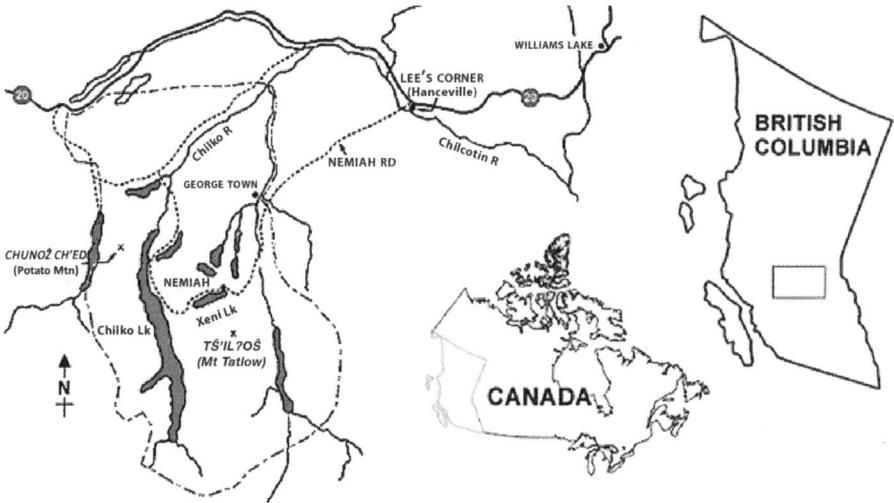

Nemiah Valley. Courtesy of Friends of the Nemaiah Valley

From Map 3, *Tsilhqot'in Nation v. British Columbia*, 2007 BCSC 1700

Place Names

Chief Roger William

Before European contact, we never stayed in one area. We couldn't, because we'd do too much damage by overusing the area. Families, Nations, communities all understood who did what where, and there were areas where we all collectively stayed together. So depending on what area we went to, families from other communities were there as well. Before the road was built in the 1970s from Stone community to Nemiah, the main road went out to what we call the Brittany Triangle and Tsuniah. Then, you'd go across Taseko to get to Stoney. Where Taseko Lake, Chilko Lake, and Chilko River meet, we call Tachelach'ed. There's a place called Far Meadow, Nusay Bighinlin, but no one lives in the

Brittany Triangle today. There's all sorts of Tŝilhqot'in names, where different members of our communities used to live. My understanding is that people used to commute between Yuneŝit'in, Tl'etinqox, Tŝideldel – so we're saying Stoney, Anaham, Redstone. Xeni Gwet'ins went from Stoney.

There's a place called Scum Lake. It's between Stoney and Anaham, on the west side of Taseko River. We call it Tŝintŝan in our language, and communities sort of camp out there. As soon as the snow melts, everybody goes out on the Land and starts camping. There's a crossing on Taseko. Taseko is glacial, and you can't see through, but our people know the trail that gets them to the river. Even at the mouth of Taseko Lake, they know how to follow the sandbar just by the landmarks and by their horse. Their horse knows too. You go on the sandbar to cross and if you get off the sandbar, you sink and you'd be swimming! At the mouth of the river, they call it Nadilin Yax.

Down here there's Elkins Creek Junction – it's kind of a tough name. I was just corrected by an Elder during our panel hearing. He took me aside, and he said Naba ʔelhnaxnenelhʔelqelh – it's kinda hard to say, eh? There's a pretty rough trail going down to Elkins Creek Junction with Taseko and a crossing, so that's one, and then there's another further down, Far Meadow. Far Meadow is where my uncle, late Eugene Sammy William, used to raise cattle. His uncle was Eagle Lake Henry, ʔElegesi. And then there's our former Chief Sil Canim, who lived in the area and built a cabin. So that's Far Meadow, Brittany, Brittany Lake, all that area. There's Captain Georgetown on this side – they call it Captain Georgetown. Those are sorta like the little communities, families, that people from Yuneŝit'in Stoney, Anaham, Redstone would go through, and they would stop because that's family for them too. There's different families, intermarriages. So that was the major highway, if you wanna call it that, and they would branch off to Nemiah, and they'd go back to Tsuniah, and there would be family there too.

Then when this road was built, Nemiah Road from Stoney, and technology, vehicles, came, I guess people just kinda abandoned those places, because of government policies, government legislation. Even in the 1980s when they did the Constitution Express,[6] our Rights were still suppressed so much that you couldn't even eat in certain restaurants. You couldn't buy alcohol. There's a lotta things you couldn't do. And I always joke about it with our people because I like eating Chinese food. Chinese restaurants used to accept our people all the time, so our people got used to that food and a lot of our people eat Chinese food today. Before that you didn't even have any rights to live on the Land, and wherever they could, governments tried to control where we camped and how we camped.

When I was growing up, I heard stories from some of our Elders who were worried when they hunted and fished that the government wasn't going to agree to it. They really respected that authority, and they didn't wanna get in trouble. I learned this as a child when I was growing up, and hearing these stories, I wondered, okay, midugh – midugh, we say, non–First Nations government – dictate what we should do and where we should do it. Who *are* these people? I found out later, talking to more Elders and leaders. I was going to school and started asking more questions, and our Elders – my mom, my grandparents, uncles, and aunts, different Elders – would talk about the Tŝilhqot'in War. Before contact we were a group of people who lived off this Land through our legends, our history, our stories and rituals. We didn't own it per se, but we were part of it. There were place names, and we protected those areas and place names. There are connections with other First Nations and sometimes conflict and wars between Nations. There was a leader named Sil Canim, and he died in a fire. They said he had papers that had the whole Nemiah Valley as reserve and had all the way up north as reserve.[7] We looked high and low and couldn't find the papers.

Nenqay The earth

Chief Roger William

In our language, Nenqay means the earth. The earth itself is a being, it's alive, and we co-exist with this being. We've been part of changes on this earth. In our ritual beliefs, you were taught while you were inside the mother's womb, when you were being born, and when you became an adult. Some of those teachings, like the teachings about twins, are very powerful. Every Tŝilhqot'in person has power because when a baby's inside the womb, the mother and father eat, see, and do certain things. You have to be careful. And when the baby is born, they save the ts'iny [umbilical cord] because they want their child to have a certain skill. For example, if you want the child to be a hunter, a fisher, or things like that, that's where you would put the ts'iny when the child is old enough to know what they're doing. They know the time to do it from the stories and legends that they teach the child. You smudge with juniper bush and sage and do an honour song before the sun comes up, and you put the ts'iny somewhere. The ts'iny is the connection from the mother to the child to the earth.

To become an adult is a sacred process, and there are different areas, including Teẑtan Biny in the mountains, where we do that. Every child, female or male, goes through that process. You do this process when coming on your time or getting your man's voice. Someone, a medicine person, watches over you for protection, but you don't know who it is. They make sure you're safe, but you're also on your own. For a week, you only drink water when you need to, from the back of your hand. Only when you desperately need it. That's how they teach you. And you have dried fish, a small piece, or dried meat or berries if you really need it. It's gonna have to last you – that's when you take it. And you have to think positive and work hard during that time. Youth who are becoming adults are put in an area that's sacred, and you'll see different structures, different piles of rocks out there in the Tŝilhqot'in marking where they were. They say that week dictates what you do for the rest of your life. Our people say that if someone was being negative, lazy, or stealing during that week, that's how they'll be for the rest of their life. The sacred time when you're becoming an adult is so important that they put a process in place for you so that you're positive and everyone gets their power.

Every Tŝilhqot'in had some kind of power. A deyen, a spiritual medicine person, has multiple powers, and these powers can be received through dreams, through different rituals, or passed on by another. My great-grandfather Sit'ax passed on a portion of his power to my grandfather Sambulyan, who was a deyen. When you become an adult, a certain animal becomes your power, depending on what happens during that week. We were very powerful. When you look through a window and the sun's shining through, you see the light and the little specks of dirt floating. They say a deyen could grab a sunray and lift themself up and hang in the air. That kinda power. They could blow a hummingbird through the air to kill somebody. Stories like that.

At the end, before colonization, we were very powerful because, as Tŝilhqot'in people, we were all taught those same ritual processes and steps, like smudging with juniper and sage. All that happened all the time, every day. When you hunt, when you fish, when you gather berries, there are rituals that people can do with those berries and medicines as they move along, and that was practised all the time. That's my understanding. Now we're fractured. Now there's the Catholic Church, and there's people who don't believe in Catholicism. Different religions came into play and a different government. A lot of things started collapsing. The knowledge was there, but so many things were happening. Language is a big part of it. Knowing your culture, ritual beliefs, all that is a big part of it, but some people are not comfortable taking that on. Medicine people, deyens, still help people in Xeni and in other Tŝilhqot'in communities, but back then, deyens were so powerful. Catholics all go to a church on a certain day at a certain time when they all pray. But for us, we *lived* it. It was passed on

Lha yudit'ih We Always Find a Way

through generations, and a child would live this. If you're a woman, if you're a man, there are certain things you can't do and can do. You lived it.

Rituals

Ivor Deneway Myers xinli,[8] Yuneŝit'in

I never went through all the rituals that I was supposed to. That's something my grandfather Samuel probably went through when he first became a man. He had to go through fasting, lots of fasting. The same with the women. They were no different. They had to fast at the time of womanhood when they had their period, their menstrual time. They weren't supposed to eat any flesh when they went through that ritual the first time. And both male and female were supposed to eat dry goods. They didn't want to let any of the children eat too much because that's how they became big – carried excess weight. They didn't want to see their children like that, so that's why they went through that ritual. Once you're past that ritual, then anything in the future will become easier, but there will still be lots of challenges and obstacles that will be hard for them to accomplish.

I must've been about fourteen years old when my mum doctored me with beaver. What she did was she made a fire, and she looked at the front paws of the beaver and, one at a time, she scorched each paw, and then placed it four times on the palm and four times on the back of my hands. Then she did the same with the beaver tail. Four times she scorched the beaver tail with the fire and she'd tap it on the back. That's what she did. She finished with a juniper branch, shaking the branch, smudging it on me four times, just like she did with the beaver paw and the beaver tail. She told me the reason she did that was because she wanted me to never be lazy. She wanted me to pursue my life, to be a hard worker, become a builder like her brothers. They built their homes. That's what I've been doing most of my life – building some conventional homes, some log homes. I built a school at Stone. I did the machine work at Alexis Creek School. My mission for the future is to build an underground home.

There are lots of other rituals that Tŝilhqot'ins go through. They could be doctored with water, the sun, the trees. When you look at the back of the trees along the side of a mountain, you can use [the back branches of] those trees to doctor somebody. If you use fire, that person would withstand the cold. No matter how cold the weather is, that person wouldn't feel it as much. That's the purpose for that.

There's a lot of animals out there that Tŝilhqot'in people ate. Muskrats, beavers, lynx, rabbits, marmots, elks, caribou. Even bear – black bear, but not the Grizzly. I was told that black bears were the favourites, and the grease is one reason why. That grease could be used on the human scalp to keep the hair dark for a long time. For myself, I've been usin' hellebore root, and I also use the sun. That's one of the rituals. Before the sunrise, you walk outside. You let no one know that you're there. You face the sun where it's rising, and you have some hair in your hands. It could be from your scalp. You torch the hair and smudge it in your hands. You talk to it while you reach your hand into your hair. Talk to it in a good way. You wanna keep the root strong for the longest time, and dark. You talk to the sun when it's rising. The sun is the most powerful, and then the Ancestors. You talk to the Ancestors at the same time. And while you have some ashes in your hand, you smudge it like that [rubbing his hands together] and smudge it in your hair. And then your wrists, you go like this, and talk to it in a good way. I asked my mom [Elder Helena Myers xinli] that. I said, "Mom, can you tell me if what you told me was the truth and how it was talked about by your mom, your grandparents?" And she told me that story again. That's how the Tŝilhqot'ins do rituals for darkening your hair. There's many other ways, but that is one way.

I don't think you have to be a deyen to do those rituals. Happened to one fella. He's a forestry manager, and he was telling me he got tired of fighting fire for over three weeks. He listened to me talking about making rain. You hang a frog in mid-air and let the hindquarters turn into a stream during the summer. He asked, "Can we try this?" So we did that day. It was cloudless, and all of a sudden clouds formed where the frog was hanging from its hindquarters. It was big in its hindquarters, so when rain came, it rained for a while. Another one he saw was a bear skull. You gotta put a rock in the mouth so it's kinda open and it's sittin' there. That's how he created rain. You can do it with snow. He did it with snow.

Some other people told me about facing towards the sunrise and praying in your mind to your Ancestors, your Great Spirit. Talk to them in a good way for the future, like that. It's the most powerful. For myself, I was fourteen years old at the time when the big thunderbolt ran between my feet there, like *right there*. My mum was walking where Simon is staying, that log house. Walking to the east. Sound was starting. It was just crackling. And the sun was strong. I was walking there, and then I saw that thunderbolt coming right at me. It struck between my feet. My mum says that was the loudest thunderbolt she's ever heard in her life. I was always wondering about that. I didn't know what it meant. It almost –. And now …

Songs are you – your own identity. You don't reveal to no one. You sing your-self. Belongs to you, no one else. It's up to him, up there in the sky. You're not supposed to share it with anyone. Only time you'll ever sing to a person is when you're healing them, putting their spirit back in them sometime. Or you can use it wherever you have to go for communicating with those spirits.

Somebody in the sky somewhere would bring you that song. You have to sing that song. They'll become your power. After each fast. It could be maybe ten days after you finish the first fast, whatever. If there are five more days, they could give you another power. And so on. It's like that. Sit'ax had many songs – my great-great-grandfather. He used to cast out evil spirits.

Whoever gives it to you through the sky, the Great Spirit, they tell you how to sing a song and how to heal people. That's how it was. If somebody asked you to dance, you couldn't help but dance right in front of them. If somebody asked you to heal this child, you gotta go over there and do it, and you don't ask for any money. You don't ask for nothing but do a good deed for that person.

* * *

There's a lotta ways to prevent a bad spirit from coming to you. You use either a juniper or sage or other plants or animals to protect you by using that as a necklace. I don't want to wear it here [the hospital] but that's what you use to hang around your neck so nothing will harm you when they fire the bad spirit on you. It could be their bad power.

Remember the time I told you about taking care of yourself? Take care of your hair, take care of your clothes, take care of your shoes, take care of your spit, take care of your pee, your names. Some bad person will do harm to you. They'll grab the poop and put it somewhere and make you die from it. You don't have to be ashamed when they do that. Whoever's done that to you will face the consequences. They will hurt themselves two more times. They shouldn't be playing around with their power just to hurt other people. That's nothing to fool around with. You don't play with that, otherwise you'll harm a lot of people. They might go into the grave with it.

Whatever it is is part of who we are, what we are supposed to be aware of while we're on this earth. Some of us experience that many times in our lives. If I was a strong deyen and somebody died over there somewhere, before they died they'd give me the scent of who did it, and I'd find out where they are. That's how you find out.

I hear people. I'll hear the spirit of a person. That spirit. I do that. I'm supposed to. Say somebody touched a person here and it hurts. I just take it right off. I'm not strong like those other people, though.

See, that's the reason why you go fast in the mountains for a long time, like Deneway did, the way Moses did, the way Jesus did, the way Noah did. That's how they got their power. They fasted.

* * *

One thing I wanted to tell you that I heard from my grandfather George [Myers xinli]. Says long, long ago, a lot of people were starving, and I know there was no horses in this Land at that time. None whatsoever. People used to travel by foot. And they had dogs during those days, and they used dogs as packers to transport some things. And the bow and arrow also originated long ago.

It has been told by another Elder that one time there was a medicine man who was starving. He was gaunt, with nothing in his stomach. So this deyen man dreamt about how to make a bow and arrow and how to use it to kill animals. And in his dream, it came to him, how to make this bow. And how to make the strings. And how to make the arrowheads. And how to make the arrow stop. In his dream that's what was told to him so he made one. And in his dream, he also probably had the power of that bow. Only a deyen person that has a power of that bow could use the bow to his gain. A person just like yourself or anybody else trying to stretch that bow, you cannot with your hands, even with your two feet and two hands – you can only stretch it so far. But when that medicine man comes around and grabs his bow, he stretches it arm's length. That's how powerful that bow is [making the sound of an arrow going through the air]. So it came to be where this medicine man was able to heal with that, with how to make a bow and arrow. Feed himself and his family. He would start them huntin' with bows and arrows. No ordinary person could stretch that bow – just himself. And that arrow became very perfect where it's shooting two miles.

My grandfather told me about that one there.

* * *

Long ago when the deyen people were gonna track somebody down, they used the Kingfisher. They released the Kingfisher – that's their power – and they put a spell on people. The Kingfisher went right over toward where those people were running. It went after them, that way. Some keeled over and were killed, some survived. That's the spell that the deyen people put on them. No difference when Moses freed the slaves, but he killed a lotta people with that power.

* * *

Long ago our people used to fast for thirty days. If they wanted to become very powerful, they fasted for a long time. Each time you fast, you dream about a certain object, animal, or whatever power you're gonna carry doing your healing. Sometimes with this power you could cast out the evil spirits and put back a spirit – bring the spirit back into humans. Some people used to use fire and throw it at each other, just to find out who was the most powerful.

When you're fasting, you're not supposed to drink, or just drink a little bit at a time in the morning. I'm not sure about nighttime. You're not supposed to eat anything for the longest time. And you must sleep in the bush at the place of a juniper plant. It's one of the special plants. I'm sure there might be many other ways of becoming a deyen.

There are people that abuse their power by abusing what a deyen knows. They use it to hurt other people and that's not the right way. They're gonna suffer from the consequences that are gonna fall on someone. And they should know that. They shouldn't fool around with things like that.

One time there must've been five or six people. They didn' know what was floating in the air across the lake so they swam across. There was a deyen swimming in the air. Must've been in robes. Had a fire down the road. They made fun of 'em and they told 'em to come down and take all the packs of sticks out of the fire with his knife. He didn't hesitate. He went down and they wouldn't even help him. He set the fire and went back up to where he'd been sitting. They didn't fool around with him after that. Said they didn't want to bother 'em any more. They were hunters, I guess, from the coast people. They weren't doing the things they [should have been doing]. His name was ʔAbeyan. Died in Nemiah during 1918 [the Spanish Influenza]. He was just a very powerful human. He had a power of the sun in 'em.

That's just one of them. You know that staff that was displayed in the TNG [Tŝilhqot'in National Government] office in Williams Lake? There's red and white on it. It belonged to a shaman. That shaman had a power to un the dead. When he puts that staff down, you die in a short time. If he wants you to revive, he brings that thing up. That's how powerful he was.

There are a lotta them that had the power to drive in mid-air when they're running. And they were distance runners, comin' big distance. They could go from Nemiah to Williams Lake and back in a half-day.

Some people had the power of a hummingbird. They grabbed the bird like this with their hands, and they chucked it right at you. You couldn't see that hummingbird going through. It hit you hard, and you'd die instantly. Not that long ago that happened.

You acknowledge the Ancestors through the fire. You give 'em tobacco. You say to them, "Smoke with me" or "Eat with me." They be right there. They be sitting there eating. So when you're fasting, once you're done, when you go back home and you find out that you're not powerful enough, you go back up [into the mountains]. You're not strong enough, you go back up. That's what they told me, a lot of these youth. So whether they like it or not, they're gonna [go back up]. When they decided they had enough power, youths would come down to reveal themselves in front of their parents. "I'm strong enough now," he'd say or she'd say. So that's how a lot of people used it for good things, but a lot of them used it for bad things, pretending to use it for their people's benefit, just like Moses did with the Red Sea. Just like when those Warriors drowned in Chilko Lake.

It was told to me through some Bible that I read, or I saw the movie about Jesus walking on water. No difference in our country. One time, one of our shamans walked across the river carrying a feather. You know how swift the current is. They walked on the surface of the river. And they'd come back, and it'd be the same. Some of them used to walk right across. One time, my dad told me that when some of the shamans were bathing in a really swift current in the river, they used to be waist-deep no matter how deep the water was. They used to walk on water. They used to have fun like that.

When I was a teenager, I never went through some of the things that a lot of our people have gone through. But I heard stories from Elders, my uncles, my aunties – William Setah, Madeline [Setah]. A young person, whether female or male, is like nothing at the beginning. You're a nothing, and you're not ashamed. It's just like putting a small little turd in your stomach. That's who you are. Nothing. But if you go through the wilderness and fast for a long time, you have your power. And whoever that is that gave it to you, you do it according to what that person tells you. That's how you're supposed to carry yourself, by healing people. Jesus himself fasted for forty days, forty nights. At the end he went back home and that's when people found him, right? Even the blind. And that's the same thing here – if you fast for a long time, you let everything go in the right way. Everything will fall in a good way. It helps lots of people that have problems inside themselves – their spiritual beings, their physical beings, their emotional beings. And they could put their spirit back in them.

During the time when I was growing up, my mum and dad used to always tell me be very careful where you go. We don't care where you go but always sit down and talk to us. If you're gonna punch a man at different gatherings, go somewhere else. Be careful. Careful with your belongings. Where somebody doesn't like you and pretends to be your friend, they'll do something to you. Somebody's actions are gonna meet you. Maybe somebody wanted to do me in for doing spiritual work. I practiced Catholicism. I forgot my old traditional ways. I even forgot my language.

CHAPTER 1 ENDNOTES

1   The first two sections of this chapter are based on a talk that Chief Roger gave in UBC's Musqueam 101 series on October 23, 2013. We're grateful to Leona M. Sparrow, Director of the Treaty, Lands, and Resources Department, Musqueam Indian Band, and to Dr. Susan Rowley, UBC coordinator of the series. Thanks to sʔəyəɬəq Elder Larry Grant, the late Delbert Guerin, and the xʷməθkʷəy̓əm Musqueam community for a warm welcome, and to xʷməθkʷəy̓əm archivist Jason Woolman for a copy of the event video. Thanks also to Sophie Royle for transcription of Chief Roger's talk.

2   Chief Roger is commenting whimsically on the Defendants' desperate argument that Title be denied the Plaintiff and his community on the basis of their connection to Chief Nemaya. By insisting on using the anglicized term Chilcotin, the Crown asserted its own territorial claim over Tŝilhqot'in Land regardless of the Plaintiff's arguments in support of Title and Rights. If Chief Nemaya was an "outlaw," as the Crown alleged, then Chief Roger proudly argues that he's an outlaw too since he was doing no more than Chief Nemaya in defending his Land against the incursions of settlers.

3   Saint Joseph's Indian Residential School (known as "The Mission") in Sugarcane, near Williams Lake, BC.

4   Kamloops Indian Residential School in Kamloops, BC.

5   A milestone achievement, the underground electrification project in Xeni will bring power to households in the community in 2022–2023. In the 1970s, Xeni Gwet'in successfully resisted the threat of the construction of a massive hydroelectric dam, which would have inundated what is now Title Land. See Titilope I. Kunkel, "Aboriginal Values, Sacred Landscapes, and Resource Development in the Cariboo Chilcotin Region of BC" (Ph.D. diss., University of Northern British Columbia, 2014), core.ac.uk/download/pdf/84871589.pdf.

6   For a vivid account of the Constitution Express, see Louise Mandell, "Tracking Justice: The Constitution Express to Shared Sovereignty," *BC Studies* 212 (Winter 2021/2022): 72, doi .org/10.14288/bcs.no212.195688. Vicki Lynne George has compiled a collection of filmed interviews with leaders of the Express: *The Constitution Express: A Multimedia History*, "Interviews," constitution.ubcic.bc.ca/node/133 (joint project of the Union of BC Indian Chiefs and the First Nations Studies Program at the University of British Columbia).

7   Justice Vickers writes that "Chief Roger William testified about a persistent oral history among members of the Xeni Gwet'in that Chief Sil Canim was murdered in 1932 in order to prevent his securing Xeni as an Indian reserve. According to the oral history, Sil Canim had a paper by which the Federal Government set all of Xeni as a reserve but, before he could accomplish this goal, he was murdered by Andy George who had been hired by one of the Purjue brothers" (*Tsilhqot'in Nation v. British Columbia*, 2007 BCSC 1700, 192).

8   Ivor Deneway Myers xinli (1955–2016) was a highly respected Knowledge holder who spent many years recording the Elders in Tŝilhqot'in. He served his community, Yuneŝit'in, as Nits'il?in for fourteen years and as Councillor for four years.

Dada chugh[1]
The Big Sickness (1862)

It's how you put this story between English time and Tŝilhqot'in time ... In my mind I think, well, smallpox is just 1862, right. Like the way they say it in English, you know. "During pioneer times." That's it. "Pioneer times" is when the Tŝilhqot'in War happened. In Tŝilhqot'in we say it was yesterday. I mean, white people have been here just a blip, and look what happened to our world.

—MARIA MYERS (Yuneŝit'in)

When Smallpox Hit Our People

Chief Roger William

When smallpox hit our people, in some cases a whole community was wiped out, and in other cases, a quarter or half was wiped out. Maybe 80 percent died. We lost a lotta people. Before contact, there was a celebration when somebody died. We were taught that you respect everyone, the earth, the wildlife, and after you get food, you offer some to them. When somebody visited you, you would give them food, you would give them your bed, you would take care of them because the ritual belief is that it paves the way for you to a better life. There's a spirituality in our thoughts, our way of life, a greater eternity. They celebrated the death by burning the bodies. There was a process for that – drumming, singing.

In some communities where everyone was gone, families on the outskirts tried to help. In some communities, there were only a few people left. My understanding through stories is that non–First Nations people with good intentions – Catholic, in our area – helped them. There's no way they could burn everyone, so they buried them, and that was totally against our way. But the whole community was gone, and the families around them tried to help survivors accept burial. One quarter of them did, but the other three quarters were outraged. We didn't know what was gonna happen. We were all dying and some people were saying that it was the blankets doing it. A lot of our people were thinking we're gonna all get killed, all of us.

We lost a lotta good leaders, medicine people, and families to smallpox. Some who died were the really important people, like the Ivors [Myers], the Gilberts [Solomon], and the Henry Solomons. The ones that were left, some were good, but they were hurting. They were trying to pick up the pieces but didn't have that leadership skill or that culture. They were trying to survive and to remember.

It hurts a family and a community whether you lose one person or many people but imagine when you lose 100 percent in some places, 20 percent in other places. There was fear. Everybody was in survival mode. That means throw each other under the bus in some places, you know. To survive.

What my uncle, the late Henry Solomon, talked about is that after the smallpox, there were three divisions of people, beliefs, everything. Some hung onto our culture, some accepted the European way, and some were in the middle. There was a group that totally didn't agree with what was happening, seeing burial as against our legends, history, and tradition and believing it was wrong. There was a group that accepted because they had no choice, and there was a group that was in the middle and could go either way but blocked both sides. It's the same for a lot of First Nations. That's what we're trying to bring back together now, and that's the cumulative impact from 1862 to the present time.

Today, if you lose a person, it's hard on the community, especially the family. Imagine 1862 – your whole Nation is impacted, and then two years later it's the Tŝilhqot'in War. There's Tŝilhqot'in people now who don't know enough about our culture, and they go back to when the smallpox hit our people. Everybody was trying to survive, and we had far fewer people. Tŝilhqot'ins and non–First Nations started coming together, having children, fencing off areas, making a cabin. The other Tŝilhqot'ins, because they're Tŝilhqot'in, kinda let it happen, so they never really mourned. It was catastrophe.

Dada chugh

Ivor Deneway Myers xinli, Yuneŝit'in

The first one was called "dada chugh" [the big sickness] – the smallpox. It was deliberately brought, deliberately so they could wipe us out of our Land and our resources, including natural resources – game, water, air. Late Henry Petal told me there were two non-Natives who brought smallpox into the country at that time. They used a horse to do that, and they used infested blankets wherever they went. They'd put the blankets right there, and then it spread. There was a lotta Tŝilhqot'in people living there. Each one of them had lots of knowledge of the Lands. Each one of them had lots of knowledge of the rituals or legend stories. That's when they brought the missionaries as well. They used to call our people down to the lowest, so they brought the priests to calm us down.

During the period when the smallpox came, a lot of people used to live around Tatlayoko, Tatla Lake, and also Chilko Lake, Chimney Lake, Puntzi, Toosey, ʔElhdaqox – Fraser River, Chimney Valley, Williams Lake, Beaver Valley, Lac La Hache, Horsefly, the Slow Creek area, back of the Meẑdem, Anaham, where Anaham Reserve is. Our Territory didn't go as far as ʔElhdaqox. It went further east from there. We utilized all the countryside at one time, and a lot of our place names were destroyed. Could've been tens of thousands of people died in Tŝilhqot'in Territory devastated by that smallpox. History went with them. There were very few Tŝilhqot'in people left.[2]

A lot of people survived that smallpox because they were in the mountains. If there was a shaman in the bunch, they used their power to scout. They went to find the people who were suffering, but they didn't wanna go down to that place, because they'd die too. They didn't want to come near the villages where the people were dying left and right from the plague. People that had the disease sometimes came close, but they spoke from a distance. There was a time when a young boy was crying, starving, sucking the nipples of the mother who was dead. This happened.

Our people used to be cremated where they died. That's why there are hardly any burial sites in the country. When they died, all of our people were put on a high place on the ground, and that's where they were cremated. After the smallpox, a lot of people were buried in mass graves, and to this day people are buried in graves. When the first European people arrived, they tried to tame the people, and they allowed the priests to come in the country to neutralize us. Then they forced foreign names, English names, on a lot of our Tŝilhqot'in people, and identity and culture were lost. The priests manipulated the minds of the Tŝilhqot'in Nation by forcing names upon people. It was a cultural genocide which began during the time of smallpox, when the European people came in.

And then this [Chilcotin] Reserve. Governor [James] Douglas was enacting a policy of some sort. "You shall claim any land that's not inhabited after the smallpox." That was one of their tricky ways to expropriate the Land. The colonial government wanted our resources and our Land, and that's why they wanted to get rid of us with smallpox. They almost succeeded. Secrecy – a bunch of European people who came together behind closed doors. They had a meeting – how to annihilate the population of British Columbia. The smallpox was deliberate. It was done on purpose. Smallpox was like an attack without letting people know. It was an eye opener for the Tŝilhqot'in Warriors.

How Smallpox Came to the Tŝilhqot'in

Tom Swanky

Smallpox came to the Tŝilhqot'in when the Douglas administration in Victoria licensed colonists to introduce the disease where Tŝilhqot'in communities had granted access for roads. Thus the the smallpox genocide in the Tŝilhqot'in became tied to the history of colonial roads.

The road developers intended to create a Northwest Passage by land, linking Britain's North Pacific colonies to its colonies across the continent. Three projects were proposed. The first would have originated at Q'umk'uts (Bella Coola), reached the Chilcotin Plateau at Nagwentlun (Anahim Lake) and followed a trail to Chiscot, a large Tŝilhqot'in community at Cheẑich'ed Chezacut (Chilcotin Lake), before proceeding northeast to reach the Fraser River at Lhatko (Quesnel). A second version of this road would have left Chiscot eastbound to the Fraser at ʔEsdilagh (Fort Alexandria). A third version would have reached the Chilcotin Plateau at Sutless (Nimpo Lake) and then proceeded east to Bendziny Puntzi, before meeting the Fraser at ʔEsdilagh. This last version is what was known as the Bentinck Arm Road during the Tŝilhqot'in War.

Attorney General George Cary fronted the Bentinck Arm Company and MLA Robert Burnaby and Hudson's Bay Company (HBC) insider Ranald McDonald were directors. McDonald and George Barnston received a charter for a toll road through Tŝilhqot'in Territory from Douglas in 1861, even though the Crown had made no arrangements for access with the Tŝilhqot'in authorities. Cary also fronted a land syndicate dominated by HBC insiders associated with the Puget Sound Agricultural Company. Before the Crown negotiated for the purchase of any Aboriginal Title, Cary, his syndicate, others hoping to capitalize on the road, and the road's contractor staked Land under several Indigenous villages, including Q'umk'uts, Chiscot, and Lhatko. So they had a private financial motive for distributing smallpox in addition to the underlying public motive of needing to displace Indigenous authority for the purposes of evicting and dispossessing Indigenous people on their own Land. In late 1862, the Bentinck Arm company collapsed when the road builder, William Hood, had a falling out with George Cary.

Bute Inlet was the second place from which developers approached the Tŝilhqot'in over roads in the summer of 1861. In this case, MLA Dr. William Tolmie, general manager of the Puget Sound Agricultural Company, and MLA Dr. John Helmcken, also an HBC manager, provided funding and personnel for an endeavour fronted by MLA Alfred Waddington. As agents for Waddington, Captain Price and surveyor Robert Homfray separately secured approval from Tellot's Homathko Valley community for a road from Bute Inlet to intersect with the Bentinck Arm routes at Puntzi or Chiscot. Captain Price gave Tellot a magazine cover showing the 1847 Franklin expedition leaving London to explore the Northwest Passage. Perhaps he used it to explain the concept of a Northwest Passage by land and received permission for such a project to be built in the vicinity of the village. However, neither Price nor any other agent reported seeking consent from Tŝilhqot'in communities elsewhere on the route.

The Crown chartered the Bute Inlet Wagon Road Company for a toll road before Waddington accompanied a crew of almost one hundred men to advance the road during 1863. However, the Crown had still not negotiated with the Tŝilhqot'in authorities for access, and this lack would be the basis of a claim by Waddington for damages after the Tŝilhqot'in closed the road in 1864. Although the Bute Inlet Company was bankrupt by the end of 1863, Waddington remained committed to the project. He sent a small crew to Bute Inlet in March 1864, and the threat to spread smallpox had been made even before Waddington bought the Company's assets for his own account at the dispersal auction in April.

After the Tŝilhqot'in destroyed the 1864 Bute Inlet crew in April and executed McDonald and his Puntzi partners in May, the HBC advertised that it would complete the Bute Inlet Road from Puntzi to Fort Alexandria if others financed its completion in the Homathko Valley. In August 1864, a unit of regular soldiers from the British Navy occupied Tellot's village to secure any new road crew. However, Waddington was out of money, McDonald was dead, others with interests at stake – such as MLAs Helmcken, Tolmie, and Burnaby – were unwilling to risk more, and no new investors could be found. So the Bute Inlet Road collapsed in the end from a combination of amateurish engineering, a poor financial plan, and a colonial disrespect for Tŝilhqot'in authority.

The history of colonial roads in Tŝilhqot'in Territory shows that the source of conflict behind the Tŝilhqot'in War was never the fact of roads per se – even though the Bute Inlet Road sometimes is used as a marker symbolizing the greater issue. Instead, the conflict began – and has continued since – over the locus of legitimate authority in the administration of resources.[3] Before the

Tŝilhqot'in War, acts of colonial aggression had already caused a series of violent confrontations, the deaths of Tŝilhqot'ins and their Indigenous neighbours by the thousands, and the death of perhaps five colonists at the hands of Indigenous communities defending the integrity of their legitimate authority.

Before the colonial community revealed its willingness to inflict genocidal policies on the Indigenous population – beginning with smallpox in 1862 and continuing through the residential schools – the Tŝilhqot'in who approved roads obviously expected their communities to benefit from these developments. After 1862, an overwhelming sense of grief and despair for the future brought a recognition that some battles could not be fought, and others would have to be delayed.[4]

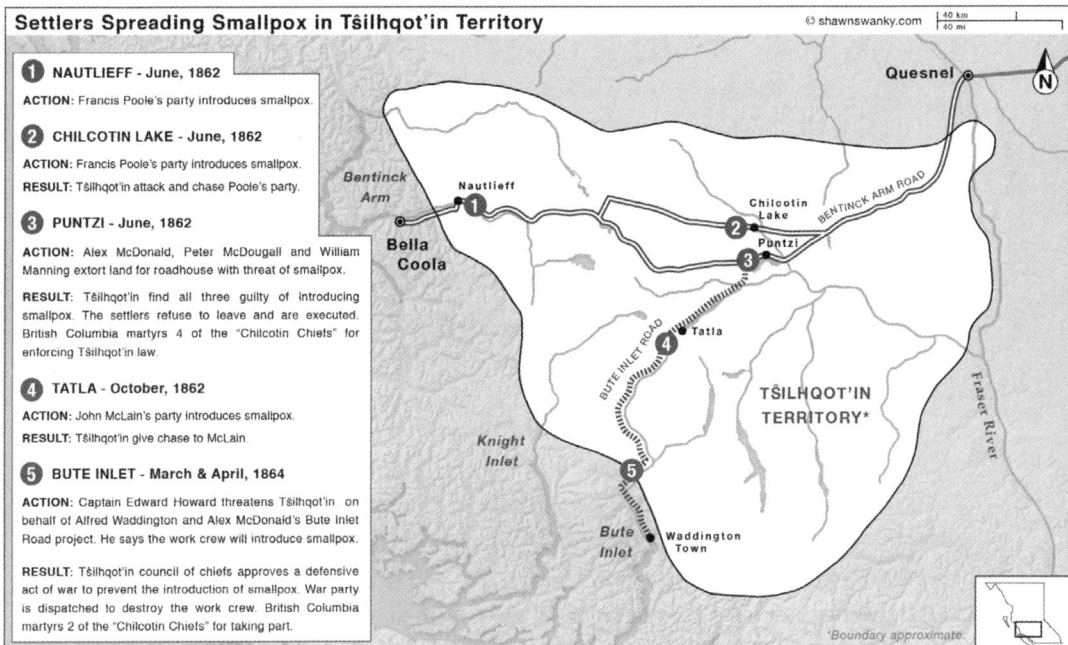

Settlers Spreading Smallpox in Tŝilhqot'in Territory © shawnswanky.com

1 NAUTLIEFF - June, 1862
ACTION: Francis Poole's party introduces smallpox.

2 CHILCOTIN LAKE - June, 1862
ACTION: Francis Poole's party introduces smallpox.
RESULT: Tŝilhqot'in attack and chase Poole's party.

3 PUNTZI - June, 1862
ACTION: Alex McDonald, Peter McDougall and William Manning extort land for roadhouse with threat of smallpox.
RESULT: Tŝilhqot'in find all three guilty of introducing smallpox. The settlers refuse to leave and are executed. British Columbia martyrs 4 of the "Chilcotin Chiefs" for enforcing Tŝilhqot'in law.

4 TATLA - October, 1862
ACTION: John McLain's party introduces smallpox.
RESULT: Tŝilhqot'in give chase to McLain.

5 BUTE INLET - March & April, 1864
ACTION: Captain Edward Howard threatens Tŝilhqot'in on behalf of Alfred Waddington and Alex McDonald's Bute Inlet Road project. He says the work crew will introduce smallpox.
RESULT: Tŝilhqot'in council of chiefs approves a defensive act of war to prevent the introduction of smallpox. War party is dispatched to destroy the work crew. British Columbia martyrs 2 of the "Chilcotin Chiefs" for taking part.

Settlers spreading smallpox in the Tŝilhqot'in. Map courtesy of Shawn Swanky

Galín and ?Imili

Lorraine Weir

Galín and her sister ?Imili were the sole survivors of dada chugh in Bendziny Puntzi. According to Elder Henry Solomon xinli, Galín was seven and ?Imili a year or two older when they "were rescued by someone from a camp at the other end of the lake who had come to visit with Galeen's people."[5] Solomon's mother Mariah died of tuberculosis and his father Timothy died "during the measles epidemic that swept through Indian communities with a vengeance equalled only by smallpox,"[6] so he was raised by Galín. Henry's son Gilbert has spoken of the anger which they must have felt, wanting to "battle the white people," to "pay them back":

> Today we carry that. Our mom and dad gave it to us. We don't know what to do with it, we just carry it. Our mind and our heart tells us not to do that. But we still carry it. People are turned into rock.[7]

In Tŝilhqot'in filmmaker Helen Haig-Brown's powerful film *My Legacy*, as in his many contributions to this book, Gilbert Solomon has called for a healing process for Nenqayni deni and has worked to support it for many years.

We are grateful to the Solomon family for allowing us to include one of the founding stories of the modern Tŝilhqot'in Nation, Se?intsu My Grandmother. Elder Henry Solomon xinli (Xeni Gwet'in) was renowned as a gifted storyteller, and this story brilliantly demonstrates his stylistic virtuosity. Like the great creation story Lhin Desch'osh, Se?intsu tells of the transformation of the Tŝilhqot'in People, their Land and animals.

At the time of her death, ?Etsu Galín was the last living connection to dada chugh the big sickness. In the first part of Se?intsu, Henry Solomon uses the language and style of sadanx gwenig the stories of long ago to elevate Galín's story and the story of smallpox, placing the power of colonial destruction in the context of the forces of creation which shaped the Tŝilhqot'in world. In the second part of the story, the storyteller tells of his own upbringing by ?Etsu Galín.

In the version of Se?intsu which follows, a three-line interlinear gloss transcription has been used in order to provide (1) Solomon's Tŝilhqot'in words, (2) a literal translation, and (3) an adapted translation which is the basis of the edited version presented first. The literal translation will enable readers unfamiliar with the Tŝilhqot'in language to identify some of the characteristics of the language, like word order (that is, syntax, reversed in comparison to

English), careful specification of time and place in relation to proximity to or distance from the speaker, and careful attention to direction on the Land. These spatiotemporal mapping coordinates are characteristic of Dene languages like Tŝilhqot'in but have been mostly lost in modern English. When Tŝilhqot'ins say that "English is backwards," they are observing both the different word order and the vagueness which results from the absence of spatial indicators by comparison with their own language. Time is a river in Dene languages, but space is minutely calibrated as befitting peoples who have always lived on the Land.

Se?intsu My Grandmother (Part 1)[8]

Elder Henry Solomon xinli, Xeni Gwet'in

> Two young girls were found among all the dead people. ?Etsu Galín, Kathleen, was the one that raised my dad. She was there for a long time, eh, raisin' him. She was in part of the Toosey area, that's where ?Etsu Galín went, but the other sister went to Anaham. Had a family there. That's ?Imili. On my dad's side, they were the only ones.
>
> —RONNIE SOLOMON (Xeni Gwet'in)

I will tell a story in the ancient way. It is brief.

Long ago my grandmother was a Bendziny person. People lived near the waterfall at that time. Then a big sickness came among the people. It crawled out of the body of the sick person. Smallpox it is called. It was that sickness. Then the people who lived there in the pithouses all died. My grandmother, Galín, and another person stayed there for one week among the dead people. I don't know for certain if that other person was ?Imili.

Then, a week later, people who lived not very far away walked past the place where the others had died. Then one person was walking there and he found us, my grandmother said. Then, she said, he brought us over to where people had been living in the pithouses and where our family had died. There, at the Bendziny waterfall, the people in the pithouses had died.

Then a wolf took the dead people out of [the pithouses] and scattered the bodies of the people all over the ice, near the waterfall. The wolf scattered the bodies of the dead people around. The wolf was different. It had long fur. It ate all the people. We looked back there and saw that it had eaten all the people in one week. All of them. People's hair was strewn all over the ice. That's what really happened.

We were brought back to people who lived over there in the pithouse. We did not go back to the pithouse over there [where everyone had died]. Someone else raised us over there, where many people live. The sickness did not spread there. Nothing happened to no one [anyone]. That's why we were not affected, my grandmother said.

She lived more than one hundred years, a little more than one hundred years, and then she died.

Left: ʔEtsu Galín xinli. Photo by Chief Roger William of an archival photo, courtesy of Gilbert Solomon
Right: Elder Henry Solomon xinli. Photo by Roland Class

Yagh guntsel jid sadanx gwanagwetasnig.
Um it is brief ancient I will tell a story.
I will tell a story in the ancient way. It is brief.

Seʔintsu yax Bendziny deni ghinli yedanx.
My grandmother over there Bendziny [Puntzi] person she was long ago.
Long ago my grandmother was a Bendziny person.

ʔEgu yax nadilin ʔeyedah ts'edilhtŝ'ih hagughinih.
Then over there waterfall there people lived there it was.
People lived near the waterfall then.

ʔEgu dada nenchagh nitedeniẑed.
Then sickness it's big it came among the people.
Then a big sickness came among the people.

Deni ghaxalhʔas xangh.
Person it crawls out of the body it was.
It crawls out of the body of the [sick] person.

ʔAsmaẑl fugŝ ts'edinh xaghini, ʔeyi dada.
Small pox it is called, it was that sickness.
Smallpox it is called. It was that sickness.

ʔEguh hink'an yax lhiz-qwen-yes ts'edilhtŝ'ih ʔegu,
Then and over there pithouse (eath-fire-under) people lived then,
Then the people who lived there in the pithouses,

deni gatŝ'in ch'eleʔesggan.
People all of them they died.
all died.

Guyen Galín ts'edinh xanih, seʔintsu ʔeyen.
That person Galín she is called it was my grandmother is her.
Galín (Catherine), my grandmother,

ʔEyenah ʔegun ʔinlhed ch'ilhghilh ʔegunah datsagh towh jaghinqi.
She there one week there dead people among them they (two) stayed.
and another person stayed there for one week among the dead people.

ʔImili   ghinli   ʔeguh   lha   su   ʔegwiyeneŝen.
ʔImili   she was that   not   properly   I know.
I don't know for certain if that was ʔImili.

Gan   ʔegu   ʔinlhed   ch'ilhghilh   ghinli.
But   then   one   week   it was.
But then a week later,

ʔEguh   hink'an   bagweʔanz   lhaʔaguŝed   ts'edilhtŝ'ih   hagughint'i.
Then   and   beside it   quite far   people lived   it was.
people who lived not very far away

ʔEgu   ʔegun   yax   deni   ts'en   nanatsʔeghadansh.
Then   there   over there people   toward   people walked.
walked past the place where the others [had died].

ʔEgun   ʔinlhanx   ʔegun   nalgash deyenẑ   ʔeyenah
Then   one person   there   he walked   he
Then one person [who]was walking there

nanexwinlhtin   denish,   seʔintsu.
he found us,   she said,   grandmother.
found us, my grandmother said.

ʔEgu neyax   deni   ʔets'en   ʔegun chuh lhiz-qwen-yes ts'edilhtŝ'ih
Then over there people somewhere else there too   pithouse   they lived
Then, she said, he brought us over there to where the people were living in
pithouses.

ʔegun   nanexwenilhtin   denish.   ʔEgu   chunchuh   ʔinlhed
there   he brought us   she said. Then   again   one
He brought us there, she said. Then,

ch'inlhghilh   ghinli   ʔeguh   yagh   chuhchuh   ʔegun   yax
week   it was   then   um   again   there   over there
one week later,

nexwedesniqi   ts'elesggan   ʔegun   nanexwets'enilhtin
our family   they died   there   one brought us
he brought us to where our family had died,

denish.   ʔEyed   guyed yagh   Bendziny   nadilin   ʔeyed.
she said. There   there   um   Bendziny   waterfall there.
she said. There at the Bendziny waterfall,

Hink'an   yagh   ʔeguh   lhiz-qwen-yex   ch'elets'esggan
And   um   then   pithouse   people died.
the people in the pithouses had died.

ʔeguh   guyi   nun   gant'i   deni   ʔegwenz   xadaŝelex.
then   that   wolf   that type   people   from there   it took out.
Then a wolf took the [dead] people out of there.

ʔEgu   yad   gweneŝ   tench'ed   hagughini, nenk'ed
Then   there   in front of   sheet of ice, it was   [?]
Then [the wolf] scattered the [bodies of] the people

nadilin   nenk'iyed, gweneŝ   tench'ed   gagunlhchugh
waterfall   there,   in front   sheet of ice   all over that
all over the ice, near the waterfall.

deni   nabedelex.   Deni   ch'elesggan   ʔeyen   nun
people   it scattered them around. People   they died   them   wolf
The wolf scattered the bodies of the dead people around.

xagwebaghilish. **ʔEgu** **ʔeguh** **nun** **ʔeyuwh** **gant'ih** **begha**
it brought them out. Then there wolf different its fur
The wolf was different. It had long fur.

dinaẑ **lant'ih** **xaghint'i.** **ʔEyi** **deni** **gatŝ'in**
its long it looked like it was. That people all of them
It ate all the people.

ch'eleʔezan. **Hink'an** **ʔegu** **nagwenaghilʔin.** **ʔInlhed**
it ate. And there we looked back around there. One
We looked back there [and saw that] it ate all the people in one week.

ch'ilhghilh **ghinli** **deni** **gatŝ'in** **ch'eleʔezan.**
week it turned people all of them it ate them all.
All of them.

ʔInlhes **tench'ed** **ʔegu** **ʔinlhes** **gan** **deni-gha,** **deni**
Really (in reality) sheet of ice there really then over there, people
That's what really happened.

tŝigha **gatŝ'i** **ʔeguh** **naŝdeẑ.** **ʔEgu** **yugun**
headhair all of it around there it is strewn. Then over there
People's hair was strewn all over the ice. Then over there

deni **ts'inlin** **ʔegun** **nanexwets'enilah.** **Lha** **gwech'iz** **ʔegun**
people exist there we were brought back to. Not after it there
Then we were brought back to people [who lived] over there in the pithouse. We
did not go back to

nanadelh. **Yugun** **lhiz-qwen-yes** **ʔegun,** **ʔeguh** **hink'an**
we went. Over there pithouse there, then and
the pithouse over there [where the family had died], then

yax **deni** **ʔeyun** **nexwenentilhyan,** **yax** **deni** **lhan**
over there people someone else raised us over there people many
someone else over there where many people live.

dilhtŝ'ih ?egun. ?Egun, ?egun lha dada
they live there. There there not sickness
The sickness did not spread there.

nitexdiżelh lha deni ?inlhanx hulnil. ?Eguh jid
it did spread there not person it happened. That's why
Nothing happened to no one [anyone]. That's why

lha huldinl, nih hadaghini se?intsu ?eyen. ?Inlhed
not we happen, she said my grandmother that person. One
we were not affected, my grandmother said. She lived

handed gu?an xi ghinda. Nenk'ed ?inlhed handed
hundred over (that) years she lived. [?] one hundred
more than one hundred years. A little more than one hundred years

gu?an ŝelin ?eguh hink'an ch'adejagh ungh.
over that it's become then[9] and she died it was.
and then she died.

Suk'antsel ch'adejagh.
A little while ago she died.
A little while ago, she died.

ʔEtsu Galín's Basket

Elder Mabel Solomon xinli, Xeni Gwet'in

Elder Mabel Solomon remembered that ʔEtsu Galín "had a basket like this strapped to the side of her horse at Toosey, and she came to a village where [there was] a house, and they offered to feed her, and she would go to this basket and put some food in there. And then, later on, they realized that she had a young child in there, in the basket, that was hanging off the side of the horse, and it was the late Henry Solomon" – Mabel's husband.

Genocide

Lorraine Weir

After first contact in 1774, smallpox came in waves up and down the coast, and historian Robert Boyd documents smallpox epidemics in the Pacific Northwest shortly after, during the late 1770s, then in 1801–1802, 1836–1838, and 1853, as well as in 1862–1863 in the Tŝilhqot'in. A successful vaccine using cowpox was discovered in 1796, but Boyd writes that it "had no effect on mortality rates in Northwest Native American populations until the epidemic of 1836–1838."[10] Between April and December 1862, Boyd estimates that fourteen thousand people – half of the Indigenous people living on the coast from Victoria to Alaska – died. At the same time, vaccine was in good supply, and the white population was familiar with basic prevention strategies: vaccination (and inoculation in the case of smallpox), quarantine, social distancing, and hygiene. Practicing these measures ensured that there was low incidence of smallpox among non-Indigenous people in Victoria during the same period. On one hand, city-dwelling settlers largely escaped the epidemic due to privileges of class, education, and access to medical doctors, while Indigenous Peoples bore the brunt of it due to the same negative determinants of health now easily recognized as structural expressions of racism.[11] Historian Mary-Ellen Kelm writes that "if Aboriginal bodies were weakened by contact with non-Natives, it was not just the fault of faceless pathogens but also of governmental policy-makers, civil servants, and legislators who consistently sacrificed Aboriginal bodies for 'provincial development' ... [S]acrificing was not inevitable but rather the result of a careful weighing of interests."[12]

When Tŝilhqot'in Warriors were threatened with smallpox by Waddington's roadbuilding crew, they were not only familiar with the terrifying power of the virus to wipe out whole villages as it had at Bendziny, but also with the racism and sexualized violence directed at them and their families. The issue for them was not roadbuilding but sovereignty. Months later, resistance to the Crown's assertion of control over Nenqayni deni would evolve into the Tŝilhqot'in War, leaving the horror of six Tŝilhqot'in Warriors hanged and the abyss of genocide for survivors to endure. As Elder Eileen Sammy William has said, "People were afraid to give information about the generation who lived during the Tŝilhqot'in War, so very little was handed down" about those relatives.[13] When an Elder passes away, a whole library of cultural, historical, and linguistic knowledge goes with them. In the wake of genocide, what was left?

Elder Theresa George xinli

Betty Lulua, Xeni Gwet'in

Elder Theresa George xinli was in her eighties. Kinda like a stepmom to my husband. [Long ago] she was out, just out in the bush, just like travellin' with teamhorse and wagon. And horseback. And she said they used to wash their blankets. They made sure their blankets were really washed thoroughly, 'cause I guess disease was spread through blankets, you know, human contact with people that are sick. She watch[ed] somebody that's been sick and she want[ed to] wash their blanket, and you rub it really hard and you hang it. That's regardin' the smallpox. They had these big tin tubs that they put over a campfire and see that they get the water as hot as they can get it. Let their blankets boil in that hot water to get rid of the disease. And hang it up to dry, air-dry.

I asked her if she would tell me what did you ever do when any kind of sickness came into a community, gettin' people really sick and some may be dying. She said we never did stay when they were there. We moved away from anything that will harm the family. And they really took it to heart to live off the Land. Pack water, you know. Make wood. Use kindling. There was wood – fir trees – and they use it for fire starters. And there's pitch-tree gum. Like, the pitch, they use that as a fire starter. And if there was [a place] where those wagons couldn't go, they take the other horse and lead the packhorse. They used to travel to all the areas where there's wagon trails.

Deni Daẑtŝan Graveyard Valley[14]

Elder Martin Quilt xinli, Xeni Gwet'in

Graveyard Valley. There used to be ten thousand over there. They all died. Dogs can find hidden bones. Lotsa bones scattered all over in the bush over there. Take about a day's ride with a saddle horse. They musta died from smallpox I guess.

They used to get lots of pores in their face, eh. A lotta pus came out, I guess, to the face. Some people, they just walk in the bush. They die. They don't wanna die at home, eh. They go in the bush and die.

The Big Flu (Spanish Influenza)

Lorraine Weir

Dada chugh was a decisive sign of dispossession, but it was not the only disease to fracture the Tŝilhqot'in world. Spanish Influenza or the Big Flu was a pandemic, but when it arrived in the Tŝilhqot'in in 1918 it was understood by Nenqayni deni as another blow directed at them from outside, just as smallpox had been. For Maria Myers, the Big Flu was "germ warfare," as she says in her statement below. Current studies show that "deaths among Indigenous peoples were of an order of magnitude higher than among the non-Indigenous: 6.2 out of every thousand non-Indigenous Canadians died of influenza, while on-reserve Indigenous death rates ranged from 10.3 per 1,000 in Prince Edward Island, to 61 per 1,000 in Alberta."[15]

White People Are Shooting at Us in the Air

Maria Myers, Yuneŝit'in

You know what our old people used to say about the Big Flu? They used to say white people are shooting at us in the air. My uncle Eugene [William] was only born in the bush because my grandfather [Sambulyan] was a deyen and he told the family, "Don't go back to Nemiah. It's scary there." And that's what my mum [Helena Myers xinli] told me. Eugene was born and there was a certain place – Dasiqox [where he was born].

And then at a certain time, the sickness was gone, and it was okay to move back. When they moved back, my grandmother Annie [Elkins] felt like crying, because everybody she knew had died. My mum was only two. Ronnie Solomon sings that song. It's a song to my mum.

Helena[16]

Ronnie Solomon, Xeni Gwet'in

Helena yedanx ya ʔan Dasiqox
Helena, long ago, over at Dasiqox

ʔegu dalhtŝ'i ʔegun,
where you once lived,

Xeni Gwet'in dada gutedeniẑed.
A sickness reached the people of Xeni.

Gwechugh deni lhan ts'elasggan.
Too many people perished.

Deni lhan gatŝ'i jeẑlin.
Many people were no more.

Gwech'iz deni tuh najendil.
Later your family moved back among the people.

Be ʔinkwel bedzi denisdagh.
Her [Helena's] mother grieved in anguish

Gwechugh deni lhan ts'ajedejagh.
Too many people had passed on.

Ba desniqi gatŝ'i jeẑlin.
Many of her family were no more.

Hulht'i ʔaguŵet'i, hulht'i ʔagulhʔin.
It cannot be helped, there is nothing you can do.

Lha nendzi denidah.
Don't let it hurt you.

Gan baghents'a gughult'i.
We will just pray for them.

Hulht'i ʔaguŵet'i, hulht'i ʔaguŵet'i.
It cannot be helped, it cannot be helped.

Lha nendzi denida.
Do not grieve.

Spanish Flu

Ivor Deneway Myers xinli, Yuneŝit'in

In 1918 Spanish Flu came in the country, and a lot of our people died again. A deyen decided to help, one powerful medicine man. There was another medicine person who was livin' at Stone, and when they went, they both died. Their spirits came together in a place on the road just below where Simon is staying at Stone. Their spirits came, and they flew into the sky.

When they came to the sky, they saw themselves amongst a whole flock of people, all naked, and they were placed right in the boiling water. Tickled their hands with forks. If you were trying to escape, they'd fork you back in.

And one of the deyens had the power of sunlight that clung to his hair and he was lifted from that area, brought back to the boundary, and he was going down.

He said, "Henry," he said, "I was goin' down. My blood was drippin' from me. But I was hearin' a deyen calling for help!"

I asked my dad, "Why was he crying?"

Says, "Maybe he was crying because he was doing all kinds of bad things to other people with his power. When it came to his turn, they punished him in that way. Maybe that's why he was crying."

So when the one came down to earth where he was lifted at the beginning, he said,

"Here I was walkin' back home. I walked towards the door and I was gonna open it. I went right through the door," he said. "My spirit went right through the door, and here my body was in the corner, so I walked towards my body, and I'm back in my body. I woke up, and I told the people next door."

It was my grandfather and my grandmother, George and Pauline.

Then a week later, that guy died. The Spanish Flu. That deyen died, buried in Nemiah. The other one died, probably buried at Stone.

That's how my dad told me, and that's how I know the story today.

For the ʔEsggidam Ancestors

Lorraine Weir

Whether white people were shooting arrows of smallpox or the Big Flu, the source was the same from Elder Eugene William xinli's perspective, and it was the Tŝilhqot'in War,[17] the first volley in the colonial genocide which claimed anywhere from 80 to 90 percent of the Tŝilhqot'in population in slightly more than five decades. Historian Mary-Ellen Kelm writes that "the Big Flu broke down the boundaries between the living and the dead. Such boundaries, which include the limits between the inside and the outside of the body, are crucial and must be maintained for both individual and social health. The four main causes of disease in Aboriginal etiology relate directly to the breaching of these limits and involve: soul loss, spirit intrusion, object intrusion, and witchcraft. The breaching of these boundaries, then, denotes not just profound physical distress, but the kind of spiritual disorder that can only lead to continued disarray."[18]

This "spiritual disorder" is what Gilbert Solomon refers to as negativity associated with the sustained colonial attack on the Tŝilhqot'in world. Apache/ Tewa/Lakota psychologist Eduardo Duran calls it soul wounds[19] and spiritual torment, as well as other forms of imbalance and illness. Stories of the diseases that white people were and are shooting through the air, as Maria Myers says, are as much stories of physical illness as of the pain of world loss and the wounding of the Nen Land and of Nenqayni deni the people. In this sense, it's not only the diagnostic terms which are mobile but also the memories, one catastrophe overlaid on another. The ʔEsggidam Ancestors are everywhere, the sense of violation as fresh as yesterday. Gwenig stories are their resting places, place names their homes.

Tsíqon

from Terry Glavin

"Eugene William xinli remembered a Nemiah man called [Tsíqon] who returned from Stone with the Spanish flu. He and another man had been told not to go because there was a dangerous flu going around, but they still went. So this disease got to Nemiah and wiped out half of the Chilcotins." [Tsíqon] "felt bad" and used lumber intended to build a dance floor to build coffins instead, and "later on the people helped him bury the rest."[20]

Burial

Patrick Lulua, Xeni Gwet'in

Smallpox. The only one that really spoke to me about that was the late Francis Setah, my father-in-law. Conway Setah's brother – they call 'em Tsíqon in our language [Tommy Setah xinli]. He's the one that buried a lot of the smallpox victims. He didn't get the smallpox – I dunno why. Probably shallow graves, right. They were afraid, 'cause what midugh used to do was take those people up and then spread the disease again, and that's why, before that, they had cremation done. But if so many of them died at one time, they didn't have much they could do with all the dead ones. Buried in Nemiah. There.

Xeni Biny, looking toward the unmarked burial place. Photo by Lorraine Weir

CHAPTER 2 ENDNOTES

1   Pronounced "dada cho." Dada means "sickness" and chugh means "big."

2   After sweeping across the Tŝilhqot'in Plateau, smallpox "completely wiped out the six Shuswap [Secwépemc] bands on the west side of the Fraser River and cut the overall Shuswap population to a third of its former level" (Elizabeth Furniss, *Victims of Benevolence: The Dark Legacy of the Williams Lake Residential School* [Vancouver: Arsenal Pulp Press, 1992], 40).

3   Compare John Sutton Lutz, *Makúk: A New History of Aboriginal-White Relations* (Vancouver: UBC Press, 2008). Lutz argues that Tŝilhqot'in "insistence, in the nineteenth century, that Europeans enter their territory on Tsilhqot'in terms meant that the Chilcotin Plateau was one of the least settled areas in British Columbia," and maintains that in the case of Xeni, if "early resistance to capitalist relations did not protect their economy in the long run, it would seem that it did protect their culture" (161). From a Tŝilhqot'in perspective, it might be argued that while genocide was inseparable from colonial capitalism, self-determination is rooted in culture and language and grows from roots in the Nen Land. See also chapter 8.

4   See also by Tom Swanky, *The True Story of Canada's "War" of Extermination on the Pacific, Plus the Tsilhqot'in and Other First Nations Resistance* (2012), *The Smallpox War in Nuxalk Territory* (2016), and *The Smallpox War against the Haida* (with Shawn Swanky, 2023), all published by Dragon Heart Enterprises in Surrey, BC.

5   Terry Glavin and the People of Nemiah Valley, *Nemiah: The Unconquered Country* (Vancouver: New Star Books, 1992), 88.

6   Glavin, *Nemiah*, 88.

7   Gilbert Solomon's words, from *My Legacy*, a 2014 documentary directed by Helen Haig-Brown. See femfilm.ca/film_search.php?film=haig-brown-my&lang=e.

8   Seʔintsu My Grandmother, parts 1 and 2, was recorded by Maria Myers (Yuneŝit'in) on July 26, 1981, transcribed by June Williams (Xeni Gwet'in) on February 20, 1982, and first published in *Chilcotin Stories* (School District 27, Chilcotin Language Committee, 1982). We are grateful to Dr. Patricia Shaw, director of the BC Breath of Life Institute for First Nations Languages at UBC, Vancouver, who made it possible for Maria to spend a week (May 14–20, 2017) at UBC, working with Lorraine Weir and student assistant Ben Chung on the transcription and translation of the story. Permission for the English translation was given by Dinah Lulua on behalf of the Solomon family. Permission to use Maria Myers's translation, based on her own 1981 recording of Henry Solomon, was given by Maria Myers. The edited translation is by Lorraine Weir and based on Maria Myers's close translation and on her teachings about this story shared with Weir and Ben Chung in May 2017.

9   Maria Myers outlines the layers of time in this story as follows: sadanx = ancient times; yedanx = long ago: the smallpox time = 1862; sukʔan = a little while ago. Galín's lifetime: she was one hundred years old. Sadanx is the whole story, yedanx is the smallpox time, and sukʔan is when Galín died.

10 Robert Boyd, "Smallpox in the Pacific Northwest: The First Epidemics," *Anthropology Faculty Publications and Presentations* 141 (Spring 1994): 6–7, pdxscholar.library.pdx .edu/anth_fac/141. See also Robert Boyd, *The Coming of the Spirit of Pestilence: Introduced Infectious Diseases and Population Decline among Northwest Coast Indians, 1774–1874* (Seattle: University of Washington Press with UBC Press, 1999).

11 For more on smallpox on the coast, see, for example, Greg Lange, "Smallpox Epidemic of 1862 among Northwest Coast and Puget Sound Indians," HistoryLink.org (website), February 4, 2003, www.historylink.org/File/5171. This article includes a wide-ranging survey of racist speech in the journalism of the day, documenting the public currency of racism against Indigenous Peoples at the time.

12 Mary-Ellen Kelm, *Colonizing Bodies: Aboriginal Health and Healing in British Columbia, 1900–50* (Vancouver: UBC Press, 1998), 177.

13 From notes made by Linda R. Smith in September 2016 during a visit by Elders to the Museum of Anthropology at UBC. Similarly, Emily Ekks xinli is said to have told her grandchildren not to speak to white people because "they're trying to get information off of you so they can use it against you someday." As a child, she remembered being "snuck around the mountains" so she wouldn't have to talk to midugh about the Tŝilhqot'in War.

14 Deni Daẑtŝan Graveyard Valley is the site of the last battle between the St'at'imc and the Tŝilhqot'in. Peace was declared in the 1840s. In 2007 the two Nations constructed a monument to honour the memory of the Warriors. The St'at'imc population was decimated by smallpox, which laid waste whole villages, as in the Tŝilhqot'in.

15 Esyllt Jones, "Surviving Influenza: Lived Experiences of Health Inequity and Pandemic Disease in Canada," *Canadian Medical Association Journal* (*CMJA*) 192, no. 25 (June 22, 2020): E688–E689, doi.org/10.1503/cmaj.201074, and "Recollecting Influenza: Pandemic Disease, Health Inequity, and Social Change," with a poster by Karen Jeane Mills, part of the Graphic History Collective's online Remember | Resist | Redraw: A Radical History Poster Project series, December 17, 2020, graphichistorycollective.com/project/poster-27 -1918-1919-flu-pandemic.

16 Transcribed and translated by Maryann Solomon with permission from Ronnie Solomon. Copyright Ronnie Solomon. All rights reserved. This song records the impact of dada chugh on three generations, from Elder Helena Myers xinli (Ronnie Solomon's aunt – his mother Mabel Solomon xinli's eldest sister) back to Elder Helena's mother, Annie Sammy William xinli (Ronnie Solomon's grandmother). It was Annie Sammy William who survived the smallpox genocide and wept on her return home to find such devastation. Helena Myers's sister, Eileen Sammy William, is Chief Roger's mother and Annie Sammy William xinli his grandmother. Her husband, Roger's grandfather, was Sambulyan xinli.

17 Glavin, *Nemiah*, 91.

18 Kelm, *Colonizing Bodies*, 42.

19 Eduardo Duran's term. See Duran (Tiospaye Ta Woapiye Wicasa), *Healing the Soul Wound: Trauma-Informed Counselling for Indigenous Communities*, 2nd ed., Multicultural Foundations of Psychology and Counseling series (New York: Teachers College Press, 2019).

20 In the version of this story which Eugene William xinli told Terry Glavin, ʔElegesi used Lysol and rum as disinfectants and antidotes to Spanish influenza. See Glavin, *Nemiah*, 89–91.

The Tŝilhqot'in War (1864)

Maybe things are very critical now because our people were decimated with smallpox in the past. It was another way of annihilating our people, and the survivors were able to fight no more. Maybe they [midugh] were threatened and they hanged our Tŝilhqot'in Chiefs. Lhatŝ'assʔin said, "We meant war, not murder," and they hanged our Tŝilhqot'in Chiefs without a fair trial. After that, people were afraid to even speak about war.

—IVOR DENEWAY MYERS xinli (Yuneŝit'in)

Then Everything Broke Out

Chief Roger William

Two years after smallpox caused the death of 80 percent of our people, the Gold Rush into the Tŝilhqot'in began from the coast, from Homathko and Bute Inlet up through the mountains. Our people used to go down to the coast with First Nations down there, and the Gold Rush crew, the Waddington crew, wanted to build a road up. Some of our Tŝilhqot'ins worked for them but were mistreated, and some of our head Warriors were saying we shouldn't let them do this. Then the others said that our people were working there and making it work. Later, some of the people from the camp said this is how we're being treated. When the Warriors found out that Tŝilhqot'ins were being mistreated and there was a smallpox threat again, the war broke out. Then everything broke out. Our Tŝilhqot'in Warriors warred with the roadbuilders and wiped them out.

As early as 1808, Simon Fraser saw a Tŝilhqot'in riding a horse, but during the Tŝilhqot'in War, our Warriors were on foot purposely in order to stay ahead of the soldiers. The soldiers chased them and they just kept moving. We had cachepits, and our Warriors knew where all the food was. They weren't packing [carrying] anything. They were on foot and in good shape. They led the soldiers on into a place. We had bows and arrows to get big game like mountain goat, mountain sheep, deer, or moose, and we were good at putting ourselves in a place and setting up to hunt an animal for food. So that's what happened here. Our Tŝilhqot'ins led the soldiers into a place and killed their leader, McLean. Then the soldiers packed up and left.

Asking for War

David Setah, Xeni Gwet'in[1]

Our people tried to work for them. When people who worked in the same camp were lining up to eat, they came out and said, "You guys hungry? You guys wanna eat?" And they just threw the food down on the ground. Our people weren't gonna eat that, so they went hunting, and they had no choice but to leave their wife and kids behind. While they were gone, the miners and all those people who got drunk back in those days messed around with the women. You're asking for war when you do that to people, and that's how the war broke out. Nobody was gonna stand back and let [that abuse] happen. There was a Chilcotin Reserve sent out here and later taken back, but foreigners were still scared to come into the area.

A lot of our people achieved what they did even after all that was done. If we wanted to own a piece of land out here on our own, we had to give up our status to do it. We had to say that we were no longer Tŝilhqot'ins. That's the only way we could get a piece of *our* land. And after all that, we didn't have the right to vote, and we weren't recognized.

How It All Started

Rita Lulua Meldrum, Xeni Gwet'in

My name is Rita Meldrum, and I'm a granddaughter to Nimazya (Tommy Lulua), who was the brother of Gene Lashway Lulua, one of the first elected Chiefs and also a hereditary Chief of Nemiah. The government made my great-uncle Lashway a Chief, but my grandfather and dad refused to move to Xeni, because they didn't want to live in a cage.[2]

Nimazya's wife was Inez Lulua. The first story that was imprinted in my mind is the story my grandmother Inez told me about when she was a teenager and she was at Table Mountain, and the McLean crew used to come into the camp and kidnap all the young, beautiful Native girls. In order to prevent that, they would dig a hole in the side of the mountain away from their [Tŝilhqot'in] camp and hide all the girls there and cover them with mud if they came out, so they didn't look beautiful. The McLean crew was camped on the other side of the mountain, on the Tatlayoko Lake side, and they used to kidnap young girls and sexually abuse them.

During one of these raids, the McLean crew kidnapped the Chief's daughter, and I think they kept her for about a week or two – a week to a month, I think my grandmother said. They brought her back to trade her in for other young girls. And what they did with these young teenagers was they gang-raped them. Used them as slaves at the camp. And the group brought her back, and then the Chief saw how dead she looked in her face – there was no life left in her. So he took a gun and shot her in the head in front of the McLean crew, 'cause he didn't want her to suffer like the other girls and the other families did.[3] The Chief stood for his family and his Land. That's when the McLean crew thought the Chief was retaliating. They didn't steal any more girls. They rushed home.

My grandmother told me that's how it all started. It can almost make me cry to think that. I went to residential school from age five until thirteen, and I was raped, so I can understand. I got post-traumatic stress because of that. So I can understand why he did it. No More Stolen Women started back then and is still going.

Jinadlin

Ivor Deneway Myers xinli, Yuneŝit'in

There was a man by the name of Jinadlin. During the time when they didn't know what his name was, they call 'em Lhatŝ'assʔin. Lhatŝ'assʔin means we don't know him. His real name was Jinadlin. That's where he was born. That's where the mother came from and ended up going insane. I've never been to that place, but I've been through there. It kinda switches, it goes back in the same creek again.

Jinadlin came of age, and when he was old enough, he had a son by the name of Biyil. And Biyil had a son and the son was from Tatlayoko. And he had a son down at Bute Inlet, where he met this other woman. Maskwas, she was. So he had a child there.

Waddington and his crews were going to build a road through there. They met Tŝilhqot'in men who were willing to build a road through the Tŝilhqot'in country. They had no qualms about it until the crews started abusing their women, using some of the girls as prostitutes and starving the people at the same time.[4] Never gave them their fair earnings. The leader [Lhatŝ'assʔin] had a daughter, and they probably sexually abused her. That's one of the things that escalated the situation. Then one of the road crew members threatened them with smallpox. That alarmed them, 'cause they had witnessed thousands and thousands of Tŝilhqot'ins dying from that.

A young boy used to come to their camp. This fellow didn't like it, so he spilt boiling water on this child. That's what escalated everything. They said they'd give 'em more smallpox, that's what they'd do. Here were Tŝilhqot'ins who were willing to help build a road, and they got threatened with more smallpox.

So that's why Lhatŝ'assʔin and his Warriors had a War Dance that night. They danced all night until early morning before sunrise. None of the people [who were dancing] were supposed to sit down, or they would get executed. That was their law then. When they'd finished, early morning came, and another shaman would drop something near the fire. They looked at it and saw they'd win the battle. It was the start of a war, and they went to attack that camp because Waddington's crews were at fault for all the things that had been going on. Some non-Natives were not involved with the smallpox episode, and they were let go.

Lhatŝ'assʔin was appointed by his people. Grand Leader they called 'em in my language. It's nenchagh. At that time the deyen people mostly made decisions about who should become the leaders. It was told to me many times by different Elders how they picked their leaders. It was done the traditional way using the deyen people. The men were no [more] powerful than the women, the women were no [more] powerful than the men. So they were supposed to work hand in hand and respect each other. That was told to me by quite a few Elders but not the younger generation today. Even the women could join the force and become enlisted in that war with their boyfriends or spouses or whatever you call 'em. They danced around the fire all night. They were given some tobacco and smoked it. It was part of their rituals. When he went back to the homeland, Lhatŝ'assʔin and his Warriors said, "I dunno what's gonna happen after this."

So Lhatŝ'assʔin was in Chayses's camp. They were gonna be given something – they were gonna honour 'em as a High Chief. It was told to me by one Elder – no other Elder told me but this one Elder – he didn' wanna reveal it in public because he might get attacked. It had something to do with Anahim. This one Elder said to Lhatŝ'assʔin, my great-great-uncle, "They're gonna give you something called tsagwish [beaver trap].[5] They're gonna honour you as a High Chief if you come to Chayses's camp. If you don't wanna go to it, all the people that you love will be no more." A year before, Lhatŝ'assʔin had come to

Lha yudit'ih We Always Find a Way

Chayses's camp, and his ankles were hurting – giving him pain. So when he went to Chayses's camp, they were waiting for Chayses and his men to negotiate, talk in good faith. When he went to Chayses's camp, he said to them, "You should go back in the bush, run back in the bush. If you don't, you're gonna be apprehended."

One young girl, a teenager about sixteen years old, came all the way from – not Telhiqox, she ran from there I think. And Lhatŝ'assʔin said to her, "Aren't you just jealous 'cause we're gonna be honoured as the High Chief? We're gonna be given an award." That young girl said, "I didn't come all the way here for nothing. This doesn't just come from my mouth. I'm a messenger here. I keep giving the message to you from a deyen. A deyen told me to come here and tell you." After that, she left.

Not long after, there were guns pointing – "Whether you like it or not, you have death. Let go the rifles." They put some cannonballs along their legs, but Lhats'assʔin didn't realize they were cannonballs, and he called [them] tsagwish. That's when Lhatŝ'assʔin knew to go.

So they either walked or were put in a wagon all the way to Quesnel. They were put in that small little cabin, all five of them. I dunno all their names. It was five of them involved. [War Chiefs] Chayses, Biyil, Lhatŝ'assʔin they called Jinadlin, and there were two others [War Chiefs Telad and Taqed]. The priest used to come there and talk to them. He wrote down everything that was said.[6] Judge Begbie didn't know what to do. Sent a telegram or letter to Governor Seymour. I believe Governor Seymour replied and told them to hang 'em.

They believed in what they did. They got hanged without a fair trial. They are martyrs of the Nation. To this day, some of the stuff that was supposed to be for them was crossed out in black. It's what they queried. 'Cause the white people that were involved didn't want to be to blame all those times. So that was a mystery in itself.

One of the Elders from our country told me how the chieftainship was given to Hoseli in prison after that. Hoseli didn't want it. The last person that it was given to was Anaham. That power didn't go nowhere after that, because it's very traditional. It should be given to somebody that's very knowledgeable – good heart, good mind. Somebody that's fair, honest. Somebody who hasn't done anything wrong in the past and somebody that has lots of knowledge regarding history and the Land and how they're speaking from it – both worlds, both societies. They speak at the level of the people and the governments, other governments.

After the hanging of our Chiefs, the colonial government expropriated some Land and pre-empted some Land without our consent so all the stuff that's been happening since 1864 is illegal. The federal and provincial governments have no jurisdiction whatsoever over the Land that the Tŝilhqot'in Nation utilizes today. When our population got reduced by smallpox, we couldn't use the whole area, but today we use and manage it. There has to be some kind of a long term agreement with the federal government and it has to be done fair and in a good way. That's what I'd like to see in the future.

Dignity and Trust

Chief Roger William

Some people were divided already. They didn't trust the Chiefs, they didn't trust the Warriors, they didn't trust anybody. And when the Warriors were hung, there was a big division in the Nation. But without the Tŝilhqot'in War, I don't think we would be what we are today. The Tŝilhqot'in Warriors put dignity back into our people. They put hope back into our people. During those two years, everybody thought they were all gonna die, and they were all tryin' to survive. You know, I think about all the stories that I heard. Every [Tŝilhqot'in] child knows about the Tŝilhqot'in War. And I think about survival skills. To see the whole Tŝilhqot'in being scared when the Warriors started to come back after they wiped out the crew and they were wiping out the rest of the people in the Tŝilhqot'in. There was like a celebration almost, and a scare at the same time.

When we go to war, there's a ritual. There's singing, dancing, and a sacrifice, because you may not come back again, but it's for the honour of your Land and your people that you protect. But when somebody dies because of your actions, that can become an addiction. That can become overbearing, and that might be a bad thing. That's why there's a ritual, a ceremony with dancing, sage, and juniper. So when you're doing this for a cause, you're ready spiritually, mentally, and physically. And when you survive the war, you come back, and it's wiped away. There's a process for that. And if it ain't done right, then what happens – and you see it today – is if somebody kills somebody for a reason, that person keeps killing. It becomes an addiction, like a drug, like alcohol. You gotta do it, you don't know why. It's rage, because there's an adrenalin rush that's probably not normal. It's just like riding a bull or mountainracing: it's an adrenalin rush, but you gotta do ceremony to control that.

Late Henry Solomon talked about how the Warriors got uneasy and angry. They had to do something, and they'd go out there and kill someone and feel good again. He talked about the Tŝilhqot'in War Dance and War Song that are a ceremony so you don't have to do that. He said they would dance all night for their family, their people, their Land. They were honoured to fight, and they might not come back. They danced all night to be prepared and to be honoured. They weren't scared, they weren't out to get somebody in a war. They were out to protect who they are, their Land, for their people. And if they didn't come back, it's an honour, it's meant to be.

Late Henry Solomon talked about the power of that. He explained that even though you have to kill someone, it's still not right, but if you don't, you're gonna go [die]. He said when you kill somebody, it's an adrenalin rush that can take you over, so once you kill somebody, you've gotta do it again and again, for whatever reason, whether it's good or bad. When you kill someone – if that happens for whatever reason – you're taking a being, a spirit, away, and if you don't dance, pray, and do ceremony for it, it'll take control over you. That's how I understand it. When my uncles and the Elders talked to me about this, they said those are the high points in life that could control you. They said that when you become a deyen and you've got medicine, medicine's got a life of its own, it's got a personality, whether you've got bear medicine, beaver medicine, whatever. The medicines have got their own character, and you've gotta be able to control that by doing the right things. You have to be honest, you have to be prepared, and you have to treat everyone with respect. If you do all the right things, you've got a better chance of controlling the power, so if you had to kill somebody in a war, you could control that.

In some of our rituals and in our culture, we're taught that you do everything in your power to prepare yourself to do something. At the end of the day, if you don't succeed, it's okay. It's meant to be, don't worry about it. Somebody dies on account of what you're trying to do or whatever, it's meant to be. It's an honour. It happened. So that's what our Warriors were taught back in the day, and that's what I'm taught. You do everything in your power to do the right thing, and if it goes south, our people say it's meant to be. But if you cheated, if you did this and that, then it comes back on you, and you're gonna live with it. That's what I've been told. You created that. It's not Creator. You didn't put yourself into the hands of the Creator. But if you did all the right things, and then it didn't work, you're okay with it, you can live with it, you can move on. Didn't work, that's the way it goes. But if you did something, and then the Creator did something, you gotta live with it. There are procedures, there are rituals. The leadership will try and help you get outta that.

Back in the day, punishment was much stronger, because, before you were born, you were in the womb of the mother and the father, and they were teaching you all the right things to do to become an adult. Then you go do something wrong. There's gotta be something that's going on. We can't trust you. They get rid of you, ban you – that's how serious it was. Today, you go to court and get a sentence for two, three years. If you were in jail for those two three years, that helps you in the future with the time served, because twenty days in jail means forty days off your sentence. But in our culture, in our way back then, because you lived it and then you chose to go the other way, it was really serious. You can't be trusted – not by your family, not by your community, in some cases not by your Nation. They wanna get rid of you, whatever that means.

Exoneration

Lorraine Weir

On March 26, 2018, in the presence of the six Tŝilhqot'in Chiefs who joined him and performed ceremony in the House of Commons in Ottawa, Prime Minister Justin Trudeau made a speech exonerating the Tŝilhqot'in Warriors. Trudeau was careful to stress that the Warriors "were attempting to repel a colonial road crew that wanted to build a road through Tŝilhqot'in Territory without any legal agreement with the Tŝilhqot'in Nation" and that "the rights of the Tŝilhqot'in people to the land, and their right to maintain and uphold their cultural and legal traditions, were not considered by the colonial government of the day." The Prime Minister's speech has been excerpted at length here, not only because it provides a summary of key aspects of the history of the Tŝilhqot'in War, but also because it marks a long withheld acknowledgment by Canada of its historic role in attempting to subjugate Indigenous Peoples and of its obligations to address the damage done and contribute to positive change now and in the future.

> In the spring of 1864, the Tŝilhqot'in chiefs led a war party, in defence of [their homeland] ... The chiefs were attempting to repel a colonial road crew that wanted to build a road through Tŝilhqot'in territory without any legal agreement with the Tŝilhqot'in Nation. The rights of the Tŝilhqot'in people to the land, and their right to maintain and uphold their cultural and legal traditions, were not considered by the colonial government of the day. As settlers came to the land in the rush for gold, no consideration was given to the needs of the Tŝilhqot'in people who were there first. No agreement was made to access their land. No consent was sought. At the same time, along with settlement came smallpox, which devastated Indigenous communities across the continent, including the Tŝilhqot'in.

Some reliable historical accounts indicate that the Tŝilhqot'in had been threatened with the spread of the disease by one of the road workers. And so, faced with these threats, the Tŝilhqot'in people took action to defend their territory. After convening a council to declare war, they attacked the road crew near Bute Inlet and removed all settlers from their lands, before taking refuge in their territory beyond the reach of the colonial militia. Not long after, one of the leaders of the colonial militia, Gold Commissioner William Cox, sent the Tŝilhqot'in chiefs a sacred gift of tobacco and, with it, an invitation to discuss terms of peace. Head War Chief Lhatŝ'assʔin and his men accepted this truce. As a show of good will, they rode into the camp to negotiate peace. Instead of being welcomed as leaders and respected warriors, they were arrested, imprisoned, convicted, and killed. On October 26, 1864, five Tŝilhqot'in chiefs were hanged for murder: Head War Chief Lhatŝ'assʔin, Chief Biyil, Chief Tilaghed, Chief Taqed, and Chief Chayses. They are buried in Quesnel, BC. Later, Chief Ahan was also hanged. He is buried in New Westminster, BC.

Today our government acknowledges what the colonial government of the day was unwilling to accept: that these six chiefs were leaders and warriors of the Tŝilhqot'in Nation, and that the Tŝilhqot'in people they led maintained rights to land that had never been ceded. Even though the colonial government did not recognize these rights, the chiefs acted in accordance with their own laws to defend their territory, their people, and their way of life. They acted as leaders of a proud and independent nation facing a threat from another nation. When they came to meet with colonial officials, they did so on a diplomatic mission, expecting to be treated with dignity and honour. Their capture and arrest by the colonial government demonstrated a profound lack of respect for the Tŝilhqot'in people, as did the refusal to recognize Tŝilhqot'in as a nation.

Those are mistakes that our government is determined to set right. We now understand that the treatment of the Tŝilhqot'in chiefs represented a betrayal of trust – an injustice that has been carried by the Tŝilhqot'in people for more than 150 years. And so, as an important symbol of our commitment to reconciliation, we confirm without reservation that Chief Lhatŝ'assʔin, Chief Biyil, Chief Tilaghed, Chief Taqed, Chief Chayses, and Chief Ahan are fully exonerated of any crime or wrongdoing. In the words of Chief Lhatŝ'assʔin, "They meant war, not murder." We recognize that these six chiefs were leaders of a nation, that they acted in accordance with their laws and traditions, and that they are well regarded as heroes by their people.[7]

When five of the six Warriors were hanged in Quesnel, Lhatŝ'assʔin's black horse "escaped from the site of execution … swam both the Fraser and Chilcotin Rivers, and returned" to Lhatŝ'assʔin's village and his family.[8] At the request of the Tŝilhqot'in National Government, when Trudeau made a formal visit to Xeni in November 2018, he rode in on a black horse. Gene Cooper's Quarter Horse X Thoroughbred, Indinʔ (Thunder), was chosen for this ceremony.

Indinʔ resting during a ride on Tl'etŝans Xadalgwenlh Bald Mountain near Tl'esqox Riske Creek. Photo courtesy of Gene Cooper

Arrows

Chief Roger William

I don't think we ever recovered. We were always told what to do. You know, here's the Indian Act, here's the residential school. "Go there – that's where we're gonna fix you." They never said "Okay, what do we do to help you? What does your culture do? What do you do?" You know? Like, "What's your ritual belief? What do you do?" That wasn't even given a day. I think of some people now and what they're goin' through. People born into what the government created – residential schools. Thinkin' they were gonna assimilate us from our culture so that they didn't have to kill us, but they could "kill the Indian in the child."[9] But that never happened. So here's a person who was born into a chaos, so she didn't know *her* world, the Tŝilhqot'in world. She doesn't know it. She doesn't know the Western world. She's stuck in between and just like a victim. She probably knows a lotta survival skills – that's DNA. But we don't have the people we used to have that could help out. That's gonna take years, generations to come back, because right now you see gangs and you see leaders and you see people who are doin' good, but they still can manipulate if they need to, to survive. They know the language, they know how to hunt, they know how to respect and honour, but still, it's as though they can flip a switch and turn on somebody to survive.

I think a lot of it is so deeply ingrained because of how we were treated from the smallpox to the Tŝilhqot'in War to the Indian Act to the residential school. Many leaders say we've got a lotta arrows in our back. People outside recognize you more than your own people. There's some jealousy. If you were to interview everybody about a person, I think the majority would like that person and respect how good that person's doing, but there's a minority who make lots of noise, and that makes it sound like everybody feels that way, but they don't. And the ones that don't say anything, they don't want to stick up for you or me. They just stay quiet, but they like you, they like me, and they believe us. But they're not gonna get up and say, "That's not right what you're saying! That's so not true!" You know, they wouldn't even get up. There's a few that will get up and say, "Hey, that's not right!" But there's a lot that just – kinda like they're not gonna, you know, they're probably thinkin' of the repercussions, thinkin' of their kids, their grandchildren, so they don't. People in our community that are close to me say some people are jealous of me. It's like they think I'm showing off, acting better than them. But that's just a few people, that's not everybody. It's like there's a majority that's saying, "Yeah, I like what you're doin'," but they're not gonna stick up for me. Our Elders told us that there are things in life that you have to do, but if you don't do it right, you could affect yourself, your family, your people. And back then, the way I understand, breaking the law could have meant losing your life or being abandoned by your community. Sometimes losing your life is a lot better than being abandoned, being out on the Land by yourself, and dealing with everything, including other First Nations.

So that's the feeling and understanding that I grew up with and what I heard from many of my uncles, aunts, grandparents, Elders, different leaders. That's the quickest way I can summarize how we as Tŝilhqot'in people were and how that changed and what we're trying to do to bring back the way it was before contact. When the Tŝilhqot'in Warriors went ahead with the war, it threw another rift into us, but I think it made us stronger. For us, the Tŝilhqot'in War is a celebration. We celebrate on October 26, going to each part of the Tŝilhqot'in where the War took place and doing drumming, prayers, and presentations.

Feeding the Fire, Feeding the Ancestors

Chief Roger William

We were taught to feed our Ancestors. Our people believe that when you feed the fire or you put food out for wildlife, you're feeding your Ancestors who have passed on before you. If you feed them, they stay healthy, and if they're healthy, they're gonna help you, they're gonna protect you, and they're gonna move on into the next dimension, the next world. We were taught, "Don't eat all your food." You always leave something on your plate, and you feed the fire. You don't look at the fire because if you do, your ancestor is not going to eat. It's like when people look at you when you're eating. You get this feeling that you're eating too much, or you're doing something wrong. So they say don't look at the fire, so the Ancestors can eat. You just feed the fire, and you walk away.

Healing

Chief Roger William

I believe there's a lot of our people who wake up and understand why they were raised the way they were and why they're here today. Now they want to heal. But there are some people who wouldn't even accept that they need to heal. They call it superstition. "I don't care, doesn't bother me." They wouldn't admit it. There's those kinda people, and there are people who don't know. They don't know their culture, they don't know. They know about computers, they know about the internet, and that's what they like, and they're proud of it, but they don't know anything about where they come from, so they don't wanna really be there. That's a human reaction, but they're still angry about the Chief and Council who made a decision, and they're not in there, they're not one of the few that were chosen to do whatever. They're angry about that, they'll call down the Chief and Council every chance they get. They know some of the traditional laws, and they know how to escape the law around here. Some of them are just trying to survive. They've got no choice, that's where they come from. They want to learn, but they don't know how.

Sometimes trying to tell somebody what's right and wrong is not really honourable. I try to set an example, just being nice to them and shaking their hand and smiling at them and telling them "You're doing a good job" when you see them and then leave them alone. And when they really want to do something about it or understand, then they'll come to you or someone else and learn. I really believe that. We go to treatment to get help – alcohol and drugs. For me, we need to also, on top of that, learn our culture, our rituals. Go back to when you were in your mom's womb. What happened? This is what's supposed to happen, but what happened? Where did that mom come from? What did she go through?

When I was growing up, some of the Elders and people that I respected were controlled by government laws. For example, it was against the law to hunt mountain sheep because of the numbers. We're not supposed to hunt swans because of the numbers. And when I was growing up, old-timers followed government laws. People were scared to be charged. When they hunted, I remember people then, and even now sometimes, quickly shooting an animal for fear of being arrested and losing their gun or their meat. My grandma [Annie Sammy William] used to tell me, "Be careful who you talk to." She told stories about how the government tricked our Warriors into peace talks, and then when they came in, they were tried and hung. People didn't trust government or authorities because of that. She always said, "Be careful who you give information to. They could turn you in, and you'll be charged and go to jail." Our Warriors lost their lives because of government lies, so our old-timers – and even some of our people today – don't trust anyone.

My great-great-grandfather was Qaq'ez, the older brother of Lhats̓ass?in the Head Warrior Chief, so that's where I'm coming from. And there's some other leaders who talk about their great-great-grandfathers who were the scouts for the enemy. And that's part of where we're coming from, and we're trying to bring this group back together. There's jealousy, there's hurting, there are trust issues amongst ourselves, but to me, we're just coming back stronger. We're starting to trust each other, starting to work together. It's a long process. I'm talking about from when I was a child, watching and listening to my grandma telling stories, to now where I am today, and I see changes. I still see a lotta hurts out there, but I see good changes coming too. It's gonna be a while.

To me, reconciliation is not only dealing with the Land question. From smallpox in 1862 to the Indian Act, residential school, and provincial and federal laws, there have been many impacts on us. We need to be recognized as the self-governing Tŝilhqot'in People. We need to bring our language and our traditional law back. We need to heal. Past hurts, I think they're always going to be there. But I think, slowly, we'll get stronger, we'll understand, we'll get better. There'll still be people out there that have other beliefs, another religion that dictates their life. Some of it is good if they're a good person. Mostly religion teaches you to be honourable, to treat people with respect. They don't teach you to lie. All religions talk about honour, including ours. They've got different gods, different names, different ways of doing things but at the end of the day, it's the same. Our youth are getting back to the Tŝilhqot'in language and starting to practise it and use it today. The healing will start coming quicker. Now we're at war within, trying to get back not only our Lands and resources but that feeling, that understanding of being part of the Land and moving forward. For me and my children, it's about getting back to the language, the ritual beliefs, and then there's a new process – computers, vehicles, that angle on life. The war is to be able to use what we know, what our culture is, and accept what's coming down and move forward. That includes the Land question, the damages that were done to us for generations, and our young people understanding, reading, feeling, and knowing what that was.

A lot of our young people don't know what we went through. We protected them from that, we wanted to make sure that they didn't have to deal with it, but at the same time now, we need to say, "This is what it was, this is who we were." We were over there, then we came here, and now we're over here, and you need to understand that history so you can move forward.

When I hear someone saying, "Mission? I never went to the Mission. Doesn't bother me" – and you ask that person, "Okay, speak to me in your language." They go, "My mom never taught me."

"How come your mom didn't teach you?"

"I dunno why."

"Well, maybe your mom's mother didn't teach her because she was in residential school and this is what they were told. You ever think of that?"

"Oh, really?"

"Okay, you've never been affected by residential school, you never went, but because your mom didn't teach you, she didn't know her way of raising you. Your grandmother raised your mom the Tŝilhqot'in way, and then your mom didn't teach you."

That is a factor – never mind physical, sexual, emotional abuse. That's over and above what we gotta deal with down the road. But just the fact that you can't tell me in Tŝilhqot'in about who you are, that's big damage right there. That's probably the biggest damage, because you're going to have children, and there's no way you're gonna teach your children how to speak Tŝilhqot'in, let alone understand it. When I hear people say, "Oh, I never went to the Mission, it never affected me," you just ask them those questions, and they'll be thinking, "Oh." Honour comes with Tŝilhqot'in, the connection to the Land.

The Women's Mourning Song

Joyce Charleyboy, Tŝideldel

Elizabeth Jeff is the one that sang the women's song that she called "The Mourning Song," and I was never able to sing that song. It was funny because we were there at Hudson's Bay Flats, and she got me to stand in the centre of this field where the Fort used to be. She said, "We're going there today." It's close to Bayliff Ranch out west. She said, "I want you to stand right here, and I'm gonna sing this song for you. When I sing the song, lots of things are gonna happen to you."

And she said, "This is where our Warriors were captured," at Hudson's Bay Flats. She said, "They came in for peace talk, but they had a couple women warning them, 'Don't go in. As soon as you go in, they're gonna take your weapons, they're gonna shackle you, because then you're in their hands. We can't do anything for you if you guys go in. If you walk through those gates, we can't.' But Lhatŝ'asʔin believed that there were still good people in the world, and they were gonna have their peace talk, and they were gonna say their part and then walk away.

"Then what happened," she said, "as soon as they went through the gate, they were asked to hand over their weapons, and as soon as the weapons got taken, the women knew. The Warriors had mothers and probably aunties and wives that had travelled with them. By then they had been on the run," she said, "for almost a whole year and they couldn't gather anything because they were on the run. They weren't able to gather for the winter months, and it was getting down to the fall time when they had been asked to come in. And so," she said "the women waited outside the confines of the Fort," and I think she said three days they waited.

I can't remember what day it was, but she said they knew something was up when they saw the scouts coming in and out with horses, and she said that the one woman that was around that Fort told them that they're actually moving them today. "They're not gonna try them in their own courts. They're not gonna even listen to them." And I don't know if she knew the language or if somebody had been translating to her. She said, "There's word that because of the number of people that they've killed, they're gonna be tried; not here, but they're probably gonna be moved somewhere else." And Elizabeth said, "One of the women said it was a war. It was not. They're the ones that started it, you know. And they tried to argue and nothing. So they sang this song as they were leaving."

Elizabeth started singing this song. You could hear the echoes in that little valley we were in and the way the river carries the sound back. It was amazing. I cried. She said, "The women left before the men were moved, because they didn't want [them] to see where they [the men] were gonna be going. They knew that they weren't comin' back." I believe Lhatŝ'assʔin's mom and his wife were leading, and they left. So I just cried, and she finished the song, and she walked up. She had a hard time walking, and she walked up to me and grabbed both my hands, and she said, "You know what? It's not about those women you're crying, not about what happened to your Nation that you're crying. You gotta figure out who *you* are. I know you've been lost for how long. *You* have to figure out where *you* come from." And I'm thinking, "Yeah, right," 'cause you know you feel all that emotion. And she said, "When you can sing the song with no emotions, then you're there. I want you to know that. If you can sing this whole song, and nothing affects you, you've figured out who you are. It's gonna take a number of years, but you have two families that you have to be proud of. You're not here because of mistakes that have been made. We learn by those mistakes, but we don't continue doing them." It wasn't until about four years ago that I was able to sing that whole song with no emotion. That's when I realized I know who I am, I know where I'm going.

What the Women Went Through

Joyce Charleyboy, Tŝideldel[10]

What the women went through when our Warriors were taken wasn't really talked about. I know there was a lot of hardship, a lot of anger. We come from a long line of really strong women that can stand firm. We need the healing [which] is the songs that we sing. When you stand on this ground, that's the most powerful.

We have to come back to our own communities, 'cause sometimes when you're out there in that outside world, all the energy gets sucked outta you, 'cause you're fighting everything, but when you come back to your Territory, that's where you're re-energized to take on the world again.

"This Is Where *Your* Warriors Are Buried"

Joyce Charleyboy, Tŝideldel

Eliza [William, Joyce's aunt] was the one that took us to the possibility of where the Tŝilhqot'in Warriors were buried. My grandmother and her were babies when their mum died of the Spanish flu, so she grew up with somebody that was from the Nazko area. She said they would take her and tell her, "This is where *your* people are buried, this is where *your* Warriors are buried," and so she knew. So that's where the history came from.

A Dark Story

Nits'il?in Russell Myers Ross, Yuneŝit'in

One reason I put a dark story on the Tŝilhqot'in War is because it's not something that people talk about all the time, or they don't know that about us that makes up our character.[11] So there's a reason why there's a level of darkness to share. Like how a person was shaped or how a nation or a community is shaped, but I think it's only a highlight. What I wanted to represent in my story was that keeping on looping back because I think even growing up, you kind of realize, "Oh, I live in this modern context. It's all gone." But then, no matter what, I kept seeing pieces of it, and then, reflecting back, going, "Oh, I guess what I did was something similar to what my family member did here," or even encapsulating the whole "Salmon Boy" story. I was living out that story that I didn't fully understand till I came home.

It's only with the loss of my mother that I realized that there is this trend through our whole Nation. A lot of us are still reeling from post-traumatic effects and slowly recovering but always dealing with loss in some way. It's the ripple effects of death coming from the Tŝilhqot'in War which is probably the most devastating – losing most of your Nation and then never being able to really recover from it and not knowing how to heal from a longstanding grief. Even though your parents are strong, your grandparents are strong, you're still dealing with some level of grief in some way. The Tŝilhqot'in deal with it in a different way. I think a lot of the time it ends up going inward, and it's not like we have a lot of collective ways of dealing with it. It's hard just trying to think through it.

But there's other things too, filling that space where we might've lost a song or a story. I think we need people to take responsibility to say that we're going to fill that space. I know I did by default with my mother's Teẑtan Biny song. It's my mother's healing song. I always listened in the background. She was teaching it to women in the family, and I always figured they're the ones learning it, they're the ones who inherit that song, but I don't think they fully embraced it or caught on to it. I felt obliged to try to take it on and try to remember to carry on all of my mother's songs.

I felt like my mom [Madeline (Meline) Myers xinli] would never have become a singer if my grandmother [Elder Helena Myers xinli] hadn't passed. If someone was to open something in our community, it was my grandmother who did a prayer or a song. But after my grandmother passed, my mother kind of took it on herself, especially when honouring Teẑtan Biny. She showed up at every event with her drum with the expectation of singing, and she wasn't shy anymore.[12] She just took up that space. I don't know how conscious it was either, but that's what I saw, and I see it again even for myself with Ivor's passing. More and more I need to reflect on what Ivor did and what he contributed so that I make sure that I'm doing it or I try to encourage others to do something similar. I think of the really tangible things that you're able to do every day. It's really hard, and it's stretched. Some people think there's a lot of power within the position of Chief, but there's also a lot of space for other people to show leadership for other things. I'm trying to encourage people to demystify their sense of this position as being all-powerful, but it is difficult. I think there's always mixed blessings in it and trying to figure out how to grieve, how to move forward, and then being able to perform as best you can like your parents did.

We Survived

Trina Setah, Xeni Gwet'in

We survived the smallpox.

We survived the Tŝilhqot'in War.

We survived the residential school.

We shouldn't dwell on it too much.

We know that we survived it.

CHAPTER 3 ENDNOTES

1   David Setah testified at trial for fifteen days and "endured several days of cross-examination with patience and grace" (Chief Roger William and Jack Woodward, *Sechanalyagh: A Book of Gratitude* [Victoria: Woodward and Company, 2007], 14).

2   That is, a reserve. Proposed reserves were surveyed in Xeni in September 1909 and "recognized" by the Department of Indian Affairs for the year ending March 31, 1912 (*Tŝilhqot'in Nation v. British Columbia*, 2007 BCSC 1700, 312–313).

3   Historian Tom Swanky writes that "the mistreatment of women is a foundational part of the Tŝilhqot'in narrative of the Tŝilhqot'in War. The evidence from the Tŝilhqot'in narrative and the written record mesh to produce a common narrative. In the common narrative, the rape of the Chief's daughter took place between Christmas 1863 and New Year's 1864 at the work crew's Bute Inlet camp (most likely in the Captain's cabin of the boat sent to retrieve the 1863 crew) – before the smallpox threat was made on March 22, 1864. A decision about the need to assert Tŝilhqot'in law and apply it to settlers operating among the Tŝilhqot'in – and specifically to punish this rape – already had been taken by some portion of the Tŝilhqot'in before the smallpox threat saw a subsequent larger council and the decision for a more general act of war. Although settlers distinguish between 'punishment' and 'war,' these distinctions do not have the same concreteness in most Indigenous legal systems. "There is testimony at length on this rape in the Prosperity Mine hearings. The tradition from these other sources is that the girl had been so brutally raped over a number of days that her legs had been disjointed at the hips and she could not walk. It is hard to see how she would not have been dying from the physical trauma. Some Tŝilhqot'in men – including Lhatŝ'asʔin's brother – had to carry her up the valley towards home. The girl then disappears from both narratives. It is quite conceivable that 'she looked dead in the face and that there was no life left in her' and that her father killed her as an act of compassion to end her suffering. [This testimony may also indicate that the death of the girl's spirit had already occurred.] Genocide is unbelievably violent and it forces people into horrific situations" (Tom Swanky, personal communication, May 12, 2023).

4   Tom Swanky quotes from an account by Bishop George Hills of "the child sex trade" in Victoria in 1862: "They [settlers] were in the habit of buying and selling these [Indigenous] women and ... children 11 and 12 years old and keeping them until they could succeed in their seduction" (George Hill's Journal, March 17, 1862, quoted in Swanky, *The True Story of Canada's "War" of Extermination on the Pacific*, 201). Swanky also notes the incidence of prostitution in exchange for food at the Bute Inlet camp and of people "competing with their dogs" for scraps thrown on the ground (203).

5   "When [Governor] Seymour left Tŝilhqot'in territory for a tour of the Cariboo gold fields, he put in charge the colonial police chief, Chartres Brew, and authorized him to conduct trials and summary executions. Seymour left Gold Commissioner William Cox as second in command ... The oral tradition as conveyed by Ivor Myers shows that negotiations between Cox's camp and Lhatŝ'asʔin took place along a conduit from Alexis and Ulnas in the colonial camp to a camp established by Chayses somewhere within range but hidden from the colonial forces ... As an incentive to induce Lhatŝ'asʔin's party to attend a conference, Cox's agents promised that the Governor would make them rich with a large gift of beaver traps. Yet when

Lhatŝ'assʔin first visited Chayses's camp at Bute Inlet the year before, his ankles had begun hurting. This hurt foreshadowed a future in which Cox would have shackles made from beaver traps to put around the ankles of the Tŝilhqot'in ambushed at his camp ... Lhatŝ'assʔin and those considering whether to attend the promised conference faced a choice. On one hand, condemning all the Tŝilhqot'in to a seemingly desperate future of facing an incessant threat of extinction at the hands of a colonial community that already had engaged in an act of genocide through spreading smallpox. On the other hand, putting themselves at risk of harm while grasping at the straw that Governor Seymour might represent non-Native parties of good faith who would see Indigenous communities treated with honour" (Tom Swanky, personal communication, December 22, 2021).

6   See R.C. Lundin Brown, *Klatsassan, and Other Reminiscences of Missionary Life in British Columbia* (London: Society for Promoting Christian Knowledge, 1873), dx.doi .org/10.14288/1.0056091.

7   Listen to Prime Minister Trudeau giving this speech here: John Paul Tasker, "'We Are Truly Sorry': Trudeau Exonerates Tsilhqot'in Chiefs Hanged in 1864," CBC News, March 26, 2018, www.cbc.ca/news/politics/pm-trudeau-exonerate-tsilhqotin-chiefs-1.4593445. Trudeau's words are based on Tom Swanky's historical research. See, for example: Tom Swanky, "Puntzi Lake and the Martyrdom of 'The Chilcotin Chiefs,'" Shawn Swanky (website), October 16, 2013, www.shawnswanky.com/articles/canadas-war/puntzi-lake-and-the-martyrdom-of -the-chilcotin-chiefs, and School District #27 Curriculum Team, in direct consultation with the Tsilhqot'in National Government, *The Chilcotin War: Unit Plan and Resources* (2019), www.tsilhqotin.ca/wp-content/uploads/2021/02/TNG-Chilcotin-War-Unit-Plan_2020. pdf. See also William J. Turkel, *The Archive of Place: Unearthing the Pasts of the Chilcotin Plateau*, Nature | History | Society series (Vancouver: UBC Press, 2007) and Tina Merrill Loo, "Bute Inlet Stories," in *Making Law, Order, and Authority in British Columbia, 1821–1871*, Social History of Canada series (Toronto: University of Toronto Press, 1994).

8   Chief Joe Alphonse, "When He Exonerated Six Tsilhqot'in War Chiefs, the Prime Minister Recognized Our Truth," *McLean's*, November 14, 2018, macleans.ca/opinion/when-he -exonerated-six-tsilhqotin-war-chiefs-the-prime-minister-recognized-our-truth/.

9   Long attributed to Duncan Campbell Scott, though now thought to have been the words of an American military officer. See Mark Abley, *Conversatons with a Dead Man: The Legacy of Duncan Campbell Scott* (Vancouver: Douglas & McIntyre, 2013).

10   Joyce Charleyboy speaking on behalf of the Tŝilhqot'in Ts'iqi Dechen Jedilhtan Tŝilh- qot'in Women's Council, Lhatŝ'assʔin Memorial Day, Hudson's Bay Flats, October 26, 2019. Transcribed by Lorraine Weir.

11   Nits'ilʔin Ross is referring to his unpublished graphic novel "Deyenz Lhuy Belh Nandlagh: A Story of Transformations" (M.A. thesis, Indigenous Governance, University of Victoria, 2005), docplayer.net/174903590-Udeyenz-lhuy-belh-nandlagh-a-story-of-transformations .html.

12   Madeline Myers xinli was a leader in the protest movement against the proposed gold and copper mine (first proposed as the "Prosperity Mine" by Taseko Mines Limited and subsequently as the "New Prosperity Mine") which would have destroyed Teẑtan Biny Fish Lake (see chapters 10 and 11). Nits'ilʔin Myers locates his work here in relation to that of other family members, including Nits'ilʔin Ivor Deneway Myers xinli, and traces part of his lineage.

Residential School:

Trinkets and Reconciliation

Some of the stories in this chapter contain details of experiences of bullying, assault, rape, and psychological abuse, and may be triggering for some readers. Support for Survivors and their families is available. Call the 24-7 free crisis line of the Indian Residential School Survivors Society at 1-800-721-0066 or 1-866-925-4419.

"Every Night You Hear a Fire"

Lorraine Weir

On January 25, 2022, Kúkpi7 Willie Sellars of T'exelc the Williams Lake First Nation announced the preliminary results of nine months of archival work, interviews with Survivors, and a geophysical survey of fourteen out of 470 hectares of the land surrounding what was Saint Joseph's Indian Residential School, near Williams Lake. Using ground-penetrating radar as well as aerial and terrestrial lidar (light detection and ranging) sensors, the investigation team identified ninety-three sites that show "reflections" suggesting the presence of human burials. Six months earlier, Kúkpi7 Rosanne Casimir of the Tk'emlúps te Secwépemc First Nation had announced the discovery of 215 potential unmarked human burial sites on the grounds of the former Kamloops Indian Residential School. Both of these investigations are ongoing in 2023 as only a small portion of the two sites has been surveyed at this point. On January 25, 2023, Kúkpi7 Sellars announced the discovery of an additional 66 reflections identified during the Phase 2 investigation of a further 18 hectares of land. In her speech during the papal visit to Canada in July 2022, TRC Commissioner Dr. Marie Wilson spoke of the deaths of 3,201 children at the schools, "another thousand who were sent home to die within a year," and more than a thousand unmarked burial sites near various schools. Another estimate indicates that "6,000 of the 150,000 who attended the schools between the 1870s and 1996 died or disappeared. The numbers are not precise because neither the schools, the churches that managed the schools, nor the Indian agents kept accurate records."[1]

St. Joseph's Residential School, the school which most Xeni Gwet'ins were required to attend until it was closed in 1981, was "one of the most well-publicized and notorious residential schools in Canada"[2] and one of the first schools in the Indian residential school system. Known to generations of students as the Mission, it began in 1891 as an industrial school by means of which the Oblate Fathers intended to restrict the movement of Secwépemc people whom they sought to convert to Roman Catholicism. Tŝilhqot'in and Dakelh children were also sent to this school, and from early on, children sought to escape. The case of eight-year-old Duncan Sticks was the first to be publicized. He was one of nine boys who ran away from the school on a dark winter night in early February 1902. All of the boys were "captured and returned," as the inquest later put it, except for Duncan. He was heading home to Esk'etemc Alkali Lake, and his body was found the next day near the roadside, thirteen kilometres from the school. The boys had complained of bad food and beatings, but their complaints were dismissed and continued to be dismissed for many years until summer 1920 when another group of nine boys entered into a suicide pact, eating poisonous water hemlock to end their suffering. One of those boys, Augustine Allan, died and was buried before his family was even notified of his death. When Augustine's father feared for the safety of his other son and wrote to the Department of Indian Affairs to ask that he be released from the school, Indian agent O'Daunt explained to the superintendent that "Indians are very much adverse to any kind of restraint, and to put it mildly, are not to be believed, as a general thing when they complain about Schools or similar Institutions, as they let their imaginations run riot, if they think that by so doing it will help them to gain what they happen to want at the moment."[3] In fact, the children at the Mission were not only beaten but starved, as the inquest into Duncan Sticks's death showed. By the mid-twentieth century, Interior "schools achieved financial solvency through agricultural production, while their students remained hungry ... Schools with successful farms [like St. Joseph's] sold their produce while their students went hungry."[4]

Convictions for sexual assault by priests and Brothers at the Mission began in 1986 with Oblate Father Harold McIntee, convicted of thirteen charges of sexual assault committed between 1959 and 1963; Father Hubert O'Connor, sentenced to two and a half years in jail after being convicted of the indecent assault and rape of two Indigenous women at the Mission between 1961 and 1967; Brother Glenn Doughty, convicted of five counts of indecent assault and five of gross indecency in 1991, with an additional thirty-six offenses charged in 2000 related to crimes at St. Joseph's and at Kuper Island Indian Residential School; Edward Gerald Fitzgerald, a dorm supervisor, charged in 2003 with ten counts of indecent assault, three counts of gross indecency, two counts of buggery, and six counts of common assault in relation to his time at the Lejac Residential School and at Saint Joseph's. Intergenerational violence is evident in the case of one of O'Connor's victims, Marilyn Belleau, who is the sister-in-law of former Esk'etemc Chief Charlene Belleau, Augustine Allan's great aunt.

These are the well-documented offenders at the Mission but far from the only ones, as several of the stories in this chapter indicate. Abuse took many forms, ranging from bullying to starvation and from assault and sexual abuse to dispossession of language and culture, all in the name of "taking the Indian out of the child." Stories from four generations of Xeni Gwet'ins and Tŝilhqot'ins who survived the Mission are included here, beginning with Elder Martin Quilt xinli, who was sent to the Mission in 1945, and concluding with stories from the years before the school was closed in 1981. Violence takes many forms in these stories and each storyteller shares their experience in their own way, sometimes contrasting positive memories of food, or learning new prayers, or even sword dancing, with memories of beatings, bullying, humiliation, and sexual abuse. All of the stories of genocide in this chapter bear witness to the systematic and purposeful attempt by the Canadian government and the churches involved to "eradicate all aspects of Indigenous cultures and lifeworlds,"[5] and often Indigenous children themselves. Within the Tŝilhqot'in Traditional Knowledge framework presented in chapter 9, Gwenig stories are Dadaben medicine, sometimes caustic and astringent as part of the healing process, and sometimes jagged and contracted around the memory of atrocity. As Elder Martin Quilt xinli says, "Every night you hear a fire."

Brother O'Neill and the junior boys in the dorm before bed (mid-1950s at the Mission). Courtesy of Archives Deschâtelets-NDC, Fonds Deschâtelets, St-Peter's photographies, Williams Lake Residential School

The Prize

Elder Martin Quilt xinli, Xeni Gwet'in

When I went to school, we get whipped for talkin' our language. [laughs] St. Joseph's Mission. I was six. I was down there about ten years. I didn't speak no English that time when I first went in there. Took me about a couple of years. [laughs]

They use a big hook, [if] we get caught talkin' our language. [laughs] They were about that long. The sisters had that kinda hook. *Sister Superior.*

They use a strap that wide. Some kinda sawmill belt. Pretty heavy too. They hit you, and then you'll straighten out!

The boss is always sneakin' around too, tryin' to catch you doin' something. They whip you, eh. Duncan Amut he got whipped. Some kinda whip they had, a bullwhip. They almost killed 'em. He run away, goin' towards Alkali. He pass out along the road. Shuswaps, they find 'em. Bring 'em back to Alkali. Doctor 'em up. Fix 'em up.

He passed out on the road. I guess he was really hurtin'.

Some of them kids, they went to Coqualeetza [Indian Hospital]. They never did come back. Their bodies came back.

I seen one guy, he eat pretty quick what he throwed up. He had TB. Jimmy Murphy from Anaham. Ed Stieman from Toosey. One woman, they pretty near died in Mission. She got sick. That's what Jacob Roper[6] was tellin' me. She got kicked out of school. Went home. They don' want 'em to die in the Mission, eh. No. Send 'em home.

There's cat dung in our flour. They had a cat pee in there, and they make a flour with it like that. That's what Jacob Roper told me. He said someone see what the cats were doing, eh. We caught lots of cats. Put 'em in gunny sacks. Bring 'em way out in the field. We'd throw 'em in the creek there. [laughs]

Lotta snakes on the railroad too. Kids would catch lotsa snakes and bring it back to school. Must be about ten, twenty snakes in one can. [laughs] They just turn 'em loose outside.

That Mission in Williams Lake, it burnt down.[7] Oil stove exploded and burnt down the church and the boys' dormitory and the priests' house. They're all joined together. We stand quite a ways [away], far off in our yard, and we still feel the heat from off burning buildings. There's quite a few kids got burnt up, over twenty.

They still use that house, eh. They build 'em back up.

It's kinda haunted. Every night you hear a fire.

I think I went to school in 1945. 1954 I came outta there. You get some kind of prize. I got a pocketknife. [laughs] That's what I won.

Elder Martin Quilt xinli. Photo by Lorraine Weir

Working with the Negative

Gilbert Solomon, Xeni Gwet'in

Gilbert Solomon. Photo by Chief Roger William

Me, I did ten years in the Mission. There's lots of negative people in there, and all the supervisors were negative. Very negative. So we learned how to work with the negative to survive. So somehow we could work in a way with that negative 'cause I can *see*. 'Cause I don't do the things that they could still *look at me all the time* or *check me out*. I don't go there anymore. They stopped swearing at me.

Or they'll have this guy that's putting our number down. He's watching us. Being the boss, you know. He would be given a notebook. Has it in his pocket, and he knows who it is, and if you said some kind of word or anything, out comes this notebook, and your number goes on. He's probably watching everybody if they're doing [cleaning] shoes. He puts it in the notebook.

And then the boss gets this book at the end of the day before we go to bed: "Everybody, listen! I want these numbers to come right here. Over in the front, right there. And we're gonna make a line right here. Number lalala-lala."

And you'd go up there in front, and they're standing there. And then he'd get each of the kids to line up over there.

"Okay, you see those chug-a-lug n*****s there?"

He'd give them each two slaps in the face. Right and the left. Go down the line, slap each one of those people.

"All of you line up, and do that."

And he'd slap those people over there. You know, they'd go like that to us.

And [he] will slap us, some [of us] harder, and then we'll go after. Or he slap really hard. He said,

"Well, um, you make me slap you hard. You make me slap you again because I did it too lightly, so I did it *hard*, you know, so I did it again." [smirking]

You get like that there. And I said,

"I dunno, in your eyes, in your mind, I see you just wanted to hit me, that's all. You just wanted to."

You know. Whatever. Like that.[8]

We had to deal with each other like that. We keep each other away.

"Yo, don't do that, you'll get us in trouble."

"*Don't do that!*"

"Stop doing that!"

If you don't stop doing that, then somebody's gonna hit you or gang up on you or something, you know.

You have to be in a gang in order to be safe over there. Sometimes the gang's not there. They're tired of following you around or whatever. But sometimes they need to be together. Sometimes, all of a sudden, everybody in their group, you know. Sometimes they're not there.

Okay.

All of a sudden, people group up.

It's automatic.

Gang attack.

Teachers are not visible.

Wreckin' our school, our office, the green. The schoolroom.

Make barricades.

We got knives, teachers got knives. Messin' it up on us.

Just to survive.

We want to fix it, and we're not allowed to fix it.

Then we got smart one time. They used to muss our hair so we used soap and water and put it in our hair to make it hard so they couldn't do that. She's [the nun] like, "What are they doing?" Hot, hot, hot water. Spilt it on her skirt. [laughing] We had to work like that, you know, to get by and just to survive.

We acted together to attack one person. One time we almost did. We were going for a walk way out there and gonna attack this person, the Supervisor. He was a First Nations – Shuswap or something. And these were Tŝilhqot'ins. They gonna go kick the shit out of this guy over there in the woods, you know. We were gonna do that, like, till it's all gone. We're gonna do that [combat sounds] already. But we didn't hurt each other up there on the hillside. We didn't laugh at the teacher or make fun. Our parents taught us about respect.

You know what we got? You know that Mission school we were in? They said to work there. Well, check that timeline.

Mission.

And it's called a Reform school.

They'll put you there.

"If you guys go there" – do you know what they're thinking? What they're gonna do?

"You'll end up in this other school." And they didn't do that.

So they're like, "Huh." They'd calm down.

So they would do that, you know.

So we'd protect each other even like that.

"YO! WHOA! Stop crying! Don't cry!"

Or "Somebody's gonna come and beat you up for that! Make you cry more. Something to cry about. Stop doing that."

So then, you know, they listen. But I think some of them, they just need somebody to, like,

"Hey, talk to me, I'm not gonna do all that and get us in trouble."

"Stop crying or you'll get me mad, and I'll kick the tsan [shit] outta you!"

∗   ∗   ∗

So when we get back home, there's things happening. Alcohol and stuff. Everybody's doing stuff. We're learning by doing. When you grow up, you need alcohol.

I'm not gonna do that. I'm not gonna do what they're doing. I'm not gonna copy that. I'm gonna go this other way.

And then you say – when you grow up, you say, "You see that Chief there? I'm gonna change that Chief. You'll see. Watch." He's gonna grow up. He'll change the Chief. He'll try and fix it.

So we put Roger there. He's a young kid then. He'll listen to us. He'll hear our talk. What we say, he'll do. He'll listen.

He turn around and do whatever.

But you gotta listen to Elders. That's how it goes. That's how it is.

"We're gonna have Title Land." Yeah yeah yeah.

You listen. You can't be gone like these other Chiefs 'cause we're gonna get rid of those guys. They're just not doing nothing for us. They're just la la la la. Whatever. So we're gonna put you there and you're gonna listen to us.

It worked. But in the meantime, it still kinda didn't work, but we left him in there.

I Lost My Language Twice

Ivor Deneway Myers xinli, Yuneŝit'in

Me, I lost my language twice there. When I was a child, I spoke nothing but Tŝilhqot'in language, and what was told to me by my mom and dad all the time was, "Don't retaliate on anybody, no matter what the consequences are. Whatever happened here, we'll see made right today. Don't retaliate." Strong words from my mum.

I was at the residential school. They brought me to Coqualeetza Hospital. I had something wrong with my left foot at the time. They brought me to Coqualeetza Hospital, and I dunno what they did to my left ankle, my left foot. My calf cannot grow any more. I tried my best, and it hasn't grown. They musta cut some tendons or muscle or whatever or maybe take some bones out. I don't know what they did. It's called clubfoot, I guess. They made it very tender, and I have to be very careful how I use my left foot. So that's when I was in the Coqualeetza Hospital. After I came back from Coqualeetza Hospital, I went to the Mission, St. Joseph's Mission. I couldn' even say one word of Tŝilhqot'in. I totally forgot my language because they spoke nothing but English language there.

When I got back to St. Joseph Mission, all the community boys were teasin' me that I didn't know one word of Tŝilhqot'in. Not a word. And I said I did. In actual fact, I didn't. *I couldn't even remember one word.* So they teased me like that. That really bothered me. It's a good thing I had my brother William Myers xinli. He was my big mentor. I always asked 'em, how do you say this? how do you say that? He told me how to say it. And I retained my language. It happened twice. Went back to Coqualeetza Hospital again and came back, same thing. *Didn't even know one word.* So I had to depend on my brother William again. To this day, I'm very thankful that he's there for me.

I was at the Mission about nine years. Some bad things happened there. I was ashamed for a long time. Even later I carried that shame. I managed to shrug it off when I went through the Choices [youth] program. I want to thank a counsellor there, Dorothy Montgomery, for introducing me to the Choices program, and I completed it. I got a lot out of it, and I wasn't afraid any more even to mention it in public. But it hurt me, and it took me away from my mum. I took it to heart. Maybe that's why I'm like this today – all the surgery, stomach cancer.

It escalated when I had my first relationship. I loved her with all my heart, but she didn't want to live in Stone. She said she was gonna go and get educated for a year, and we went our separate ways. When that happened, I was torn to pieces. I didn't know who to turn to, so I'd go see my mother, Helena. That's who I went to. All those years I forgot how it felt when I was taken away from my mum. End of nine years, I'd go see my mum.

I didn't recognize myself. She told me, "You'll get well. We love you. We care for you. We like you. Don't go there." It was the first time she'd held me in her arms for a long time. I'd forgotten how it felt. How I yearned to go back home when I was in residential school. *Every* year, especially during Christmas, I wanted to go home. I was in St. Joseph's Mission. I was in the Kamloops Indian Residential School. All my brothers went there. I was left alone, behind. That's how lonely I was, how I wanted so much to be with my mum and dad. It's like a penitentiary. That's how it felt.

In the Mission I couldn't even speak my language. They didn' allow us. And when I was in Kamloops Indian Residential School, I had nobody to talk to, but there was a few that was from Stone that I was able to talk to in my language. But even then, the supervisors weren't there for me. Even though I told the truth, I got punished. Nothing but the truth, and I got punished for that, something I didn't do wrong. So that's the story of what I endured through all those years when I was in residential school.

To this day I speak fairly well. To this day I know my language. When I record my Elders, I know what they're saying. There are a lotta words out there that are very foreign to me – never heard of before. And there's lots of stories out there that I probably don't know about. And I recorded some of them. I said Wow! All in Tŝilhqot'in!

Take a look at me. I've got cancer. I never thought of havin' cancer. I don't drink alcohol or take drugs. 1981 was my last time with taking marijuana. The year before I had a family, I said to myself that's it. No more of this. I treated it as a priority. That's who I want to be a role model to. To this day I never took a drop, never took any of that stuff, and I'll try my best to stay away from that as long as I live. This stomach cancer escalated from a lot of stuff. During residential school you keep bottling everything inside here. That became the form of cancer. The stuff that you eat, the stuff that you drink. It came from a lot of stuff.[9]

Four Years

Elder Marvin William xinli, Xeni Gwet'in

I didn't [go to] school that long. Four years I was in the Mission. I was too old to go back.

Some people were Shuswap, so they beat you up.[10] Try to fight you, and you don't know. That's why, when you're outta school, you fight to win.

Father Brown, he was around here. Prey-er [predator]. A lot of us went to school from around here. He was a sicko. Long-time. You can't stay that long with a sicko.

My dad pass away. Worked out this way, chase our cattle. That last cattle. But he got hit. Mum, my mum was still alive [until] must be three – three years ago.

My mum in the mountains [showing me a photograph]. Ride horse.

Elder Marvin William xinli gathering berries. Photo by Betty Lulua

In Traditional Mind

Elder Catherine Haller, Xeni Gwet'in

My name is Catherine Haller, and I'm from Xeni Gwet'in. My traditional name is ʔEniyud. Since I was eight years old, my focus was on being a really traditional person. I was comin' from and raised from traditional ways and beliefs. I've been speaking Tŝilhqot'in all my life. I was at St. Joseph's Mission, Williams Lake, from 1958 to 1964. I didn't accept being at the school. I was eight years old when I started.

I didn't understand a thing those DIA [Department of Indian Affairs agents] said when they came from Williams Lake, picking us up. I was wondering what they were saying. My mum was crying – she wasn't ready. She had to prepare us to go. We couldn't understand them, and they were yanking us to get our coats on. I told mum in Tŝilhqot'in, "Don't cry. I'll pick up some English words, and then I can stand up for you. I should just go to the Mission." I didn't cry – just a teardrop. They thought we were scared, but I wasn't scared. There were three of us – my older brother and my sister and myself. I told them, "Don't be scared, just grab your coat and close this hut, and we'll change some of the experience. We're gonna face this. I know it's gonna be tough, but we have to face it. It's already happening so we're just gonna have to go forward and maybe be a different person for a time." When they were yankin' us and puttin' us in the back of the truck, I just did that to them – pfft! I thought, good, I'll take this in a good way, I'll take what they've done to me in a respectful way. I can't understand English to pick up that word. I'll figure it out, you know. In traditional mind, I thought, I'll pray for myself and I'll just go on with what I believe in. So that was painful, but then I thought, I want to learn how to pray and use my Catholic ways of believin' in my own traditional way. If I start understanding English, I'll communicate in a good way. Maybe it's just because I spoke Tŝilhqot'in, I never learned how to use my tongue to communicate back. It was really hard.

The roads were like snake roads comin' from Lee's Corner in those days. It's not like that road you travel on now. It takes a few hours to get in now, but at that time it probably took them the whole day, and then they stayed here and started looking for the students out here. We were like in huts, here and there. It wasn't like this. There was no house here [at the ʔEniyud Health Centre in Xeni] at that time. And no Natives' gas station.

When we got to the Mission, my sisters and brother were crying, but I wasn't. There was a bunch of kids around us lookin' at us, but it didn't scare me. I was always able to stand up for myself and my people. I still speak out if I need to say something and Elders are not saying it. So I kinda know what I have to say and really think about it before. I pray on it before I say it, so I don't have to hurt anybody's feelings. So that's how I was, and I told my siblings not to cry. My brother was on the boys' side, and I told 'em you hang in there, and even traditional men will be happy when you get home from the school and you've picked up some English. Pick up what you believe in yourself to be. That's your choice, I thought in Tŝilhqot'in. I thought, I'll take what they're doing to me in a respectful way. If I can't understand English, I'll figure it out, you know. I was emotional. In traditional mind, I thought I'll pray for myself, and then I'll just go on with what I believe in.

I wanted to know how to pray and use Catholic ways of believing in my own traditional way. Non-Natives would tell you to communicate in English, and I thought, I'll communicate with them in a good way, for understanding. It was really hard. Maybe it's just because I spoke Tŝilhqot'in and never learned how to twist my tongue to communicate in English. A tear fell, but then I lifted it up and changed it. It took me almost a week to begin to understand English. Sometimes we connected with our own Nations. We had coats over our heads to talk to each other, because we were being hit over the head with the teachers' hands or anything. They used to bang our heads together if we spoke Tŝilh-qot'in, and they said, "You speak English!" Whenever they did that, I prayed. And I'm so happy that after all we went through, we learned English. I learned prayers I really like. This is how I wanted to be: to go forward. It's like what they say in Tŝilhqot'in – Lha ʔeneh ŝint'is. Guneŝ dzanh yetugh ʔin. It means I don't wanna look back. I wanna go forward.

I was always the active one of my sisters. I used to ride my horse early in the morning. First thing, I'd get up, put on my loose clothes, and go riding. So at the Mission, I wanted to get into sports. At that time I didn't run, but I'd see the big baseball field open. As soon as I got up at seven, I ran. Then they asked me if I wanted to get into sports. I said yes, I wanna play baseball. Guess why I wanted to get into baseball? So I didn't have to spend time with the rest of the kids who were being emotional and getting into fights.

Sports were more challenging after you got really good. You had to play a lotta homeruns. You know, I was pretty good at baseball. I started pickin' it up, I didn't give up. I just started goin' forward. I just stuck to it. And then I started to get into skating too. I could really skate. I had to get in shape. Every time I went to Vancouver [to play in baseball tournaments], the supervisors were always so emotional and angry with us. A couple of times, I'd sneak into church and pray, to be on the safe side for my health and for my brother and my sister. I was pretty skinny, but I was growing. Then I started knowin' everything that was going on with us. 'Cause this was gonna happen anyways. Many years on, I found out what was happening.

It was a whole year we were at the Mission. We never came home for Christmas. We stayed all year till June. June 20th. And we were so happy to come home. It's like this month we'd be dancin' around, happy. It was so nice to see Mom. I told her everything about the good things, not the bad things. I didn't want her to know them. I'd already confessed it in church, so I thought Mom doesn't need to hear that. So I just kept it to myself, and I thought, when I'm ready, I will tell her but not right now.

Elder Catherine Haller.
Photo by Linda R. Smith

The Green Jeep

James Lulua Sr. and Dinah Lulua, Xeni Gwet'in, with Lorraine Weir

Dinah: Do you remember the green Jeep?

Jim: Yeah, it went all over the back roads to find kids.

Dinah: Yeah, they went on the back roads when it suited them. Had to get the kids to school on time.

Jim: They took the back seats out so they could get more kids in. Musta got a lotta kids that way.

Lorraine: Why didn't you run away from the Jeep?

Jim: They punished us, so we didn't try.

Dinah: Parents would sometimes hide their kids. Some did avoid the Mission, like Mum [Elder Mabel Solomon xinli]. But most went.

Jim: We used to hope the tires would go flat. Musta been pretty solid wheels. Gilbert and Dinah put nails on the road once, just up there, near Roger's place, but it didn't work. Even the bad roads around Ts'uni?ad Tsuniah never got those tires.

Dinah: Yeah, Father Brown. He used to drive that green Jeep. The Jeep always got through. It took them two days to pick up all the kids and take them to the Mission. We didn't get home until one month in summer. We stayed at the Mission through Christmas and Easter. They gave us a Christmas gift, and we went to midnight Mass and had dinner. In June some kids got to go right away, but we lived far away, so we waited two weeks to be picked up and taken back.

We were only taken as far as Yuneŝit'in. The Jeep left us there. Father Brown always drove that Jeep. They left us there, and we were on our own to get home. Some kids knocked on the doors of their parents' friends to get a ride, but most kids just waited for somebody to notice them. They got us to school pretty quick, but they didn't care if we got home safe.

When you got to the Mission, the first thing they did was coat you in white powder. It smelled bad and stung your eyes. To delouse you. Then they cut your hair, straight across the back of your head, from ear to ear. [tracing the line with her index finger]

Jim: I did try to escape once. Late Jerry Charleyboy and I were going to escape in the middle of the night. We had to jam the door so it wouldn't automatically lock on us. We got away a bit, but then we decided to go back. He wanted to go back, so I went too. We snuck back in the dark. We were afraid we'd be punished. And then we just stayed there at the Mission until school was out on June 15th. I was fourteen when I left and turned fifteen that July. Then they couldn't force you to go back.

—Transcribed from memory after a conversation with James Lulua Sr. and Dinah Lulua, June 9, 2015. Revised by James Lulua Sr. and Dinah Lulua.

First Journey

Eila Quilt and Laura Setah, Xeni Gwet'in[11]

Eila: That was my first journey to residential school and my first time passing through Stoney. I had never been there before. I was pretty young. Five or six years old. And seeing all the houses close together, 'cause Nemiah wasn't like that. You had to ride to go visit anybody. What really fascinated me was the gravesites and seeing the baby baskets hung in the trees – the baskets of babies who had passed on. I had relations there that had passed on and some of their precious stuff was hung in the trees like baskets, and even their hunting tools or things. I remember driving through and seeing that and being in awe of that.

I dunno when I started noticing that they weren't there anymore, you know. I think when our sister Pauline passed away when she was on her way to residential school. Just above Stoney, our driver flipped the truck. And my sister who was just a year younger than I am, Pauline, passed away.

Laura: It was her birthday.

Eila: Right on her birthday, yeah. It was then that I noticed all that stuff was gone. We realized, you know, 'cause what could we put up for Pauline? But when I looked around, there was nothing up. I thought to myself, they don't do it anymore, so we don't need to do that. Pauline had just turned ten, so I would've been eleven. The first time I went to residential school was when I was six, so in that span of time, how many of those things got stolen or taken – but I didn't miss them till that day.

Laura: I often wondered about that, 'cause I used to see them in the trees too. I was four years old when I was taken to residential school, and I was tall for my age. So sad, eh! You got taken away from your parents and no matter what kind of things my mother told them – she's only four winters! – still I got taken anyways, 'cause they just look at your height and they think you're an age. I was pretty tall even at twelve years old […] Our younger brothers were sent to Kamloops Residential School. Just imagine how far away they were taken and what effect it had on them.

Eila: That was the year our mum died. I remember when they were gonna get sent to Kamloops Residential School. That's Rocky, Larry, and Joyce. I begged Father Lobsinger, "Do not send them, send us in their place, 'cause they're too young to be that far from home." But no, 'cause there was no room left at St. Joseph's, so they had to send them to Kamloops. They wouldn't listen to us. And that's the year our mum died. But it still affected our younger siblings, 'cause we were so used to not being with our parents until summertime, 'cause we lived so far out. We never got to go home except summertime, whereas other families got to go home Christmas and Easter. Well the army didn't build this route [the Nemiah road] till the early '70s [1973].

Laura: We were before '70.

Eila: Then we got to go home Christmas and Easter, but before that, no. The younger siblings got used to not seeing Mum for a while, so I know, one of them, it still affected him. He thought Mum was just gone for a little while. I think it all finally set in after two or three years. I remember them playing and telling them that their mum was gone. But they were too young. They didn't understand what death was.

*   *   *

Eila: There was just the oatmeal. Some kind of porridge that we didn't like. There was some that was wholewheat that we weren't used to, and we couldn't eat it. *I* couldn't eat it anyway! The regular hot oatmeal I would eat or the cream of wheat, but it was the different kind of porridge that I couldn't eat. But scrambled eggs, sometimes they made us scrambled eggs for breakfast. We all loved the scrambled eggs! The supervisors and all the staff used to eat bacon, eggs, and potatoes, toast – all the good food! We used to get soup sometimes and sandwiches at lunchtime. I can't remember the supper stuff. I know we used to eat all our food, all. We had bread, and our favourite was puttin' pepper on there and then eatin' it with butter on our bread!

*   *   *

Eila: I learned lots, yes! My alphabet, my numbers. We didn't speak English. We had to go to Kindergarten A and Kindergarten B – that's what they called it – so we learned how to speak English. And then I was too smart for grade two so they put me in grade three.

I was there for ten years. I don't remember why we had to get strappings every day after school, because I didn't understand what we were gettin' strapped for. It was with my cousins – we were all hangin' around with each other at residential school. Maybe it was because we spoke our language, 'cause that was the only language we knew. And then, by the time our hands were so tough from getting strapped on the hand most of the time, they started pulling our pants down and strapping us on the bum. And sometimes we'd end up kneeling in a corner of the dorm. I have no idea why I had to kneel in the corner of the dorm, but it was for so many hours just kneeling there, and we weren't allowed to move or anything from the corner.

My uncles were humiliated for running away from the residential school. When they got caught, they had to wear a dress and get their hair all shaved. That was probably in the 1920s. I never tried escaping from the residential school. I used to get homesick a lot, but I wouldn't dare run away all by myself. It was too scary!

We kept our language for some reason. We never lost our Tŝilhqot'in language, even when we were in the residential school. We used to come home during the holidays, during summer time, and then our parents only spoke Tŝilhqot'in, so we used to go into Tŝilhqot'in mind when we got home.

Tuberculosis[12]

Eila Quilt, Xeni Gwet'in

The tuberculosis took many of our people. It took some of my aunts and uncles from my dad's side of the family. The only one that survived was my dad. I was too young to even remember. I don't even remember how many aunties and uncles I have from my dad's side of the family. I see pictures of them every now and then. My parents never really talked about it. Maybe it was too much for them to talk about it. They were probably still grieving.

English

Chief Roger William

English is like driving down the road compared with riding a horse down the road. That's two different things. You can hear, you can smell, you can see on a horse. In a vehicle, you're going so fast, you're numb. You know nothing of what's going on on the Land when you go through in a vehicle, where by the time I get to Stoney on horseback, I'll have a different understanding and feeling of what that is.

English is a language in which some people don't understand me. I think I'm expressing myself, but people misunderstand what I'm trying to say. I'm getting good at trying to explain in English the picture that I'm trying to create for the person to really understand at the same time. If an Elder is talking to me in Tŝilhqot'in, it's so different than somebody telling me the same story in English. You read Lhin Desch'osh, and then an Elder tells you the story: it's totally different. That connection, that flow is so different than in English. Because in English you can interpret it in many ways, right? Your understanding of a word in English compared to someone else's understanding of the same word in English. You put it together with other words: pretty close, but it's not the same. It's like reading a book and watching a show. You read a book about something, and it tells you what the person's thinking, right, what the person's smelling. You watch a show, and the same thing's happening, but you don't know what the person's thinking or smelling or feeling. You just see that person sitting there.

Midugh White People

Chief Roger William

When I was young, midugh – white people – were seen as authority figures. Even if it was just a visitor, people were thinking, "Oh, that must be government." In our community and in our Nation, there were attitudes that we don't share certain things with these non–First Nations people, and there were stories that went around, when the government took our rifles or took our cattle if we didn't pay the range fee. Back in the 1970s and '80s, midugh said there were too many horses and they were having a negative impact on the ranches, so the horses were caught and sold. It didn't matter if your horse had a brand but was wild – if it got caught, it got sold. So there was this fear of midugh, and it used to be important to our people that they not work outside the community with companies that were going against the community's wishes. That sentiment was stronger in those days than it is now.

We need to remember that alcohol was involved in those days, as well as the changes in food and the emergence of the three groups of Tŝilhqot'in people I mentioned earlier [traditionalists, modernists, and those in between]. All of that was still happening in Xeni and the whole Tŝilhqot'in, but in our community, there were more of the group that hung onto their culture and their ritual beliefs, but alcohol was still involved. A person could be respectful, strong, and very traditional when sober, but abusive when drunk. Residential school told us that we could go to church and ask for forgiveness on Sunday, and whatever we did last week was gone. We could move forward and be healthy again, even if we were drinking.

Remember that three-quarters of the people in the Tŝilhqot'in died from smallpox. In some places, it was 100 percent. Then came the residential school, and people were still confused, hurt, and divided in powerful ways. Some people went the new way and became important figures and leaders because they did well in the Mission, even though they were being abused. There was all kinds of abuse, including cultural abuse. Ten months of the year, you weren't practising your culture, you weren't on your Land. You were somewhere else going to school, where you were told that your way is not right, and you had to pray to somebody else's god.

So there was a lotta mistrust for a long time. Today I see our people being stronger, and when they see a non–First Nations person saying a certain thing, they're like no, it's not right. Any Tŝilhqot'in will say, "We know who we are, we know what happened, you can't lie to us, you're just another person, you're not an authority. I know my rights." They tell the Chief, "I know my rights, you can't do that to me!" Even today there's some mistrust, but I think our youth and a lot of us are starting to work together more, putting the three groups back together and looking at the big picture. So we're stronger in a sense, but that strength is without the culture.

You've got this power, you know your rights, but you're already lost. You've lost your ritual beliefs and your honour, and whatever you do bad is gonna affect your family. Now you've got strength, but you don't respect the culture, and you don't believe that whatever I do, I'm gonna survive in this life – I know my rights. Instead, whatever I can do to create a job or get something done, I will do, even if it means that I have to cheat here and there. And the attitude, in many cases, is that the government has done a lot of damage, so whatever I steal from the city of Williams Lake, they owe that to me anyways. They stole my trees, they stole my resources, they took away my hunting, they put a lodge there, they put a private property there, they logged us all out, they ... So if I steal from the city of Williams Lake, that's just a drop in the bucket. And then that attitude builds up. Then they have kids who don't really know why their parents think the way they do, so those kids not only steal from the city of Williams Lake but also from their parents and their cousins from another community, because that's what their parents did but for different reasons. Those other reasons aren't passed down. Another negative never makes a positive.

My Grandmother

Rita Lulua Meldrum, Xeni Gwet'in

I was eight years old, and I was going to residential school, and we came home for the summer holidays. I was the darkest out of my family until my other siblings came on, so they used to call me "Crow" and "n****r" and all that. I was bullied and called names at residential school, and it happened when I got home too. I was ridiculed and shamed by my dad's first cousin, who was left to die in a hollow tree because she looked white. She had a white father. My grandmother [Elder Inez Lulua xinli] had a dream about her and went and saddled one of the horses and left, telling my grandpa that she was going to pick up the little girl that his sister-in-law left to die.

My cousin would call me "lazy n****r" and make fun of me until I cried. She would just laugh at me and call me crybaby. I was black as a crow, so I could eat leftovers after everyone had eaten. My sister jumped onboard with my cousin to call me those names, and I was so heartbroken that I welcomed death one summer morning. I decided, oh, I'm gonna kill myself. I don't know if you can understand, but I was really, really happy when I decided how.

My grandmother lived right next door. I think our houses were *that* far apart, overlooking the lake and facing the mountain where the Tŝilhqot'in War started. I got up, and I was gonna go to the corral and get my horse. What I was gonna do is take my horse, get a rope and tie the rope on my horse and put it around my neck and let the horse go, and I could hang myself that way. I was all happy, and I was running to the corral, and my grandma heard me. I was walking in moccasins, going to the corral. And she goes, "Rita." I just stopped and didn't say anything, never took another step. And she goes, "I know you're out there. Better come in." And after a few calls, I finally said, "Okay."

So I go into her house, and she says, "Oh, I want you to make me some tea." I kinda went, "Okay." Then I started to get water out of the bucket that was in the house and I started pouring with the aluminum pot. And she goes, "No, no, no. I want you to go to the lake and get me fresh water." And I went, "Oh, okay." So I went running down to the lake, which seems like a mile when you're a little kid, but it wasn't that far down. So I went down and got fresh water, and I poured the water out in the pot. And then she goes, "No, no, no, no, no. I want the hot water in the cast-iron one." And I went, "That's gonna take *forever* to heat!" And I kinda went, "Okay." So I poured it, and then I would start to leave – I still hadn't forgotten my plan – and she goes, "No, I want you to sit down with me." Then I went, "Oh," and she told me to get a bowl of water, 'cause we also use water for healing. So I got water for her and put it in front of her. And she actually wanted the fresh water from the lake so she could work on me. She didn't want tea. So she got this fresh water that I'd just brought, and she's using that, and she starts working – spiritually working – on me, and I went into a trance. I swear. Ten o'clock. I didn't come out of the trance. And I looked at the clock when I came to. It was 3:30 in the afternoon. It took her all that time to bring my spirit back. She turned my spirit and my being, I guess, around so I didn't have to commit suicide. It took that long for her to convince my spirit, my soul.

That's the most amazing thing I remember from Grandma, and she told me that my family is only treating me that way because my mom is gonna die. My mom's gonna pass away, and she said that they're my teachers, and they're spiritually and emotionally preparing me for the day when my mom dies. Because I need to be there for my brothers and my sisters. I said, "Grandma, we don't have brothers," and she said, "Oh, they're coming." And I, "Oh."

She raised my cousin as her own, but I remember one time when Grandpa was so mad that he grabbed ribs that were roasting on the open fire and he hit my grandmother. He said, "Why did you bring her into our house and our family?" He called my cousin's family untrustworthy and said they were thieves. Then she [my cousin] was disowned, because she'd gone over to the enemy camp.

My grandma had another vision of a young child who was lost for about a week. In her vision she found exactly where he was, and she saddled up her horse. After a few rides, she found the child. She had many patients from all over, from Anahim Lake, Xeni, and as far as Riske Creek. Sometimes they arrived in the middle of the night when it was minus fifty. Some rode for a week to see her. There were some funny stories. One was of my grandpa Tommy who came to see her because he'd been drinking for days or weeks, and he asked Grandma to work on him. She started singing and holding Grandpa for spirit healing. After a short while, she grabbed his hair and bounced his head off the floor, and she told him, "You're just hung-over!"

She told me I'm gonna move to a place where the buildings are gonna be as high as mountains. She goes, "Some buildings are gonna be so high you can't even see the top." And she goes, "People are gonna be like salmon going up the river." Still thinking she's crazy! And I kinda, "Okay!" And she goes, "And then you're gonna be there working with people." We call yatu – it's ocean – yatu. Yatu tes hyagh means you're gonna go live close to the ocean. And help people there. And all the emotional pain that you suffer here at home, you're gonna use that knowledge to help people who are less fortunate than yourself. I work at a halfway house for external inmates who have been in prison for anywhere from six to forty, fifty years. And I've worked down on Skid Road with the homeless and addicted. And I worked as an addiction counsellor for ten years. So now, if I'm stuck and don't know where to go or what to say to my clients, I always remember my grandma, and I go, "Answer's somewhere in there! Please help me! You're the one that sent me here!" [laughter] So I'm quite connected to my grandma and all the things she taught me. Yeah. She lived off the Land until she died. She was a powerful woman.

My grandmother gave me the future, what it was gonna look like and where I'm gonna be and who I'm gonna help. And after she told me all that, I went to residential school, and I'd come home and tell my grandmother, "That's the devil's work. You can't be talking like that." I was already brainwashed by the Church. She was an awesome healer, the most religious person I ever knew and also the most amazing. It still hurts me today that I said that. I accused her of being evil, and I abandoned her. The damage I must've done to her for judging her for practising what she was chosen to do by the Creator and for helping her people. And I went and turned around and said that to her. I was going home for her. I feel really, really bad, even today. She was still trying to teach me, and I know why she stopped teaching me.

I think she was sad. She felt that she lost us then. I was the one that she was training to be the next her, and she lost me. For me to turn around and say that to her, that was a slap in the face. If my grandkids did that to me, I would feel so devastated. Today I know how she felt. It's so painful to think of that. After all the things she taught people. I'm grateful for her.

Elder Inez Lulua xinli. Archival photo courtesy of the Lulua family

I Remember

Rita Lulua Meldrum, Xeni Gwet'in

Well, I don't remember much. I remember running away from the residential school the first time because I was molested by Brother Spruyt.[13] I swear I was eight or nine, and me and my cousin were playing in the playground by the swings, and then Brother Spruyt caught us and he tells me, "If you wanna play with the boys, you might as well sleep in the dorm with them too." I don't know how long I was in the boys' dorm, but it seemed like *forever*.

I remember peeing my bed and then tucking the blankets underneath myself so I would be sleeping when Brother Spruyt came along. He would take me into his room – it was in the junior dorm on the boys' side, and I remember the smell. Years later, every time I remembered that smell, it would make me sick. He would take me into his room to have oral sex with him and vaginal sex. I remember bleeding and being really sore. And even to this day, my body memory. At the time of the year when I was molested, I would get pains down there, in my vaginal area, and it feels really sore for no reason at all.

I remember I was about fifteen when I went to see the doctor – Doctor Weinrib was his name. He's an old doctor that used to be here in Williams Lake. He was my doctor, and he did all of the exams, and he told me I probably would never have children because I was so damaged down there, and I went, "Oh, okay." I was surprised when I got pregnant with my oldest. I was only sixteen or seventeen. She passed away a couple of years ago. And then about four years later, I had my daughter, and three years later I had my son.

Some of the older girls or the intermediate girls were assigned work during the day to either clean the brothers' or the workmen's or the sisters' dining room. I was cleaning the workmen's dining room, and somebody must've peeked in the brothers' and the fathers' dining room to see if they were finished eating, and [two boys] blamed me, saying I did it when I didn't. After they were done eating, I was still cleaning the workmen's dining room, so Brother Spruyt came and told me, "Never open that door again." I told 'em I didn't, and he got mad, and he threw me over the dining room table, and I bounced off the wall, and he kept kicking me and kicking me around my stomach area, my chest area. There was a workman still sittin' there eating, and he told 'em, "If you kick her one more time," he goes, "I'm gonna start beatin' the shit out of you." So he quit. I don't remember finishing cleaning that room. I was all bruised up from my chest right down to my pelvic area.

A few days later, I went up to Father O'Connor's[14] office, and I said, hey, I says, we were told to report any abuse or whatever, and I told 'em what Brother Spruyt did, and he just looked at me and said, "Oh, you must've deserved it." I went, "Okay." So I walked out, and then every time he saw me, he would punch me, 'cause he knew I was all bruised up. He would reinjure my ribs every time he walked by me. Then one day I finally looked at him, and I go, "You know what, one day I'm gonna grow up, and I'm gonna come looking for you." And years later I went to visit old Sister Devlin a few times to build some trust and stuff, and I said, "By the way," I says, "where's Brother Spruyt?" "Oh," she says, "oh, his plane crashed a couple years ago. I guess him and Father Lobsinger were both in the same plane when they crashed up north two years before." And I felt so crushed. I felt *ripped off.* I felt so ripped off. I don't know what I would've done to him if I'd seen him. I would probably still be in jail somehow, yeah.

You know what I learned at the residential school? I realized not to fight back. Do like I'm a dog. I don't want to feel pain no more. You know what I mean, where that feeling comes from? Like, okay, I give up, I dissociate. All this was just before I turned six when I got there, and I was small for my age, and I didn't leave there till I was thirteen – that was my last year there. Thirteen is when I begged to go back to school because I wanted an education. I promised to be so good, I promised not to talk back, I promised to assist with the younger kids. Blah blah blah, you know, please take me back. I lasted a few months. I went to school here in Marie Sharpe [Elementary School, Williams Lake], right across the street from where I am now. I don't know how long I was there. One day we were in the gym, and one of the girls musta kicked another girl in the head, and she blamed me for kicking her. I said, "I'm sorry, but I wasn't the one that kicked you in the head." She goes, "Yeah, it was you." And I go, "No, it wasn' me." I always stood my ground. The teacher was really upset: "You need to apologize to her because you hit her." And I said, "I didn't."

What do you think I did? I apologized, but why did I apologize? Because I punched her in the head in front of the teacher? I said, "I punched her in the face," and I *did*. I said, "I'm sorry." And they go, "Well, then you need to apologize for just hitting her." And I says, "Do you want me to punch her again?" And they go, "No." "So I don't need to apologize then, right?" And they go, "No, but you're goin' to the principal's office." So I sat there in the principal's office. Nobody looked at me. I looked around, tapped my toes, tapped my fingers. I walked out the front door, got to Highway 20, thumbed a ride all the way back to Tatlayoko the same day.

That wasn't the last time. I must've run away twice. The first time I got caught. I ran away with another student – I can't remember who she was now – but anyways, we took the railroad tracks into town, and we were looking for rides, so we were peeking in the bars to see if we could see people that we knew. Some of the ex-students from the Mission saw us, so they phoned the Mission. "Oh, we know where they are." They called the cops. They chased us all over town. There were tires lyin' beside the road, so I jumped in there and hid, and then I got caught. They put us in jail, and I don't know how long we were there, but they phoned the Mission and got them to come pick us up. I didn't wanna go with them, but I kept hangin' onto the cell doors to tell 'em to keep me there. Who *does* that?! [laughs] And the police said, "We can't keep you." I said, "Well, you arrested me for a reason. You know, like, I could be charged, you know." I don't know where the fuck I get my shit from! Yeah, they finally got my hands ripped from the bars, and they dragged me off to the Mission. My back was bruised for quite a while, like, I couldn't sit on my ass for a while. I think maybe I was eleven or twelve at the time.

I've talked to a few people about my abuse and the people that were present. And I think for all of us, we only remember *our* pain. We don't remember witnessing other people gettin' abused. I said to my brother, "Do you remember that?" And he goes, "You know what, I was an alcoholic for years after the Mission, so I can't remember." And I went, "Oh, okay." So.

When professionals interview people who've gone through so much pain and if they witness something that happened, you just shut down emotionally right away. You act like it's just a normal thing. "Oh, yeah, that's what happened." Because you already experienced something worse, but you emotionally shut down just to survive that incident that just triggered you.

I never grew up on reserve. I never grew up around the worst part of it. Like, my dad beat up my mom. That was harsh too. You know, we got kicked outta the house in the middle of winter. Dad would shoot at us. You know, it wasn't pleasant. We would hide in the hay just to hide from Dad, and he would go through the hay with a pitchfork to see if he could find us in the haystack, and like, I mean, he would just miss us. I'm thinking he *knows* we're here, why would he miss us if he didn't know we're right *here*? And yeah, it was unpleasant, but you know, we weren't the only ones, and it wasn't *constant*. It wasn't like a month-long party like it was on the reserve. Like the whole month of April was the holiday for them. The whole month at Christmas was the holiday for them. Like, these kids, they got to go home. What did they go home to, the ones on the reserve? Parties, homebrew, sexual abuse, physical abuse, emotional abuse, lack of food. Having to become a mother to your brothers and sisters when you're only like six or seven. And you're [people on reserve] telling me that you know more than I do? What did your grandmother teach you? What did your mom teach you when she sobered up? Is the information right? You know, when did she start drinking? When did your stories get distorted? Did she hear it from somebody else that didn't know the story? Yeah. Like my grandfather and my grandmother and my dad and my mom, we all grew up off reserve. Everybody else that I know grew up on reserve as far as I know. We never depended on Band funding. We never knew that our teeth were paid for. We didn't know our medical was paid for. We had to pay for our own medical, because off reserve nobody tells you nothing. You're like out of the loop, and then I go to the dentist here in town one day, and he goes, "Oh no, it's paid for." "Who paid for it? [laughter] You mean *all this time* I didn' have to pay for dental or medical?" Did *they* experience that? No.

I ended up with PTSD. I never learned about PTSD until I was like fifty, fifty-five, sixty. I just learned about myself and how residential school affected me and all the shaming abuse that just continuously went on. It felt like residential school at home, so it felt like it was continuous, and because I was the second oldest or whatever, I had to parent and do a lot of the work for the younger ones that somebody else couldn't do. And it's affected my relationships, my partners, my kids. I didn't belong to a gang or a group of people at school. I didn't even have my own family to support me. I've always been a loner. I was a loner at residential school, and I'm a loner now. My family, we stood our ground not to move to Nemiah, even though they nominated my uncle Lashway to be Chief, just so my grampa could go follow him. My grampa said no, I'm stayin' here. Don't wanna live in a cage [a reserve].

Our Way

Ivor Deneway Myers xinli, Yuneŝit'in

Walkin' in the bush, we talk to the trees, we talk to the spiritual world. We used the Sweat Lodge, we used the fire to communicate with the spirits. That was our way. We didn't have churches back in those days, like the priests you have today. Imagine doin' what they did in the Mission – the teacher touching the children. That's not our way.

Where Do You Come From?

Chief Roger William

I always remember a couple of things from when I was going to school. I was in Williams Lake Junior Secondary, and I had non–First Nations friends. We were sitting together and the teacher was asking, "Where do you come from?" Students were saying, "Oh, we come from England, from France, Italy," and they got to me. I was like "Oh man!" I was like, "Where do I come from?" And my non–First Nations buddy said, "Are you kiddin' me? You're from the Chilcotin, you're from here! You're from this Canada." And I was like, "Yeah! Yeah, I am!" But the system, you get lost in it. I remember that moment, and I keep thinking of all our children. We're kinda lost. If someone like me, who only knew Tŝilhqot'in and learned English in the Mission, can't say right away where they're from, imagine what our people are going through today. I was raised up our Tŝilhqot'in way, and still I was lost. Imagine.

Another moment that I remember from high school is when I was back home at a General Assembly and the Ministry of Forests guy was talking, doing a presentation and saying that they were gonna do clearcut logging, they were gonna come into this valley "whether you like it or not." I remember that, and I remember thinking "Yeah, right. That's not gonna happen." I was probably in grade eleven or twelve when I was thinking that, and then my older brother, Gene Cooper, ran for Council when he was in grade twelve and nineteen years old. He got in, and I used to listen to him tell me about his meetings and about how many Xeni Gwet'in members he knew, what they did, what their intent was. I was blown away. I couldn't believe how much my brother Gene knew about other families in Nemiah, in the Tŝilhqot'in. I thought, Wow! I had fun trying to get to the other end of the valley riding a horse or hitchhiking – we didn't have a vehicle – and yet he knew that much. And when the Ministry of Forests guy told us whether we liked it or not, I remembered the question that teacher asked in school.

Parents

Maryann Solomon, Xeni Gwet'in

In residential school they traumatized all the children plus the parents. They didn't even have a chance to say I don't want my children to go. The parents were threatened, and they were left behind.

I was at residential school here in Williams Lake for ten years, beginning in 1968. It was hard. I remember leaving home, and I was scared and thinking about my mom and dad and thinking how is she gonna survive with us gone? Because she needed us too, helping out. Life back then, there was no running water. We were always packing water. We had to help out, you know, cutting wood for the winter. Putting up hay by hand for the cattle. It was complicated, all the work, and I used to miss that. You know, you should be at home doing the work.

I didn't know what jail was like, but residential school seemed like jail. You had to do things at a certain time as a group. We always had to line up, and it was terrible. There was a lot of different kinds of abuse. Yeah.

My mom [Elder Mabel Solomon xinli] waited for us. We weren't at home and, like my mom always says, "I couldn't teach you guys. Your culture, traditions, your language were all taken away at the Mission, and you came back speaking English, and I don't know English." She didn't understand what we were saying. I came back, and that was life. That's pretty sad.

When I started working with the Elders, that was healing because they were teaching me the traditions, the culture, our laws, the language.[15] I was glad that I was still able to speak Tŝilhqot'in when I talked to the Elders. I was able to share stories and listen to them, and they were teaching me. And the things they went through – it was a hard life, but it was *their* way of life. Today, I can't imagine having to go out and live off the Land year round, you know. That's how they survived. Yeah.

The Mission

Dinah Lulua, Xeni Gwet'in

Must've been around '63 or '64 when I went to residential school. I was excited about going. We had new clothes, new shoes. I was gonna go to school with my sister Emma and my brothers. When we got closer to the Mission, I wanted to go home. I didn't want to carry on! At the Mission they cut all our hair off and put stinky stuff in our hair and let us sit there without clothes on in the bathroom for I dunno know how long before they rinsed our hair off.[16] They assigned one older girl to you if you're just a little child. That person had to look after you, stay close to you, make sure you go to bed, make sure you eat food, make sure you got to school. I was around five or six when I first went to the Mission.

The Sisters lived up on the top floors. One supervisor stayed in the dorm. There was a little room on the side where they stayed. I stayed in the dormitory, and the classroom was in the same building. The priest was in what they called the Principal's Office. We went to grade 1A to grade 1B there before we went to the other school. Grade one was in the other building. When I was going into grade three, they started to put us in the public schools, so I went to 150 Mile School for three, four, five, six, and part of grade seven. Then they brought us back to the Mission every day after school. Mom took us out of school in the springtime, just before school was out, so I went home and helped her out, my sister Emma and I.

I joined all kinds of sports at the Mission, just so that we could leave the building once in a while. We played baseball, basketball. The other game was ringette, they call it. It's something like ball hockey. You have just a straight stick that you use, and there's a ring. I also was taught how to do Scottish dancing on the swords. I used to travel around with a Pipe Band. I remember going to Lillooet, Kamloops. We were on TV in Kamloops, myself and Daphne Petal, the two of us. That's the Pipe Band I travelled with. There's a picture that they had when they had the residential school thing happening at TRU [Thompson Rivers University, in Kamloops, BC]. They had photos of the Pipe Band, and there's four girls in front of the Band, and I was one of them.

I joined everything and anything to get away from that building. I dunno if the nuns came from Scotland or how sword dancing was brought to them.[17] Jim said he was in the Cadets. I even joined the Girl Scouts, and they used to bring us to Williams Lake, and we'd go to this church basement, and we'd join other girls, and we used to sell cookies. Yeah, that's some of the things they used to teach the Boys and Girls Club.

The Cariboo Indian Girls' Pipe Band. From left to right in the front row: Inez Setah, Georgina Mary Johnny, Dinah Solomon (Lulua), and Daphne Petal. Circa 1964–1965. Archival photo courtesy of Dinah Lulua

The Cariboo Indian Girls' Pipe Band. Postcard photo by Ken Buchanan, courtesy of Archives Deschâtelets-NDC, Fonds Deschâtelets

Text annotations on the photo read: "Girls", "Seniors", "Junior (B)", "Junior (A)", "Intermedia", "Basement playroom", "Intermi.", "Boys", "Juniors", "Seniors"

Dinah Lulua's annotations on a reproduction of "The Cariboo Indian Girls' Pipe Band." Postcard photo by Ken Buchanan, courtesy of Archives Deschâtelets-NDC, Fonds Deschâtelets

This part here [see map above] was the juniors. Here was the intermediates. These were the younger ones, but these were the little older ones and then the next one would be the intermediates, and the seniors were up here. This was the line [dividing the school by genders]. And grade 1A and grade 1B class was towards the boys' side on the other side of the building. The girls' playroom was on one side of the basement, and the boys' on the other. This part here was the dining room in the basement. At first the food wasn't good, but when they hired this one cook, we started havin' good food like bacon and eggs and pancakes and porridge and all that stuff. But before that, I remember eatin' soup that didn't have anything in it, just what looked like one little piece of some kind of meat floatin' around in it. We ate a little bit of crackers with that soup.

The bad food. Yeah, I must've been a bad kid. I was strapped every night. Sister always had a little pad in her pocket, and as soon as you stepped outta line a little bit, your name came down on this paper. And if your name came down three times on that paper, you lined up at night before you went to bed and you got strapped. I got so tough that I couldn't even feel that strap anymore. And if you didn't cry, sometimes they're standing on the side, and they'll make sure, they'll make sure they whipped the strap around your wrist. Then I got smart, and as soon as they hit me, I started goin' "Whaaa!" and the nun stopped hitting me. They give you another couple, but if you stand there and act like you don't feel nothin', you got it worse. So I just kinda played baby!

Sometimes they pulled your pants down, and they'd strap you. That happened to a boy right in front of the whole grade one class. That's the only time I saw it. I dunno if I got that at the school, but I got it at the dorm, and we were only the five-to-nine age group. And then we were in the intermediate. Once I got older, around age ten, we were put into the intermediate dorm. I got it in the dorm, but I know that was the beginning part, and that's where I got a lot of strapping.

I think the worst that happened to me was probably the peer pressure. Gettin' put down by other students. Because I wasn't a fighter at school. For some reason I just got beat up lots. Some people remember gettin' picked on by a Shuswap or a Carrier, but my experience was my own people were the worst ones, 'cause they're the ones that you're around, and if they got mad at you, they picked on you. They'd punch you or take your food away from you. I never saw the supervisors sit children down and discipline them for their actions. They just let it happen.

We were put outside at certain times of day, and it didn't matter how cold it was. In the cold of winter, we weren't even allowed to come back in the front door to warm up on the steps. Outside for two hours, and that's where you were for two hours. They put skates on you, and your feet might be half frozen from being out in the cold so long. They had these mittens, these furry mittens that got wet and froze, or they got lots of snowballs on. You couldn't take them off, and sometimes you'd cry from the cold and the freezing, but you still had to stay out until it's time to come in. You weren't allowed to come in until the whistle blew.

I was at the residential school for eight years. A lot of things that happened I don't recall. One of my cousins who grew up with me at residential school has a lot of memories of what happened, and sometimes she tells me things and I don't recall them. I got whacked over the head with a yardstick by my teacher, Sister Ann, when I was in grade two. In those days the yardsticks were much thicker than they are today, and they had metal on one side. I got hit over the head, and it broke on this side of my head. I don't remember cryin'. I don't remember if I got knocked out. I talked to a lawyer in Kamloops, Alana Hughes. That's the first thing they ask you. Did you get knocked out? Well, I don't know. Maybe. But I remember the ruler broke when it hit my head. I remember being in the hospital for a long time, and I don't recall why I was there. I remember gettin' lost and couldn't find my room at the hospital. And I found the nurse, so I sat beside her, and she gave me something to scribble on, so I just kinda played with it, and then she finally put me back in my room, and I never remember why I was there. I dunno if they keep archives of those things. Maybe they destroy it after a certain number of years.

One of the lawyers told me, "Well, you don't look like you're affected by it. You look like a smart woman." I didn't say anything. Just, okay, I know where I stand here. I'm not getting any help from you, I'm thinking in my head. You're supposed to be knocked out, you're supposed to be somehow handicapped to be able to collect compensation for what happened to you? They say that's "common experience." They say that just being at the residential school is "common experience."[18] But to get strapped and abused is part of common experience? I don't think so. I think that's abuse. A lot of girls were sexually abused by priests and brothers. They snuck into the girls' dormitory. Even the priests themselves.

My dad [Elder Henry Solomon xinli] used to talk about the Mission building before this one, where he went to school. He talked about how a lot of the girls there had babies, and somehow the priests and the nuns got rid of the babies, so a lot of the babies are buried in the basement of the place that burned down – the old Mission building.

Old St. Joseph's Mission building. Courtesy of Archives Deschâtelets-NDC, Fonds Deschâtelets, St-Peter's photographies, Williams Lake Residential School

He talked about how there was a creek across the fields on the side of this building here, towards the railroad track. That's where a lot of babies were buried that the priests and the brothers fathered. So those are the type of stories that my dad [Elder Henry Solomon xinli] used to talk about. My mom [Elder Mabel Solomon xinli] was saying my dad used to say he started running away from Mission, him and another person, and when they were brought back, they were whipped. They were whipped till blood was splashin' off their backs, and they continued to run away even though they got whipped hard. They were left bleedin' and they kept running away, kept running away. There was two of them. And Lennie [Solomon] was saying that Tony Myers from Yuneŝit'in used to talk about it, and he said he did that with our dad. He ran away. Yeah. I dunno what grade he was. We assume he was in grade three maybe when he didn't go back anymore. He just kept runnin' away. He didn't wanna be there. No matter how much they abused him, he kept doing it. They must've wanted it to end because they finally gave up and stopped chasin' 'em! [laughs]

A lot of times when we were growin' up, Dad didn't really discipline us. Our mom did all the disciplining, 'cause if Dad did, you were sorry if he had to discipline you, 'cause he was pretty harsh. So I think that's why he chose mostly to be away, and he guided for other guidin' outfits and did odd jobs. Mom was home doin' all the raisin' of the children. They needed money too, so Dad had to go and work, but Mom stayed home and cut the fields and put up the hay for cattle and horses for winter. They would feed the animals and survive in the winters.

In the Mission

Chief Roger William

I went to residential school when I was six, and three years later, I was able to go to school at home in Xeni after Chief Marvin Baptiste xinli set up the school there. I knew Tŝilhqot'in well and was almost having fun with my language trying to communicate, and I could understand my Elders well. In our language there's a different word for your older sister and for your younger sister. Same thing with your uncle and your aunt, older and younger. So basic Tŝilhqot'in I was good at, but when it got to those details, I was struggling, because I lost them in the Mission. They didn't want you to practise your language, and if you did, you were punished. To make your life easier, you learned not to speak your language, because you were already away from home, and you were struggling. It was a lot easier to just go with the system.

I think my older sister Agnes was in residential school for nine years. She can tell you a story of what she went through and what she had to do to survive. When Agnes was going to school, she could protect our older stepbrother, Gene Cooper, and Gene protected me every way he could in the Mission. But there was no one who could protect my sister except for other relatives. I feel fortunate to have had Gene and Agnes. I grew up with Gene and another cousin, David Setah, whose mother, the late Madeline Setah, delivered me and called me her son. So David's sorta like my older brother too. He's two years older than me, and Gene's four years older, and we did everything together – chasing horses, rodeo, hockey. In the Mission, I was shielded by them to be able to grow, where I feel my sister had to fight to do everything, but she never really could grow the way we could, because she was busy protecting herself and fighting and stopping being picked on, stopping people trying to take advantage of her. She really fought, and today you can tell she's a Warrior. Like me, she was brought up in the Tŝilhqot'in language, but she had a tougher life because there was really nobody to protect her, where Gene and David and I had her, but also a whole bunch of people, like Simon Setah, Gilbert Solomon, and James Lulua Sr.

Bullying in school can change a child's life. You stop learning because of bullying, because you're either scared, angry, or you're getting in trouble. I felt all of that, but I was protected enough to breathe through it whether I was in the Mission or going to school back at home and learning my language again, because in the Mission, I lost it a bit. I understood it but I had a tough time – my tongue couldn't really work. As time went on, I learned my language again, and I learned to hunt and fish and to be with the Elders.

Protecting

Gene Cooper, Xeni Gwet'in

I'm a stepbrother to Chief Roger. We grew up together. Eileen started raising me when I was about twelve, when my grandmother passed. My dad was from Nemiah. He's the one that brought me over and gave me to my grandmother, and my grandmother raised me since I was about a month old. So I was raised out in Nemiah.

Roger was the one I was packing on my back to school through deep snow. Protecting him in residential school. He was small for his age, so I used to have to defend him all the time. For some reason, he seemed to be a target of people's aggression, so older boys – they were sometimes twice as big as me – used to come and make 'em cry, and I used to defend him. Doing the fights for him, getting beat up for him, so they'd keep their concentration off him. I used to do a lot of the fighting for him in residential school, protecting 'em. Sometimes it was an Anaham Tl'etinqox member that was fighting with him, or sometimes it was a Redstone Tŝideldel member. Shuswap Secwépemc, yeah. It didn't matter who it was. I stood in front of them, and I fought for him, just to make sure that they'd leave him alone. And David as well, David Setah. We grew up together. I protected them, put myself there just so they'd leave them alone. I'm a year and a half or so older than David and about three years older than Roger. We found out much later that a lot of the ones that were bullying him were in a home where their parents were abusive to them, so making somebody cry at residential school made them feel good. If you're a quiet person, and you keep to yourself, a lotta times you'd fall victim to them. But if you're aggressive, you talk back, you fight back, then they know you're gonna be noisy if something goes haywire. The tough thing – whether you were Shuswap, Carrier or Tŝilhqot'in – was to make your parent believe that the priest was bad. They'd say, "There's no way that can be. *You're* the bad one. You're not seeing things the right way." That's what you'd get. So they had to find another way to expose those priests.

I never had the abuse that a lot of them did, but I had a lot of emotional abuse, emotional effects from it, because I was dragged away from my grandmother, who needed me at the time. And, you know, even after residential school, when there was funding provided to assist with counselling, I was – I used to think I was a tough guy. I never needed counselling and didn't believe in that stuff. But I thought, no, for once I'm gonna walk it and see how it is. So I went to a counsellor in regard to my residential school experience and the effects it had. I didn't know I was carrying that much emotion until I went into that, and I crashed a few times. It took a while to get on my feet and be able to deal with it. But once I finished the counselling, I felt really good coming out. I walked away from the counselling – like, it was an experience, and I gotta take the positive outta that and use that. It made me find out that I learned to adapt to the situation all the time. I never thought about that. You kinda get in survival mode. To survive whatever's going on now, you adapt to it. You find out where it's wrong for them, where it's right for them, and you find that middle, and you just survive.

Some of our leaders wanted to be more aggressive, but I was saying, "I know what you're feeling, but we need to beat them at their game, understand their paperwork, and use that against them." It took a lot of convincing, but they got on board, saying, "If it doesn't work your way, then we can do it our way." So we really did our best to make all the paperwork, and that's where a lot of success was: trying to follow the rules, follow the steps. Don't get outta line anywhere, do something wrong. And because the Nation was focused on this Title case, we had to be careful at the community level. That's why we wanted to decide what we do until this court case came through. So, yeah, people had to hold back lots on economics and all that, just so this court case could go through. There was a lot of sacrificing by a lot of people.

"What Did She Say?"

Elder Eileen Sammy William, Xeni Gwet'in

I know my language at Mission. He's [Roger] the one that lost *all* that when he went to school at Kamloops. He come back, and I'm talking to him in Tŝilhqot'in. "What did she say?" And then I told him, and then he start talking like that, using Tŝilhqot'in.

I didn' know it's so easy to forget your own language. That's when in school you don' use language. You just play with other people like that. Lose it *all*.

If Residential School Hadn't Happened

Chief Roger William

I guess how the residential school affected me more is, for example, the teaching my mom got from her mom and dad that I didn't get. I know a lot of stories, but I think my mom skipped six years of it from when she was in the residential school. She didn't have a husband, so she had to do everything herself. My mom watched my grandma and grandpa as they got old, and I was raised around them. She helped them, and I lived with them, the same as my older stepbrother Harry Setah, my sister Agnes, and my older stepbrother Gene. The late Harry Setah was a big part of my life, and my grandfathers, and a lot of my uncles. I watched how they walked, how they got on a horse, how they hunted, how they cut the meat, how they had their family. That's who I grew up watching and admiring.

When I was going to school, hockey was my interest. We always skated on the creeks and the lakes. Not everything was bad in residential school, but there was enough damage there to create a black mark for all of us, but there was some stuff we learned. Like an Elder telling me that I'm lucky to be able to speak English when they can't speak English or communicate with anybody outside the valley.

I used to hear my uncle Eugene Sammy William xinli and my uncle Henry Solomon xinli telling stories, and if I'd had them in my life every day, I think I would've known more. I blame residential school for that, because I didn't have that, and also for the fact that, although they were really good people, they were also hurting people. Alcohol affected them, and when they were under the influence and not knowing what they were doing, they would say stuff and do stuff that was not very good. My mom also had to deal with Catholic influence from residential school creeping in, and her brothers and sisters saying that she was living in sin because she had no husband and was a single parent. That affected me and my sister and stepbrothers too, but as time went on, it reversed. Gene's working at the Nation office, my sister's working here at the Band office, and my brother's working in Fisheries, so people began to say that my mom was doing well, doing hides and baby baskets.

If residential school hadn't happened, imagine what we could've had in terms of more legends, stories, rituals, and living our culture. If I hadn't had to stay in the Mission ten months of the year, if I'd been out here all my life and actually harvesting like I'm supposed to do and using the Land and moving around, imagine all that before contact. I always think my kids are smarter than me, and their kids can be smarter than them. And I think if I'd been raised in the old way, we probably would've prospered more, all of us in my age group. But at the same time, we've been adapting.

Our younger ones are saying that they wanna know more of the language, the legends, and the stories, because they're reading and seeing it and it's good. Now the pride is coming back. The three groups are starting to say the Catholic Church has hurt us for such a long time. My auntie and uncles who went to the Mission have addictions to alcohol that they just can't kick and are now going through the process. When I was growing up, my uncles and aunts feared what the government, the police, the game warden were gonna do to their stuff, but today, we've got pride. I think we're making this turn, you know, making this shift. And once people start – and I see that happening with the youth – we're gonna really turn this around. I think if we hadn't protected the Land, we would be hurting even more. Brittany Triangle would've been logged out, and there would've been logging down the Taseko mining road. All that would've been logged.

Reconciliation and Trinkets

Chief Roger William

All the money and stuff that Canada provides as reconciliation from residential school, I think it's a joke. I see my aunts and uncles suffering. They got money from it. I got money from it. That's a slap in the face. That's the worst thing you could do – erase taking them away from their home, never mind abusing them physically, emotionally, sexually. Just taking them away from their home and telling them that's not the right way to live. That's wrong. Teach 'em your culture, make 'em go back home. My baby coming back to me from the Mission and saying, "ʔAba, Dad, what you taught me's wrong. Where I come from is right." So my child's got a different attitude. They don't respect me the way they used to; they don't look at me with a sparkle in the eye. They look at me different, like I did something bad. So if Canada wants to do reconciliation, they gotta deal with the Land question, they gotta honour the damage they've done to our people.

We have to heal ourselves. Give us the resources so we can do that. We've got people in our community, in our Nation, in BC, and in Canada who are First Nations people and are professors that could counsel us, that could heal us. Give us the resources to bring them to help us out. We know what's right and wrong. Let's put money into course material, let's put money into a Tŝilhqot'in immersion that's gonna be all Tŝilhqot'in with English later, and teach our legends, history, our leadership, our rituals, our law. I call our rituals our constitution. If you wanna do reconciliation from residential school, you're looking at that, but they didn't even touch that. It's like they're saying, "Okay. Here. We affected you. We don't care about your kids and grandkids. That doesn't matter. They didn't go to school here so we'll just give you money, we'll give you a counsellor, we'll give you money for healing." But the damage is done with these kids already. This person's children, grandchildren – they're all damaged from the residential school. You give me money, but that money's probably not even going to help me, my bills, never mind reconciling with my kids and my grandchildren, never mind all the damage I did to them. That's just me. You didn't even deal with the Land and the resources that you affected. You didn't even deal with teaching me my own language, my own rituals and beliefs, and my ceremonies. You didn't give me money to find someone in my Territory to teach me that again, to live it again. You just threw money at us and said we're putting millions of dollars into First Nations. The general public's in an uproar, saying we still have problems, and you put all this money into First Nations, and you never solved it, it's still a problem. You've got political parties running for seats in Parliament, saying "We wanna treat everybody the same," like the old Reform Party. "You shouldn't have special rights, you don't pay tax, you don't do that" – you know. "You get your hospital paid." Yeah, you live with us and you find out that before I'm finished doing my teeth, the dentist says, "Sorry, I've got no money for you. The INAC [Indigenous and Northern Affairs Canada] money ran out. I'm not gonna work on your teeth anymore." Two years later, more damage. Three months' work on a job that was only done three months before. Now you've got no teeth. Just a rough example. That's what we have. Our people still have to pay for their eyeglasses.

You know, we get this certain amount for housing – $38,430 subsidy per house, and that's it. The rest will be a loan. Twenty years ago, you might have built a house for that amount. Today a house costs at least $150,000. I can't even get a loan to do business here on this reserve. The bank's not even gonna give me a loan, because it's on reserve. I'll never own my house on reserve. I can't even start a business. I just have the right to stay here, the right to be in a house, but that house is nothing for me. No collateral, nothing. I don't have any rights to put against a business I might wanna run. All my life. I pass that same problem to my children. They can stay here but can't do anything with it. That's not reconciliation. It's a joke, really. It brought up the hurts of our people, gave 'em a little bit of money. Some of them perished. They're gone today. If they'd never gone to residential school, they'd still be alive today. But when they got that money, it's a new thing. They've never had that much money. Money gets a person into trouble. Money can be a bad medicine if you don't use it right, and it makes you do things that you wouldn't normally do, especially if you're not healed, if you've been hurt by the system so bad that you gotta drink alcohol just for me to be able to talk to you. Otherwise, no confidence – "I'm shy, I feel inferior, I don't feel confident, I just … Give me some alcohol, I'll be so smart and so powerful, and when that's not there, you won't even see me sitting here." That's what some of our people that got money say today. People and businesses out there took advantage of them, knew that they got money, sold 'em stuff they didn't need. Gone. Now they're sitting here, they used to be on this healing journey, and now it's way off the healing journey. They're angry. By the time they realize that somebody tricked them, their own children tricked them by using the money in a certain way, they're hurting, they're mad. Then they just start drinking, and they don't care if somebody tries to say something. Just give them the finger. They don't care, and then, pretty soon, they're gone. Could be that they flipped their vehicle, could be health. In some cases, it was a little better. Some people used it wisely, and then it's not all bad, but I still think it's just more trinkets, you know. Just keep giving out more trinkets for the damage they did to you.

CHAPTER 4 ENDNOTES

1   See Williams Lake First Nation (website), "St. Joseph's Mission Investigation," www.wlfn .ca/about-wlfn/sjm-investigation/. The last residential school in Canada was closed on December 31, 1997. You can find a useful timeline in the online *Canadian Encyclopedia*: www .thecanadianencyclopedia.ca/en/timeline/residential-schools. The Truth and Reconciliation Commission of Canada (TRC) "concluded that residential schools were a systematic, government-sponsored attempt to destroy Aboriginal cultures and languages and to assimilate Aboriginal peoples so that they no longer existed as distinct peoples." The TRC further characterized this intent as "cultural genocide" (National Centre for Truth and Reconciliation, "Residential School History," nctr.ca/education/teaching-resources/residential-school -history/). For an authoritative overview, see the Truth and Reconciliation Commission's summary of its final report, *Honouring the Truth, Reconciling for the Future* (2015) at ehprnh2mwo3.exactdn.com/wp-content/uploads/2021/01/Executive_Summary_English _Web.pdf. Dr. Wilson's speech is at National Centre for Truth and Reconciliation, "Dr. Marie Wilson's Full Speech in Maskwacis for Papal Visit," posted by Karolyn Xie, July 25, 2022, nctr.ca/dr-marie-wilsons-full-speech-in-maskwacis-for-papal-visit/. The blog by Working Effectively with Indigenous Peoples® provides a cumulative total. See Indigenous Corporate Training Inc., "The Indian Act, Residential Schools and Tuberculosis Cover Up," May 17, 2016, www.ictinc.ca/blog/the-indian-act-residential-schools-and-tuberculosis-cover-up. The national Memorial Register for residential school students is at National Centre for Truth and Reconciliation, "Memorial Register," nctr.ca/memorial/national-student-memorial/ memorial-register/. See also Bev Sellars's memoir of her experience at the Mission, *They Called Me Number One: Secrets and Survival at an Indian Residential School* (Vancouver: Talonbooks, 2013), and Phyllis Webstad, *Beyond the Orange Shirt Story* (Nanaimo, BC: Medicine Wheel Education, 2021).

2   Elizabeth Furniss, *Victims of Benevolence: The Dark Legacy of the Williams Lake Residential School* (Vancouver: Arsenal Pulp Press, 2011), 115. See the detailed narrative of the Mission at archives.nctr.ca/uploads/r/National-Centre-for-Truth-and-Reconciliation-NCTR/8/2/a/8 2a2efc77cc5be3334c4666a83b14df3157b4cbf56791f091b14896dc780b0e9/NAR-NCTR-020 .pdf.

3   Furniss, *Victims of Benevolence*, 93.

4   Kelm, *Colonizing Bodies*, 73, 71. – The TRC notes that "children were sent to what were, in most cases, badly constructed, poorly maintained, overcrowded, unsanitary fire traps. Many children were fed a substandard diet and given a substandard education, and worked too hard. For far too long, they died in tragically high numbers. Discipline was harsh and unregulated; abuse was rife and unreported. It was, at best, institutionalized child neglect" (Truth and Reconciliation Commission of Canada, *Honouring the Truth, Reconciling for the Future: Summary of The Final Report of the Truth and Reconciliation Commission of Canada*, 43, irsi.ubc.ca/sites/default/files/inline-files/Executive_Summary_English_Web .pdf).

5   For an excellent overview, see Erin Hanson with Daniel P. Gamez, and Alexa Manuel, "The Residential School System," Indigenous Foundations (website), 2009, updated 2020, indigenousfoundations.arts.ubc.ca/residential-school-system-2020/. Tamara Starblanket's

book, *Suffer the Little Children: Genocide, Indigenous Nations and the Canadian State* (Atlanta: Clarity Press, 2018) provides a powerful analysis of residential schools in the context of genocide. Two of the key works of scholarship on the history of the residential schools are J.R. Miller, *Shingwauk's Vision: A History of Native Residential Schools* (Toronto: University of Toronto Press, 1996), and John S. Milloy, *A National Crime: The Canadian Government and the Residential School System, 1879 to 1986*, 2nd ed., Critical Studies in Native History series (Winnipeg: University of Manitoba Press, 2017). For more information on McIntee, Doughty, and O'Connor, see Suzanne Fournier and Ernie Crey, *Stolen from Our Embrace: The Abduction of First Nations Children and the Restoration of Aboriginal Communities* (Vancouver/Toronto: Douglas & McIntyre, 1998), and Ward Churchill, *Kill the Indian, Save the Man: The Genocidal Impact of American Indian Residential Schools* (San Francisco: City Lights Publishers, 2004).

6   For more of Jacob Roper's life story, see Lorne Dufour, *Jacob's Prayer: Loss and Resilience at Alkali Lake* (Halfmoon Bay: Caitlin Press, 2009). For more information about the Indian hospitals, see Maureen K. Lux, *Separate Beds: A History of Indian Hospitals in Canada, 1920s–1980s* (Toronto: University of Toronto Press, 2016), and Gary Geddes, *Medicine Unbundled: A Journey through the Minefields of Indigenous Health Care* (Victoria: Heritage House, 2017).

7   "A 1945 building inspector's report concluded that the Mission buildings posed an extreme fire hazard. The inspector insisted that renovations would be futile, and that the school either should be shut down or a new facility built on the site. Finally, in 1954 funding was provided to construct new school buildings and residences. Two weeks before students were scheduled to move into the new facility, fire broke out in the old buildings …" (Furniss, *Victims of Benevolence*, 112). The old school building was demolished in 1987.

8   One of the TRC reports writes that "student victimization of students was an element of the broader abusive and coercive nature of the residential school system. Underfed, poorly housed, and starved for affection, students often formed groups based on age, community of origin, or First Nation. Such groups gave students a measure of identity and status, but also provided protection to their members and dominated more vulnerable students" (Truth and Reconciliation Commission of Canada, *What We Have Learned: Principles of Truth and Reconciliation* [2015], 79, publications.gc.ca/collections/collection_2015/trc/IR4-6-2015-eng .pdf). In this story, the racism which was the foundation of residential schools is literalized in the conduct and language of staff towards students.

9   Historian Ian Mosby has demonstrated the connection between the chronic hunger and malnutrition imposed on many residential school students and their subsequent experiences of diabetes, hypertension, and cardiovascular disease. See, for example: Ian Mosby and Erin Millions, "Canada's Residential Schools Were a Horror," *Scientific American*, August 1, 2021, www.scientificamerican.com/article/canadas-residential-schools-were-a-horror/; Ian Mosby, "Administering Colonial Science: Nutrition Research and Human Biomedical Experimentation in Aboriginal Communities and Residential Schools, 1942–1952," *Histoire sociale / Social History* 46, no. 91 (May 2013): 615–642, doi.org/10.1353/his.2013.0015; and Hon. Dr. Mary Ellen Turpel-Lafond (Aki-Kwe), *In Plain Sight: Addressing Indigenous-Specific Racism and Discrimination in B.C. Health Care*, Addressing Racism Review Summary Report, November 2020, engage.gov.bc.ca/app/uploads/sites/613/2020/11/In-Plain-Sight -Summary-Report.pdf. Stomach cancer belongs on Mosby's list, and its incidence among residential school Survivors is well known in Indigenous communities, though still largely ignored by medical researchers. Ivor Myers's perspective above is cross-cultural, reflecting his knowledge as a deyen traditional healer, as well as his experience of allopathic medicine.

Had he encountered a similar openness in his journey through the hospital system, perhaps his last months would have been easier.

10   See volume 1 of the *Final Report of the Truth and Reconciliation Commission of Canada* on the Schools' "long-term legacy of continuing division and distrust within Aboriginal communities" (108–110).

11   Eila Quilt and Laura Setah are sisters who recorded together about their experiences at the Mission.

12   "Of all diseases, tuberculosis, by far, cast the longest shadow. Among the First Nations, the disease took mostly young people. In 1935, over 80 percent of its victims in British Columbia Aboriginal communities were under the age of thirty, 70 percent were less than twenty years old" (Kelm, *Colonizing Bodies*, 10). The residential schools played a well-documented role in this process, demonstrated as early as 1907 by Dr. Peter Bryce, Chief Medical Officer for the Departments of the Interior and Indian Affairs. In his *Report on the Indian Schools of Manitoba and the Northwest Territories* (publications.gc.ca/collections/collection_2018/aanc-inac/R5-681-1907-eng.pdf), Bryce wrote that within the first fifteen years of the schools, 24 percent of the children had died due to tuberculosis, which thrived on malnutrition, weakened immune systems, dirt, poor ventilation, and no heat. Bryce's recommendations were ignored, and by 1918, Duncan Campbell Scott was able to affirm that "Indian children lose their natural resistance to illness by habituating so closely in the residential schools" and they "die at a much higher rate than in their villages," thereby contributing to "the final solution of our Indian problem" ("The Indian Act, Residential Schools and Tuberculosis Cover Up"). So common was TB in the residential schools that it became known as "Indian tuberculosis," and infected students were sent to the segregated Indian hospitals where, as Geddes writes, "when they showed signs of recovery, [they] were sent back to the residential school. This mutually beneficial arrangement maintained the numbers and funding of both organizations" ("The Indian Act, Residential Schools and Tuberculosis Cover Up," based on Maureen K. Lux, *Separate Beds: A History of Indian Hospitals in Canada, 1920s–1980s* [Toronto: University of Toronto Press, 2016], 8). Ivor Myers xinli's experience of being sent back and forth from the Mission to Coqualeetza Hospital is an example of this practice.

13   Brother Hoby Spruyt was a dorm supervisor and music teacher at St. Joseph's Mission. After several years there, he moved to Kuper Island Residential School, eventually following Father Thomas Lobsinger, who moved from the Mission to Dawson City, Yukon. When Lobsinger became a bishop, Spruyt was his "administrator." They died in a plane crash while Lobsinger was returning to Dawson City with Brother Spruyt.

14   Father Hubert O'Connor was principal of St. Joseph's Mission (January 1961 to August 1967), became Bishop of Whitehorse in 1971 and of Prince George in 1986. In 1991 he resigned when he was charged with rape and indecent assault of two young women students at St. Joseph's. He was convicted of these crimes in 1996 and served only six months of a two-and-a-half-year sentence. He appealed, and the assault charge was acquitted, while the rape charge was dropped when he participated in a healing circle at Esk'etemc Alkali Lake. He died in 2007 in Toronto.

15   Maryann Solomon has written two books based on the Elders' teachings: *Xeni Gwet'in First Nations Traditional Medicines* (2004) and *Xeni Gwet'in Ancestral Laws and Customs / Xeni Gwet'in ?Esggidam Dechen Ts'edilhtan* (2012), both published by the Xeni Gwet'in First Nations Government.

16   The Truth and Reconciliation Commission notes that "despite the fact that Indian Affairs had given orders to abandon the practice, students were still having their hair cropped into the 1970s. In the 1990s, students at the Gordon's, Saskatchewan, school were still being struck, and pushed into lockers and walls by one staff member. The failure to develop, implement, and monitor effective discipline sent an unspoken message that there were no real limits on what could be done to Aboriginal children within the walls of a residential school. The door had been opened early to an appalling level of physical and sexual abuse of students, and it remained open throughout the existence of the system" (*Final Report of the Truth and Reconciliation Commission of Canada*, vol. 1, 104–105).

17   The girls' pipe band was created in 1958 by Father Alex Morris, who became principal of the 150 Mile Elementary School in 1946. He started a music program and persuaded the provincial government to fund the purchase of bagpipes (Margaret Whitehead, *The Cariboo Mission: A History of the Oblates* [Victoria: Sono Nis Press, 1981, 132–134).

18   See the Government of Canada's description of "Common Experience Payments" at www .rcaanc-cirnac.gc.ca/eng/1100100015594/1571582431348. The *Final Report of the TRC* notes that "the number of claims for compensation for abuse is equivalent to approximately 48% of the number of former students who were eligible to make such claims" (vol. 1, 106–107).

Naŝlhiny Horses and Growing Up

Naŝlhiny Horses

Chief Roger William

I grew up with horses. My mother rode horses. She had teamhorses, and she chased cattle, chased wild horses, and I travelled with her in a baby basket on her back since I could remember. Horses were a means of transportation for our people for years. Horses are naŝlhiny in our language. I always thought and felt, and I still feel, that horses were a part of our Tŝilhqot'in way, but when you learn through history books in high school and elementary school, horses are said to have been brought in. I grew up with horses being a part of us.

My mom told me a story about my uncle Jimmy William – some say Jimmy Bulyan. (My grampa Sammy William was also known as Samforyam or Sambulyan.) Jimmy lived in Teẑtan Biny Fish Lake, raised a family in Teẑtan Biny, Yanah Biny, Wasp Lake, Jididzay Onion Lake, Dasiqox Taseko, Yeqoxnilin, all of the Taseko River. He moved around in that area, had his wife, children – most of his children were born and raised there. My great-uncle, Jamadis, lived there before him, and my mom told me stories about Jimmy.

Everyone had the power of an animal, bird, or fish, but a deyen had multiple powers. That's what my uncle Jimmy Bulyan was. He was a deyen, and he had the spiritual power of a horse. That was his power. He could train, he could catch any wild horse, and the horses he had were always good horses. To me – and my understanding was from my mom – great horses came from Teẑtan Biny. Jimmy Bulyan trained them, and one time he came to visit the place where I was born, Naghataneqed. It's at the east end of Konni Lake, in the meadow where the cabin's still up today, a two-storey cabin with a warehouse. It's not livable today, but the structure's still up. My mom was telling me that her older brother Jimmy Bulyan came over and got off his horse and decided to go down on his hands and knees and was slapping the horse's legs. This horse was just green-broke, just trained. The horse shook, and my mom got scared. "You're gonna get kicked!" But he told her, "The only time this horse'll kick me is if it's gonna kill me." So that's a story that I grew up with.

I was raised with horses, and they were always a part of me, my family, grandparents, siblings. I was taught that a horse can feel how you're feeling, whether you're upset, angry, excited, or if you have bad intent. The horse feels you. I was always taught that a horse can even feel a fly on its back. The horse shakes, and its skin twitches as soon as a fly lands on it, and I used to watch that when I was a child, watching teamhorses or horses in the corral or tied up in a meadow. I used to watch the fly land and the horse shake it off, and I always understood. I was raised to understand that when I'm dealing with a horse, it feels me, and there is a spiritual connection. Because they're on the Land all the time, they feel the cold, hot, wet, winter – they feel all that year round. They smell, they see, and they hear the Land. Today I always think about how we Tŝilhqot'in people, Xeni Gwet'ins, we were like that too. That connection and communication is so important. I was always taught that we honour the Land, the resources, the water, the wildlife, the fish. We pray for and we honour everything that we do and get from the Land. And that's the same with horses.

A lot of our members were brought up that way. My uncles, my siblings all felt the horse, connected with horses, and horses connected with them. It's almost spiritual. When you're riding in the dark, you feel danger, just like a horse. I was taught that when you're riding, you always pay attention to the horse. The horse is always out on the Land, and they can smell, hear, and feel fear, feel danger, so when I'm riding, I'm always aware of how comfortable the horse is. If I can feel his body winding up, something's not right, and I'm ready automatically for any action that the horse may take. It could be an attack from something, or sometimes something just comes out of nowhere, and the horse reacts. You're with the horse, you feel the horse when it winds up quick. All of a sudden the horse just jumps, and you're there with the horse. That's what I grew up with, being around horses when they're in a corral, when they're tied up, one of them hanging out. I see the horse reacting to something, and then I'm looking around to find out what's going on, and the horse warns me what's happening. If the horse is calm, there's nothing wrong, but if the horse is starting to get edgy, then you're getting ready for it, whether you're riding the horse or you're on the ground. It could be a wild horse, or a teamhorse out in the meadows, or a horse tied up or in a corral. You understand the horse, and you feel the horse. That connection, that understanding is how many people train their horse. It's an understanding that's built up inside you as you grow up. You hear stories from Elders, uncles, aunts, cousins, friends – stories about horses. And that becomes normal to you.

Qayus wild horse at Lhizbay, near Tsilhqox Biny Chilko Lake.
Photo by Chief Roger William

Gwenįg Stories and Discipline

Chief Roger William

To discipline a child – because children forget, or they challenge things – all you have to do is remind them about a story. "Remember what happened in this legend?" And they're like "Oh yeah!" If your parent sees you do something, they'll remind you, maybe tell you a story, and if you do it again, they'll remind you again, but then they may skip. So if there was a snack or a meal, it would be skipped. Things like that, that's how they taught our people. You're told legends and stories, and you're taught these ways. Then if you don't follow them, then they would skip something on you, and you'd know right away what you did wrong. If you're a little kid, you're reminded by different things. You would be reminded by a story. A lot of it is body language and actions, like the action of doing or not doing something. But when you get older, depending on what you've done wrong and whether you had intention and all that, the punishment is severe. When you're growing up, a lot of your discipline is through stories, through body language, and through actions.

I noticed that in my upbringing, and I still see examples of it today. For example, my uncle, late William Setah, and my auntie, late Madeline Setah, had cattle, and they taught their animals in this way. They had horses in the corral and cattle outside it. We live fifteen, ten, five miles apart, and everybody's the same, but sometimes we eat, and then we feed our cattle earlier than others. Sometimes a cow would go astray and take off. Late William Setah would come down to the corral and look at the cattle. He'd see one cow that wasn't his. He'd walk back up, and those cows wouldn't eat. They'd miss a feed. He fed at the same time every day and, depending on the weather, three times a day. Usually, he fed morning and night, but maybe three times if it was really cold. So he came back down that night, and the one cow that wasn't his was still there. He walked back up and didn't feed them. He fed the horses, fed the cow that's inside that needs it for the calf, but the cows outside, they were pretty well on their own. They were strong enough and didn't have little ones to look after. They'd probably have babies later. So he just walked back up. He'd do that several times, and then those cows kicked that cow out, the cow they knew didn't belong to them. They'd actually kick that cow out.

It was not too long ago – I think it was a few years back – and one of their horses was a mare that would get in heat. There was a stallion outside the fence, and she'd try to encourage him to come in, but there was an old horse – it was probably thirty – that chased the mare. The old horse stood there watching, and chased the mare away from the fence to keep her away from the stud. Couple times my cousin went down, and if the stallion was still there, he didn't feed the horses. The mare kept doing that, and the old horse just watched. Next time, when my cousin went back down to feed, and the mare was doing that again, he left, didn't feed them. Then the old horse chased the mare away from the fence and kept her away so he could eat.

The ranching way of life complemented our culture. We had to move around to different meadows to harvest hay, to put hay away, so that our cattle and horses could eat, and we knew where all the meadows were and all the water, the water table, the creeks, rivers, lakes. There are years when you don't harvest enough hay, so you let your saddlehorses go to fend for themselves. You may keep one or two horses, and then you feed the cattle. So that was my understanding as I grew up.

There's trapping, hunting, fishing, berry picking, medicine gathering, our community gardens – in my upbringing all that was very normal. We'd go out and get the horses when we needed them to hunt moose and deer and to trap. Horses get to a point where you can't use them anymore, so you have to catch another horse if you need to. You catch horses and train them. Our people used to bring in different stallions, and they chased horses, culled them, cut [castrated] them, trained them or sold them to keep the herd strong. It's like ranching, but you don't cut hay for these horses – they're out there on their own. We understand their role, we understand how they survive out there on the Land. You have stallions that have so many mares, and you have young stallions that hang out together because they have no herd, until they get strong enough to take over another herd. The elders and the youth survive together, so when the youth become strong enough to take over a herd, they know from the elders how to live off the Land. And the elders are taken care of in the herd with the younger stallions. Then you have herds with stallions and mares. Our leaders and people knew about these groups, and they chased horses every year to train, to sell, and to use. Sometimes we'd let some of our saddlehorses go and get them the next year. We knew where the herds were, where they hung out, their trails. When you chase them, you know where they're gonna run, because our people were always out on the Land with horses to go hunting, to go fishing, berry picking, ranching, gardening, everything. All of that was complementary to our culture and way of life, physically and spiritually, for a long time.

Seniya Money

Chief Roger William

I remember the first time my mom got a welfare cheque and what welfare did in many ways to our people. Before that we hunted, fished, trapped like we'd always done, but now there was money involved. We'd go to Lee's Corner [store]. There was even one of our Chiefs who had a store in the valley and sold dry goods. Our people traded or made deals with the Chief. Europeans came in, and then there were reserve lands. Welfare was one of the most devastating things to our people, because after it began in 1975, they didn't have to go out and ranch, fish, and hunt. Now you've got a cheque every month. You got a home, and you hunted and fished once in a while to make ends meet. The need to go out year-round was not there, and because fur prices dropped, trapping slowly fell off. There was more dependency with the welfare cheque coming in, and eventually people threw ranching away. Then the youth were impacted because their parents or, in some cases, grandparents didn't have horses or cattle. They stopped using horses.

My grandfather and my uncles always built cabins for ranchers, tourism operators, and their own people. They would get materials from Indian Affairs, or they would cut their own, but as time went on, all that started to change. Gradually there was more dependence on the Band office. The more money came into the community and the more services came from the Band office, the less our people were dependent on the Land and its resources. From the time of the Declaration in 1989 to the roadblock at Henry's Crossing and the filing of the Trapline case in 1992, to the Chilko study which became Tŝ'ilʔos Park in 1994, one of our goals was to bring horses back, and we did that by having gatherings with youth and Elders. Riding to these gatherings and having gymkhanas, rodeos, and mountainraces was a way to get our youth involved again.

A lot of ranchers in the Tŝilhqot'in fenced off our traditional use areas, including fishing areas and in some cases our earthlodges, the pithouses. This process started separating everyone. So did ranching as non–First Nations people's ranges got bigger because they needed two hundred head to survive, while ours stayed the same and, due to our lifestyle, we needed only fifty to a hundred cows. Pretty soon, more of our ranchers had to range in one area. Then the price for cattle stayed the same while the costs for branding, making hay, and all that kept going up. Eventually our families just stopped ranching and trapping. Some still hunt and fish, pick berries and gather medicines, but horses got lost in the shuffle.

Welfare

Marilyn Baptiste, Xeni Gwet'in

Some of our people say they remember the day when some of our Elders refused welfare. They remember their grandmother crying and saying, "Do not take this welfare, 'cause it will destroy our people."

Lha yudit'ih We Always Find a Way

Another Perspective

David Williams

When the ranchers were given the Land, First Nations were crowded into concentration camps that were called reserves. The ranchers wanted the wild horses that were numerous in those days off the range so it would be for their cattle. The Indigenous people didn't have enough land to run cattle because they had to raise hay and they couldn't be out on the Land in winter. But horses could go out on the Land and survive in the winter, so they went to horses. So they had hundreds and thousands of horses, many of whom went wild. And so there's always that tension. Of course what the government sees as their primary responsibility is keeping the range for the cattle. The ranchers are obviously a much more powerful lobby, so it's always been that hatred of wild horses by government people. And that's why they slaughtered ten thousand of them over the years for their colony.[1]

Mountainracing

Chief Roger William

The mountainrace is a time when our wild-horse chasers show off their skills. When you try to catch a wild horse, they come down the side of a mountain, go through straight stretches where there's a lotta rock, and they hit trails, mudholes, creeks, and beaver dams to get away from you. Our mountainrace is much like that.

Through my mom, grandparents, uncles, and aunts, I heard stories, and I watched how our people trained their horses and how they managed, rode, and chased them. When the mountainrace came in, there were role models in my community that I looked up to, like my first cousin, Ronnie Solomon (the son of my mother's older sister Mabel Solomon xinli). Ronnie was always chasing horses and cattle and had a nice horse named Trigger that he trained. That horse is amazing. When Ronnie mountainraced, he always won. He was my hero whom I looked up to, and at age sixteen, I did my first mountainrace.

We used to have a whole bunch of cowboys like Roy Lulua, former Chief Benny William, former Chief the late Marvin Baptiste, Raphael William, Walter Lulua, Sonny Lulua, and the late Harry Setah. A whole bunch of them would chase horses and, down at Naghataneqed, they built a little rodeo ground where they had horses and cattle on the hillside. Once a week or every two or three weeks, they'd chase horses in and have a jackpot. They all paid in a bit of money. We used to watch them riding saddlebronc and bareback and cow-riding. And we'd watch them chase horses off the hillside and through the creek and everything. That used to be pretty neat! I remember my brother, the late Harry Setah, was always asking us if we wanted to get on some steers, and we'd always be scared. We didn't want to, but one day we did, and we kept riding. Then we got into rodeo, so by the time I was sixteen, I was riding some steers, but I'd already been riding cows. I started riding bulls when I was eighteen. Today kids are riding bulls by sixteen – fourteen, some of them. Way out in the boonies, it was a little different. Horses, I was always on a horse.

This year marks thirty-two years since I first started mountainracing, and I've wiped out on the trail, in the mud, in the creek, in the beaver dams. Just this past year, I wiped out at Williams Lake Stampede at the bottom of the hill, before the racetrack, so I feel pretty lucky to still be doing what I love today.

Shannon

Chief Roger William

We met on Valentine's Day, February 14, 1993. Shannon is from the largest community in the Tŝilhqot'in, Tl'etinqox. Her brother and her uncle were both Chiefs, but she didn't want anything to do with politics. She made that clear when I met her. It's pretty crazy that she ended up marrying a Chief! Kids love her and connect with her just like that. Shannon went through rough times in her community and her family. Like many First Nations communities across Canada, her community had problems with drugs and alcohol, the impact of residential school, and all that. She had a tough life, but she learned to advance from it, and after we met, she quit everything within a year. Shannon's a very strong Tŝilhqot'in and really family-rooted. She's worked since she was thirteen, getting jobs while she was going to school because her mom couldn't give her the money that she needed. Shannon graduated from high school and then got her diploma in business.

I was married when we met but separated from my first wife, and I had a son. There was a transition period between relationships, and I told Shannon that she should find someone who had no children and raise a family. She said yes, but every time we saw each other, it was all out the window, and we were back together. During the second year, we started getting serious and decided this is it. Eleven years after we met, we got married, in June 2004. She was a Tl'etinqox member, and after we got married, she became a Xeni Gwet'in member. We have two sons and a daughter.

Shannon worked for the school district for three or four years. Then she applied for a job in my community. We have policies about conflict of interest, so I didn't get involved in interviewing or hiring her. The Council hired her, and she made a lotta changes in social work in relation to children and family. Everything was still paper-based when she arrived, and she updated to a digital system with reporting online. As a result, she was able to use all the funding programs from Social Assistance, where previous social workers had trouble keeping up with the paperwork so they weren't able to use all the funds from different programs that require reports and getting clients' approval. Shannon worked really hard and got a lotta stuff going for the social development clients, children, and family. You could tell that members in our community really liked her. She was hired in 2006 and kept working until January 2013.

Shannon is really smart. She can negotiate with anybody for her clients, for her vehicle, for her house. She puts up real good arguments, and it's pretty hard for you to turn them down. And she goes to bat for you, goes to war for you. So I think Xeni lost a really good staff member, but because I was in conflict of interest, in terms of evaluating her, hiring her, I couldn't do anything. She made sacrifices for our young children, for me, the Title case and Fish Lake. I was gone a lot, and although our families helped us out, she pretty well raised the children by herself. She saw how hard I had to work during the election, and she had to work hard to do her job and watch the kids while I was gone a lot. Shannon is an amazing, strong, dedicated lady, and when I didn't get back in in the 2008 election, it just blew her away. She couldn't believe it. What were the people thinking? What did they want? I think she probably worked overtime for years between 2008 and 2013, and she was working in a place where she wasn't happy, but she still did amazing work for our people. If anyone in leadership wasn't addressing her concerns and issues, I couldn't do anything. She went to bat for me, and she sacrificed for me, and I couldn't even help her.

I used to ride bulls. I rode bulls for fifteen years, and Shannon met me when I was riding bulls. During the first year that we were together, I won the overall bull-riding championship. She loved the bull riding! We shared it and were on the road together. That was probably the fun time for her, with all the rodeos, dances, and bull riding. Then, when I quit in 1999, those trips were gone, and I think it was a little different for her. She loves mountainracing, which is only three times a year, but I'm still gone for the same amount of time to train my horse. So, yeah, I feel guilty. We talk about it. She probably doesn't want to hurt me and say, "No, you should just stop all that and make more time with us." We always talk about not wanting to stop each other's dreams, and I think she probably sacrificed more than I did in terms of that. I think I'm a bit selfish there. We talked a lot, but after being in politics for a long time, I probably knew what to say, and she was kinda like, "Okay." But when I couldn't do anything for her, that was probably one of the main reasons why she just couldn't last one more month before quitting. I always try to keep politics separate from personal life, but sometimes you can't, right? I learned to debate, I learned to express what I want, why I want it, and how I want it, and because she isn't into politics but she agrees that this Title case is for her kids, our grandkids in the future, she knows it's only good. But I think it's all taken its toll.

David and Goliath[2]

Shannon Stump, Xeni Gwet'in

People sorta had an idea [at the beginning of the Title case], but they're like, "Yeah right. It's like David and Goliath. There's no way in hell this little four-hundred-member community in the middle of nowhere is gonna win Rights and Title that's gonna affect pretty much all across Canada." The racism is just crazy, and we're not educated to know this stuff. And that's how people thought of themselves after the residential school. They're like, "Yeah, right, whatever, we'll give it a shot, but I don't think so." But Roger kept explaining: "This is what we're gonna do, this is how we're gonna stop the logging. Let's get educated on this." After a while, once they'd seen what he was doing and the domino effect with different mills and the government, then they realized that yeah, Nemiah means business. 'Cause a lotta them [logging companies] just come in and don't even inform the Bands. When they stopped the logging, and then Fish Lake, and then the Rights and then the Title, it was getting bigger and bigger, yet the goal was still the same from day one. People were like Wow, this is happening!

I think they probably don't understand it [the Title case], or they don't wanna understand it. Like anybody, they just want results now, you know. But Rome wasn't built in a day, or something like that! [laughs] I never really followed along with the politics part, but as his wife, it was tough, you know, there were a lotta ups 'n downs. He kept the same momentum right from day one to now [2014]. I always tell him he's not normal! [laughs] I cannot function like him! Like delivering on three-, four-hours sleep, travelling, endless hours.

He's amazing. There's a lotta backlash, and he's still positive about it and has the same vision at the end of each day. He always put himself last. It's always, "This is what I want for the community, this is what I want for my kids, this is what I want for my grandkids." He was thinking long term about the logging and mining. He did his homework before he presented anything. Every time he talked to somebody, he had a vision, he had a statement, and he ran with it, which is amazing. [You've gotta] let people know what you're doing, what has been done, what's gonna be done. Roger was really thorough on that.

*　*　*

At the beginning of our relationship, it was all new to me, but it was a challenge that I was willing to take on. I supported him in anything, whatever he wanted to do, but it's so weird, me 'n him have nothing in common! [laughter] The only thing I would say we had in common was our communication skills, and our end goals have always been the same. With all the chaos of him being on the road five days a week, we always communicated one way or another. And, you know, I didn't drop everything to be with him from day one – I still worked in Anaham. I worked at Alexis Creek for ten years. For the first half of our relationship, I was in Anaham, he was in Nemiah. I just went to Nemiah on weekends. I raised my kids, my kids were with me, they were in Nemiah daycare Tŝilhqot'in [language] immersion. We went back and forth. We made it work. I'd say I had more support in Nemiah than I had at Anaham.

Being a Chief is not a nine-to-five job – most days, it's twenty-four hours, so there were some days I was okay with him doing paperwork and others when I was really hard on him. Like, I wanted to throw his computer out! [laughs] "You need to know your boundaries, you need to have a life, you need to not be just married to your work, you know, you've got me and the kids." And we were foster parents, so it wasn't just our three kids. I had a boy that was living with us for a year. Sometimes I was home alone with eight kids. At Alexis Creek, I was a liaison worker. In Nemiah I was a social worker, a family-support worker, and a foster parent. But the expectations of a Chief's wife and of your kids, you're sort of put on a pedestal. It was tough. You know, I have a big heart, and it was always about kids, 'cause I grew up in a rough home, I grew up with the violence and the drugs and alcohol abuse, residential school. I had a front-row seat on all that. So being a foster parent, I wanted to do better for the kids, and I wanted to do better as a person myself, too. Our three kids weren't an accident, they were all planned. Roger and I talked about it right from the get-go. Is this what we wanted, 'cause where were we gonna live? Am I still gonna be in Anaham, and he's in Nemiah? Like that one year he was on the [witness] stand from September till January, he came home only on weekends, and it wasn't every weekend. It was like I was a single mom. Everyone's like, "Oh my god, how do you do it?," and I said, "Well, I still communicate with him." You know, this is what we agreed on, it's not like he just up and left and I don't know where he is. We did it as a team, and he supported anything I wanted to do.

When I go into any job, I don't just do it for the pay. I had a vision of what I wanted to gain for myself as a person. When I worked with the youth in Alexis Creek, I got burnt out. I was only dealing with all the troubled youth, and there was nothing positive. They were amazing kids, but there's just a point where you need to change the scenery, to relook at your goals. In Nemiah, I did social work dealing with adults and families. It was a good experience, and I loved it. I love helping families choose the better road. But, in the end, it was just too much, and my heart wasn't in it. I was burnt out, I had eight kids with me, and I was in court almost every Wednesday, so that meant leaving the house at six in the morning and making my sitter come then or me packing all the kids, and it was just crazy. Then I'd be done court around four, do what I needed to do and be on the road by six, get home by 8:30, 9:00 at night. So being up, like, almost around the clock, and I was on the road every two days. There were some times Roger was home more than me. My last year working, I was gone more than him. My two oldest ones were going to school in town, and there was no bus run, so every Sunday I drove them into town, did what I needed to do, but that was just in and out, and that's still a seven-hour trip. Sometimes I'd come in on Tuesday nights for my court Wednesdays, go back home, and then come in on Thursday nights 'cause I had to pick up my kids Friday after school and then go home. I put about 6,700 kilometres a month on my truck. I never drove anywhere in my life where you hit rain, snow, sun, thunder, and lightning in one trip! [laughs] I know how to change a flat tire now! I'm an expert!

Brothers

Chief Roger William

I'm very fortunate that I rode horses all my life, chased horses since I could remember with Gene Cooper, my older brother. I learned a lot from Gene. David Setah's another person I learned a lot from. Gene and David are both older than me. David's mom is my mom's older sister, Madeline Setah. Her husband,

William Setah, whom I looked up to, was always guiding, riding horses, and he told stories about my grandparents and my uncles chasing horses. So I grew up around Gene and David, and we did a lot of horseback riding. We chased cattle and horses for our families. Gene and David did most of the horse training, and we learned how to shoe horses and all that. Our uncles and cousins passed on that knowledge to us.

At that time, there were logs across the trail during the mountain race, logs that were low enough for you to jump or high enough for you to duck. There was a creek that had a tree right in the middle of the entry. On one side, the trail went into the creek. On the other side, they'd dive off the bank, so depending on where you were and how you'd hit the bank, you could be on the right side of the tree or on the left, going into the Nemiah Creek. Then when you got across, there was a trail that winds through the willow bushes and it was muddy. So that was my experience when I was sixteen and I first raced. I remember my horse that I was riding was a mare. She had been my older brother Gene Cooper's horse, whom he got from our auntie Lucy Lulua. Because he was training horses for her, she gave him that horse. He called her Shadow, but we always called her Black. I'd always ride her, and I quickly learned that Black Shadow was a very fast horse, small but fast. Gene and I used to race each other, and I'd always win with her. That was pretty cool.

My mother had a horse named Little Grey, a qayus [wild horse] and a fast horse. Gene liked that horse, so we made a deal and he gave me the mare and I gave him the gelding, but Black was younger than Little Grey. That was our deal. I used to do a lotta riding with Gene and David, and we'd chase horses and ride horses every day, all the time, throughout the valley. I did the same thing with my older stepbrother Harry Setah. He was given to my grandparents, but my mom ended up watching him a lot, so we all called each other brothers – Gene, late Harry Setah, and myself. David Setah always hung out with us, stayed with us, and we were always doing things together. I was fortunate to have them in my life, because I was the youngest, learning from them how they did everything from fishing to hunting and riding horses. Everything they did I watched and learned and followed. I hung out with the older group because it was just easier that way.

So that's how I was brought up. That's probably what really helped me in doing what I love – mountainracing, playing hockey, riding bulls, rodeo, saddle-bronc riding, team roping. These are things I love doing, and they're a challenge but they're not risky. You can't pass your day. That's what I'm thinking, you know. Today that's how I feel.

Mischief

Elder Eileen Sammy William, Xeni Gwet'in

Oh, this one time they [Roger and Gene] get into mischief. They broke the window of an old cabin! [laughs] He must have been five or six. Always gettin' in trouble? Yeah, but he was pretty smart in school. He wasn't a problem.

When he was younger, he always rode horses. Him and David [Setah], Gene [Cooper], they always rode horses. Sometimes they go down the Chilko [Lake] late at night. They don't come back until one in the morning! [laughs]

Patrick

Chief Roger William

There's a story about him and me. [laughs] My late stepbrother and godfather Harry Setah xinli kept buggin' me and Gene [Cooper] and a bunch of us to start ridin' bulls. Finally I said, "Yup." He gave me all this equipment. Whatever bull ropes he had, he gave to me, and I started riding. I kept comin' up and out. Maybe one, two, three – boom! The front end. One, two – one, two, three, four, maybe. Boom!

We were at Anahim Lake Stampede and Patrick said, "Go!! Shoot, Roger! You gettin' on? I'll pull you up!"

"Okay, over there, sure."

And then I got on, I'm ready to go, and he's "Are you ready?"

I said, "Yep!"

"No! You stick out your damn chest! Where's your goddamn boots? Put them in front of the bull rope!"

"'Kay!"

"'Kay! Now you're ready! Nod your head!"

That was my first ride. Eight seconds and I took off. I started ridin' all my cows and my bulls after that. Patrick just told me what to do right in that split second, and I listened to him, and after that I never looked back. I started ridin', I started winning, and I always told Patrick thank you. Thank you, Patrick. He made me get over that hump. Harry's the one that got me goin'. Hangin' out with David and Gene gave me confidence, but it was Patrick, that one ride, Anahim Lake, and I kept fallin', fallin', fallin' the same way at almost the same time, and once I did that, I got it.

Chief Roger on the way to winning the Chilcotin Rodeo Association Bull Riding Championship for 1993. Archival photo

Getting into Politics

Chief Roger William

I think our people found it was like a breath of fresh air for a young person to get into politics and be as aggressive as I was. When I ran for Council the first time, I was nineteen. I only got seven votes! Two terms later, I ran again, and they tried me and liked how I was as a Councillor. Then I ran for Chief, and I got in and stayed in. I was young, spoke the language, could connect with the outside world and bring it home, and could connect with our Elders in the language. Our Elders' meetings and General Assemblies were all in Tŝilhqot'in. That was unheard of. There had been good Chiefs in the past, but I don't think they'd ever seen anyone who was able to connect with out there, who had graduated from high school, was skilled with horses, and spoke the language. In terms of role models for many kids growing up, this is what they wanted to be. I think it was all honeymoon for a while.

I come from leadership before me and I always use our previous Chief and Council to help make decisions. I talk to them and I come from them. I learn from their mistakes, and I learn from their successes. Benny William and Adam William are my cousins, and they were in before me and Marvin Baptiste xinli for a long time before them. Benny was in for six years, and his father is my mom's brother Eugene Sammy William. Adam William's father is my mom's brother. My predecessors knew about the culture and were really strong, but they couldn't create a picture with the outside world, what it means in the present, and what it could mean in the future. I think I came from the people more. We tried to meet the needs of our people, included staff members in decision-making, and helped them with managing money. For example, we looked not only at money but the impacts of money and of their jobs on their hunting and traditional uses of the Land. Money provides for food, so you want to put your effort into working and forget about hunting, fishing, and berry picking. In a money economy, it's not necessary to be out on the Land as much, but people kind of forgot about that fact. All this was part of helping our people to see the big picture. When it came to Aboriginal Rights and Title, harvesting, logging, and mining, we tried to create the best picture we could. We tried to look at all the angles.

I was really fortunate to have Council that understood what I was trying to do, and although they didn't agree with everything, we could debate and argue about how to do it. The one who was in leadership the longest was David Setah, and the two of us debated a lot. Even today we still debate, but we understand each other, we know where we're coming from. His mom and my mom are sisters, so we've been like family since we were young. Even when we were kids, David, Gene Cooper, and I were thinking and talking about Chief and Council. We talked to our older cousins Gilbert Solomon and Simon Setah, and they asked what we would do to change things. But there's no way when I was a kid that I was thinking of being Chief or Councillor! I was gonna be a bull rider or a hockey player! In high school, when the teacher brought someone in to speak to us, I used to think, "How the heck am I gonna get up there and make a presentation?" I'd be all shy and choked up. It's amazing how things change in a short while.

After David graduated, he worked as a Band planner in our office, and then he got hired at Stoney to be Band manager. Gene was a Councillor while he was going to high school, and then he got back in on Council, and I got in as Chief. Then Gene started working at the Nation level, and I got in leadership, so the three of us were all involved whether at the community or Nation level, and I was able to talk to them – "Are we on the right track? Was that a good speech?" I was Chief for seventeen years, and David was in Council for fifteen years, so I was able to be gone a lot, and he would hold down the fort and make decisions at home. Before 2000, there was only the radio phone system, and I didn't even try to phone home when I was out at meetings, because I had to wait so long before getting through to somebody at the Band office. But just because of how we were raised, David's decisions were pretty close to what I thought. A blessing in disguise.

I think the way Gene, David, and I have lived is pretty close to the way the Elders lived. And the Elders before them lived pretty close to the way their Elders lived. But when you hit technology, it just shoots up, and you've got this whole other thinking. As technology came in, we were trying to hang onto our culture. Sure, you've got culture and language, but then you see a bigger picture. You've got a store with a few things on the wall compared to a big store with everything, and even if you stayed all day, you wouldn't be able to see or understand everything. When technology comes in, it opens up everything. You can travel around the world with this new technology, and you can learn from around the world, but you've also got some Tŝilhqot'in understanding and culture. Now you've got more to deal with out there as well as here. When Gene, David, and I were kids, what we saw in front of us and what was behind us were pretty close. But now my kids are growing and what they see in front of them is *huge*. So I guess the focus becomes broader. Although we're doing lots of cultural activities like gatherings, and that's much stronger than when I was a kid, technologies advance way more quickly than we do, and that opens up the world. When I was a kid, I would see a hockey book and a rodeo book, and I would dream about it, but now a kid can get on a computer and dream about many things. It's a lot different.

I call myself a lucky individual because I speak my language, I went to residential school long enough to get a taste for what was done and how it is to feel like that and to give me respect and energy to know what I later learned residential school was about. And then I've got people in my family, cousins and brothers, who are really significant to me and whom I rode horses with and got into cowboy. I rode bulls for fifteen years and mountainraced for thirty years – I'm still mountainracing today [2013]. I played hockey. I never wanted to be a Chief. I wanted to be a bull-riding star, and I wanted to be a hockey star! But I think that helped me because, when you're riding bulls, you're riding something that you've got no control over. You've got to ride with it. If you play hockey, and you try to do it by yourself, they're gonna lay you out, right, so you gotta pass the puck, and you gotta do teamwork.

When I woke up is when I had a child. You never really understand what your members who have children are going through – alcohol, drugs, teaching, culture – until you have your own child. Then you find out what you can teach and what you can't teach. I grew up really fast when I had a child, just like night and day. I had my first son, Colten, in 1989. Colten is twenty-four now, and I got in as Councillor when I was twenty-two and Chief when I was twenty-five. I remember my first election. I was thinking I'm gonna be like my brother Gene, but I got seven votes! Wow! So I went back to school and did a lotta work, and then I ran again when I was twenty-two, and I got in as a Councillor. And then I really started practising my language more – we never spoke it much because of residential school. I remember when I was growing up, as children with my cousins and older brothers, we always said, "Let's keep speaking Tŝilhqot'in, we can't lose it." So when we were playing, we were trying to speak Tŝilhqot'in. If we spoke English, we'd penalize ourselves. You had to do this or that penalty if you spoke English. When I got in leadership, I had to speak the language to communicate with the Elders and home-visit them. And the Chief and Council I was with talked about using the language more in the General Assembly, bringing all that back. So that was my first taste of what they call politics, but to me, it's like a war, like investing. It's our life. It has to be done.

The Drum

Elder Catherine Haller, Xeni Gwet'in

You see Roger's drum with the Native design on it? My friend made it. I put a word in, and I prayed. I got that drum made all the way from Fort St. John. My friend Henry John made it, and I paid him in trade. He's dead now.

Do you know why I picked the design that was painted on that drum? Guess. Tŝʼilʔos and ʔEniyud. We belong, we're human, we're traditional, we're ʔEsggidam.[3]

I was the one that kept shovin' the drum at Roger when I came back from healin'. And offering him the drum to get him started. He didn't know that. I never told 'em. He's gonna make his own choices. Gave 'em a drum. And Roger kept – I felt like he was playing. He kinda left it on the side when I offered him the drum. At that time, I felt like Roger didn't even know why I was givin' it to him. Later on I saw those kids playin' with that drum, picking it up in kinda the opposite way. I prayed really hard. The next thing, I heard he picked it up and put it away on those kids, and he was thinking. He said to himself, "I know why Catherine has given this to me. There's gonna be a challenge pretty soon. And to get me happy." All that time that I put a word in, prayed for him, to get that drum made all the way from Fort St. John.

Roger's drum, with an image of Tŝ'ilʔos. Drum bag by Elder Eileen Sammy William. Photo by Lorraine Weir

So this was all planned, and not very long after, Roger started wearing traditional moccasins. Once you get into moccasins, once you start singin' and pickin' up a song, you're a man that leads the community, and you have to find strong resources in yourself. When I offered that drum, I told Eileen, "Give him a branch and he'll –." She caught on to what I was saying and started makin' traditional clothes for him. This was in 1996, I think it was.

It was time for him 'cause he was so happy offerin' himself doing the traditional, but he wasn't gettin' that far, so I thought this will lead the way for you. This will be your heart and protect you. But you need traditional clothes, I was tellin' him, in order to be ʔEsggidam, people generations before us, and be a leader. I spoke to him in my highest Tŝilhqot'in. At that time his English was a bit tough in the English-speaking way, but I told him you have to learn both, the Tŝilhqot'in way and the English way. I started talkin' to him in Tŝilhqot'in all the time, from nine o'clock till three for almost ten years, and he started speaking the way he speaks now. He got fluent. He was speakin' English all the time when he was first Chief. I used to tell him that you only have to trust me, just be traditional. Dress in the traditional way, and sing like ʔEsggidam. Make yourself like you're one of the people that belong here. If you trust them in the choices you make, if it's just like how you wanna be, they'll come to you.

That's why he's dressed that way, and that's what I saw in him. When people were votin' Chiefs in, I looked around the four corners of the room where everybody was sittin'. The first year, when Roger was gettin' nominated, he was pretty young. And then I started quittin', on and off, so I didn't attend community meetings. When I sobered up, I started looking at the leaders who mistreat you every time you ask for support. And I thought if I get there, I want to go to the leader, and I pray to the Lord that I'm gonna really stand up to them now and fight back the way the Chiefs fight back. This is what I'm gonna do. So I did! And those people that mistreated me, they're not here now. I was the Councillor who nominated him, and I thought there's time for him to grow as a leader. I was watchin' him for many years, and I thought if I get on my feet, I'll see where he's at, and he was at the highest level. His manner is respectful. He trusts us when you ask. He doesn't try to push you away. He tries to earn your support – even meet your needs. He's all traditional men the way they are now. He's got ʔEsggidam under there. Tŝ'ilʔos. At the time when he got in as Chief, he wasn't seekin' anything.

My grandfather was Freddie Johnny. He used to dress in traditional clothing, and he spoke Tŝilhqot'in a lot. I was lookin' at my grandpa when I was about seven years old, and he sang a drumsong and said I'm Nits'ilʔin. It means I'm a Chief. Nits'ilʔin stands for cradle. Nits'ilʔin could be standin' in front of a church, you know, preaching to people. Nits'ilʔin could be everywhere where it protects you if you ask for it. Nits'ilʔin could be anything in your Sweat Lodge – that's our church, long time ago, that Sweat Lodge. It could appear in there. And all the questions I was askin', that's what he told me. He said we have to have traditional clothes, and my grandma dressed my grandpa in the way Roger dresses [in buckskin], except Roger has mukluks. My grandpa was in the position for a long time. Dressing traditionally, I think Roger's honouring all the earth, the water, his own country, and the work he's doin'. And the valuable work his mom put in. It's really hard to make those clothes. How long does it take her? Sometimes she stays up all night. That's how I understand from my grampa being a Chief a long time, a very long time.

Chief Roger with Cecil Grinder (Tl'etinqox), Supreme Court of Canada, November 7, 2013. Photo by Jeremy Williams

War

Chief Roger William

I remember during my upbringing that alcohol affected our leadership at that time, not only in Xeni but in different communities. We didn't see them, and we didn't know what they were doing. Alcohol was taking control of them, and they'd be gone for weeks on end, for a month, and we didn't know what was going on. They'd go to meetings and not come back for a long time, and then you heard stories, the moccasin telegraph from all over the Tŝilhqot'in, about what was going on. We were like, "That's not right. We can't do that." I remember talking with my older cousins like Gilbert Solomon, Simon Setah, and a whole bunch of people about how we needed to change that, our leadership couldn't be doing that. It wasn't good for our kids or our Land. I remember everybody our age talking about the loss that we were feeling.

They say politics is my motivation, but for me it's investment in our community, in our Nation. That's the motivation that I grew up with, learning from my mom as a single parent, and from my older brother Gene and late Harry Setah and David Setah. I used to watch Gene in meetings, in General Assemblies, talking. And I used to think about who we are and about my whole upbringing. I guess, for me, in leadership, speaking Tŝilhqot'in became important, protecting Land became important. And coming from our people was very important to me. Every day that I breathe, that I talk, our resources are leaving our community, our Nation. Our language is leaving, our culture is leaving, and the Elders who taught me all this are going. Maybe it depends on your definition of politics, but I didn't see it that way. I saw it as war. War to protect our Lands and resources, our Aboriginal Rights and Title, our children, our Elders, our way of life, Xeni – Nemiah, the lakes, the smell. I remember when I was a child, I knew when I was getting to a certain place by how it smelt, how it felt.

CHAPTER 5 ENDNOTES

1   For more on this theme, see John Thistle, *Resettling the Range: Animals, Ecologies, and Human Communities in British Columbia*, Nature | History | Society series (Vancouver: UBC Press, 2015). On connections between rodeo and politics in Indigenous contexts, see Mary-Ellen Kelm, *A Wilder West: Rodeo in Western Canada* (Vancouver: UBC Press, 2011), chap. 6. On horse culture in Xeni, see Jonaki Bhattacharyya, "Knowing Naŝliny (Horse), Understanding the Land: Free-Roaming Horse in the Culture and Ecology of the Brittany Triangle and Nemiah Valley" (Ph.D. diss., University of Waterloo, 2012), chaps. 5 and 6, hdl.handle.net/10012/6521.

2   Goliath is Canadian and settler law for some Xeni Gwet'ins, but for others Goliath means the other five Tŝilhqot'in communities (Tl'esqox, Tŝideldel, Yuneŝit'in, ʔEsdilagh, and Tl'etinqox). Whatever the source of opposition or lack of support, Xeni is always imagined in the position of David, and that has proved true to its history throughout these battles.

3   ʔEsggidam (sometimes pronounced "ʔEswydam" or "ʔEswydan") are the Ancestors, the people from long ago. See chapter 12 for the sadanx gwenig traditional story Tŝ'ilʔos and ʔEniyud.

Logging Coming Closer:

From the Declaration to the Brittany Lake Forest Management Plan (1989–1998)

Clearcuts and the Declaration

Chief Roger William

When I was growing up, we used teamhorses for haying. A whole bunch of us, family and relatives, would be out there cutting, raking, and hauling hay. There'd be three, four, five of us working, but when you get a tractor and mower, pretty soon there was only one person out there, and the rest of the family'd be doing something else. It seemed like logging turned out to be like that, only one person compared to a whole bunch of people out there. Our people in Xeni had been comfortable hunting, fishing, doing ceremonies and prayers, and ranching was pretty close to that life, but when logging came in, a lot changed. When I was young, my mom first saw welfare, and then the economy changed and machines started taking over human labour. Our members saw the timber going out and the clearcuts growing. Then they started hearing their relatives in the Tŝilhqot'in saying, "I can't even recognize these places. The berries are gone, the medicines are gone," but someone else would say, "No, I've got a nice truck, good TV, nice house." This happened in the '90s and while the Tŝilhqot'in Nation and the communities were starting to think about timber leaving our Territory, people in the cities and towns were saying, "First Nations people aren't working, they're lazy." Meanwhile, leaders were thinking about job creation, doing the harvesting ourselves, because we know the Land better and will protect more of our traditional uses as well as our archeological and heritage sites.

If you could see snapshots of Xeni before European contact and today, it would look pretty much the same. There's no logging. There's no mining. A lot of timber is the way it was. But if you start going out into the Tŝilhqot'in, then you start seeing the changes. There's a lot of clearcuts. In our area as well as others, there were mining explorations. And flood in 1980, that's when the threat of flood was still real. BC Hydro was planning to connect three lakes – Taseko, Chilko, and Tatlayoko (a fifty-mile-long lake, a twenty-five-mile-long lake, and a twenty-mile-long lake) – to create a big dam to produce hydroelectric power. All the mining exploration, all the mining roads, commercial road building – you know, our people were like, wow. The Elders were pretty clear about logging, and they didn't agree with mining. We wanted to handle our permits. All that was fresh in people's minds, and first and foremost was we don't want those things happening, and we wanna protect and control. That kinda language came from our Elders and our people. And we were like yeah, that's what we want to do.

Annie C. Williams was Chief at that time, our first woman Chief in Nemiah. She's my second cousin. Her mom, Juliana Lulua, is the daughter of my uncle the late Eugene Sammy William. When Annie got in as Chief and I got in as Councillor, we replaced Benny William, who stepped down as Chief, and Sonny Lulua, who stepped down from Council. We finished that one-year term with former Chief Adam William, who was also a Councillor then. I remember travelling to many meetings, listening to the Elders, and watching the harvesting of timber coming closer. Our initial concern was to look at specific claims with reference to loss of reserve lands, because at that time Nemiah Valley was part of the [BC] Hydro reserve. That was in my mind getting into leadership, and not only mine but all the other Xeni Gwet'ins in leadership. We were concerned about the Hydro dam and also about heli-skiing – choppers bringing skiers to the mountains. I remember all that stuff happening during that time, and the logging coming closer to Nemiah, and our members telling other Tŝilhqot'ins, "Now we can't even recognize some of the places where we used to camp and live. It's all clearcut. I don't even know where it is."

We were first interested in a Declaration in 1983, the Chilcotin Declaration: "We are the Chilcotin and we declare to all men and women that we are an independent Nation, proud and free." Remember that?[1] Annie's predecessor, Benny William, had met Jack Woodward at meetings and talked with him. Jack knew Cindy English, who was training Xeni Gwet'ins to do cultural research at that time.[2] Cindy started the Friends of Nemaiah Valley. We also connected with Paul George of the Western Canada Wilderness Committee who knew about what we were trying to do in Nemiah and what was threatening to come into the valley.

Lha yudit'ih We Always Find a Way

Chief Annie C. Williams

Lorraine Weir

In his book *Reserve Memories: The Power of the Past in a Chilcotin Community* (2002), anthropologist David W. Dinwoodie highlights the contribution of Annie C. Williams to the Tŝilhqot'in Declaration of Sovereignty. He remembers that, while she was away at business college, she "became familiar with the place of public lands in the economy of British Columbia. She became convinced that aboriginal citizens could effectively intervene in the industrial exploitation of public lands." She ran for Chief on her return home and became the first woman Chief of the Nemiah Indian Band (as Xeni Gwet'in First Nation was then known). Dinwoodie was a graduate student learning the Tŝilhqot'in language and living in Xeni at that time, and his discussion of the Chief's strategy reflects his sense of the politics of that period:

> The Band's case was difficult to make at the local level because the issue polarized the local population along ethnic lines. Indians formed a minority and most non-Indians favored logging. Williams realized that the issue took a different shape at the provincial level where environmentalists and social activists help [to] even the numbers ... Gaining support from non-Indians became a real possibility with the change in the arena of contest.[3]

When Chief Williams "enlisted the assistance of Cindy English, then a graduate student in anthropology at the University of Victoria[,] English began working with community members to consider how the memories of elders might be documented. She also contacted a prominent Victoria specialist in Indian law [Jack Woodward]."

First Meeting

George Colgate[4]

When the Title case started, Annie C. Williams was Chief. Cindy English, I believe, was the contact to Jack Woodward, so I think Cindy was instrumental in getting this whole thing going. It started off with the Trapline [case]. I can remember Jack coming here [Xeni]. What he was trying to do was get something that would win, but you can't bite off too much: then you're not gonna win. So I think that's why he went for the Trapline, and I think Annie was on board with that. Then something happened. *Carrier Lumber* came in, but *Delgamuukw* also expanded it. I think that may have given Jack – say, let's go for a little bit more than just the Trapline.[5]

I remember the first meeting. We went down and met in Jack Woodward's office in Fan Tan Alley [in Victoria]. They were figuring out how do we proceed with this. There was Roger, myself, Annie. Cindy was there. I remember going up that elevator, and then someone had to go down and put more money in the parking meter, so I went down with Annie's son Erik, who was just a little guy. So we went down and put money in the parking meter, got back in the elevator, and the elevator stopped at one floor, and it was the wrong floor. The elevator opened on this side sometimes and then on the other side. Erik got out, the door slammed, and off we went! I'm goin', I just lost Annie's son! Now how am I gonna find Erik? What was I gonna tell Annie?! [laughter] But we found him.

I remember the first time Jack was out here talking to people, and I remember him getting up and saying, "You know, every time a white person comes to this valley, they take something away from you, and I am now gonna be the first white man to tell you that I can get some of your land back." Okay. And for me, in the back, I'm goin', Well, I don't think I've taken anything away. So I was a little bit dubious about Jack for quite a while. And he was sorta making statements and deals of all sorts, but it turned out that he was good. Jack was always very pumped about this sort of thing. This was, I think, what he saw as his legacy, and it turned out it was.

Friends of Nemiah Valley

Cindy English[6]

That first meeting was really the beginning of the long road toward a Title case. It established who was going to do what and who was going to help pay for it. It also initiated the discussion about the need for Friends of Nemiah Valley to be formed. The original Friends of Nemiah Valley was really a vehicle for a coalition of individuals and organizations to assist Nemiah [Valley Indian Band, subsequently the Xeni Gwet'in First Nation] in their efforts to protect their Land from clearcut logging and to protect their culture and way of life. This organization had people from Sierra Club, who paid for a researcher, Linda Robertson, to do forestry research to keep an eye on what was happening in terms of the licences and the policy that was leading to logging coming into Xeni Gwet'in Territory.

It also had wildlife biologists, non-Indigenous landholders who had an interest in the area, and interested parties such as the Aboriginal Rights Coalition, who wanted to help. It was used as a research, education, liaising, and fundraising vehicle for the original Trapline case.

When Nemiah and Jack first met to discuss how to structure a case to protect their Territory from logging, Jack laid out who could probably do what jobs. WC2 [Western Canada Wilderness Committee] would pay legal expenses, and Sierra Club would provide a student to help do the forestry research that an expert witness on forestry would need, and I would be the coordinator of the case, so I would do all the liaising with Nemiah, research, fundraising, and whatever else needed to be done. I shared the job with Barb Souther, since both of us had young kids at that time. She coordinated the forestry and wildlife side of Nemiah's effort, and I coordinated the anthropological, historical, and liaising side of the effort, which was to stop clearcut logging in their trapline. We had our expenses paid by WC2 but never a salary, which was difficult in those days.

Friends of Nemiah Valley closed down after many years, and a new, slightly renamed Friends of the Nemaiah Valley started several years later, when the legal climate had developed enough for Xeni to proceed with more legal action, as the case law had developed to the point where they had more legal precedents to help them. Friends of the Nemaiah Valley did a great job in the ensuing years. It's a hard road and they had a good board of people who did all kinds of research and fundraising to protect the region.

Making a Statement

Chief Roger William

Declarations are not our way, but I think it was Jack Woodward, Cindy English, and Paul George who said, "You guys gotta make a statement," because they'd seen our fight and our challenges. Jack said let's work on a declaration. We all sat around a table and talked about seeing clearcuts coming and logging coming on Nemiah Road and wanting to protect this beautiful area. So, six years after the first Declaration, our strategy was to create another declaration, and it needed to come from the people. Whoever ran for Chief and Council had to abide by the declaration, and it would create continuity.

When we got support for the Declaration from the Western Canada Wilderness Committee, the David Suzuki Foundation, and Friends of Nemiah Valley, I heard stories at meetings with other First Nations about environmentalists taking over and First Nations going to the back, while their Land got protected and their interests got lost. So when we met environmentalists, we said right from the start that we wanted their support, but we were in control, and if they didn't agree with that, then we didn't want to work with them. We were always very clear about our Aboriginal Rights and Title, and they agreed to support us and not dictate how things should be done. We were gaining experience with communication and consultation.

The Declaration Nenduwh jid guẑit'in was made by the people, by the Elders. We hired people to go to the Elders' homes and interview them about what was going on in our caretaker area. Illa Setah was one of the people who did this work. She's David Setah's older sister and my late auntie Madeline Setah's daughter. She took notes, which helped us come up with the wording. Diane Lulua was also involved in this, as well as Inez Setah and Gilbert Solomon – they dealt with archeology before this, so I think they were probably all involved one way or another. Patrick Lulua's another one. Patrick Lulua and Gilbert Solomon worked on the wording in both Tŝilhqot'in and English in consultation with the Elders who were interviewed about their wishes. Cindy was the main proposal writer, getting the money, and Patrick interviewed and helped out. Chief and Council and the lawyers, Western Canada Wilderness Committee, Friends of Nemiah Valley, and the different staff members who were working on it: we came up with the wording of the August 23, 1989, Nemiah Declaration. The Western Canada Wilderness Committee paid for the graphic designer and covered costs for making copies. Our people wanted control, and that was what they told the interviewers when they went around. They didn't want logging, mining, or damming and flooding for BC Hydro, but people could come in and take pictures, and we'd give permits to use the Land, as long as people respected it.

The Declaration said, in short, nothing's gonna happen here without our involvement. The English wording is not that much different from the Tŝilhqot'in. You can't go word for word in Tŝilhqot'in and English. You need to understand Tŝilhqot'in, understand English, and then explain it from one language to the other. If somebody's speaking Tŝilhqot'in, I'm not gonna say word for word in English. I'm gonna understand what's been said to me, and I'll say it in English. I'm not gonna worry about word for word because it's impossible.

In our language, it's not that complicated. In Tŝilhqot'in we've got words I don't even know, words I haven't heard very often unless somebody uses them, and I'm like, "Oh yeah, I remember that word now!" but if I spoke to you in Tŝilhqot'in, I probably wouldn't have come up with that word. Some Elder says that word and I say "Oh yeah, I heard that word somewhere before." But it's fairly simple because, if you look at our alphabet, it shows how to pronounce words, where in English, you've got some letter that's in there that you don't even hear. It's a *silent* letter! It could mean this, but it could mean something entirely different in another word that's exactly the same except for that letter. Our language is pretty specific, it doesn't change – not like English. In Tŝilhqot'in, a word might mean a few things, but if you add another word, you figure out what it means right away. In English, it could take three or four sentences before you know what that word is actually saying.[7]

As time went on, the Declaration became more and more important. Xeni Gwet'ins wanted to be able to recognize their home and not see the whole landscape change.

The Wilderness Committee and the Declaration

Lorraine Weir

When I asked Joe Foy, executive director of WCWC at that time, why the Wilderness Committee had gotten involved in the Declaration, he replied that as an organization they "liked declarations" and had encouraged other environmental protection groups to adopt that strategy. "A declaration defines an issue and a strategy," he said, "and that's a good way to get others involved." Paul George was president of WCWC when Jack Woodward visited him in the summer of 1989 seeking financial support for research "into the Aboriginal Rights to trap and how those rights relate to wilderness preservation." In his book *Big Trees Not Big Stumps*,[8] George says it was a "hard sell" for some of WCWC's directors, and the solution was for them to support Xeni Gwet'in in the same way as they had supported Meares Island and the Stein Valley: a Tribal Park Declaration. They agreed to financial support of $17,000 to be paid in instalments. George attended a meeting in Xeni and "told them bluntly about needing a tribal park declaration document in order to satisfy WCWC members' doubts as to the Nemiah peoples' true intentions regarding the use of their traditional lands. The declaration had to have a map of their traditional territory with the portion to be included in the tribal park and the rules of the land use within that park. Without this we could not provide any financial support. I gave out samples of the Meares and Stein declarations. I left the meeting with the understanding that they would think about it, and get back to us."[9]

Woodward brought George the results about a week later: "the text, a hand-drawn map, and a design sketch of how they wanted their finished document to look." The Declaration was to be in Tŝilhqot'in on one side of the page and

English on the other. George remembers Woodward explaining that "[t]here might not be an exact one-to-one correspondence in meaning between the two versions" because "some of the Xeni Gwet'in concepts did not easily translate into English." As both Benny William and Annie C. Williams remembered, the Tŝilhqot'in version was drafted first, although on the Declaration it's dated "1 December 1989" and the English "23 August 1989."[10]

Chief and Council had rejected the idea of a tribal park and wanted the title "Nemiah Aboriginal Wilderness Preserve."[11] Cindy English visited the Museum of Anthropology at UBC for inspiration after the original sketch was made by Nelson Williams (Xeni Gwet'in), based on the Elders' ideas. Graphic designer Dave McGregor did the layout for print, basing it on the sketch.

Nenduwh jid guẑit'in The Declaration

"Let it be known that:

Within the Nemiah Aboriginal Wilderness Preserve:

- There shall be no commercial logging. Only local cutting of trees for our own needs, i.e., firewood, housing, fencing, native uses, etc.
- There shall be no mining or mining explorations.
- There shall be no commercial road building.
- All terrain vehicles and skidoos shall only be permitted for trapping purposes.
- There shall be no flooding or dam construction on Chilko, Taseko, and Tatlayoko Lakes.
- This is the spiritual and economic homeland of our people. We will continue in perpetuity:

    o To have and exercise our traditional rights of hunting, fishing, trapping, gathering, and natural resources;

    o To carry on our traditional ranching way of life;

    o To practise our traditional native medicine, religion, sacred, and spiritual ways.

- That we are prepared to SHARE our Nemiah Aboriginal Wilderness Preserve with non-natives in the following ways:

    o With our permission visitors may come and view and photograph our beautiful land;

    o We will issue permits, subject to our conservation rules, for hunting and fishing within our Preserve;

    o The respectful use of our Preserve by canoeists, hikers, light campers, and other visitors is encouraged subject to our system of permits.

- We are prepared to enforce and defend our Aboriginal Rights in any way we are able."[12]

Translating the Declaration

Lorraine Weir

In order to reflect on the significance of some of the differences between English and Tŝilhqot'in versions of the Declaration, David Dinwoodie undertook a literal translation of the Tŝilhqot'in.[13] It's clear from his translation that the intention of the original framers of the Declaration was not to provide a precise equivalence between the two languages but to address each community of readers and speakers somewhat differently, while conveying the same list of prohibitions and permissions.

The Declaration laid down the law for those who would trespass the borders of Xeni, clearcut the trees, destroy the Land by mining, build unauthorized roads, dam and flood the Land, damage habitat and destroy the Land with Ski-Doos, and use ATVs for fun rather than for trapping. It also clarified the terms of "sharing" with visitors who are "non-natives." After the Supreme Court of Canada victory, the Declaration was proclaimed as the First Law of Title Land, in effect marking the point when Dechen ts'edilhtan Tŝilhqot'in law supersedes settler law, although the Declaration had been enforced from the time of its proclamation in 1989. It is the Tŝilhqot'in language portion of the document that most clearly attaches the document to cultural knowledge and practice of the Nen the Land.

On the next page is the Declaration in Tŝilhqot'in with David Dinwoodie's close translation. Sentences that are not found in the Declaration's English translation, only in the Tŝilhqot'in original, are *italicized*.

Nenduwh jid Guẑit'in. Xeni Gwet'in First Nation. Courtesy Chief Roger William.
See page G of the colour insert for a larger colour version of the Declaration.

Nenduwh Jid Guẑit'in
Thus we want it.

Nenduwh k'an dzi Gwelu za, ʔinlhi 1989.
Here this day of December [ice only] 1, 1989.

Nenduwh gadidinh:
We proclaim this:

Xun tsilhqox gwet'in, Xeni deni nidlin,
we Chilcotin people, being people of Nemiah Valley,

nenduwh jid guẑit'in
thus we want it.

Yedanx xwedeni nen jeʔanajest'in
The land where our people moved about long ago

jedaltsi taʔagunt'ih ʔeyed
where they lived well

gwenenazijez ʔeyed
where we lived

nenduwh gadidinh jid guzidzin:
this is how we want it addressed:

Xeni Gwet'in Xa Gwenanisjez
Nemiah Valley [Xeni Gwet'in] People's Territory.

Nenduwh Gadidinh,
Thus we proclaim,

Xeni Gwet'in Xagwenanisjez ʔeyed:
in regard to Nemiah Valley [Xeni Gwet'in] People's Territory:

1. **Lha xedecen bid seniya ʔanats'edulyi gut'in.**
   There will be no making money with the use of our timber.

2. **Lha tsi ts'edulhduz cuh gat'in.**
   There will be no drilling in the mountains [rock].

3. **Lha ʔeten nats'egutsi gut'in.**
   There will be no road making.

4. **Yes qi nazus gadant'i ʔeqats'etat'ilh dza beʔanats'etat'in.**
   Motorized snowshoes [snowmobiles] and off-road vehicles can only be used for hunting.

5. **Tsilhqox bin, Dasiqox, hink'an Telhiqox ʔeyed lha ts'egulhbanx hink'an nats'uʔilh, gut'in.**
   At Chilko Lake, Taseko River, and Tatlayoko Lake no damming or flooding there will be.

6. *Yedanx dzah nenduwh gat'in deni nidlin nenk'ed ʔeguh gataghat'ilh.*
   As it was done here long ago, that is how people will continue to live now.

7. **Midugh xwenenjiyetayalh nenk'ed seʔagunti'ih, gan xun gwebaʔan-adetaghadilh.**
   It is alright for non–First Nations [Midugh] to use our land only if we grant them permission.

8. *Xun xeni gwet'in xwenen gweqaʔadidih xuh, lha ʔilhax xwets'ah tasalh xuh.*
   We people of Nemiah Valley [Xeni Gwet'in], we will fight for our land, no one will be able to take it.[14]

The emphasis on place and time is very obvious in the *italicized* sentences and phrases that don't appear in the document's official English translation: "*The land where our people moved about long ago / where they lived well / where we lived.*" Here the ʔEsggidam Ancestors are connected to contemporary Xeni Gwet'ins, the "land long ago" to the Land now, and "living well long ago" to the implied future of living well as a result of the enactment of the prohibitions and permissions that follow in the document. Yedanx long ago reaches back toward the long-ago time when Ancestors did as people will do now if necessary: "we will fight for our Land, no one will be able to take it." Mining and forestry and hydroelectric power are the fierce beasts of the modern world, requiring new forms of fighting, but the same courage and determination as in yedanx past. "As it was done here long ago, that is how people will continue to live now" is a principle of Nen stewardship that comes with a clear set of updated rules – things that will not be done. People will continue to live here as they did long ago if these prohibitions (as well as permissions) are followed.

By using the traditional language of time, place, and Land, the Elders and their document-writing helpers expressed a vision deeply rooted in Dechen ts'edilhtan Tŝilhqot'in law. However, the idea that "some Xeni Gwet'in concepts ... don't translate easily into English"[15] seems less accurate now than it did in 1989, thanks to the testimony of Elders at trial and to ongoing work on Dechen ts'edilh-tan in the Tŝilhqot'in (though translation itself is seldom easy). In any event, one of the writers' strategies was to avoid trying to convey traditional concepts by omitting these sentences from their version of the Declaration. Instead, they state that "This is the spiritual and economic homeland of our people," thereby grounding prohibitions in economics as well as spirituality and omitting considerations of "As it was done here long ago, that is how people will continue to live now." When the concluding statement of fighting and winning is transformed into a statement of enforcing and defending and of Aboriginal Rights, settler law is explicitly invoked. However, the original text of the Declaration also reads as a map of much of what was to come in terms of the challenge of conveying fundamentals of Dechen ts'edilhtan Tŝilhqot'in law to settler courts. By the time the Declaration was proclaimed as the First Law of Title Land on March 19, 2015, it was no longer necessary to bridge the gap between languages, and so separate documents were prepared, one in Tŝilhqot'in, "Xeni ʔeguh jid Nits'egugheniʔan," and one in English, "Affirmation of the Nemiah Declaration."[16]

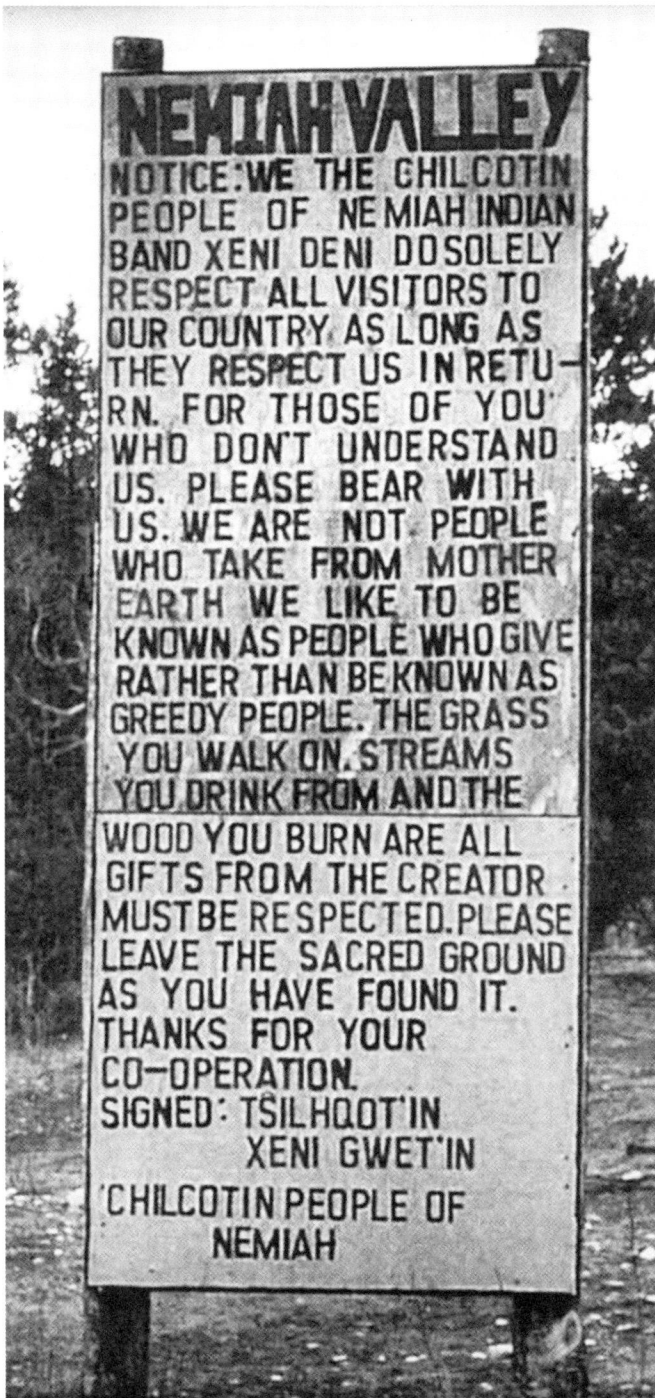

Boundary sign from the same period. Wording by Patrick Lulua. Archival image, courtesy of Chief Roger William

The Thirtieth Anniversary of the Declaration (August 23, 2019)

Lorraine Weir

During the annual Brittany Gathering at Henry's Crossing, the thirtieth anniversary of the Declaration was celebrated with speeches and drumsongs. Gilbert Solomon made a speech which became the prayer opening this book, and Roger shared his memories in relation to the victory in the Title case. As Chief, Annie C. Williams had played a key role in the Declaration. In her speech, she reflected on the origins of the Declaration and of the Title case in her community and stressed the important role played by Xeni Gwet'in Elders:

> Our Elders took what they wanted people from the outside to see so they would know what we have and how we're gonna go about protecting it. They wanted to know that this place and this, our land, was going to be protected, and not just for us but for our generations to come. When our Elders sat down with us, they said we don't have anything written down for anyone to go by, for them to see what it is that we're trying to protect and why we're trying to protect it. So we came up with what we called "Nenduwh jid guẑit'in," and that is just "This is the way we want it." And that's the Declaration. In Tŝilhqot'in, it says more than in English. They said we need to write down, and we need to know that we can protect [against] any kind of encroachment of resource extractions. They wanted to protect the rivers, the fish, our animals that we have here and our way of life, not just for us to enjoy, but to make people aware that this is why we're protecting it for everybody.[17]

Clearcut Out

Chief Roger William

The [mountain pine] beetle kill was used by Forestry as a rationale for clearcutting, and the Elders were concerned that, as one put it, they were "gonna be clearcut out … We said we don't mind them cutting one or two trees in the bush, that's okay. That's how we do it if we want wood or house logs. We don't cut down the whole forest to make a house." Forestry went so far as to visit Xeni, bringing Chief Ervin Charleyboy with them, as well as some members of the Chilcotin Tribal Council, in order to try to persuade Xeni Gwet'ins to log, but they were not to be persuaded. Just as in the 1970s, when Chief Marvin Baptiste xinli had tried to stop logging by mobilizing all of the Bands in the area in support of his cause, the other communities were all involved in logging as a way of creating jobs for their people, so there was very limited support for logging then, and the same in 1989. Together with Councillors William Setah and William Lulua, Chief Baptiste had successfully gotten all of the trappers together and amalgamated each of their individual traplines into one Xeni Gwet'in Trapline, and thus into one boundary, which Chief Annie C. Williams deployed in the Trapline case in order to keep logging activities out of Xeni. When the Trapline case was amalgamated into the Title case,[18] the trapline boundary became one of the boundaries of what would become Title Land.

Water Powers

Lorraine Weir

In the 1970s, Chief Marvin Baptiste xinli dealt with the threat of a hydroelectric power dam that would have flooded Tŝilhqox Biny, Dasiqox Biny, and Xeni Biny. Euphemistically referred to as the "Chilko-Coast Diversion," the threat went back to 1938, and the report which outlined it, titled *Water Powers: Fraser River*, is a good example of the fusion of racism, capitalism, and big industry that was seen as the proud foundation of settler British Columbia and still turns up today, slightly altered, in the advertising of many resource-extraction companies. Premier T.D. "Duff" Pattullo wrote in his foreword to the report that:

> Power, mechanically produced and widely applied, is the basis of our present civilization and culture.

> Primitive man [*sic*], who depended on his own physical effort to supply his needs, was never able to accumulate a surplus, and never had the leisure to give effective thought to his future well-being.

Slavery and the domestication of animals relieved a favoured few from incessant soul-destroying toil. But until man learned to use a power which did not compete with him for food, which could be developed in large units and effectively controlled, he was never able to make real progress toward comfort and security.

A great inexhaustible source of such power is the energy in our falling streams.[19]

The "falling stream" which the province had its eye on was the largest natural high-elevation lake in North America, Tŝilhqox Biny Chilko Lake, and they proposed various strategies to create the "Chilko-Coast Diversion," including one called the "Taseko River (Diversion N)" that "would require the waters of the Taseko River to be added to the waters of Chilko Lake, a tunnel built to Elkins Creek, and low dams built to a point from which the water can flow by gravity through Konni Lake and Nemaia Valley to Chilko Lake."[20] This "real progress," as Pattullo called it, would have inundated the Nemiah Valley and subsumed Tŝilhqox Biny, Xeni Biny, and Dasiqox into one vast "surplus" at the expense of Xeni Gwet'in people, Land, waters, animals, fish, and plants, all in the name of "civilization and culture."[21]

Although Chief Marvin Baptiste xinli had successfully opposed this project in the 1970s, it was still in the background, "rumbling around" as one person put it, at the time of the Declaration in 1989. It had remained a threat for forty years while similar plans were violently enacted on the Lands of other Indigenous Nations in the province. To take one example:

In 1952, the Cheslatta [Dakelh] Nation peoples were evicted from their homes on two weeks' notice and forcibly resettled outside their traditional lands. Their lands, villages, cultural and spiritual sites were then flooded as the newly built Kenney Dam filled what is now known as the Nechako Reservoir.[22]

Sixty-five years later, the BC government finally entered into an agreement to provide restitution and redress to the People for impacts suffered.

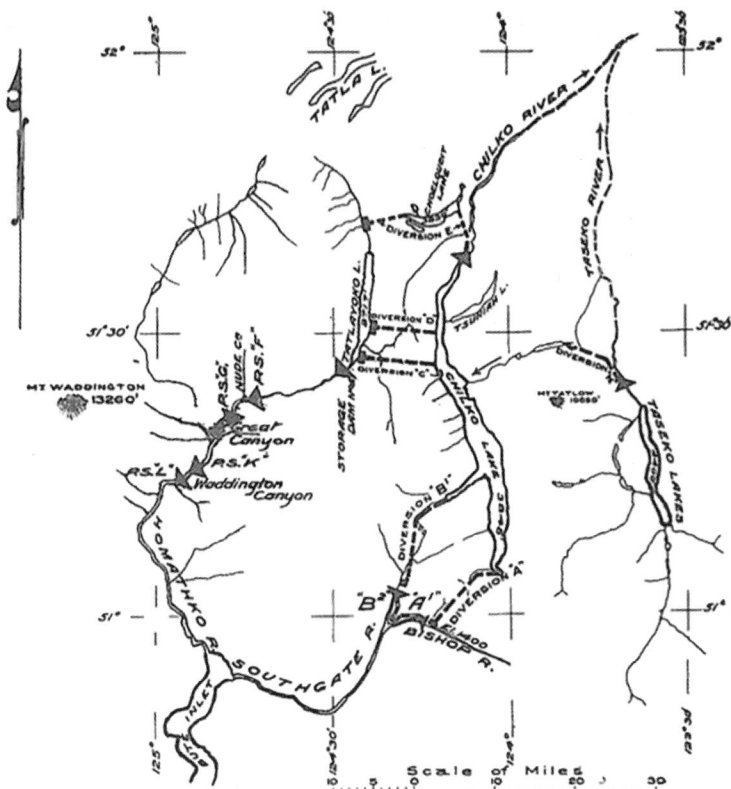

Plan of Chilko-Coast diversions.

From *Water Powers: Fraser River* (BC Department of Lands, 1938)

Meeting Ovide Mercredi (1991)

Cindy English

Annie C. Williams was Chief and she came down to Victoria. We went on a campaign to meet with allies to raise the $15,000 necessary. We met with several organizations and came up empty-handed, but then we went to a meeting of the First Nations Summit where Ovide Mercredi, the newly elected National Chief of the AFN (Assembly of First Nations), was making an appearance. I had been researching Ovide Mercredi since he'd become National Chief, and I knew he was from a trapping background. I felt that if anyone would know what Nemiah was facing it would be him. We set up a table outside the meeting and started up a slide show that drew attention to our cause. We talked to whomever would listen. I saw Ovide Mercredi there, and I went up to him and told him what was going on, and he held up his hand. He said, "Hold that thought! I have to go speak, and I'll be right back." [laughs] And so he came back and listened to Annie and me about what was going on and said he would help.

He was travelling for months after that, and I kept phoning his office to make good on his promise. They said they didn't know anything about it because he was travelling, and there were no cellphones in those days, but they also said if he said he would help, he will, so I kept trying. One day I got a phone call from his office saying that Chief Ovide was going to be at the First Ministers' Conference being held that week at Whistler. Could the Chief come to meet with him? Roger was then the newly elected Chief. Roger and Gene Cooper drove on the Duffy Lake Road all night long to get down to Whistler. I wanted to be there to see it happen because I facilitated it, and of course Jack [Woodward] wanted to be there, so Jack and I went together, and we were there for the meeting with Roger and Ovide, and they solidified the deal to get their money. Later they hired lawyer Joe Arvay.

Backing Up the Declaration

Chief Roger William

It's good to have a Declaration, but you've gotta back it up. That's the tricky part. How do you do that, and how do you move forward? Back in 1989, there was harvesting in the northern part of our trapline, and we took action. In 1990 Cindy English connected us with AFN National Chief Ovide Mercredi,[23] who was a former trapper. He was in Whistler at a meeting, and Cindy thought we should meet him. Gene [Cooper] and I went down to Whistler and had a very short meeting with Ovide Mercredi. We sat down, ate, did an update, and he said, "Yup, I'll fund this." So he hired lawyer Joe Arvay, and we took Carrier Lumber to court.

On December 11, 1991, Carrier Lumber had an out-of-court settlement with us to stay out of our Xeni Gwet'in Trapline for five years. Tachelach'ed the Brittany Triangle is outside our Trapline but inside the Xeni Gwet'in Caretaker area, and Carrier Lumber wanted to harvest beetle timber there.[24] They kept coming in without involving us, even though we said no over and over again. We met with them and said that before taking the next step, we needed to meet with our Elders and our people. There's a lot of timber in Tachelach'ed and also wild horses, moose, and deer. We have families that live there, in places like Nusay Bighinlin Far Meadow, Niba? elhenenenalqelh Captain Georgetown,

Natasewed Brittany Lakes, and Tsalgen Chaunigan. For a *long* time, the only way you could get in there if you wanted to harvest moose, deer, or do any commercial activities was by a trail, on the river, on horseback, or on foot. We told them we were willing to come to an agreement or we would take legal action, and we showed them the Declaration and asked them to work with us. When they decided to go ahead with or without us and log in Xeni, our people said that we had to back up the Declaration. The company had challenged us, so we had no choice. We tried to communicate and consult with them, but they said, regardless of our Declaration, that they were going to log.[25]

From *Tsilhqot'in Nation v. British Columbia*, 2007 BCSC 1700

[22] It was the season for tislagh (steelhead salmon). According to their oral history and traditions, Tsilhqot'in people have gathered at this time of year in the custom of the ʔEsggidam (ancestors) since the time of sadanx (legendary period of time long ago). Tislagh returned to the Tsilhqox (Chilko River) and, as they had for generations, Tsilhqot'in people returned to the river crossing at Biny Gwetsel and to Tsi T'is Gunlin, just south of Henry's Crossing, to gaff tislagh. They left Xeni (Nemiah Valley) and other parts of Tsilhqot'in territory and travelled the ancient trails set by the ʔEsggidam, passing Tsuniah Biny (Tsuniah Lake), onto the crossing of the Tsilhqox at Biny Gwetsel, making their way further down river past Tsi T'is Gunlin and onto Henry's Crossing.

[23] In May of 1992, during the season for tislagh, approximately 100 Tsilhqot'in people returned, not to gaff tislagh at Tsi T'is Gunlin and Biny Gwetsel but to establish a blockade at Henry's Crossing. Their purpose was clear. There would be no improvements to the bridge at this important crossing over the Tsilhqox that would allow clear cut logging to occur in Tachelach'ed (Brittany Triangle).

[24] Xeni Gwet'in people (people of the Nemiah Valley) are charged with the sacred duty to protect the nen (land) of Tachelach'ed and the surrounding nen on behalf of all Tsilhqot'in people. They were determined that any logging in Tachelach'ed would be on their terms. The nen and their Aboriginal rights were threatened. The seasonal harvest could be interrupted in order to discharge their duty to protect the nen.

[25] Tsilhqot'in people were frustrated and angry. What they considered "their wood" was leaving the community without any economic benefit to Tsilhqot'in people. Over 40 families were on the Xeni Gwet'in housing wait list. The wait for housing was upwards to 25 years on Tsilhqot'in Reserves. There was also high unemployment. Forestry provided very few jobs for Tsilhqot'in people and the profits from harvesting the wood did not flow to their communities.

[26] The forecasted clear cut logging was expected to interfere with their Aboriginal right to hunt and trap. Insufficient consideration had been given to sustaining their communities in the model for sustainability employed by British Columbia.

[27] These were the central issues that interrupted the 1992 season for tislagh. The events that year on the bridge at Henry's Crossing, just down-river from Tsi T'is Gunlin and Biny Gwetsel, subsequently spiralled into these long and costly proceedings.

The Bridge at Henry's Crossing

Chief Roger William

By the time we found out that they were doing a bridge expansion at Henry's Crossing so the big logging trucks could cross the river and go into Tachelach'ed and the Trapline, they'd taken the deck of the old bridge off. My older step-brother, Gene Cooper, was on Council at that time, and we were both at the Tŝilhqot'in National Government office on May 6, 1992. We found out about the bridge when one of the operators at Henry's Crossing messaged us at TNG about what was happening. They wanted to get heavy equipment like logging trucks over, and they needed to replace the centre beam of the bridge to do that. It's amazing that they removed it without telling us.

Gene and I left the meeting and radio-phoned home, but it took us a while because there was only one line, and staff were using it to contact Aboriginal Affairs and so on. Many times I didn't even bother calling home, because the line would just be busy, busy, busy, but we got through that time and told them that we were gonna have a meeting that night and to make sure that everyone got the message. When we got home, everyone was there, and the meeting went from around seven o'clock until eleven-ish. So we said we were gonna roadblock. Like it or not, we're gonna go, we're gonna move to Henry's Crossing and roadblock. Then a bunch of us jumped into a vehicle and went to Henry's Crossing, getting there at two or three o'clock in the morning on Wednesday, May 7. Minnie Charleyboy and her husband, Patrick Charleyboy xinli, travelled with us. As daylight came she sang a drumsong about Tŝ'ilʔos and ʔEniyud's people of Xeni.

The Henry's Crossing bridge with its deck removed. Archival photo courtesy of Chief Roger William

Everything had been taken off the bridge, so no one could travel across it. Seven o'clock that morning, the bridge crew came, and we turned them around. They left, and the roadblock started. The rest of our Xeni Gwet'ins caught up with us that day. We had choppers come here with government, and we had all the Chiefs here. I remember Chief Francis [Laceese] brought two forty-five-gallon drums of fuel. During the roadblock, there were ceremonies, there was drummin', and we had a lotta meetings in our language, and it always came from the people. We also met the non–First Nations people here because they used both sides of the river and this bridge had the centre beam gone. Carrier Lumber were trying to create chaos, and we sat down, and we met with them. We couldn't call a lawyer to help us write letters and file an injunction against Carrier Lumber, because we didn't have any money for lawyers. Back then, we only had a radio phone to be able to communicate, and we didn't get legal advice, we just said, "No! We gotta back up our Declaration."

I remember movin' there and being there for two months, not coming back home for two months. When we got there, we set up the antenna for our radio phone in a tree and connected it to a battery. Then I phoned Jack [Woodward] and told him where we were and what we were doing. He was like, "What?! You're roadblocking?! What?!" He was freaking out! "All this is piss in the skies!" But we stopped them. We roadblocked them.

The bridge at Henry's Crossing is important for our people and for the non–First Nations ranchers and tourism operators as well as off-reserve Xeni Gwet'ins who live there. We thought the company knew there were tourism operators along the river as well as ranchers that used the river or that bridge. They tried to divide and conquer by taking that centre beam out and then creating pressure so there would be conflict between First Nations and non–First Nations if we roadblocked. When we did, both non–First Nations and First Nations sacrificed the use of that bridge to be able to do the right thing. For the most part, both the Nation and non–First Nations people supported us. We had a meeting with non–First Nations right at Henry's Crossing, where the roadblock was, and we all agreed that we didn't want any timber harvested in the Brittany Triangle. We had choppers [helicopters] coming from the company and from government. Government also realized that they needed to come to some kind of agreement. Conflict could've happened but didn't, because we communicated that we were looking at the big picture.

Tŝilhqot'in Chiefs came and the Ulkatcho Carrier community came to support us and Chief Francis Laceese came from Toosey Tl'esqox. Then people started to mobilize themselves at camp and set up a Sweat House. People hunted and fished, dried meat and fish, cut firewood and stayed there. It was May, and the snow was melting. We had fun too because that's who our people are, and they've always been on the Land. All their lives, Elders moved out and camped as soon as it was warm enough, and this is what they always wanted to do. We also had a lotta youth who had heard the stories and gone camping all the time. It was great!

The roadblock lasted for two months, until July, and came down after the Ministry of Forests gave us a letter that they would not replace the two bridges on the south side of the Brittany Triangle without giving us two weeks' notice. Our primary concern wasn't that we couldn't cross the bridge. It was logging.

Roadblock

Gene Cooper, Xeni Gwet'in

I became involved when I was a councillor, back in 1991. Roger was the Chief. We were in a meeting in Williams Lake and didn't get home till 6:30 that night, and we got word from community members that the bridge builders were starting to do construction on the bridge so Carrier Lumber could come across and cut some timber. At that time, we thought that instead of making it a political thing, we'd better have people behind us whatever we were gonna decide. So we put word out that we needed an emergency meeting, and we had a bunch of Elders come, like Patrick Charleyboy, Minnie Charleyboy, Joyce [Charleyboy] and Juliana Lulua, Ubill Lulua xinli and family, Dennis [Lulua]. Quite a few came to the meeting, and we asked 'em, "What do you guys want us to do?" We were in a situation where they were gonna build that bridge, come across, and log in that area under the Ministry of Forests guidelines, which entailed too high a harvest rate for us, and we didn't think that the guidelines included environmental concerns. But we told people, "Whatever you guys decide, that's what we will do."

The Elders said: "Roadblock. We need to roadblock, we need to stop them now." So we said, "Okay, we're gonna do that. These are the things we need." We put little groups together, some of them to get the camping stuff ready and bring it in, and a few families decided that we better get over there right away. So we went on ahead with what camp gear we could gather, and we must have gotten here at two in the morning. Around nine or so, we met the construction crew and told them, "This bridge is gonna jeopardize what's gonna happen over there, so we're here to stop you. We have more people coming," we told them, 'cause there were six of them and just Chief Roger and I at the bridge. They said they didn't want to be involved in conflict, and they respected our decision to roadblock, and they left. For two months after that, we were here at Henry's Crossing.

We found out that Carrier Lumber wasn't doing any silviculture applications[26] in that area, so that really concerned us. It was just straight harvesting, and we mentioned that to 'em. They were always accommodating. They said they'd do silviculture, and we said, "Our People are not getting jobs out of this," and they were accommodating with that as well. They were so accommodating that it kinda started to scare us! [laughter] We thought gee, you know, there's something we're missing here. I said to Roger at the time, "You know, this is bigger than you and I as Chief and councillor. We need to get our people involved." So we struck a ten-member committee, and we told them, "This is what Carrier Lumber are saying. What do you guys think?" They'd give us feedback, and we brought that back to the table every time. It got to the point where Carrier Lumber felt they weren't getting through to us and we were holding back, maybe because of the people, and they tried to arrange meetings away from the people. They'd say, "It's a business meeting, and we should have it in a neutral area." They were trying to use that to move us forward to make an agreement with them.

We had not only our people come in but also people from Redstone, Stoney, Anaham, and the Carrier Nation and other Nations supporting us in the fight to try and stop the logging. We decided that we were going to get the rate of logging reduced so it was more environmentally friendly. We were also looking at a three-month moratorium in the Redstone area because the Redstone Chief at that time, Ervin Charleyboy, was supporting us. So that became the platform when we left Henry's Crossing. At the same time, we'd been looking at lawyers to seek an injunction because we found out that a roadblock was not how to stop them. A week or so after our meeting here [at Henry's Crossing], we all went back to our own communities.

We got back to Nemiah around 6:30 p.m., and our Band manager at the time, Annie C. Williams, said that the AFN Chief [Ovide Mercredi] was going to meet us in Whistler the following morning at 10:00 a.m. to see if we could use one of their lawyers. So Roger and I changed our clothes, packed up what we could, and took off to Whistler. We got there at about two in the morning, got up at eight, then we met him at ten. It was only a ten-minute meeting. We explained to him that we had had meetings before the roadblock with the Ministry of Forests, so they knew what was going on. It took us three meetings and we had warned 'em, "If you guys continue at this rate, we *are* gonna roadblock." If they'd gone ahead at the rate they were planning, it was gonna affect our trapline, our traditional activities around here, and our Rights as well. So the AFN Chief listened to us for about ten minutes and said, "Okay, I'll provide you a lawyer." The lawyer's name was Joe Arvay. He was pretty aggressive, and he got onto Carrier Lumber right away. Dick Byl was the lawyer for Carrier Lumber, and they were negotiating. Eventually, Dick Byl stumbled quite a bit and our lawyer used that to our advantage and got an injunction. We were able to stop the logging, so we could relax and start doing other things.

During the roadblock here, a lot of the non-Natives in the area thought that we'd just all of a sudden started roadblocking, and it created some inconvenience because some of them had to chase cattle across here. So they got mad about it. I was attending the Cattlemen's meeting [Cariboo Cattlemen's Association] 'cause I was a rep for Xeni, and they brought that up. I guess they had brought it up before, so they were mad, and I got up and told them, "For three months we've been meeting with the province, and we put a warning out: we *will* road-block if there's no change. So it should be no surprise that we have a roadblock here, and if you're inconvenienced and can't get your cattle across, that's not our fault. The Forestry workers should've given you warning." They try to shine a light on First Nations because they're accustomed to trouble all the time. So that helped us steer them away from that and get other non-Natives involved, saying to Forestry, "No, you guys are wrong. You're the ones that are making mistakes, and that's why these things are happening. You've gotta smarten up in how you deal with First Nations." So we changed things around a bit, and it was good 'cause we gained allies as the process went on. That's been our foundation to succeed to where we are now [2014].

Tŝilhqot'in logs speeding out of Farwell Canyon to Williams Lake.
Photo by Lorraine Weir

Unity

David Setah, Xeni Gwet'in

I was working at Stoney when the roadblock came here [Henry's Crossing] – but every weekend I always came out to support 'em and go back to work. The thing Roger did really good there is that he always had the door open to Forestry, telling them, "If you wanna go inside the Brittany Triangle, you meet with us and you tell us how you're gonna do it – everything about your logging practices and all that. We want to sit down and we want to be able to include our ideas in it." So leaving the door open like that while you're trying to work with them so they won't affect your ways. There was no way we were gonna – or even Roger himself – was gonna sign an agreement that was gonna destroy his Aboriginal Rights. And so with that door being open, and trying to work with them, and knowing what they did back then is think, "Yeah, they're probably only First Nations trying to get in our way. We'll just go at things as we usually do and go into the area and go as planned. And we'll take the logs outta there." That's been their attitude all the time, and as soon as they tried that, Roger got all the people together and asked for directions. He updated 'em on all the things he [had] tried and he just asked his people, "With all that in mind, what should we do?" And the people said, "We'll roadblock 'em. We'll go over there and get in their way, make sure they don't get into the area until we're satisfied with what they want to do."

So after Roger and them had that meeting that night, they moved over here [Henry's Crossing] in the middle of the night. I think they were here by one or two in the morning with a few people following them, and they set up camp. The first camp was on this side. In the morning, they just waited for the guys that were building the bridge to come over, and they stood in their way and gave 'em a piece of paper and told 'em all the things they tried with Forestry. "They're not working with us, they're just going the way we are. That's the reason why we're here. We're here to roadblock." Good thing the company said they understood and they just stopped everything. They left, fortunately.

A lotta negotiations started happening, and the good thing about it is the unity in the Nation at that time. Everybody from the Nation came over. The Carrier Nation at Anahim Lake – we've got Tŝilhqot'ins there too – they all came over and supported the roadblock. The non-Natives around here, I mean, in these areas, we're the last of the untouched. We can actually see what's going on out there, and we know what's coming. That's a good thing about being so isolated, or maybe if we weren't so isolated, we would have made the same standstill. But with the devastation happening out here, we knew what was coming. Leadership did a lot of different things to stop it. Annie C. Williams with the Declaration did lots and ever since then, the leaders that have gotten in went by it – protect the Land. That's a good thing, that consistency of protecting the Land.

If the bridge at Henry's Crossing had happened, there would have been a big mill not too far from here on Eagle Lake Road. They were all set up for it. That thing where they actually burn the wood [beehive burner for kiln drying] and all that is still sitting there. You could see evidence of what they were gonna build there and that would've happened, 'cause then it was more economical for them to take wood outta here. But right now it's too hard for them to come in here and haul it all the way to Williams Lake. They would still have to put a mill there. It'd change a lotta things. Even the Tatla Lake School District built a bigger school because of that, and then there were hardly any kids in that brand new school. That's how confident they were that they could walk over people.

That's one thing I like about my community, is that they're not scared of industries, they're not scared of government, and if there's something out there coming towards us that we don't like, then we just say, "Yeah, we'll fight it." With that attitude, we won lots of battles. And when another one comes, we always remind our people we've never lost a battle. We keep going with that, and it brought us a long ways. Unity in the Tŝilhqot'in community is awesome. I dunno how it is with other Nations. I know they lose some battles. But your whole Nation has to stay together, and you fight with one voice. Once you do that and they see the unity, they'll back off. Anything'll back off. You could take the meanest, biggest grizzly bear around here, and if it's one on one with one person, probably he'll win, but if he sees a bunch of people in one area coming towards 'em, he'll take off. He knows he's gonna lose. With unity you can make a lot of big things back away from you.

The Lion at the Door

Cindy English

The reason for the roadblock was the bridge expansion at Henry's Crossing, which would have meant that big logging trucks could cross the river and go into the Brittany Triangle and the Nemiah Valley Indian Band Trapline. Other First Nations were doing roadblocks, and perhaps Nemiah thought, "This is the line the logging cannot cross," and so they roadblocked. This meant that they stopped the loggers, but their lawyers were having a fit about it because it might lead to activity that would harm their legal action acting in good faith, or the lawyers might have to get an injunction against the proposed logging, but an injunction would have cost money that Nemiah did not have. At that point, WC2 had stopped paying legal fees and Friends of Nemiah Valley had only managed to fundraise $500 during an entire summer of hard fundraising effort in the Tŝilhqot'in. It was imperative that the Nemiah people get their injunction because of the then imminent threat of logging in the trapline, which meant that money was needed to fund that action, but Xeni and Friends of Nemiah Valley had unsuccessfully tried fundraising for this action for several years. I remember Paul George saying at one point, "Well, the Band will have to have a bake sale!" Right. Now the lion was at the door. Nemiah needed to have legal representation who could pull out all the stops.

"Can't They See What They're Doing?"

Joyce Charleyboy, Tŝideldel

I remember William Setah looking at me and he said, "It's not gonna happen. I don' know why they keep comin' back." He said, "You look at the whole Territory" – 'cause I believe they had 'em on a flight a few times. "Everywhere they've taken and taken, and there's just this little area where we're livin' right now is all that's protected." Because of the ties I had with Nemiah and because that's where my mom's from, and being there in that community, it was always somethin' that I believed – you know, my kids and my grandkids are gonna see the pristineness of it because our Territory [Tŝideldel] was almost gone at that point in time.

I was getting lost in my own Territory because of all the roads that had been put in. From the time that I left to when I came back, it was just gone. There's nothing really left. And Dad [Chief Patrick Charleyboy xinli] takin' me out there and sayin', you know, "Is *this* what they want? And if we continue," he said, "we're gonna have nowhere else to go for hunting. What're we gonna do?" And a few of the other Elders that had a hand in raising me were in negotiations, I believe, with Riverside (which is Tolko today) at the time. One of the Elders said, "It takes how much water for one tree to grow?" And he said, "When they're cutting all of this, all our waters are drying up. There's no natural springs anymore. All the ponds are gone. Can't they see what they're doing?"

Taking Care of the Land

Ivor Deneway Myers xinli, Yuneŝit'in

I never did like roadblocking, but how else can you let the public know what goes on within the Territory or in the area? Roadblocking feels like in their eyes you're a terrorist, but it's not that. It's exercisin' your Rights as a Tŝilhqot'in Nation, as Tŝilhqot'in people, because we never relinquished a lot of this Land that's being expropriated to their system. I feel that what they've done was wrong to begin with, and here they're trying to take some soil off the ground to their benefit and not really the benefit of the Nation. Like I said before to them, we are 100 percent owners of the place you surveyed. Let's negotiate from there.

I was working for Nemiah as a journeyman carpenter supervisor, teaching some members of the community there how to do basic work on beam carpentry. And there was talk about roadblockin' Henry's Crossin' and I was wanting just to ask members, so I was told to go there and build [inaudible] so I did. How it came about was they were gonna harvest trees on the south side of the river. My mum [Elder Helena Myers xinli] used to live around that area. My great-great-grandmother came from Tahliqox, lived there after a lot of their people died, you know. She moved to Stone. It's multicultural in Stone [i.e., people from different Tŝilhqot'in communities live there] for part of it. That's why I'm saying no one owns a piece of Land – they're caretakers. They take care of the Land. The owners are the Nation.

Sacrifices

Chief Roger William

I really want to commend our Xeni Gwet'in Elders, parents, and youth for being proud, for not logging, because when their friends and relatives next door had a nice vehicle, a good Ski-Doo, a quad, motorbike, and a nice house, they still said, "No, I don't agree with clearcut logging the way the Ministry of Forests wants to do it." And they kept saying no. We followed the Declaration even though we saw that for our family out there in other communities, there were some benefits. I always remember the time I went to a restaurant in Williams Lake, and I saw an Elder from another community. They asked me, "Why are you for protecting chendi [jackpine]? They're good for nothing. Why are you fighting, doing everything you can, to protect this skinny stuff?" I could see a youth who's making a lotta money working saying that to me, but an Elder? I always remember that.

Imagine the Elder who said that to me talking to another Elder in Xeni. That's gonna be a big clash! Material goods weren't very important to our Xeni Gwet'in people. They stuck to their guns and said, "No, we don't agree with the way government and industry are destroying our Land. We're not getting anything out of it even though Tŝilhqot'ins down the road are making money." To me, that's a big sacrifice and I always remember that today.

I think back to Elders and members who are gone, and their children and grandchildren are still saying, "We don't agree with logging the way it's come down." To me that's amazing. They've kept on even though they've sacrificed jobs, opportunities, and a materialistic life.

You know, our children shouldn't be fighting the fight we are. I see baby pictures of my kids and now they're grown up and I can't take any of those years back. But they still care and love me. It's a sacrifice for our future children and I coulda been doin' way more things with my kids if I hadn't been doin' this kinda stuff. Maybe Linden, Liam, and Chiʔela will be able to do it with their kids, even though their dad didn't do it for them. I'm hopin' at least one of them will be able to. It's impacted us in unimaginable ways.

Taking Control

Chief Roger William

Since way back, our people have harvested timber, whether to build pithouses and other kinds of structures or for firewood. Some logging and mining exploration were happening before the logging industry touched here in the 1970s and '80s and opened up the country. There are places in Nemiah where you can still see mining roads, and some of those roads were built on our own trails. People used chainsaws, teamhorses, and tractors to log in those days, and it took a long time to fill a logging truck. In the 1980s we had our own mill at Tl'ebayi, between Xeni Biny and Xexti Biny. I remember when I was going to school, some of our members were making lumber and building log homes with it, until DIA [Department of Indian Affairs] housing regulations changed and we had to stop building those homes and upgrade.

Then the logging went down because the timber – jackpine – was too small and companies couldn't make money hauling it to Williams Lake. So the mills ended up getting bigger in the city, while the smaller mills went under with the rising cost of living and the price of timber. It was quicker and cheaper to cut logs in a mill in town, so people using chainsaws and doing horse logging got left behind. Working in the bush, you could make a pretty good living, but no comparison to somebody piling lumber in the mill, machine-cutting timber, and driving truckloads to the mill in town. Because of the market and the cost of living, there wasn't much logging at that time in Xeni, Tatlayoko, Tatla, and the logging started getting closer to the mills in Williams Lake, but when the technology changed and they finally had a machine which milled faster, there was a lot of interest in the timber in Xeni and Tatlayoko.

Other Tŝilhqot'in communities, leaders, and members decided to take control of the economy in their own backyards. They felt that if they did that themselves, it would be better than having someone else come in who just wanted the money and didn't know the Land or really care about it. So when the Nation started moving forward on this issue, the idea was that they would clearcut but protect and be careful. The leaders agreed to support each other as a Nation and we started the Tŝilhqot'in Tribal Council, had retreats, discussed governance and how to get our Land back and take control. We wanted to get away from "Bands," the Indian Act, the DIA. We're not "Bands," we're Xeni Gwet'ins. Tŝideldel. Tl'etinqox. Yuneŝit'in. Tl'esqox. ʔEsdilagh. We're Tŝilhqot'ins. DIA [Department of Indian Affairs] gave us anglicized names. For example, Nemaya was the first Xeni Gwet'in Nits'il?in that Europeans met so they decided to call our community Nemiah or Nemaiah, and because it's in a valley, they said, "Nemiah Valley."

Those things had happened, but we had our language, we were still strong, and we wanted to take over our area. The question in the '90s was how we as leaders were going to do that. The first step was to call ourselves the Tŝilhqot'in National Government and claim our own name. Before we were known as "Chilcotin" because governments anglicized our name. They couldn't pronounce "Tŝilhqot'in," and you still see "Cariboo Chilcotin" road signs out there today. We said, we're not Chilcotins, we're Tŝilhqot'ins.

The next question was how the six communities comprising the Tŝilhqot'in National Government (TNG) were going to support each other and move forward together. We all said we will let each community decide what's best for them. We're not going to dictate to each other. We're gonna support each other. We said each community is the caretaker of their own area, and they know their area better than other communities do. In Xeni, we know better than Yuneŝit'in and Tŝideldel what's happening in our area, what's best, and what our interest is. There are also some overlapping interests, because some families living in those areas went to Xeni and some went to Yuneŝit'in or Tŝideldel, or there are intermarriages.

My direction from my people was that they didn't agree with commercial logging or mining, and that's why the Declaration was created in 1989. Some of the other Tŝilhqot'in communities are closer to town, and there had already been a lot of harvesting. Being further away, we felt that we had a chance to do something different. There had been some harvesting on the edges of our caretaker area so we defined two boundaries creating the Xeni Gwet'in Caretaker

Area and the Wilderness Preserve, which is inside the caretaker area. We said that there would be no more logging in the Wilderness Preserve, but we would take over logging in our caretaker area and do a joint venture or whatever was necessary in order to create jobs and be involved. The Nation agreed to support us.

Logging in Tachelach'ed: The Brittany Lake Forest Management Plan (1992–1997)

Chief Roger William

Between the roadblock in May 1992 and 1997, we worked out the Brittany Lake Forest Management Plan, and that was another process in itself. We call that area Tachelach'ed in our language, but somehow it became Brittany in English. We applied for a licence for timber in the Brittany Triangle, and the government opened one up. There were 1.8 million cubic metres to be harvested over five years, and that's what we applied for, but we only got 250,000 a year over five years, significantly less than the 1.8 million. Working with Tŝilhqot'in Forest Products and Tŝilhqot'in communities, we negotiated the total to 1.1 million cubic metres allotted to all of us to log the Brittany Triangle ourselves over five years. We met five different mills, and after many meetings with our Elders and members, we created a joint venture called Natasawed (Brittany Lake) with Lignum [Forest Products company] because they gave us the best deal. We went as far as the legislation would take us, and the Ministry of Forests people who worked with us did everything they could within their power, policy, and the legislation to make it work.

Lignum agreed to give us ten dollars a cubic metre, and then whatever money was left over, we'd go half and half. That's the only way timber companies will give us money. But if we weren't involved in a joint venture with them and we wanted money for a piece of Land, they'd say, "Well, we gotta pay taxes too, stumpage fees too. The Ministry of Forests can give you guys money." That's what they say, right? It *is* a rip-off. What's the alternative? The alternative is they keep logging. They might do a joint venture with us, they might hire our people. I mean, the alternative is probably nothing. That's why Tŝideldel decided to log. They've got a joint venture. They've been logging over twenty-five, thirty years now. Their thinking was that if we log it, we can protect our sites.

I believed in the Brittany Lake Forest Management Plan enough to bring a referendum vote to the people to decide, because we felt it was an Aboriginal

Rights issue. The first vote was a close "yes" for two reasons: we had the right of first refusal, meaning we had the first opportunity to harvest the timber; and we had the right to shut down the harvest if we didn't agree that it was going well. After the first vote, the Ministry of Forests said that their policy didn't allow the right of first refusal to anybody. It had to be open-market bids or any company they selected. We responded that our people had voted based on the right of first refusal and the ability to shut the harvest down, as stated in the Memorandum of Understanding we'd negotiated with them, so we needed another vote. On a second vote, the people turned it down.

There were five referendum votes where Chief and Council said that the government could deal with staffing, funding, education, and health dollars, and economic development, but when it came to Aboriginal Rights, our people were the ones who decided how we would deal with logging. We went back to the table with the Ministry of Forests and kept making changes and voting, until the last two times when we restricted logging in the Brittany Triangle to Tŝilhqot'in communities, but our people still turned it down. We reduced the amount of timber to be logged from 1.8 million cubic meters to 1.1 and protected a lotta areas. We planned for only Tŝilhqot'ins logging there, and we were gonna mimic the wildfire somehow. We made it clear that, at the end of the day, our people had to look at the plan that we'd created and decide whether they agreed with it. We told the Ministry of Forests it's up to you how involved you get our people and Elders, and how much money you put into this to keep us involved. You put in less money and less involvement, and you're gonna get a no.

Our community process is that when we make a decision through a vote, we all have to back up whatever the majority says, whether the vote is in the affirmative or the negative. We can't say okay, 60 percent of us are gonna fight for it, and the other 40 are gonna try everything they can to fight against it and get their way. We said that wasn't healthy. Throughout the negotiations on the Natasawed joint venture with Lignum, we did different kinds of silviculture training for our own members, so we'd be ready to go if there was a yes. We had plans for how we were gonna get the equipment, and we even had a plan for a single, gated bridge coming into the Brittany Triangle. Anyone who wanted to hunt in there would have to go another way, whether by horseback, on foot, or using the river. No one with a gun was gonna get past that bridge. We were gonna hire people to monitor the bridge 24-7, and we planned to train people for that job.

We also talked about money as bad medicine. Money's not our tradition. It's something that's brought in. Money can hurt us. We wanted to have money-management training, because we saw that people were already having challenges with money before logging came in, and that would only get worse if the joint venture went ahead. Our experience was that people had trouble managing their dollars, and some would want an advance on their salary if they bought a vehicle and it broke down, or if they had an alcohol problem and forgot to buy food, or even if they had a flat tire and forgot to bring it in to get fixed. Staff would get mad at Chief and Council if they wanted a raise and got turned down. Imagine if we had two or three times more people because of logging, and they all had the same problems with money management! So we had training with our staff. The training covered budgeting – this is how much you make, this is how much gas is gonna cost you for a month, this is how much food's gonna cost you a month, this is how much you're gonna have left over. Yes, you've got a big cheque but how much of it's spent already? Don't put yourself there.

We were also talking about the social issues and looking at everything we could. For example, we were saying nine dollars a cubic metre for every metre that's logged, but what're we gonna do with the money? In addition to funding for education, sports, culture, and language, some people thought that youth should get money when they got to age eighteen. What criteria would we have for payment? Practising your hunting and fishing, high-school graduation, and going to college? Or would there be an incentive scheme, so a certain amount of money on graduation and a certain amount for each year in college? What if an election happened, and somebody said forget about all that red tape – just vote me in as Chief and I'll give you your money. How would we deal with that? We talked to the Elders about that and we talked in the General Assembly and at a Council meeting and with Lignum. We decided to have a referendum vote for each stage of the process, from when the money comes, to when a youth hits eighteen, to when they graduate, so when a new Chief and Council got in, if they wanted to change this process, they'd have to put the change to a vote. We wanted protection, because money can do more damage to us.

In the end, our people thought it was too much, and that's the sacrifice we made. We could've taken over the joint venture and had a company and made money for five years, but our people said after five years, what? More logging? We said if we do this for five years and achieve our goals while not exposing wildlife to danger, maybe we could do it in other areas too. But our people said no. There were fires, and they turned the plan down. We – Xeni Gwet'in and Lignum – agreed to separate, and we sold our joint venture to Lignum. It all turned out to be a blessing in disguise when our people said no to the Brittany Lake Forest Management Plan in April 1997. We gave it our all, and it went the other way. As our Elders say, it was meant to be. We were maybe two months away from the beginning of the Trapline case in BC Supreme Court, so that was the best decision our people could have made.

Sustainability

David Setah, Xeni Gwet'in

We did our sustainability study on the Brittany Triangle. You only could take 69,000 cubic metres a year out of there every year to keep it sustainable, and we sat down with them to try to make an agreement with Brittany Lake Forest Management Plan. It was 1.8 million cubic metres in five years, but we knocked it down by creating protected areas like wildlife migration routes, sacred sites, and wet zones so it went down to 1.1 million cubic metres. We tried hard to change all that to make it sustainable. We looked at their logging – they got us to design their power-logging practice according to what they want outta there. At the end of the day, nothing worked.

They were hallelujah for mountain pine beetle to come in so they could cut a lot more and then they could spend more money. I think you can manage jackpine beetle. There's different ways if you put all your effort into it. Then it would still be sustainable right now [2014]. From day one we've been telling the Ministry of Forests and all the industries, "It's not sustainable," and they say, "Yeah, larger scale it's sustainable, but not in your community." But we told 'em, we always go by the saying that you've gotta look at every community to make sure it's sustainable there too. You can't overcut one area and then go to different areas. You've gotta make sure you sustain every area, every community.

We showed it to the people and the people said, "No, it's not gonna work." We had maybe five referendum votes on that, and we consulted our people. If there was a question we couldn't answer, we had to go out and find the answer. And then we told our people that, and they expected that of us. They said, "You guys don't know?" We said, "No!" "Then find out!" And then we'd go and find out and bring it back. We always talk to our people, and they give us directions on which way to go. That's how every leadership has to work out there: just listen to the people. Not listen to one person or another or a group of five people. If there's something coming into your area, you throw a big meeting, you talk about it lots, you talk about it until they've got no more questions. And once you know everybody understands it, then you ask for a referendum vote. The people vote on it, and that's your direction, you go with that.

Being in leadership is not easy. You could be going through the process, consulting with our people like we did with Brittany Lake Forest Management. We hear our people saying something that's not right and we have to tell 'em. Once we do that, the people say, "Oh, you guys are selling out." We tell 'em, "No, we're communicating all this to you, but if there's something you're not seeing, that's all right, we'll tell you." We're also gonna tell the opposition if they're not saying the right thing. It's just like crossing your t's and dotting your i's. Then you win at that level, and it leaves you in court.

Understanding Forestry

Gene Cooper, Xeni Gwet'in

At the time this court case was happening, we were making a big push to make them downsize their clearcuts, 'cause they were allowing 'em at eight hundred hectares, and we were trying to get 'em down to two hundred. Within that two hundred, we wanted to see a lot of wildlife tree patches, so wildlife doesn't have a long distance to run, and they can get across the clearcut without being seen or getting shot. And also creating bigger buffers along waterways, because our wildlife use waterways as a corridor ... A lot of the agreements made at the time were made under duress, 'cause they were pushed. They needed workers, and our people were trying to find a way to survive, but we didn't understand forestry enough to see how we could fit in and still have the goal of making sure we save all the animals and the environment at the same time. So.

Salvage (2017)

Nits'il?in Russell Myers Ross, Yuneŝit'in

Logging has been one of the most challenging issues to deal with, from when the province puts their legislation in order and gives a direction to all their employees of what to do. They've privatized as much as they could, and they've made it sort of a rubberstamp process. A decade ago, the foresters would've actually been planning areas and doing a lot more, but the pine beetle gave this free-for-all mentality to take whatever you can salvage.[27]

From *Tsilhqot'in Nation v. British Columbia*, 2007 BCSC 1700

[71] In 1992, the Xeni Gwet'in people commissioned a sustainable forestry plan for Tachelach'ed lands. This plan was rejected by the Ministry of Forests. Ministry officials proposed various logging plans and sought the views of Xeni Gwet'in people. Between 1994 and 1997, Xeni Gwet'in people voted against logging plans for Tachelach'ed in a series of community referenda.

[72] The dispute between Ministry of Forests officials and the Xeni Gwet'in people centred on the control of logging in Tachelach'ed. Tsilhqot'in people sought a right of first refusal with respect to any logging activities. They argued that such a right was essential to the maintenance of their traditional way of life. Ministry officials declined to grant such a right, arguing that there was no legislative authority that enabled them to grant such a concession to Tsilhqot'in people. [...]

[75] On January 1, 1997, British Columbia issued Forest Licence A54417 to Timberwest Forest Limited. This forest licence permitted logging within the Trapline Territory and Tachelach'ed. On January 8, 1997, the Xeni Gwet'in filed a notice of intention to proceed with the Nemiah Trapline Action. Harvesting rights under this licence were transferred to Riverside Forest Products (Soda Creek) Limited on June 23, 1997.

[76] On March 1, 1997, British Columbia granted Forest Licences A55901 to Lignum Limited; A55902 to West Fraser Mills Limited; A55904 to RFP Timber Ltd.; and A55905 to Jackpine Forest Products Ltd., which permitted additional logging of the Trapline Territory and Tachelach'ed.

[77] In the fall of 1998, with the assistance of the David Suzuki Foundation, the Xeni Gwet'in began eco-system based planning for forestry and cultural tourism in the Trapline Territory and Tachelach'ed.

[78] On November 1, 1998, British Columbia re-issued Forest Licences A20016 to RFP Timber Ltd. and A20019 to Riverside Forest Products Limited which would have permitted further logging of the Trapline Territory and Tachelach'ed. Both of these renewed licences replaced licences of the same number dated November 1, 1993.

[79] The plaintiff commenced Action No. 98/4847 (the "Brittany Triangle Action") on December 18, 1998, against British Columbia, Riverside Forest Products Ltd. and others, seeking declarations similar to those in the Nemiah Trapline Action with respect to the lands known as Tachelach'ed.

[80] On February 19, 2001, the plaintiff filed a fresh statement of claim in the Brittany Triangle Action. On March 9, 2001, British Columbia filed a fresh statement of defence in the Brittany Triangle Action setting out British Columbia's reserve creation defence.

[81] On November 2, 1999, I dismissed an application brought by British Columbia to strike the representative claim for Aboriginal title in both actions: *Nemaiah Valley Indian Band v. Riverside Forest Products* (1999), C.P.C. (4th) 101, 1999 Carswell BC 2438 (S.C.).

[82] The parties consented to the consolidation of the Trapline Action and the Brittany Triangle Action. On February 21, 2000, a notice of trial was issued setting the trial date in both actions for September 10, 2001.

[83] On October 5, 2000, upon application by the plaintiff, I made an order that Canada be added as a defendant in the Brittany Triangle Action.

[84] On November 2, 2000, Canada was added as a defendant in the Nemiah Trapline Action, by consent.

[85] On February 2001, a fresh statement of claim was filed and, in March 2001, fresh statements of defence were filed by British Columbia and by Canada. In its statement of defence, Canada did not support British Columbia's reserve creation defence.

[86] Upon application by Canada on March 19, 2001, the trial of the action was adjourned to a date to be fixed.

[87] On April 18, 2001, a Ministry of Forests official confirmed that logging and road building in the Claim Area were inevitable, as the decision to permit harvesting in the disputed area was made at the time the licences were issued early in 1997.

[88] On April 4, 2002, an order was made consolidating the Nemiah Trapline Action and the Brittany Triangle Action.

[89] On August 14, 2002, I dismissed an application by the defendant, British Columbia, for an order compelling the plaintiff to provide notice of the plaintiff's claims to all land or resource use tenure holders, or applicants for tenure, whose interests may be affected by the litigation: *William v. Riverside Forest Products Limited*, 2002 BCSC 1199.

[90] On September 13, 2002, the plaintiff filed a consolidated fresh statement of claim. On October 22, 2002, British Columbia filed a consolidated fresh statement of defence. This new pleading did not contain the reserve creation defence.

[91] The trial of the consolidated action began on November 18, 2002. On November 20, 2002, I dismissed an application by Canada to be removed as a party: *William v. British Columbia*, 2002 BCSC 1904. [...]

[93] On February 14, 2003, I allowed the plaintiff to amend the statement of claim and dismissed an application by British Columbia for an order striking out the statement of claim on the basis that it disclosed no reasonable claim, or was otherwise an abuse of process: *William v. British Columbia*, 2003 BCSC 249.

Everything Was Happening at Once

Chief Roger William

The roadblock, the Brittany Lake Forest Management Plan, going to court with the Trapline case, and then the Title case, dealing with the proposed [New] Prosperity mine, and creating a protected area through the Chilko Lake Study Team – everything was happening at once. That team included representatives from the Ministry of Mines, Ministry of Forests, Lands, Fish and Wildlife, logging companies, mining companies, tourism operators, trappers, recreationists, and hikers. It was a three-year-long process, and we had Elders sitting with us Chief and Councillors, meeting at least once a month or more, including subcommittee meetings. Each group hung onto their beliefs and protected their interests during that process, and out of it came the protected area known as

Tŝ'ilʔos Park. Every month I was on the agenda at TNG [Tŝilhqot'in National Government], telling them where we were with the Chilko Lake Study Team and the Brittany Lake Forest Management Plan. We asked for their advice about what we should protect, and we always had something in mind when we had to deal with an issue, because we consulted so widely.

Our people had heard of First Nations being kept out of provincial parks, prevented from hunting and camping there, and we were determined to protect our Aboriginal interests in this new park. What kind of a park would it be? Would a wilderness preserve protect our interests better, and how could we do that? Out of those negotiations came an MOU [Memorandum of Understanding], which said that we could hunt, fish, and do all of our traditional activities in the park anytime. There were already some trappers, tourism operators, and ranchers in the park, and they were grandfathered in on the understanding that their interests would be preserved within the park as long as they sold to their own families. Xeni Gwet'in would also be grandfathered in should we want to go into business in the park anytime in the future. Everyone – loggers, miners, hikers, tourism operators, and governments – agreed with that MOU.

Near the end of the Brittany Lake Forest Management Plan negotiations, the Ministry of Forests got frustrated because they thought that we had a really good deal, and there was no way we could turn it down. When the referendum votes went against it, they asked if we wanted to make a deal anyway and told us they were going to log north of the trapline whether we liked it or not. In January '97 they were gonna put a road into the northern trapline by Gwedzin, and we roadblocked. The Ministry of Forests was frustrated with us about that roadblock, but we'd had meetings with them between '93 and '97. We had votes and our people had said no to logging. Tŝideldel Chief Ervin Charleyboy, Tribal Chair at the time, joined us on the roadblock and then opened up his Band office on the weekend, and we had a meeting with the Ministry of Forests. He took us in, cooked us breakfast, and we got an agreement with the Ministry of Forests to do a furbearer study. So the roadblock came down, and they chose not to come through the trapline. Then the very next week, they said they would do the furbearer study. We refused and said we'd do it ourselves and give them the report if they paid for it. They knew better than to say no again, because they knew what we would have done next. In 1998 we added the Trapline case to the Title case and made the Brittany Triangle the other boundary of the Title case.

As Tŝilhqot'in people, we want to make sure that our culture and the environment are looked after when there's any mining or logging proposed. We have to pick our fights because there are logging companies in the Tŝilhqot'in that are run by some of the Bands. Some of our members in the Tŝilhqot'in don't agree with logging, but it's still happening. In Xeni, probably 80 percent of the area can't be logged because of our court case. Because we sacrificed. I commend our Elders, our youth, our members, our leaders for sacrificing all the opportunities out there in terms of logging jobs, logging trucks, making money. They chose to say, "No, we don't agree with logging because right now, it's doing too much damage. It affects our culture, it affects our environment, we don't agree with it." So even though their relatives who are working in the Tŝilhqot'in are making good money, our people still say no. Our people are strong, and I feel really fortunate that they are saying that they want jobs, and want to hunt and fish and do our traditional activities, but not at the expense of our future generations or of our culture and our environment.

To this day, since we did the Declaration, nobody has been able to come in and log Nemiah. They've tried. There were roadblocks, court actions, direct actions, and the Land is still intact. We didn't go half into the Brittany Lake Forest Management Plan and Strategic Operating Plan. We went in full. We got our Elders involved. I wouldn't have allowed our people to vote if I hadn't thought this type of harvesting, from 1.8 million cubic metres down to 1 million, could've worked. Water, site protection, heritage, our culture, our significant sites protected, and then the hunting. We were gonna gate it. We were gonna man it so if you wanted to hunt in there, you could go by the river, by foot, or by horse, but you couldn't come in on this logging road to do that, we're not gonna allow you to. We were mimicking the fire because that's how we managed our Lands before. So we worked very hard to make it work. We tried to work with the government. The evidence is Tŝ'ilʔos Park. We're co-managers of Tŝ'ilʔos Park. At one time a Park was a protected area where First Nations could not practise their culture or their way of life, so through an MOU agreement we said that we're gonna protect this area, we're still gonna follow our traditional way, we're still gonna practise our traditional use, we're still gonna live, we're still gonna use that Land today. So that's our evidence. It's not like we're gonna go to court first or roadblock first. No. Even in light of what happened – the Tŝilhqot'in War, the treason, the government tricking our Warriors into peace talks, hanging them without legal representation and a fair trial. All that and residential school.

CHAPTER 6 ENDNOTES

1   Tŝilhqot'in National Government, "General Assembly of the Chilcotin Nation: A Declaration of Sovereignty," May 2, 1984, www.tsilhqotin.ca/wp-content/uploads/2020/12/1998 _Agreement_GeneralAssemblyofTN_DeclarationSovereignty.pdf.

2   Cindy English had met Jack Woodward when she was working on a few specific claims. Rob Tyhurst, a lawyer and anthropologist who had worked in the Tŝilhqot'in, recommended Woodward to her.

3   David W. Dinwoodie, *Reserve Memories: The Power of the Past in a Chilcotin Community*, Studies in the Anthropology of North American Indians series (Albuquerque: University of Nebraska Press, with the American Indian Studies Research Institute at Indiana University, Bloomington, 2002), 85–86.

4   George Colgate was present as Band Manager at this meeting. He and his family have lived and worked in Xeni since 1976.

5   *Carrier Lumber Ltd. v. British Columbia*, (1999) 18 B.C.T.C. 241 (SC). *Delgamuukw v. British Columbia*, (1997) 3 S.C.R. 1010. The Trapline case was the first stage of what became the Title case. See Justice Vickers's summary at *Tsilhqot'in Nation v. British Columbia*, 2007 BCSC 1700, 60–100.

6   Cindy English was a founding member of the original Friends of Nemiah Valley group. She was coordinator of the trapping case against Carrier Lumber, conducted *The Heritage Significance of the Fish Lake Study Area: Ethnography* (Harmony Human and Environmental Studies, 1993–1994; see www.ceaa-acee.gc.ca/050 /documents/p63928/87008E.pdf), and managed preliminary planning for the 2001 TNG Traditional Use Study *Tsilhqot'in Current Use of Lands and Resources for Traditional Purposes: Submission to the Prosperity CEAA Panel, November 2009* (CEAR #1397, Novembre 16, 2009, www.ceaa-acee.gc.ca/050/documents_staticpost/63928/80858/2-6-4-B_-_Part_1 .pdf). See also Cindy Ehrhart-English, "Letter of Comment to the Canadian Environmental Assessment Agency concerning the New Prosperity Project," March 16, 2013, www.ceaa-acee .gc.ca/050/documents/p63928/87008E.pdf.

7   One of the advantages of retrofitting a modern orthography onto an oral language (as was done for Tŝilhqot'in in the 1970s) is that a more or less exact (phonemic) correspondence can be created between pronunciation and spelling, at least until dialect variation and everyday speech begin to create change. In contrast, the English language in the twenty-first century bears the traces of its colonial history and its association with writing going back almost two millennia, creating all the inconsistencies and idiosyncrasies of pronunciation and spelling which come with them. All of this makes English a very difficult language to work with, but it's worth noting that coming to the Tŝilhqot'in language from English is no less difficult, though for different reasons.

8   Paul George with the Western Canada Wilderness Committee, *Big Trees Not Big Stumps: 25 Years of Campaigning to Save Wilderness with the Wilderness Committee* (Vancouver: Western Canada Wilderness Committee, 2006).

9   George, *Big Trees Not Big Stumps*, 157.

10 Annie C. Williams's involvement was to read the draft Declaration "to see if it made any sense. The Tŝilhqot'in part makes more sense." She remembered the translators as Illa Setah, Patrick Lulua, Leona Williams, June Williams, Margaret Lulua, and Roger William (*William v. British Columbia*, proceedings at trial, day 132, September 21, 2004, 00036.33–00037.15).

11 George, *Big Trees Not Big Stumps*, 158.

12 "Nenduwh Jid Guzitin Declaration: Nemiah Aboriginal Wilderness Preserve," Friends of the Nemaiah Valley (website), www.fonv.ca/nemaiahvalley/nenduwhjidguzitindeclaration/.

13 Dinwoodie, *Reserve Memories*, 86–90. When he was a graduate student at the University of Chicago, David Dinwoodie studied Tŝilhqot'in in Xeni and Tl'esqox and was privileged to be among the outsiders who were present for the development of the Declaration. Dr. Dinwoodie wishes to acknowledge that, while he worked through the translation away from Nemiah, it was based on linguistic work done with Gina Johnny and Gilbert Solomon. Our thanks to David Dinwoodie for permission to reproduce his translation here.

14 Dinwoodie, *Reserve Memories*, 87–90.

15 George, *Big Trees Not Big Stumps*, 158.

16 See, respectively, Tŝilhqot'in National Government (website), "Xeni ʔeguh jid Nits'egugheniʔan," www.tsilhqotin.ca/wp-content/uploads/2020/11/Nemiah_Declaration _Tsilhqotin.pdf and "Affirmation of the Nemiah Declaration," www.tsilhqotin.ca/wp-content /uploads/2020/11/Nemiah-Declaration_English_Signed.pdf.

17 Transcribed by Lorraine Weir.

18 Justice Vickers notes that "[t]he 'Nemiah Trapline Action' was commenced in the Supreme Court of British Columbia on April 18, 1990. The plaintiff commenced the 'Brittany Triangle Action' on December 18, 1998. Both actions were provoked by proposed forestry activities in Tachelach'ed and the Trapline Territory" and both were preludes to the Title case with the trial commencing in Victoria on November 18, 2002 (*Tsilhqot'in Nation v. British Columbia*, 2007 BCSC 1700, iii).

19 Government of British Columbia, Department of Lands, *Water Powers: Fraser River* (pamphlet), 1938, 1, www.for.gov.bc.ca/hfd/library/documents/bib50649.pdf.

20 *Water Powers*, 22–24.

21 Foreword to *Water Powers*, 1.

22 BC Government News, "Cheslatta Carrier Nation, Province Sign Agreements to Address Historic Wrong," news release, April 17, 2019, news.gov.bc.ca/releases/2019IRR0036-000704. See also: Cheslatta Carrier Nation and the Ministry of Indigenous Relations and Reconciliation of British Columbia, *Interim Reconciliation Agreement: Cheslatta Carrier Nation and British Columbia* (Victoria: Ministry of Indigenous Relations and Reconciliation, 2019), www2.gov .bc.ca/assets/gov/environment/natural-resource-stewardship/consulting-with-first-nations /agreements/cheslatta_interim_reconciliation_agreement_-_executed_-_20190328.pdf. For the story of the Kemano Generating Station, completed in 1954, see Briony Penn with Cecil Paul, *Following the Good River: The Life and Times of Wa'xaid* (Calgary: Rocky Mountain Books, 2020).

23   Ovide Mercredi served two terms (1991–1997) as elected National Chief of the Assembly
      of First Nations (AFN). An organization of Chiefs representing individual First Nations
      and supported largely by federal government funding, the AFN held its first gathering of
      Chiefs in 1982. For a detailed, if somewhat dated, overview of the AFN's history, see Tabitha
      de Bruin, Michael Posluns, Anthony J. Hall and David Gallant's article in the *Canadian
      Encyclopedia* at www.thecanadianencyclopedia.ca/en/article/assembly-of-first-nations.
      For a critical view of the AFN, see Arthur Manuel and Grand Chief Ronald Derrickson,
      The Reconciliation Manifesto: Recovering the Land, Rebuilding the Economy (Toronto:
      James Lorimer & Company, 2017), chap. 18. Legal scholar Kent McNeil writes that "Proof
      of the exclusive occupation at the time of Crown sovereignty required for Aboriginal Title
      involves enormous cost and extensive evidence in long trials – in *Tsilhqot'in Nation*, the
      only successful title case, 339 trial days spread over five years, not counting the appeals!
      The only way the Tsilhqot'in could afford this was by obtaining an interim cost order
      from the BC Supreme Court, which is granted only in exceptional cases." The late Joseph
      J. Arvay was Counsel for the Plaintiff in "*William v. Riverside Forest Products Ltd.*, [2002]
      1 CNLR 375 at para. 35, affirmed *Tsilhqot'in Nation v. Canada (Attorney General)*, [2002]
      4 CNLR 306 (BCCA), [2002] SCCA No. 295. Vickers J. ordered 'that Canada and British
      Columbia must share equally in the payment of the plaintiffs' future costs'" (Kent McNeil,
      "Has Constitutionalizing Aboriginal and Treaty Rights Made a Difference?," *BC Studies* 212
      [Winter 2021/2022]: 137–164, doi.org/10.14288/bcs.no212.192441).

24   The mountain pine beetle "infestation" began in the Tŝilhqot'in in the 1970s. In *Carrier
      Lumber Ltd. v. British Columbia* (1999) 18 B.C.T.C. 241 (SC), Justice W.G. Parrett outlined the
      Crown's involvement in the situation as follows: "Substantial volumes of timber were being
      destroyed each year and the result was an emergency in which the Crown was confronted
      with enormous timber losses, substantial timber stand rehabilitation costs and a large and
      growing risk of wild fire. [8] Between 1980 and 1983 the Crown tried to entice through
      timber offers in the area, harvesting which would begin to control the beetle infestation.
      Those efforts failed because of the remoteness of the area and the relatively poor quality
      and volume of the timber resources. [9] In late 1983 the Crown tried a new approach. In
      this attempt they offered an unprecedented sale of 5 million cubic metres of timber to be
      harvested over a period of ten years. By offering this combination of a very large volume and
      a 10 year license period they hoped to attract bids which would begin harvesting in the area,
      and some effort to control the beetle infestation." Carrier Lumber was the sole bidder and
      quickly found itself involved in a dispute with the Nemiah Valley Indian Band, culminating
      in the Trapline case. In one of the great victories of the Title case, Justice Vickers wrote that
      "Aboriginal title confers a right to the land itself, and the right to determine how it will be
      used. Legislation that authorizes the granting of rights to harvest timber from these lands
      to third parties strikes at the very core of Aboriginal title. These legislative enactments are
      beyond the constitutional reach of the Province ..." (*Tsilhqot'in Nation v. British Columbia*,
      2007 BCSC 1700, 1048).

25   Writing for the Court, Chief Justice McLachlin would later summarize this history as
      follows: "The issue of Tsilhqot'in title lay latent until 1983, when the Province granted
      Carrier Lumber Ltd. a forest licence to cut trees in part of the territory at issue. The Xeni
      Gwet'in First Nations government (one of the six bands that make up the Tsilhqot'in Nation)
      objected and sought a declaration prohibiting commercial logging on the land. The dispute
      led to the blockade of a bridge the forest company was upgrading. The blockade ceased
      when the Premier promised that there would be no further logging without the consent
      of the Xeni Gwet'in. Talks between the Ministry of Forests and the Xeni Gwet'in ensued,
      but reached an impasse over the Xeni Gwet'in claim to a right of first refusal to logging. In

1998, the original claim was amended to include a claim for Aboriginal title on behalf of all Tsilhqot'in people" (*Tsilhqot'in Nation v. British Columbia*, 2014 SCC 44, 5).

26 Silviculture is defined as "the art and science of managing the establishment, growth, composition, health and quality of forests on a sustainable basis. Silviculture is often confused with managing stands and forests for timber, but silviculture practices are also used to manage forests for wildlife, water, recreation aesthetics, or any combination of these or other forest uses...Strategic silviculture plans provide a description of the timber supply and habitat supply issues, opportunities to increase timber supply and habitat supply, and the potential treatments, treatable area and silvicultural strategies associated with those opportunities." From gov.bc.ca (Government of British Columbia), "Silviculture Strategies," accessed August 2023, www2.gov.bc.ca/gov/content?id=554DE067D67E4F4EA8BE8683B3B438BB.

27 On the connection between the mountain pine beetle and the banning of landscape burning, see Nancy J. Turner, *Ancient Pathways, Ancestral Knowledge: Ethnobotany and Ecological Wisdom of Indigenous Peoples of Northwestern North America*, vol. 1, *The History and Practice of Indigenous Plant Knowledge*, McGill-Queen's Indigenous and Northern Studies series (Montréal and Kingston: McGill Queen's University Press, 2014), 250–251. Climate change, wildfire, and the long-term impact of clearcutting are all connected to the mountain pine beetle and how the province dealt with it during these years. For a different approach to forests and sustainability, see Susanne Simard, *Finding the Mother Tree: Discovering the Wisdom of the Forest* (Toronto: Penguin, 2021) and Turner, *Ancient Pathways, Ancestral Knowledge*, vols. 1 (ibid.) and 2, *The Place and Meaning of Plants in Indigenous Cultures and Worldviews*. On wildfire and its causes in the Tŝilhqot'in, see Crystal Verhaeghe, Emma Feltes, and Jocelyn Stacey, *Nagwediẑk'an gwaneŝ gangu ch'inidẑed ganexwilagh / The Fires Awakened Us*, report (Williams Lake, BC: Tŝilhqot'in National Government, 2017), www.tsilhqotin.ca/wp-content/uploads/2020/12/the-fires-awakened-us.pdf.

Navajo Country

This Is Who You Are

Chief Roger William

In 1995, I went down to Navajo country with Chief Francis Laceese (Tl'esqox) and the rest of our Justice Committee, which had representatives from each Tŝilhqot'in community and from Ulkatcho. We were there for about a week visiting Navajo Reserve Lands, leadership, and people, including Elders. One day we had to go off reserve to a hotel after being on reserve in all these other areas for four or five days. We had to stay at a hotel that was owned by a non-Navajo. I felt depression, I felt anger, I felt unwelcome. I felt uncomfortable, almost like this is how we feel up in Canada in Nemiah all the time, but we don't even know it. We don't even acknowledge we feel that way, we're just kinda numb to it. But when we were in Navajo country, everything was Navajo. Radio was Navajo, professors teach in Navajo, and you go to a hamburger place, it's Navajo – you know, everything. That feels so good, so comfortable, and then you get to a place just outside Navajo country, and you feel angry and mad and depressed. Just one night, just one night in that hotel, and I was like wow, this is how we feel at home all the time.

We talked about it. We were in that hotel and we felt angry. Just looking at these different faces, at the clerk looking at us, responding to us, and we're like not the same, eh? We're like you know this is what it's like at home in Nemiah, in the Tŝilhqot'in, every day to our people. If you brought our people down to live in Navajo country and get that feeling of wow, then they'd realize why they were feeling this way here. A human being can take a lot – our bodies, who we are – but things come home. No matter what race you are, you can take a lot. Then you get put in a place that's so good, you realize how much you took. Wow, I didn't know I was taking all that, I didn't know why I was feeling this way, I was reacting this way. But all your life, you're feeling this way, and you get this one moment that says this is you sovereign, this is who you are, your destiny, for one week out of your whole life, and you're like wow. It puts everything in perspective, looking at the big picture. You wanna get to that one week some day, hopefully by the time the next generation is here. I always think about that.

Navajos Are Tŝilhqot'ins Too

Elder Martin Quilt xinli, Xeni Gwet'in

Tŝilhqot'ins, they go as far as Bella Coola.

Prince Rupert, I see a lotta skulls down there. Prince Rupert in that Museum. Human skulls. Some of them got bashed in. I guess there were wars long time ago.

I saw a hot spring down there too. Before you get to Kitimat, right there before the mountain. Lotsa hot water! [laughs]

I think Navajos are Tŝilhqot'ins too. They talk our language.

Right around Calgary, there's some Dogrib Indians Reserve. They speak like us.

Crazy Horse down in the States. "Tŝilhqot'ins are my best friends." Another Warrior that died.

We were on the warpath. We went down south, maybe at the Navajos. Chilkoo-tins. They burnt down Fort Vancouver too.

Even people from Yukon, they speak our language. Tlingit Indians.[1]

CHAPTER 7 ENDNOTE

1   Elder Martin Quilt xinli's poem is a statement of Dene linguistic nationalism. All of the Indigenous languages mentioned are from the Na-Dene family, with Diné bizaad (or Naabeehó bizaad, the Navajo language) being both the southernmost language in the group and the most widely spoken, with over 170,000 fluent speakers. Linguists theorize that Lingít (Tlingit) solely occupies one branch of this family, while Tŝilhqot'in, Tłįchǫ (Dogrib), Nuxalk (Bella Coola), and Diné bizaad are among the languages constituting the other, much wider branch, called Athabaskan–Eyak. From Elder Martin Quilt xinli's Tŝilhqot'in point of view, and with a strong dash of whimsy, everyone speaks Tŝilhqot'in! On a more serious note, the Chiefs' visit to Naabeehó Bináhásdzo the Navajo Nation marked a stage in the development of a Nation perspective in the Tŝilhqot'in, as the six communities worked towards the formation of what became the Tŝilhqot'in National Government (TNG).

hizbay. Photo by Chief Roger William

ayus wild horses, Lhizbay. Photo by Chief Roger William

Chief Roger's birthplace, Naghataneqed. Photo by Chief Roger William

Xeni yeqox Nemiah Creek. Photo by Chief Roger William

Lha yudit'ih We Always Find a Way

Ŝilhqox Biny Chilko Lake. Photo by Chief Roger William

ld-time equipment, Xeni. Photo by Chief Roger William

Qayus wild horses in the snow. Photo by Chief Roger William

Riding in winter, Xeni. Photo by Chief Roger William

Lha yudit'ih We Always Find a Way

David Setah in the lead, with Chief Roger second, Tŝideldel mountainrace. Photo by Shannon Stump

Mountainracing in Xeni: Roger riding Nilin through the creek. Photo by Shannon Stump

Lha yudit'ih We Always Find a Way

Roger in the lead riding Nilin at the Williams Lake Stampede mountainrace.
Photo by Laureen Carruthers

Lha yudit'ih We Always Find a Way

Logyard, Williams Lake. Photo by Sage Birchwater

Henry's Crossing Roadblock, 1992. Archival photo, Xeni Gwet'in First Nation.
Courtesy of Chief Roger William

A transcribed version of the Nenduwh Jid Guẑit'in Declaration can be found on pp. 144–145.

Elder Eileen Sammy William on the left with her sister Elder Helena Myers xinli, singing a prayer song. Photo by Chief Roger William

Elder Eileen Sammy William tanning a hide. Photo by Susie Lulua

Ivor Deneway Myers xinli (Yuneŝit'in), Knowledge Holder, Nits'il?in, and councillor. Photo by Chief Roger William

Lha yudit'ih We Always Find a Way

Teẑtan Biny Fish Lake. Photo by Jesaja Class

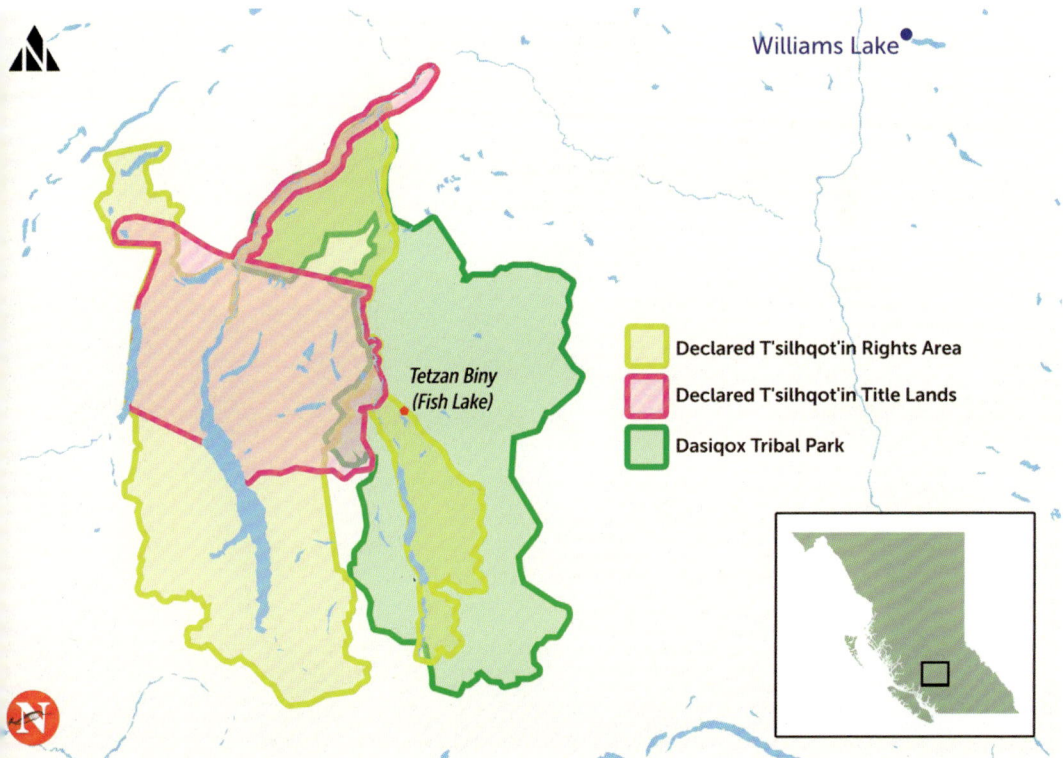

Williams Lake

Tetzan Biny
(Fish Lake)

Declared T'silhqot'in Rights Area

Declared T'silhqot'in Title Lands

Dasiqox Tribal Park

Map of Teẑtan Biny Fish Lake in context. Courtesy of Carol Linnitt / The Narwhal

Ceremony at Teẑtan Biny with Chief Roger in foreground and drummers including, from left, Peyal Laceese and Cecil Grinder. Photo by Jesaja Class

Tŝilhqox Biny Chilko Lake, looking toward Nuy chugh. Photo by Chief Roger William

ʾŜilhqox Biny looking toward Tutl'az Franklin Arm and Bute Inlet. Photo by Lorraine Weir

n the foreground, ʔEnes Biny, looking toward Chunoẑ Ch'ed Potato Mountain.
Photo by Chief Roger William

Looking southwest toward Tŝilhqox Biny Chilko Lake. Photo by Chief Roger William

Xeni Biny Konni Lake and the road home. Photo by Chief Roger William

Lha yudit'ih We Always Find a Way

"Tears of the earth." Looking toward Xeni after the 2017 wildfire. Photo by Jesaja Class

Memorial made by Lloyd Myers (Yuneŝit'in) for ten wild horses caught in the 2017 wildfire. Photo by Chief Roger William

The Elders on the way to Ottawa. First row from left: Dave Lulua, Juliana Lulua, Christine Cooper xinli, Minnie Charleyboy, and Delia William. Back row from left: Annie C. Williams, Norman George Setah xinli, Ubill Lulua xinli, David Setah, Chief Roger William, and Gilbert Solomon. Photo by Jeremy Williams

On the steps of the Supreme Court of Canada, November 7, 2013. From left, Loretta Williams, Patrick Lulua, Geri Elkins, Joyce Charleyboy, Chio Setah Alphonse, Jasmine Quilt, Peyal Laceese, Chief Roger William, and Cecil Grinder. Photo by Jeremy Williams

Drumsong on the steps of the Supreme Court of Canada, November 7, 2013. From the left, Patrick Lulua, Loretta Williams, Joyce Charleyboy, Peyal Laceese, Chief Roger William, and Cecil Grinder. Photo by Jeremy Williams

From the left, Nicole Schabus, Jay Nelson, Ardith Walkem, KC, Chief Judy Wilson, Chief Roger William, David M. Rosenberg, KC, Louise Mandell, KC, and Chief Wayne Christian. Supreme Court of Canada, November 7, 2013. Courtesy of Thompson Rivers University

Lha yudit'ih We Always Find a Way

O

Chief Roger's drum at the base of Tŝ'ilʔos, the southern boundary of Title Land.
Photo by Chief Roger William

Chief Roger holds up his drum on Orange Shirt Day, Williams Lake, September 30, 2022.
Photo by Chief Roger William

The Title Case: From the Trial to the Appeal (2002–2012)

Deʔayen
We will sing a song for the Land

—ELDER PATRICIA GUICHON XINLI (Tŝideldel)
William v. British Columbia, Proceedings at Trial, May 11, 2005

What's More Perfect for a Title Case?

Chief Roger William

After we agreed with the Declaration of 1989, there was no turning back, because if you make a Declaration and go to Vancouver and go on TV and say this is what it is, and then you go home and you don't back it up, you'll embarrass yourself, and you'll turn away all of your people. Your children will be angry because the leaders and the people were lying. We never said, "This is the way it will be," or they would've been like, "Who do you think you are? You're no better than us." I was raised to do the best thing. The Councillors that I was with were raised to do the best thing. And we wanted to make the best picture we could, so that at the end of the day, if something went sideways, nobody could say that we lied to them or hid anything from them. That was our worry. But our people had a pretty clear picture of what they were voting on, and I think that was what was really strong. I think everything we did was owned by the people and we all made that picture together. We felt we had no other choice but to file the Title case. We'd run out of options.

We'd put a lot of energy into trying to consult and plan, but we were realizing that the Ministry of Forests was gonna find a way to get the beetle timber out whether we liked it or not. That was the bottom line. The negotiations were running out of time, and they were frustrated. We'd tried everything we could, but when I did my monthly update with the Tŝilhqot'in Chiefs at TNG, they questioned why they should support Xeni Gwet'in in a Title case when they felt that it should be a Tŝilhqot'in Title case. I understood their concern and reminded them of my monthly updates, and that when we'd tried to bend to the Ministry's rules, our people had turned the proposal down. It was the Ministry's way or the highway, and it had always been that way. The Chiefs had seen the Declaration as a divide, an attempt by us to separate from the other five Tŝilhqot'in communities in the TNG, and they saw the Title case as the next step in that process of separation. We insisted that we were protecting our interests and our caretaker area inside the Tŝilhqot'in, but that didn't mean that they couldn't hunt or fish in our area just as we did in theirs. We knew full well that, as a Band, we would be shot down really fast by BC and Canada because no judge would agree with a Band proving Title. That was clear from the *Delgamuukw v. British Columbia* decision, which had come down from the Supreme Court of Canada during the previous year, and also from other First Nations cases. Jack Woodward had done his analysis and knew what the arguments of the federal and provincial governments were going to be. When our people turned down logging in the Brittany Triangle, it left a bad taste for some Tŝilhqot'in communities, because Tsilhqot'in Forest Products, a company which we all owned, was going to log 250,000 cubic metres a year for five years in the Brittany Triangle. Suddenly that was gone, and yet we were asking for their support.

There was a process with the Chiefs and I would have said the same thing they did: Why should we take *your* case on? Why don't we do a Tŝilhqot'in Nation case? Some of our leaders were struggling with supporting it, so we hired Geraldine Charleyboy, a Tŝideldel member who knows the language and is skilled at recording and videotaping interviews. We wanted her to interview the Elders in Tŝilhqot'in, asking them why they wanted to go to court to support Aboriginal Title, and why they wanted to take this Title case on. She made a video out of these responses, and we showed it to the Chiefs at a TNG meeting and said we wanted to show the video at a General Assembly in each of the communities. After much discussion, the Chiefs agreed to our showing the video in their communities and discussing it afterward. That was what got the rest of the Tŝilhqot'in Elders and people on side. Their Chiefs and Councillors had no choice but to support us. Ninety percent of the Tŝilhqot'in agreed with Xeni to take the Title case on in this area. We had consultations with our Tŝilhqot'in National Government, the Chiefs, the Elders, the members, and all the communities, and they all agreed that we should go ahead with the Title case. The Chiefs signed the BCR [Band Council Resolution] supporting our court case.

Some influential people and leaders supported the Title case from the beginning, including former Yuneŝit'in Chief the late Tony Myers, who strongly supported us. Chief Francis Laceese (Tl'esqox) was also in complete support, because he and his community were doing direct action and roadblocks during that time too. However, a couple of Chiefs needed convincing, because the case was big and we had a lot of obstacles. They wanted TNG to take the case on, and I refused. Our court case would never have got off the ground if TNG had taken over, but our Director and later Tribal Chair, Chief Joe Alphonse (Tl'etinqox), played a big part in ensuring that there was support for the Title case, because he knew that this was the way to go. He totally supported what I was doing as a Chief and as a Director, and he would back me up when there were struggles in Chiefs' meetings, knowing that one or two of the leaders might want to take him out as a director because of this. That's how much Joe believed in the Title case. Today he is a very influential, well-spoken Chief. He worked with Fisheries, way back, to start the TNG Fisheries Agreement with the Department of Fisheries and Oceans. To me, Chief Joe made a difference when he got the Chiefs to sign a letter saying they supported Xeni Gwet'in taking on the Title case. Because of that letter, Canada and BC weren't able to knock out the case from the beginning.

We had seen many cases, and we looked at different legal arguments that BC and Canada would make. We have elections every two years, and one argument we expected from them was what would happen if a new Chief and Council got in and didn't want to take on the case? The judge might agree with them, so we used my name, saying, "I'm a Chief right now, but I'm a Xeni Gwet'in, I'm a Tŝilhqot'in person," and if another Tŝilhqot'in person, Band, or the Nation didn't agree with what I was doing, they could sue me and take *me* to court. The Chiefs signed and agreed to file the case in my name, because that was the best process available at that time. That was a struggle because, ideally, you want to put a Tŝilhqot'in Title case forward looking at the whole Territory, but we were looking at maybe 60 to 70 percent of the Xeni Gwet'in Caretaker Area. We were able to move forward with this case, calling it the William case, but really it's a Tŝilhqot'in Nation case just using my name.

We filed the William case in '98, and by the time we got going, it was 2002. We were going to court. The Chiefs have stood behind us since then and are still behind the case today [2013]. During the five years in court, we had Tŝilhqot'in Elders and leaders from all six Tŝilhqot'in communities testify, and we had expert witnesses from around the province who had done any work in the Tŝilhqot'in like foresters, anthropologists, archeologists, and ethnobotanists. At the end of the day, here you've got a community with no Hydro, no logging, still preserving the traditional way, and you have Elders who don't understand English, so what's more perfect for a Title case than that little area?

Stories in Court

Chief Roger William

Court Session in Nemaiah, Carolyn Enid Sadowska.
Collection of David M. Robbins[1]

Before contact, that's oral history. You were taught the same legends and stories. In court when an Elder spoke, it would be word for word almost in terms of one Elder to the next. That's what our people say. In a story, an Elder might introduce something new because they're elaborating and trying to explain and teach. Their level of understanding of English might be a factor too, and when a story is translated into English in court, it might be a little different in Tŝilh-qot'in. Since some of our Elders don't speak English, we had to have translators in court, and that made it tricky. A lawyer would ask a question, the translator would ask the Elder, and the Elder's response was translated back to the lawyer. It went back and forth like that.

Like a lotta First Nations, we have legends that have to be told at night – creation stories where all the animals, the birds, and the fish spoke Tŝilhqot'in, and some of our people were turned into stone – so there were court sessions at night because the Elders wouldn't tell these legends during the day. One of our Elders, Francis Setah xinli, testified in Nemiah at our school, and that was historic. The Elders from our community and other communities came to hear him testify, and they knew what he was saying, but the judge and the lawyers needed a translator! It was like a celebration to have the Supreme Court of BC and our Aboriginal Title case in our own community.

During Examination for Discovery, I came to Vancouver once a week for four weeks and was asked a lot of questions about Xeni and about Tŝilhqot'in by the lawyers from Canada and BC. But they never really used that against me or the Elders at all. One day in court, one lawyer asked me a question, and I thought about it, and I answered the question. The other lawyer looked at the Examination for Discovery answer of mine and what I'd just said to the judge, and it was word for word the same. When that lawyer found out that my answer was word for word almost the same in the Examination for Discovery in 2002 and that day in court in 2003, I think they just backed off and said, "Okay, we're wasting our time here." Our Elders had said, "Don't worry about making mistakes. Tell the truth. Come from your heart. If it comes from your heart, you don't need to remember anything. You *know* it."

No Turning Back

Chief Roger William

Even during the trial, there were General Assemblies, Council meetings, news-letters, updates, Chiefs' meetings, Nation assemblies. Our members had to keep on backing up why we were going to court, because there were probably parties and gatherings where other Tŝilhqot'ins were like, "What're you guys doing? *We're* making money." I'm pretty sure if an Elder asked me what we were protecting the skinny trees for, they probably said that to a lotta members! But there was no turning back once we filed the Title case, and I think that's what kept us together. We never said this year we're gonna do this; next year we're gonna do that. It just fell into place because we were looking at everything. I never said we're gonna stop logging, we're gonna stop mining. I said what do you guys want to do? This is what it is, this is what's gonna happen. How are we gonna decide this? This is an Aboriginal Rights and Title issue. Chief and Council communicate for you, and we're gonna try to get the best agreement we can get and bring it back to you, and you're gonna tell us what you want. Then we'll talk to other First Nations, and to lawyers and environmentalists. Then we're gonna come back with that information, and you're gonna tell us your beliefs, your issues, your concerns. And then we're gonna question those too, and you're gonna question us. This isn't about what Roger wants, it's about what the community decides.

If I had said, "This is the way it is," some people would have had more reason to go against me, go behind my back, phone off reserve and visit their family and say, "This is what Roger's saying ... This is what Chief and Council are saying." And that would have been enough to throw everything off. But we weren't saying that. We were questioning them, asking them is this what *you* want? We're gonna fight – if you want yes, if you want no, we're gonna fight. If they said yes in a vote and believed in yes, but the majority said no, then they had to go out there and say, yeah, I'm good with that. I don't have a problem with that. That's a lot of pressure. You know, our kids go to school out there, they go to town eventually, and then they drink, they play baseball and hockey, and I'm sure they deal with other kids whose families are logging, and they really believe in it. Maybe they get into a fight over it once in a while or an argument. I knew what I wanted, but I also knew that we're healing.

The next step was money. BC and Canada were arguing every little statement that we made. When that happens, you start spending and wasting money, right. So a lot of times, First Nations run out of money and their case is gone so they can't go to court. We fundraised with the help of organizations like the Western Canada Wilderness Committee, Friends of Nemiah Valley, the David Suzuki Foundation, and the Lannan Foundation in the US. The Assembly of First Nations helped us out with funding to argue court-case costs. We argued that it wasn't us that wanted to log the Brittany Triangle. First we put the Trapline case in because they wanted to harvest. Then we put the Title case in, saying that we'd tried to put a plan in place but their legislation and policies had left us with no choice. Our argument was that BC and Canada had to pay court-case costs because it was their actions that had made the case necessary. Then we won our court-case costs, and that was a big victory. We thought okay, BC and Canada, you can argue all you want! If you wanna pick on every little thing, you can pay for it! Then they had to sharpen their pencils and make reasonable arguments, because they were paying for it.

Throughout this whole time, we had one law firm. We stayed with Jack Woodward, who started Woodward and Company. We fundraised together. We went hunting, we did everything together to keep moving forward. When the court-case costs decision came down, we only got 50 percent to pay legal fees for the lawyers, but the Court paid 100 percent for preparation of our witnesses, which meant the lawyers talking with our Elders and expert witnesses and different leaders, as well as their travel costs. When the witnesses had to go to court in Victoria, Canada had to pay for their travel, accommodation expenses, and food. So that was a really big win. Meanwhile, our lawyer was only getting 50 percent at the same time as lawyers for BC and Canada were getting 100 percent, but we still moved forward. Throughout the five years of the court case, BC and Canada kept bringing costs back to the table and trying to get rid of them. Every once in a while, when we were putting evidence forward, they'd return to their arguments that we shouldn't get court-case costs, and they had all sorts of crazy reasons why, but they kept losing. At one point, we were getting 80 percent of our lawyer's fee paid, because they kept bringing the argument back to the table and we argued even more. Sometimes they had to think twice before they brought back the court costs argument! You should've heard the arguments between 1998 and 2002 while we were trying to get court-case costs and stay in court, because they were trying to throw us out, saying we were the wrong people, Roger was not the right person, it should have been the Nation, or whatever they were trying to argue. They tried all that during those years, and we did our homework, because a lotta First Nations out there tried.

Delgamuukw[2] laid out a map of how you can get Title, and it was crucial to our case. When that decision came down on December 11, 1997, First Nations were able to offer oral history evidence in court for the first time. Before that, you needed to find experts like anthropologists and archeologists to bring forward evidence of occupation before contact. *Delgamuukw* paved the way for the Court's acceptance of 1846, the date of the Oregon Boundary Treaty [as the date of British sovereignty assertion in British Columbia] and for oral history evidence.[3] *Delgamuukw* also changed how governments and companies dealt with First Nations. Consultation was really unheard of when I was first in leadership. *Delgamuukw* established a six-year limitation for the filing of Title case writs, and the cut-off date for First Nations to file was December 11, 2003. We had filed the Trapline case in 1998 and were two years in to our trial by the time of that cut-off date.

As Xeni Gwet'ins, Tŝilhqot'ins, we thank the Gitxsan and Wet'suwet'en. We thank First Nations across BC and Canada for being able to be in the place we're in today, because if they hadn't gone to BC Treaty [Commission], to court, to lobby, and to roadblock, I don't think we'd be where we are now. We've also got many non–First Nations to thank too, people who talked to their government representatives and others about the need to settle the Land question, about First Nations having Title and Rights, and not denying us anymore. There's a lot of non–First Nations out there who really feel it's gotta be dealt with and that we do have Rights and Title that can't be denied, and it's crazy to continue with denial today.

When we began the Title case, our Elders said, "When you're telling the truth, there's no reason to be scared to be in front of a judge and a lawyer." On TV you see lawyers asking fancy questions, trying to trip somebody up, and then if you lose, you're in jail forever. Our Elders said, "Don't worry about that. Tell the truth. They can't trick you if you tell the truth. If you lie, oh yeah, they'll trick you. If you tell the lawyer or the judge a lie, you aren't gonna last too long. They're gonna trick you because they're smart. But if you tell the truth, they can't trick you. If you tell the truth, you're gonna win. If you don't win, then that whole system is screwed up and they're wrong." That's what the Elders were telling us, not only in Xeni but in the Tŝilhqot'in.

Getting the Land Back

David Setah, Xeni Gwet'in

When I ran for Councillor in June 1993, the first thing I talked about in my election campaign was that I wanted to get the Land back. It seemed back then like it's just right there, it shouldn't be that hard to get. But next thing I knew is that we were filing the court case, and that was quite a while later. We're still [2014] talking about getting Title of the Land back, getting it recognized and all that.

I worked for my Band for seven years, then two years as a manager of Stone Indian Band (Yuneŝit'in), and then I became a Councillor in June 1993. I had a lotta experience under me. As Councillors, we always had to leave a good paper trail on whatever we did and at every meeting we went to, we always had a notebook in front of us, and we'd write down what we talked about, what we disagreed or agreed on, and the reasons why. That's probably the smartest thing we ever did. We made sure we went to the meetings, and we came back with the notes. We let the people know what was going on.

Even before I got into leadership, I was frustrated with their court system. I remember when Annie C. Williams was Chief and she wanted to try to get the Land back. She was telling us the judge and the courts are saying we have to prove it. And all of us are sitting there – What? We're the First People here. Everybody knows that. Why do *we* have to prove it? They're the ones who came into our area. After a while, you think that it's only the government that's ignorant, but the first time you go into court, they tell you you've gotta prove it too.

From *Tsilhqot'in Nation v. British Columbia*, 2007 BCSC 1700 (Where Justice Vickers Agrees with David Setah)

[1373] I confess that early in this trial, perhaps in a moment of self pity, I looked out at the legions of counsel and asked if someone would soon be standing up to admit that Tsilhqot'in people had been in the Claim Area for over 200 years, leaving the real question to be answered. My view at this early stage of the trial was that the real question concerned the consequences that would follow such an admission. I was assured that it was necessary to continue the course we were set upon. My view has not been altered since I first raised the issue almost five years ago.

[1374] At the end of the trial, a concession concerning an Aboriginal hunting and trapping right in the Claim Area was made by both defendants. As I have already noted, that concession brings with it an admission of the presence of Tsilhqot'in people in the Claim Area for over 200 years.

Court

David Setah, Xeni Gwet'in

Court is kind of an interesting place. I knew from the first day we went into court that eventually we were gonna go to the Supreme Court of Canada before we got anything. I always kept thinking the thief judging his own theft, but I didn't really want to believe it. I was brought up hearing that all the time, and when people tried to go to court, you'd always wonder what that is. Does the government control the courts and how things go?[4]

It frustrated me back then, but I knew we had to keep trying. We had to take every little step, 'cause if we went to the first court and didn't like what we heard, then we'd say, "Nah, BC ain't gonna do nothing for us, so let's go to Supreme Court of Canada right away!" But I knew that if we did that, we'd be setting ourselves up, and the judges would say, "How would you guys know the

Supreme Court of BC wasn't gonna work for you?" I knew we had to go through all that stuff to make sure we covered all the bases.

We tried everything to challenge them to put us in court. Prior to this case, we had our members making house logs off the reserve. Forestry came and they noticed it, and they were telling me, "One of your members is making house logs on Crown land." I told him, "I think it's all right to go out there on our Traditional Territory, and using it for hunting and making shelter for ourselves is tradition. So we'll do that." They kept humming and hawing that we should fill out a permit and pay a fee, and I said, "Well, if you guys want to make a big issue of it, put us in court. Challenge us. We'll challenge you." I thought we had every right to do that. It only went two hearings. They didn't really want to challenge us, so from there on we knew that we couldn't get them to bring us to court. After that we were thinking maybe we have to file this case, and that's what happened. It was a long process.

The first time we filed the case, the lawyers set a meeting with us right away – me, Roger, and Robin [Lulua] – and they sat us down and told us, "Yeah, you got our attention. We're hoping we can sit down with you guys today instead of going through all these long processes of the court case. It's gonna cost you guys lots of money. It's gonna cost us lots of money. Let's settle outta court." That's what they asked us the first time. And me and Roger and Robin looked at each other, and we all had experience with that government. We tried to settle a lotta things in our way, but every agreement they brought in front of us was always tilted more towards them. We tried to negotiate to level it out, and then we always got the same response. But when you're going into agreements and the government's saying, "No! We've got 55 percent. You guys have got 45" – I mean automatically we know that's not gonna work. So we always talked to the government about giving us a level playing field. If you guys wanna talk about what you want to do on our Land, give us the same experts you've got that we pay for. Then they can look at your work and tell us where you guys are going wrong. We always ask for that.

Testifying

David Setah, Xeni Gwet'in

I can't remember all of my days. I wish I was as good as Roger knowing how many days I testified and how many I was cross-examined! I'd been told way before that I was gonna be in it, 'cause the court case was on forestry, and I held the portfolio from day one. Before I went in, I made a lot of visits to the testimony of a lot of the witnesses that went before me. I sat there and I listened. I did our work back home, and Roger was out there doing the big battles with the courts. I remember one of the opposition lawyers was asking what witnesses were coming next, and he said, "David Setah? Can we put 'em back a little further, 'cause I've got two weeks of cross-examination for 'em?" That's without giving any affidavit or anything! That kinda worried me, but I kept thinking maybe it's just like a test or like the horror stories about courts on TV and movies.[5] They try to get you mixed up. That worried me lots. I mean, thinking I was back in high school again, I had all my notebooks out, all the agreements we'd signed, everything, going over each one of them, making sure I remembered all of it, 'cause I was really scared that they were gonna do a trick cross-examination of me where I tell a different story than the last time. I was worried about that.

I remember going to Victoria the first time, knowing I was gonna tell my story to my lawyers. Yeah, I was afraid. When I started giving evidence, things got slower and slower, and I was always kinda worried about the cross-examination stage. I knew everything I knew, but I was worried from day one when we filed it in court and we were telling our people, "You guys are gonna have to tell your story. They're talking to the Elders, and after you tell their stories, the opposition lawyers are gonna go there and they're gonna look at it and they're gonna check to see if you're lying, or they're gonna trick you, [saying] that you're not tellin' the truth." I remember one Elder stood up, Henry Solomon xinli – the storyteller we call him. He was always sitting around and telling stories. And he got up and he told us, "If you go out there and you go to the courts – whatever you talk about, talk about the truth." He said, "Don't put any lies into it or anything, or don't make it bigger than what it is. Just tell the truth." He said, "Once you tell the truth, when they cross-examine you, then everything you said is the truth. What are you worried about? 'Cause all you talked about was the truth." When he said that, then everybody else felt at ease. Yes. Like everything else is the movies we've seen about the courts! [laughs]

As I was giving evidence, I was always worried about cross-examination, but I think what helped me is that I had respect even for the opposition lawyers. I knew they weren't put there for nothing – I respected 'em. They're people that really know their stuff. Thinking I gotta respect them as who they are. That is what really helped me out. The way I look at it is, when you stop respecting people, that could go against you. Knowing you respect 'em, you gotta be at the top of your game. With these guys, then, I think that's what helped me out quite a bit.

The other thing that helped me out quite a bit happened before the court case. I lost my mom. In a way she knew that I was really worried about the cross-examination, about the court process. On my third day, after I gave evidence, I was really tired. I went back to the room, and I just laid down. I was asleep, and I dunno if it was still a dream or it actually did happen, but I dreamt I woke up. Something woke me up. Sometimes your sixth sense kicks in when you're lying there. Something's not right and you wake up. You know someone is watching you, and you wake up. I was dreaming I was facing the other way in the room, and I pushed my upper body up, and I looked around. I knew something was watching me, and I kinda turned around, and I could see Mom standing there. I was looking at her and telling her, "Mom, you're dead. I know you're dead. What're you doing here?" I was thinking out loud, looking at her and I said, "Aw, well!" And I got up and walked over there and held her for quite a while. Then I went back to bed, and I went back to sleep. It's hard for me to know was I dreaming or did it happen?

After that, everything seemed to be okay. Like everything was really easy for me, giving the rest of my evidence, and then when the cross-examination was coming, I wasn't afraid. I just let them come, and then they cross-examined me, and I didn't get startled by anything, I didn't get alarmed by anything, or when I had trouble answering something, I slowed everything down within myself and thought about the question, got it clarified a bit more, and then I answered. I kept that process all the way through, and to tell you the truth, it was actually pretty easy!

Divide and Conquer

David Setah, Xeni Gwet'in

Judge Vickers was really good, and we're really lucky we landed 'em first. If we'd had somebody else, maybe the outcome would've been different. But I'm glad we had him, 'cause he took it to heart and he didn't discriminate against us. He was a really open person, he really tried hard to understand both sides of things, and if there was any evidence that had already been given before us and they were asking me the same thing, he cut it off and said no. But they always tried to divide and conquer. From day one, we've always had it in our Nation or in any other [First] Nation, if certain people don't agree, they just throw out a bit of money. Then some people agree and some people will still be against it. From day one, it's always been there. The lawyers tried it. When I was in court, they were saying, "And what you're talking about is Nemiah Land? Nemiah Title Land?" I told 'em, "No." I told 'em, "Tŝilhqot'in Land, it's always gonna be under the Nation. We always explain where every Band is situated right now, in case anybody else is coming into our area. That's why those places are where they are." And telling 'em, "We're just caretakers of this area." We know when we can do anything within the Tŝilhqot'in Land if it's agreed upon by those people. They're in our Nation, but they live in different communities. We always understood that, and here they're trying to tell us, "Oh, you guys are only going after Xeni Gwet'in Land, that's all you guys have got." There's six of us [communities], and we've always known it as Tŝilhqot'in Land, and it will always remain Tŝilhqot'in Land. Every Elder said the same thing. They always look to divide and conquer, you know.

I remember one question that was brought up to me is the issues between a caretaking area and the whole Nation area. They were asking me questions like "What do you guys deal with at the community level? What do you guys deal with as a Nation?" Out of the blue, they asked me, "What is the Nation issue right now?" And I told 'em about the logging – the Brittany Lake Forest Management Plan. We brought that back to the people. And the other one is mining. Taseko Mines Limited. Fish Lake, that's a Nation issue, and we had to bring that to the Nation table. I can't remember what the third one was, but there was another one. Anyways, we brought all that up, and the lawyers praised me and Roger about that. They said, "Roger was asked the same question. Maybe we didn't put it in the same format, but you guys named exactly the same things, and it wasn't rehearsed." So that was a good thing there.

I remember some of the first things about the court case. They asked me, "Why are you here giving evidence? What's the most important thing you want to get out of it?" And I told 'em, to get the Land back. The other question they asked me is, "Why would you want the Land back?" And I explained to them about all the struggles my people have gone through from way back to now. And I told 'em, "If that land was my Land, if it was under our Title, that would give our people hope for the future, 'cause right now we don't have it. We're kept at bay for a lot of things, but our people need that hope. Once you've got Title and Rights, the people have a future to look towards, and then they're gonna try hard. They know what they have to do to make sure our future is always still there once they know it's in their hands."

One of the other things they talked about was a newspaper clipping. One of the past leaders was talking about "Why should we go to court in Canada? Why should we let the thief judge their own theft?" And that leader was saying we should go to the UN and they were asking me about that. I gave 'em the same explanation, that I know we have to start where we have to start right now. I know we have to try everything with anybody that tries things with us and see where they're willing to bring us and see what they're gonna do on our Land. And if there are some things we don't like, maybe we can ask 'em to change it so we can come to what we like. If that doesn't work, we'll just keep trying, and if they don't want to look at it our way, then we'll just tell 'em, "No thanks, because it's gonna take too much away, or you guys are gonna wreck too many of our Rights. This plan ain't gonna work for us."

I told 'em, "That's the same way I see law courts. I know this is the lowest court right now. I know we have to go to BC Supreme [Court] and [Supreme Court of] Canada. I know those are there." And I also told 'em, "I've been told about what the thoughts of a lotta other leaders are about this court." I just told the judge, "People bring a dispute to this courtroom. If somebody did something wrong to them, they'll bring it here and the outcome should be the right thing, where that person gets justice. That's the same thing we expect to gain when we come to this court." We heard about that passage in the judgment where even a decision that's made is interpreted the wrong way," and I told 'em, "That's what's wrong with you guys' English, is that people can interpret it many different ways. Maybe that battle has to happen so you can make the interpretation right. One thing I know is that this place has to do the right thing. We were here first. We own the Land. The court has to do the right thing. I believe my past leaders, 'cause they've been fighting this battle a long time, and eventually we should go to the UN. I know we have to try every court, like it or not, or it's gonna cost us, 'cause once we get to Supreme [Court of Canada], they could easily ask us what we might've been asked if we were fighting the Prosperity Mine. Even though the mine is not gonna work for us, one thing we can't do is say, "No! We don't like you guys!" Without seeing any of their plans or anything, we say no and we chase 'em away. You gotta really look at the consequences when you do things like that. All a judge will do is just sit down and say, "How would you guys know if it was gonna work or not, 'cause you didn't even meet with them, didn't even try to see different things on how you want it. How would you guys know whether they were gonna say yes or no?" So they'll easily go against us. That's why we've gotta try.

We've still gotta look at every new plan they come up with again and say, "No! It's still not gonna work." And we make sure we document everything. We always had that attitude, that "Yeah, we'll work with them. If they can do it our way. Yes, it'd be nice, but if they can't, we'll ask 'em to leave. It's not gonna work." Our environment is the biggest thing and we make sure we protect everything of the environment. That's the foundation.

Proving That We Were Here First

Marilyn Baptiste, Xeni Gwet'in[6]

The way the Title case went to court, BC and the licensee weren't proving that they had the Rights to our Land and water. Instead it was the other way around, and as our people and our Elders said right from day one, they shouldn't have had to prove that we were here first. But they went through the process and they did their job and they did it well and the result is Title. If Justice Vickers could have sat for another three to five hundred days, then he would've had no choice but to declare Title for the whole court case area ... Our people did not agree that we should have to prove we were here, that we are Tŝilhqot'in, and that we are a part of this Land.

We as Tŝilhqot'in people never gave up our Rights or our Title to our Territory and that's the way it remains to this day. We never ever agreed that we should have to go into court and prove that we were here before the Europeans entered our Territory. Why would anybody in *any* legal process do that? Why did the lawyers take it forward in that way? That was one of the biggest concerns and questions, because we all know we didn't give up our Rights and our Title. If the lawyers had brought the case in a different form, it would have challenged BC to prove that *they* were here and that *they* purchased our Land. They never did. The non–First Nations in BC did *not* enter into treaty, and there were only two that I'm aware of [in 2015] – Treaty 8 in the Northeast and then down on [Vancouver] Island are the Douglas Treaties. I don't know that the lawyers even explored that kind of argument.

Justice David Vickers (1934–2009)

Gilbert Solomon, Xeni Gwet'in

I could feel his spirit getting "Yeah, that's what I'm talkin' about." He had a really open mind, a good heart. 'Cause we pray to the spirits, we help heal people that we're talking to, whether it's lawyers on the other side, the judge, or anything that's on the other side, we predict them. We practised feeling that who we think is our enemy is not our enemy. So if I thought that you were my enemy, then I forgive you, I honour you, 'cause we all have [spirits] teaching us how to unite and come together as people of Earth, all the people, and how they could awaken us in this way. We said, "No, we don't demand these things."

[laughs] They just check us, and in a way we need that, you know. We don't go there. If we honour them, they'll learn how to honour everything else around them – Earth, their life.

Talking to the Court

Elder Marvin William xinli, Xeni Gwet'in

So we speak Tŝilhqot'in all the time.

"We speak *English*!" [laughing]

Sometime some Indian people go round.

They talk to 'em.

Mixing Up Place Names

Gilbert Solomon, Xeni Gwet'in

I was talkin' to Ubill Hunlin xinli. He said the lawyers were tryin' to mix me up, tryin' to make me convinced that this place that I was talkin' about was named such and such, and I kinda like, "No, this is what it's named. I can't change that name. I can't change Naghataneqed and put it over here and call this Nagha-taneqed right here." You know. Call Lhizbay over there.

Questions

Maryann Solomon, Xeni Gwet'in

Elders, you can't just ask them questions in meetings, you know, or coach them. They [won't] share anything with you. There are some that are outspoken. Like my dad [Elder Henry Solomon xinli] would stand up and speak up, you know.

   I went down, I think, once or twice with the Elders, just to go in the court and listen. Some people can't afford to go to Victoria. It was nice to get out of the community, you know. I think a lot of the Elders who were informed beforehand wanted to go down. I remember, at the Elders' meetings, they told them, "This is what's happening: we're planning to go to Victoria for the court case and we're going down." But I know it was frustrating for some of them because of how the lawyers were in the court case. You know, they said, "Oh, they keep asking me the same question over and over." Sometimes the question's a little bit different, but it's almost the same and they didn't realize [the significance]. So they were getting frustrated. I guess that's how the process is, I dunno.

I think it was very traumatizing for them, because they're not used to that kind of "give me, give me," you know, at that level. And there's people out there watching. I would feel the same way. Everybody's watching you. And they keep repeating all the time. Probably some of them were getting tired. They can't take sitting all day, talking, answering questions.

When the Elders first went down, they weren't really sure what was happening. Like whether they'd go for logging or against it. 'Cause they didn't have direction, you know. "If we do this, what's gonna happen? We'll go for it but, oh, do we get lots of money or…?" Some people came in and stood up and let the people know: "This is what's gonna happen if you go and do the wrong thing.[7] You're gonna lose everything." Like clearcut logging. There's all the animals out there, all the birds. We have to cut wood for the stove, and nowadays you have to go further out. It's a lot of work for the winter.

In the Country

Gilbert Solomon, Xeni Gwet'in

If you ask the Elders over and over, they'll get like, "Whoa! Why do you keep tellin' me the same whatever? Heard it already, and you don' need to keep tellin' me." You know, like make 'em feel stupid or whatever. They'll get defensive. They'd be like that to you. Like if you mention something that they already understood, they'll say you don' need to keep bringin' it up. Kind of makes them feel bad. In their home, over there in the country, you can't be goin' like that, you know. [laughs] "Didn't I just tell you?"

Elder Minnie Charleyboy

Joyce Charleyboy, Tŝideldel

She [grandmother Emily Ekks] wouldn't get interviewed [for the court case], and I know why not. I had gone back to her a number of times and said you need to be part of this. "No, not doing it." She said, "It's good that it's happening," but nobody would do it, nobody would translate, nobody – they were all kinda standin' back. And I get a call from Gary Campo and he says, "Joyce, I've never met you, but somebody gave me your name and number, and if you're available, I'm your mom's lawyer." And I'm thinking, "What?" [laughter] And he said, "I'll call you back tomorrow morning. I'll be in Redstone tomorrow. I'll call you." And I'm thinking what the heck? And so I phone my sisters and I said, "What the hell did you guys do to Mum [Minnie Charleyboy] that she's got a lawyer?" [laughter] And they're all kind of like, "What?" And he didn't say he was affiliated with Woodward and Company. He just said he was Mum's lawyer. Well, okay, what the heck! Somebody did somethin' to Mom that she's suing every one of us! [laughter] I said, "This is his name – Gary Campo. He's Mum's lawyer." And they're kinda like, "Oh, because I think he left a message here as well." So we all showed up.

It was actually kinda funny, 'cause one of them, they were getting their house renovated, so they were living in another home – somebody'd loaned them a home – so we all showed up at Mum's that morning, and she's looking at us like, "What are you all doing here?" And I said, "Well, what's going on?" And she said, "Well, hang on, I gotta give tea to this lawyer." And I said, "Mom, why do you have a lawyer? Like, seriously." And she said, "No, come in here and talk to him." And I said, "No, we're not talkin' to 'em. We need to know what's going on." So there was miscommunication. So there's three of us girls – I'm the oldest of the girls – so I go in there and he's sitting there, and I turned around and I looked at Mum and I said, "Mum, he's sitting in my spot!" [laughter] And she said, "It's everybody's chair!" And I said, "No, it isn't!" And she served him before she served us! And so we were all kinda like okay, something weird is happening here. Like, we're siblings: we don't say anything, we can look at one another and know exactly what's happening. So I sat down beside him and I said, "Oh, by the way, you're sitting in my chair, and you got tea before we did, and so something's goin' on here." And he said, "Oh no, what are you thinking?" And I said, "What is she suing us for, 'cause we have nothin' to give!" [laughter] And he starts laughing and he said, "She's not suing you." I said, "Well, why are you here?" He said, "No, this is for the Xeni Gwet'in court case." And I thought,

"Ohhhhh!" Marilyn is the less political in our family, so she turns around and she says, "I'm outta here. Now we know what's going on here, I'm outta here, so." [laughs] So Gary said, "What did I say to her?" And I said, "You didn't say anything. She just doesn't like getting involved." Geraldine and I, it's our thing. Marilyn doesn't like getting involved in any of this stuff. She's a teacher, and her view is she likes to stay neutral. And he said, "Well, whatever that means." And we said, "Well, that's what *we* said." He explained to us what he was doing, why he was there with Mum.

I helped her [for] the first half. She wanted me to hear what her life was, because her life had our battles, and I had some views about being bounced back and forth between my grandparents. We had a clash about that, so I think she wanted me to hear why it was that I ended up in those homes, and it wasn't because they didn't have enough, you know. It was always that fear of when is somebody gonna come in? and when is somebody gonna take my child? You know, that's the biggest fear. And so when I heard the stories of where she came from and watching her day in and day out, it was amazing. She'd remember something that night and get Dad to call me so I'd write it down and remind her when Gary came in. I finally phoned – I think it was Ramona [Reynolds] – and I said, "How in the world did I end up here?" And she said, "I have no idea, people just gave us your name, and that's why we called you." I said, "I have another job, you know." [laughs] And she said, "Well, not according to Chief Roger." [laughs] And I'm kinda like, Roger? Does *he* make the calls here? The last half of her transcripts was done by my older brother [Orrie Charleyboy, who interpreted for the court].

Court didn' affect me as much as I knew it was affecting our Elders, because in our culture, when you're told once, you don't ask again. So you'd see the shocked look on the Elders' faces when they're being asked two or three times. You know, "Is *this* what you mean?" And I remember one of the Elders saying, "Are they just not getting it? You know, why do they want me to keep repeating it? It's on paper, I've said it three or four times. Why do they keep wanting me to answer that same question?" And it was just like wow. I think that's what affected me the most, because they had to break that tradition. When we're told once, you should remember because you don' know what's gonna happen tomorrow. I remember some of the Elders telling us that. Always remember what you're told, always figure out what it is that that other person is tryin' to tell you before you walk away, 'cause it's disrespectful to come back and ask again. That means you're not holding anything! [laughs] And so I think that was the toughest, tryin' to fit into their law.

I remember sitting in court, I think with Mum. Mum was on the stand, and I made time and went down. I was working two jobs. I finally made time to be there for Mum, because my brother [Orrie Charleyboy] was actually the one that translated for her in court. Sitting there and listening to her was when it hit me: we have to accept some things and live with the rest of the stuff in order to make headway here. In order to keep our dignity and keep our communities together, we have to accept some things. I think that was the hardest thing – that we had our laws and being brought up with our laws and then going to another level, but also seeing as I went along the way politically we're gonna have to do this *their* way to prove this is who we really are, but also never forgetting where we come from, never forgetting that we still have our laws. That was the hardest, giving in to that. Change is happening, you know, where we actually have to prove to Canada, to BC, that we're not going anywhere. And that's when it clued in. Oh my goodness, now I know what Dad [Patrick Charleyboy xinli] was talking about when he said that they'd win and we have to fight them with their own paper. "You have the mind to go there. Go there."

Going from the Culture

Eila Quilt, Xeni Gwet'in

I remember hearing someone saying it's interesting how frustrated some of the Elders were [in court], being asked the same question over and over. I always wondered, "How much are they telling?" Like when you ask them and you're pulling stuff out of them and it's not freely spoken about, like in the evenings when other things are tied into it. But people don't start a story and end it. Sometimes they go off on a tangent and bring something in and come back again, and then they go back off on a tangent [on the] other side. If you go from the culture, you'll know how that story unfolds.

Women in Leadership

Nits'il?in Russell Myers Ross, Yuneŝit'in

I remember one of our protests that we had. I think it was at Alexis Creek. Taseko Mines wanted to do a presentation there, and we just sort of undermined their plans by showing up, standing at the door, and singing. I still remember Ervin

Charleyboy there singing with us, probably singing most loudly, and I think his singing actually warmed us up on a chilly day. I learned some songs from late Ivor [Myers] there too, which was nice. And then at the end of it, we were all huddled together. Even with the Chiefs that were present – I myself not being a Chief at the time at all – everyone was huddled together, and the person in the middle was Minnie Charleyboy, a small Tŝilhqot'in woman but quite respected, and she was speaking in Tŝilhqot'in. All the men huddled right around her, and that was an image of what Tŝilhqot'in leadership looks like. So we all listened intently. So I know it's there, that respect for women leadership.

But I think a lot of Tŝilhqot'in leadership comes down to those people that we feel are honest. I described my grandmother [Elder Helena Myers xinli] as being that saintly person, and she was genuine, honest, and really giving, so I do think any type of governance system or thinking of bringing women into that place is going to require the moulding of that person to be incredibly honest, incredibly giving, like that embodiment of what some of our grandmothers were. So I'd be hesitant about some people that might have history and some of them like, "Hey, this is your chance to be pushed to the pedestal here!" But I do think if we want women in leadership, some level of re-engineering in our communities is needed, and we always want to make sure we have our balance [between men and women], even in our leadership and our governing bodies.

Becoming Title (2016)

Ivor Deneway Myers xinli, Yuneŝit'in

During wars, Tŝilhqot'ins brought individuals into the country, and they became the public domain of the Nation. Tŝilhqot'ins only had slaves for short periods, during wars, but they had some strict laws, I guess. If somebody did something bad, they would be exiled. If they'd done something wrong, they'd probably get different punishment. A slave became a member of the Nation. Even though they had very little Tŝilhqot'in blood, they would become a public domain of the Nation, providing that person wants to live in the country and wants to become a member of the Nation. In today's society, the same goes for a non-Native who went out with a Tŝilhqot'in woman or the other way. Then that person would still belong to the nation. We become Title of the Land. Our identity is the Land.

No one person ran the Tŝilhqot'in. No one community. Not even Nemaya. We are strong as a whole, as a Nation. The whole Nation owns the whole Land, the whole piece of Land. That's how it's supposed to be. If you wanna divide things up, it's gotta be done in a fair manner, whatever their compensation is. It's gotta be done by the Nation, not by each community. That's not the right way. Accordin' to a lot of Elders, what I told you was the right way. Roger breached the old law.[8]

In my mind and our Elders' minds, this Land belongs to the Tŝilhqot'in People and the rest of this country, like in British Columbia, belongs to other First Nations. All the Land in South America belongs to Aboriginal people as well. Even the air we're breathing belongs to the Tŝilhqot'in Nation, Nenqayni people. The water that comes from the mountains belongs to us still. All the game that come into our country becomes the public domain of the Nation. Our Traditional Territory belongs to the Tŝilhqot'in Nation.

People that landed in North America say it's theirs, but it's not. They found abundance of Land. Now they call it Canada, the United States. Anything they take from our Land – including resources like timber, gravel, minerals, oil, gas – is stolen property. On the other side of the ocean, whatever land the Europeans have belongs to them. When Europeans came into this country, they started developing roads without our consent. They started buying Land without our consent. They started developing Crown land without our consent. So all that is illegal to my knowledge. It was not right for them to do that. It's stolen property.

So with this Xeni Gwet'in Title case, anything within the declared Title area is our Territory, whether it's commercial properties, residential properties, industrial properties, or any other properties. And that has to be dealt with in a fair manner. Aboriginal Rights is what you can do with your Land. What you can do with your people. What you can do with anything that's living in the Traditional Territory, whether it's animals or different species. Who has the upper hand on things like that? The federal government does. Let's take an example: conservation officers. Who hired them? Not us. The federal government. And then it goes to the provincial government. And then we only have very little money that we can spend, and we don't have enough to hire a conservation officer.

Anything to do with highways, we lose our Aboriginal Rights there. At one time, we used to hunt all over accordin' to Elders like Tommy Billyboy and Norman George [Setah xinli]. We can't even hunt on both sides of the highway or along the highway. We can't even hunt on the residential properties, commercial properties, industrial properties – all those properties that've been given through their system. And even all the rangelands – can't even hunt on the other side of the fence unless you cut the barbed wire. You have no freedom like that. Let's say this sheet of paper is Tŝilhqot'in Territory. The whole area. Deal with everything that's on that sheet of paper. They could live happily over here while they're still payin' to the federal government. The federal government has to come back and pay us for that. Aboriginal Rights is another thing. The Title is another thing. You settle everything, whether it's a "postage stamp" or not. You settle everything.

There might also be some other Aboriginal Rights that we can't practise but want to practise. For example, we can't even pick berries on those properties that those non-Native people or people from outside own today. One time we were picking saskatoon berries and they pointed guns at us! My mum [Elder Helena Myers xinli] really loved picking wild chokecherries. We were on somebody's property down in Sheep Creek. He told us to come over and this one kid had a shotgun in his hand, ready to put some pellet holes in us. He said, "You better get off our property or else this one'll shoot a bunch of pellet holes right through you." I said, "Okay, I'll get off your property right now." So we did, me and my mum. The government should pay some sort of money towards things like that. There should be reimbursement.

In order for the federal government to help us out, we help them out as well, big time, and all we get is crumbs through Aboriginal Affairs. At one time they called it "Indian" Affairs. We never got our money's worth from them utilizing our Traditional Territory. With the Crown land sittin' overtop of our Traditional Territory, maybe the provincial government should start payin' a user fee for utilizing that Land. And those people that had guide outfitters, they have different zones for their areas for hunting. Hunting areas should also be ratified. Guide outfitters should pay Aboriginal people for utilizing those areas. For each animal that they shoot, they should pay a sum for reducing our wildlife habitat, because that's Aboriginal Rights, our Rights. Right now, the governments provide permits and stuff like that for people to go hunting, and we don't control 100 percent of that, unfortunately. Power, I guess.

So I feel that when they kick game out of our country, the federal government should pay a fee to Nenqayni people of the Tŝilhqot'in Nation. All those non-Natives that are living in our country today, it's okay for them to enjoy that Land, but they should have absolute respect for the Nenqayni people. Absolute respect for the Tŝilhqot'in Nation as a government. For the longest time, things have been done their way, so we just want to work hand in hand in the future. That's the way I see it. But the federal government and the provincial government should respect and recognize our Title and Land in this country. It belongs to the Nation. Every time they come into the country, they should honour it, the defining work of our Nation. It belongs to the people. Every time they sell properties, it should go back to the Nation and let the Nation know that this Land's bein' sold under their terms and should be under control by the Nation. For the

Tŝilhqot'in Nation, no individuals and no individual communities should ever sell their Traditional Territories. It should go back to the Nation and be ratifed.

We don't want a "just settlement." We want an ongoing agreement with the federal government to work hand in hand with the Aboriginal people of this country. We want an ongoing agreement about not exercisin' our Aboriginal Rights in those areas. This coexistence with the federal government – the federal government has never once sat down with the tribal Nation. They're just playing with us again. That's the way I look at it. And the province – how many years has this colonial government been in BC? The provincial, the federal government, they don't have jurisdiction in our Land. Whether it's subsurface rights or the air, it doesn't belong to them, they have no jurisdiction. They developed reserves, which was illegal from the beginning. According to their system, we don't even own one square inch of the reserve lands that've been set aside for us to use. We still own the Land, but they have to own up to what they've done and start talking about those things.

So. That's what I call Title and Rights.

Justice Vickers's Decision Comes Down

Chief Roger William

On November 20, 2007, the decision came down, but it didn't go public until the next day. Councillor David Setah, Councillor Robin Lulua, and I drove down to Vancouver and were getting updates on the phone from the lawyers about what the decision meant. We were telling our Elders and members at home, and we were strategizing, because people were gonna ask us questions – staff members, whoever – and we decided to tell them that we were still going through the decision, we didn't know what it meant, we'd let them know. That night we had a meeting, and the next morning there was a press conference. It all happened in one day!

The press conference was in Victoria on the morning of the twenty-first. It was in a room a little bigger than this hotel room [where we recorded], and there were a lotta cameras and a lotta people with mics. The Chiefs were there. The media had questions like what does this mean to you? You guys didn't win declaration of Title. What happened? Or If you win Title, are you gonna chase people out? For a long time, the media had been painting this picture that we were gonna get our Land back and kick everybody out. We were already prepared for those questions, but a lot of what I was asked during that press conference didn't even get in the paper. They might've printed half a page here and there, but I didn't say anything so controversial or surprising that it would sell. That didn't matter to me because the message was that we weren't done in court. The decision is good, precedent-setting, but we're still not done. So to us, it didn't matter what the media said, as long as we didn't contribute to their misunderstandings, but we also knew that you need to use the media, because nobody knows who we are, nobody knows about the Tŝilhqot'in War. Important people that know aren't gonna tell anybody, but if they do, they're gonna put their swing in it to make it look bad. From the time of the Declaration on, we knew that the media could be pretty bad if we didn't do it right, but if we were the ones who were communicating with the media about what we were trying to do, then it was different, as long as we were brief and to the point.

The Maa-nulth First Nations had signed a Treaty agreement in 2007 just before our decision came down, and the media were comparing the two. I said they'd worked hard for their treaty, voted in favour, and I supported them. The media wanted to make it sound as though we were critical of them, but we said we hoped that the Title case decision either didn't affect them or helped them. Not much of that got into the paper. Of course our Tŝilhqot'in Nation discussed the possibility of going through the 1992 BC Treaty Process. Today I'm glad we made the decision to reject the Treaty process. The government is probably pretty frustrated with all the money they're spending, but they can't trick First Nations or make a cheap deal, because First Nations are doing their homework and saying no. Our rejection of Treaty actually helped our case when BC and Canada asked us why we wanted to go to court. "You win or lose when you go to court," they said, "but what about Treaty? How many Treaties have been signed?" There have been a lot of Treaties signed east of BC, but very few in BC. The BC Treaty Process started right after the Nisga'a signed their Treaty. Not very many get to the third stage of the process, and by 2007, only one or two had signed.[9] BC and Canada kept asking why we wanted to go to court, but why go into a process with that kind of success rate? By 2013 we'd spent twenty years doing a court case, and during that time only 10 percent of First Nations had signed according to Canada. As of 2014, only two First Nations in BC have been able to come to an agreement. That's 1 percent of the total number of Nations entering Treaty negotiations! I really commend BC First Nations that were in the BC Treaty Process, because they stood their ground, did all their homework, and tried to come to agreement, but BC's and Canada's offers were just – I don't even want to say it. You get what you offer. They've still got 90 percent of First Nations to settle with, and their money – so-called tax dollars – is spent trying to trick First Nations into agreements that they don't agree with.

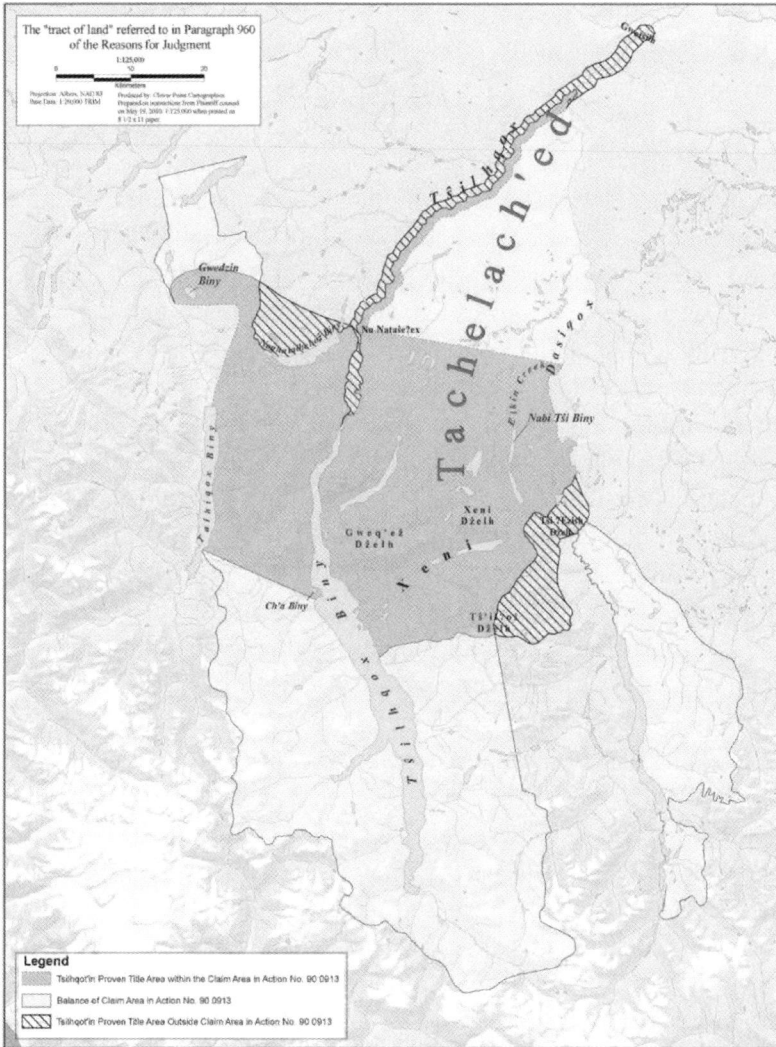

1,750 square kilometres of Title. Map of Declared Title Land, from *Tsilhqot'in Nation v. British Columbia*, 2007 BCSC 1700

This is the court case area, the darker area in the middle of the map. That's only 10 percent of Tŝilhqot'in Territory, but it's 80 percent of the Xeni Gwet'in Caretaker Area. In his decision, Judge David Vickers said that we met the test of Title, but he didn't make a declaration of Title. He found Title to almost

50 percent of the area, drew boundaries without actually declaring Title, and encouraged negotiations. On a technicality, he stopped short of making a declaration, stating that the Nation had argued for 100 percent Title, but he needed to hear more arguments and evidence in relation to what he called the "all or nothing" approach. He also wanted to hear more arguments on the boundary that he drew in the court case area. So that was a huge victory. We also achieved our goal of stopping logging to 100 percent of the area, because the judge said that the BC Ministry of Forests has no jurisdiction in the court case area. So all that was done and the only thing left to deal with was the Title.

A Summary of "Aboriginal Title" and "Aboriginal Rights" in *Tsilhqot'in Nation v. British Columbia*, 2007 BCSC 1700[10]

November 20, 2007, Justice Vickers ruled that the Tsilhqot'in people are a distinct Aboriginal group who have occupied the Claim Area for over 200 years.

The court dismissed the claim for a declaration of Aboriginal title to the claimed area, relating to the "all or nothing" way the claim was pleaded. It did, however, express its opinion that the Tsilhqot'in Nation had proven Aboriginal title to parts of its claimed traditional territory.

In summary, the Court found:

1. The Tsilhqot'in people have aboriginal rights, including the right to trade furs to obtain a moderate livelihood, throughout the Claim Area.

2. British Columbia's Forest Act does not apply within Aboriginal title lands.

3. British Columbia has infringed the Aboriginal rights and title of the Tsilhqot'in people, and has no justification for doing so.

4. Canada's Parliament has unacceptably denied and avoided its constitutional responsibility to protect Aboriginal lands and Aboriginal rights, pursuant to s. 91(24) of the Constitution.

5. British Columbia has apparently been violating Aboriginal title in an unconstitutional and therefore illegal fashion ever since it joined Canada in 1871.

"Proving" Rights

Chief Roger William

There was an expectation that we'd win at trial, and we kinda won, but we kinda didn't either. I've talked to a lotta Elders in my leadership, and they were all excited and looking forward to a huge victory, but after David Vickers's decision came down, we were all numb, wondering what the heck happened. We proved Title, but we weren't getting declaration of Title. What does that mean? We've got Rights – the Declaration of Rights – but what about Title? I think judges get influenced by what's happening during their lifetimes and by the political consequences of their decisions. They're not black and white. If they were, we would've had Title and Rights a *long* time ago. It's all about economics. It's all about the mainstream. Our goal was that no one could come in without our involvement. No one could put a logging road in the court case area, and I think, deep down, people felt we'd won because of that. That's a big victory. But the expectation that we'd prove Aboriginal Rights and Title clouded the victory. You can't *prove* Aboriginal Rights and Title. That's who we are. That's *our* Rights, *our* Title. If we can't exercise our Rights, if we can't say that we have Rights, then the government will have control.

You've gotta remember that in 1992, the BC Treaty process started. There were arguments about whether or not First Nations had Rights outside their Treaty area, and the government actually argued that people's Rights and Title existed only within the Treaty area and they'd have to give up their Rights outside it. Although the Nisg̱a'a deal didn't quite say that, because Nisg̱a'a also had Rights outside the Treaty area, there was still a big question mark beside this issue, and the BC Treaty Commission continued to say that they weren't sure whether First Nations had Aboriginal Rights outside their so-called Territory, and they weren't sure what that meant. After the Tŝilhqot'in decision came down in 2007, it was clear that we have Rights to a 100 percent of our Land, and so the only argument BC and Canada had left was about overlaps. Those arguments were political.

Negotiations after Justice Vickers's Decision

Chief Roger William

Canada said they didn't want to be involved in negotiations but they would chair. BC was willing to enter negotiations, but we knew that in the BC Treaty Process, they hadn't offered anything. So we proposed two-stage negotiations and an interim agreement in which we said we wanted economic development, shared decision-making, selected pieces of Land, and cash. But BC said, "Oh, we can't give you cash. Can't give you Land" – because Canada wasn't involved. We would not exchange Rights and Title for these items, but we did agree that if these demands were met in the first stage, we would put Rights and Title on the table and negotiate the rest, not only in the court case area but the whole Tŝilhqot'in Territory. BC responded that since Canada didn't want to be involved, the province couldn't offer Land or cash but would offer what they called a "Strategic Engagement Agreement" instead of calling it "shared decision-making." We thought that wasn't even an offer and we didn't agree to it. So we called off negotiations and went back to court to appeal. Canada also appealed, and so did BC. Between 2008 and 2009, we thought about the Strategic Engagement Agreement again, negotiated it, and came up with a consultation agreement, the Tŝilhqot'in Framework Agreement, which excluded the court case area because we were appealing. BC had a tough time with that agreement. December 31, 2013, is its last day.

What Is Title? (2017)

Chief Roger William

Title is a place where we will do what's best for the Land and for ourselves. Through our cultures, languages, and place names, First Nations have been living on the Land forever. I really believe that if there's anybody in Canada or BC that knows how to use *our* Land, it's us. We've got history and place names and trial and error on that Land, more than anybody out there, and when we make mistakes we're gonna find a way to fix them really fast and not make those mistakes again, because we know we're gonna be there forever. Politically, we're still healing. We're still three groups [traditionalists, modernists, and those in between]. But at the end of the day, people who vote leaders in are gonna have in the back of their minds what could happen because they hear it out there, because they see it in our leadership. And they wanna do what's best. And then we put pressure on leaders too – as individuals, as Xeni Gwet'ins, as Tŝilhqot'ins. And we're getting educated in both the Canadian way and in our culture. Our traditional education is coming back. We dunno what the decision of the Supreme Court of Canada is gonna say. The question is: Title, how much, and what is it? Is Title gonna be fee-simple land?[11] Is Title gonna be a country within a country? *Delgamuukw* understands Title as within the confines of Canada. So it's different from a reserve, but it's not private land. Also my understanding from the *Delgamuukw* decision is that if Canada and BC feel it's best for their people or country or province, they can override our Title, as long as they compensate, mitigate, or replace whatever they're gonna do on that Title. Is that what Supreme Court of Canada's gonna say in our case?

We First Nations were all connected and survived together in what is known as Canada or the USA or North America before European contact. We traded and we probably warred and took pieces of each other's Land for different reasons, but without each other we probably wouldn't have survived. So to make it work here in Canada, you can't isolate a Title in an area and say within these boundaries is the country of Tŝilhqot'in Nation, because we need to trade in and out of Tŝilhqot'in Nation to be able to survive like we did pre-contact. Technically, today, we're isolated because the banks won't look at us on reserve, and we are limited within our own country, within our own Land. We can't trade anything on reserve – a tiny reserve compared to our Territory – and there are actions, fights, lobbying, marketing, and a court case that are looking at that very question. You could look at Westbank First Nation, where they are having no choice but to deal with this, because they have what we call "CP land" (Certificate of Possession), where individual Band members hold the Land within the reserve, and Chief and Council have no say in that. So the leadership of the Westbank Indian Band went to court, lobbied, and won to a point where they do have a say on CP lands. Now any business on fee-simple land there has gotta pay tax to the Band, so they got around that.

Let's imagine I own a house on so-called Crown land, and I have a piece of property. I can get a loan and put my house and piece of property on the loan, so I can go into business. If I screw up, I'm gonna lose everything, so I'm gonna be sure I do it right, and now I've got money to help me do that. On reserve, the bank won't even look at me. On reserve, I can't even sell my house to somebody else, because there's not enough economic development for another member to buy it and because the federal government owns it anyway. So what would a process look like that enables a bank to loan somebody money on reserve? Maybe there might be a resolution by leadership that would say the bank can sell that piece of property to anybody out there, but whoever buys it has gotta follow the rules of that First Nations community. As long as they follow the rules, there's nothing wrong with them having property on reserve. I'm thinking of the Title case like that, where you can draw the boundaries of our Title Land, but we can market in Canada or around the world. As long as you follow the rules in this Title Land, you can stay and do business here, whether you're Tŝilhqot'in, Shuswap Secwépemc, or from wherever. So until a First Nation has developed its own law, Title would have to be defined under the laws of Canada and the province or territory.

*   *   *

In 2008 I lost the election and Marilyn Baptiste got in as Chief. She became the second woman Chief of the Xeni Gwet'in First Nation's government. Marilyn's father, Marvin Baptiste xinli, was Chief twelve years earlier, making her our only second-generation Chief.

You know, I always felt that one day I'd never get back in. You only get so much funding, and you can only do so much. Over the years when you've been in for a long time, there's gonna be people who are still a priority, but you don't get to them with funding. You end up making decisions more than once on those people, and they never forget. They're hurt and they've got the right to decide who they wanna be their leader. So I didn't get back in 2008, but Marilyn asked me and the Council asked me to help her transition. So I was working as Marilyn's assistant from February till May, and then the Chiefs all agreed to hire me because the Title case was huge. They thought the case was still very important, and they wanted me to focus on it and on Fish Lake. They hired me at TNG [Tŝilhqot'in National Government] in May 2008, and in 2009 Ervin Charleyboy lost the election for Tribal Chair, and Chief Joe Alphonse was elected.

The Appeal

Chief Roger William

On December 4, 2007, we all (Xeni Gwet'in and Tŝilhqot'in, BC and Canada) applied to the BC Court of Appeal. On April 24, 2009, the appeal was recorded and filed. The hearing began on November 15, 2010, and lasted until November 22, 2010. We had to wait for nineteen months until June 27, 2012, for the decision to come down. BC and Canada said, well, First Nations don't have Title. They might have Title to little pieces of Land, but that's about it. And we said no, it's to the whole court case area. We'd thought that maybe Aboriginal Rights to hunt and trap might be affected, or maybe Aboriginal Rights to catch and use wild horses, but in the end, all of that survived from Judge Vickers's decision. It was a victory. But in terms of Title, the Appeal Court judges didn't agree with anyone – Canada, BC, or us – but we would have to return to BC Supreme Court and pick specific areas. We still had 100 percent Rights, but they didn't give us Title, saying we could come back for small area Title, postage-stamp style, where you have Title to the place where you hide behind a blind to get your moose or deer, or the place where you stand on a rock to get your fish. The BC Court of Appeal required us to prove small-spot, postage-stamp-style Title and rejected the larger area that Judge Vickers had decided on in 2007, but I wasn't gonna go back to the Appeal Court. We decided to go straight to the Supreme Court of Canada.

Summary of the Appeal Decision, *William v. British Columbia*, 2012 BCCA 285 [12]

"The BC Court of Appeal agreed with the Aboriginal hunting and trapping rights decision of the trial judge. However, with respect to Aboriginal Title, the Court of Appeal accepted the Crown's 'postage stamp theory' – that Aboriginal Title is confined to small areas such as village sites, berry patches, fishing sites, and salt licks. However, the Court of Appeal did not accept the Crown's technical argument that this was an 'all or nothing' claim and that the Court could not declare Aboriginal title for a smaller, included portion of claimed territory. This ... cleared the way for an appeal to the Supreme Court of Canada on the issue of whether a broad territorial claim for Aboriginal Title could succeed."

Our Declaration of Rights

Chief Roger William

Clearly we're not happy about the postage-stamp-style Title awarded by the Appeal Court on June 27, 2012, but our victory is that the three judges said we won Aboriginal Rights to 100 percent of the court case area and that has never been contested by Canada or BC. It's the law. It's the first time ever in BC and in

Canada that a First Nation has won Aboriginal Rights to a piece of Land. There are a lotta cases about Rights focusing on being consulted about hunting and fishing, but BC and Canada always like to argue about overlaps and which First Nation has the Rights. Now there's a piece of Land that clearly has Tŝilhqot'in Rights, and that changes everything. Our Declaration of Rights to hunt, trap, trade, and catch and use wild horses became the law on September 30, 2012, when BC and Canada didn't appeal the decision of the BC Court of Appeal.

What this means is that from here on, BC and Canada have to define any infringement on any of the Rights we won. So they're going to have to answer a number of questions before they can do an activity, especially if it's clearcut logging or mining. For example, if an activity is approved, is it gonna affect Rights? Is that gonna be infringement? How are they gonna know? They need to know what species Tŝilhqot'ins hunt or trap. What are the numbers of those species? What about the habitat of those species? Is it healthy? Is it being impacted? How much is being used today by non-Tŝilhqot'ins? How much is being used by Tŝilhqot'ins? Are we using those species sustainably? In the case of any of those kinds of activities, they certainly have to really look, but for tourism, trail use, or ranching, probably not so much. Throughout the court case, they continued to approve permits and licences for those activities, but they certainly didn't touch anything that had to do with any referral coming from harvesting timber or mining explorations or mining except the Prosperity mine.

Appealing to the Supreme Court of Canada (2013)

Chief Roger William

When the appeal decision came down in June 2012, we hit the ground running because we only had until September to make a decision. We had one chance to seek leave to appeal to Supreme Court of Canada, and if we'd missed the deadline, the case would've been over, and the "small spot" definition would have stayed. First Nations across Canada were strategizing. The Conservative government had gotten back in as the federal government of Canada, but this time they had a majority. We decided to keep going, but only after we'd considered all the angles, including international cases involving Aboriginal people. The Haida case [*Haida Nation v. British Columbia (Minister of Forests)*, 2004 3 S.C.R. 511] was also in process at that time, but they didn't know when they were going to court. They were winning battles on the ground with the government and pretty much had control, so we didn't know whether there was any incentive for them to go ahead. We were a First Nations community putting forward our case on behalf of the Nation, with Elders in Xeni and in the Tŝilhqot'in who didn't understand English, in an area that was still pretty much pristine, with no BC Hydro and only a little bit of tree harvesting at the edges of the Territory. Is this the right case? Is this the case that we should put forward? We thought, if our case couldn't do it, then no case could do it in Canada. Our only option left would have been an international case, and by that time, Canada was involved in UNDRIP, the United Nations Declaration of the Rights of Indigenous Peoples.

Although the Canadian Environmental Assessment Agency (CEAA) panel hearing on the Prosperity mine in 2010 went in our favour, the New Prosperity project was a test ahead of us in 2012 [see chapters 10 and 11 for more on this], and we were meeting with BC about how they were gonna protect our Aboriginal Rights in relation to the proposed mine. Their response was that they were still in court and had no funding to explore those issues. We strategized about the appeal, thinking there might be a negotiation option or even that we could go back to court and go for a small spot, proving that we have Title to Fish Lake. Then the mine would be over. But we'd been in court since 2002, and we felt that we were already doing pretty well at protecting Fish Lake against the New Prosperity project, and we needed to look past Fish Lake. We got support from First Nations all across BC and Canada, so we applied for leave to appeal to the Supreme Court of Canada by the September 2012 deadline, and we were granted leave in January 2013. The Supreme Court of Canada will hear our appeal on November 7 [2013].

It's interesting that the proven Title area – almost 50 percent of the total area – doesn't include Fish Lake. To us, the judge made a political decision. We could've gone back to court to prove Title to it because we've got pithouses there and cachepits, fish, berries, medicines, and we can hunt – everything is in that little valley. Any judge in his right mind would agree to postage-stamp-style Title to Fish Lake, but we didn't take that approach. We went back to court for the court case area, and that was a tough decision with the Conservative government in power. When the CEAA panel made a decision in 2010 about the proposed mine at Teẑtan Biny Fish Lake and the federal government agreed, the Conservatives were a minority government. Today [2013] they're a majority. And there's the issue of judges who were appointed by the Liberals and are now retiring, and Conservative appointees are coming in. So we had a really tough time going ahead with the court case because we were thinking we've got the wrong government and the wrong judges. As judges appointed by the Liberals retired, the Conservative Party was putting their judges in, and the situation was changing around us. We knew this would make it a lot harder for the next First Nation to go to court after us, and we were concerned about a bad precedent. But we've been at this for twenty years, and First Nations across BC and Canada said you can't let that small-site, postage-stamp-style Title stand, so we moved ahead.

At the BC Court of Appeal, we argued for 100 percent of the Title case area, and the three judges that ruled said we have small-spot Title. We have strong evidence that it's 100 percent, but we've only filed for 40 percent of the Title case area in the Supreme Court of Canada. That's a hard pill to swallow, but we think it will move the case forward. However, our factum allows us to come back after the decision for 100 percent of the court case area for Title if we win big. You know, before European contact, we had strategies for hunting and fishing, so I guess that's what we're still doing but with provincial and federal governments. We want to make it a celebration for the days we're there, from November 5 to 8, so we'll be drumming, we'll be singing. We'll be filling up the courtroom, outside the courtroom, at the Parliament. We'll be celebrating!

Four Years

Elder Martin Quilt xinli, Xeni Gwet'in

Took us four years before we won it, this whole Tŝilhqot'in area. The people from Bella Coola, they all came over, down rodeo ground, when we won the court case.

I got some cousins down that way too, Bella Coola. My grandfather is from there. Took us four years before we won it, this whole Tŝilhqot'in area. That's why the people from Bella Coola, they all came over, down rodeo ground, when we won the court case.

One o' Jesse James's gang, he end up in Bella Coola, running from the law. [laughs] Robin Hood of the West they call 'em, Jesse James Gang. They helpin' the poor, eh. They rob from the rich, they give to the poor.

CHAPTER 8 ENDNOTES

1   The artist describes the painting as "a compilation of images sketched in Nemaiah and in Victoria, but the main scene was from a quick drawing done during a court room session being held in a Nemaiah school room. Except for the court scene, all other sketches were done directly as described by the witness through an interpreter and in the presence of a lawyer. I was able to ask questions to help me understand what to draw. In a second meeting, a drawing was either accepted by the witness as accurate or I made any changes to the drawing as necessary to fine-tune the image. As it happened, on the day of this court scene, I had finished all sketches for the case and had about half an hour to watch the proceedings. I had been totally focused on the matters at hand when I suddenly realized there were only a few minutes left before I had to leave. I quickly drew what I saw before me – Jack Woodward sitting to the far left, listening as lawyer David Robbins led Francis Setah through his evidence in reference to a map on the wall (which we do not see in the painting). I included a clock indicating the time. I had to leave at 2:30 but felt compelled to record this court moment visually during the last few minutes. The exact date is missing but not too long after, I decided to include some of my pencil drawings into a large oil painting featuring this court scene. The painting was subsequently purchased by lawyer David M. Robbins, partner in Woodward and Company in Victoria." Lawyer Maureen Mahony is seated beside Robbins. Wordspeller Bella Alphonse and interpreter Beverly Quilt look at each other in the foreground, while court reporter Christie L. Pratt types.

2   In *Delgamuukw v. British Columbia*, "the Supreme Court of Canada ruled that Aboriginal title did exist in BC after all, and that it was a right to the land, not merely to traditional practices of hunting, fishing, or gathering. In cases where the First Nations hold the title to the land, they could exclude others from it, use it for pleasure or business, and extract resources. This meant, for example, that First Nations could engage in mining, even though that had never been a traditional activity. The judgment was the most important decision yet made [1997] on Aboriginal title in Canada. It held that Aboriginal title was a communal right and not an individual one, so decisions about the land had to be made by the whole community. Lands covered by Aboriginal title could only be sold to the federal government. They could not be used in ways that were irreconcilable with the First Nations' continuing relation to the land. Like other Aboriginal rights, Aboriginal title was protected under s. 35 of the *Constitution Act* of 1982 ... Since Aboriginal title was a constitutional right, the government had to meet stringent constitutional tests in order to justify infringing on it. It had to consult with the affected Aboriginal group before acting and might have to pay them compensation afterwards. The key question after *Delgamuukw* was what lands in BC were covered by Aboriginal title" (Turkel, *The Archive of Place*, 56).

3   The criteria for proof of Aboriginal Title are laid out in *Delgamuukw* as follows: "(i) the land must have been occupied prior to sovereignty, (ii) if present occupation is relied on as proof of occupation pre-sovereignty, there must be a continuity between present and pre-sovereignty occupation, and (iii) at sovereignty, that occupation must have been exclusive" (*Delgamuukw v. British Columbia*, [1997] 3 SCR 1010, 143).

4   The Sarich Commission discussed the context of these kinds of concerns. See Anthony Sarich, *Report on the Cariboo-Chilcotin Justice Inquiry* (Victoria: Cariboo-Chilcotin Justice Inquiry, 1993), 13–14.

5   Former Chief Benny William (Xeni Gwet'in) remembers the Elders being afraid to testify, fearing that they would be jailed. Another witness recalled a concern with where all the information divulged to the lawyers went – "What did you do with that information?" The concern was that if "too much information" was shared, there could be consequences – sickness, even death – for those who had "given away" that information. When the catastrophic failure of the tailings dam at the Mount Polley copper mine near Williams Lake happened, some Elders felt that these prophecies were being fulfilled.

6   Marilyn Baptiste was Chief (Xeni Gwet'in) from 2008 to 2013 and Councillor from 2013 to 2018. She was Secretary-Treasurer of the Union of British Columbia Indian Chiefs (UBCIC) and founding member of First Nations Women Advocating Responsible Mining (FNWARM). She followed in the footsteps of her father, Marvin Baptiste xinli, who was Chief between 1968 and 1980, and is the second woman to serve as Chief of the Xeni Gwet'in First Nation, following Annie C. Williams. With respect to "proving that we were here first," Anishinaabe legal scholar John Borrows writes that "the implications of underlying Crown title are immense: Aboriginal people bear the expensive burden of proving title, and Crown sovereignty applies to restrict and discipline Aboriginal self-determination." He is referring specifically to the Supreme Court of Canada decision in the Title case and notes that while "the outcome was favourable for the Tsilhqot'in people because they secured a declaration of Aboriginal title, the decision replicates one of the worst aspects of [the] originalist fiction" of "underlying Crown title" (John Borrows, *Freedom and Indigenous Constitutionalism* [Toronto: University of Toronto Press, 2016], 141). See also John Borrows, *Law's Indigenous Ethics* (Toronto: University of Toronto Press, 2019).

7   The reference is to a July 2014 presentation by Anne Marie Sam (Nak'azdli Whut'en) and Amy Crook (now executive director for Fair Mining Collaborative), sponsored by Friends of the Nemaiah Valley. Sam talked about what the Mount Milligan mine had done to her community in the Peace River.

8   That is, by proceeding on his own as Chief of one community. Compare Chief Roger's discussion of this issue in the first section of chapter 8.

9   See the interactive map at bctreaty.ca/resources/ for information on more recent negotiations.

10   From Friends of the Nemaiah Valley, "The Tsilhqot'in and Xeni Gwet'in Court Case for Rights and Title," www.fonv.ca/nemaiahvalley/thecourtcase/.

11   Fee simple is freehold ownership, meaning that the owner will own the land forever and may dispose of it as they wish.

12   Summary from Woodward & Company Lawyers LLP, "Blazing a Trail for Reconciliation, Self-Determination & Decolonization: *Tsilhqot'in Nation v. British Columbia and Canada*," part 3, "The BC Court of Appeal," tsilhqotin.woodwardandcompany.com. Writing for the Court, Chief Justice McLachlin would later summarize this argument as follows: "[27] The trial judge in this case held that 'occupation' was established for the purpose of proving title by showing regular and exclusive use of sites or territory. On this basis, he concluded that

the Tsilhqot'in had established title not only to village sites and areas maintained for the harvesting of roots and berries, but to larger territories which their ancestors used regularly and exclusively for hunting, fishing and other activities. [28] The Court of Appeal disagreed and applied a narrower test for Aboriginal title – site-specific occupation. It held that to prove sufficient occupation for title to land, an Aboriginal group must prove that its ancestors *intensively* used a definite tract of land with reasonably defined boundaries at the time of European sovereignty. [29] For semi-nomadic Aboriginal groups like the Tsilhqot'in, the Court of Appeal's approach results in small islands of title surrounded by larger territories where the group possesses only Aboriginal rights to engage in activities like hunting and trapping. By contrast, on the trial judge's approach, the group would enjoy title to all the territory that their ancestors regularly and exclusively used at the time of assertion of European sovereignty" (*Tsilhqot'in Nation v. British Columbia*, 2014 SCC 44, 27–29).

Nen gagunlhchugh deni nidlin
We live all over this land:

Protecting the Nen

Se?intsu ghinli Emily Ekks Lulua ts'edith, gwech'etayalh
gwech'anxwelh gwalnig.
Mus gudish ghilh?az, hink'an natal?es.
Gwi denichugh ts'edih sanish, ?eyi ?egun ghanatal?es.
?Ink'an dechen, dechen gatŝ'i yadatatsez,
gan nenqay ts'alagwetak'anlh.
?Egu gadih xwelh nagwalnig ghaghint'i.

Before she passed my grandmother Emily Ekks Lulua shared this story with us.
The moose will go up north where they came from.
The elk will return.
The trees will turn red
and the world will burn up.
This is what she said.[1]

Elder Emily Ekks Lulua xinli. Photo by Sage Birchwater

Living All over This Land

Lorraine Weir

When asked about the Title case, many of the Tŝilhqot'ins who contributed to this book shared gwenïg stories and teachings rooted in their understanding of Traditional Knowledge, just as many of the Elders who testified at trial had done in order to protect the Nen Land. In this chapter, much of this wisdom is gathered and organized under headings which loosely comprise subdivisions of Dechen ts'edilhtan Tŝilhqot'in law. We begin with Nen the Land, Nenqayni deni the People, Ch'ih gudzïsh Place names, and then to Dadaben Medicine, Gwenïg Stories, Dechen ts'edilhtan Tŝilhqot'in law, and a final section on baskets as ʔEsggidam Ancestors. While this list serves to organize the gwenïg stories and teachings shared here, it is by no means definitive with respect to the categories or to their relation to the general heading of "Dechen ts'edilhtan."[2] It is a start on a much longer journey now being undertaken by Xeni Gwet'in, the other five Tŝilhqot'in communities, and the Nation as the work of revitalizing Tŝilhqot'in language, law, culture, and lifeworld is actively engaged once again after declaration of Title. Although the burning world that Elder Emily Ekks xinli prophesied has come in terms of beetle-killed trees, wildfire, and habitat destruction – all expressions of settler colonial violence – it has also awakened the People to reclaim and practise Tŝilhqot'in ways of knowing and living in the wake of the Title case.[3] As Gilbert Solomon says, "A while ago we start seeing more moose coming in and more mosquitoes, more animals showing up at our area. We finally realized they were refugees from out there, you know. They were coming in ... [to] the last green part of BC here," and the people "start singin'. We were being taught by our aunties and uncles. They knew, they still knew these songs, these sacred songs for what we have."

Joyce Charleyboy speaks of songs coming when they're ready and when the singer is ready, a synchrony of being at home in the deep time of connection to the spirit world and to the Nen Land. Like gwenïg stories, songs carry the wisdom of the ʔEsggidam, and Chief Roger explains that ʔEsggidam "means a person who had jurisdiction, who had honour, who had powerful language, who held law and rituals. When this person welcomed you in, it meant you were at home."[4] The Elders teach: "Nen gagunlhchugh deni nidlin We live all over this Land" (literally, "land all over people live"). This concept of being at home is a basic principle of place names, often the distilled essence of what happened in that place at a particular time. In the settler courtroom, place names turned into maps and Justice Vickers was challenged early on to go beyond the "metes and bounds" approach of settler cartography and to create his own "bright lines" based on the testimony of the Plaintiff and many Elders.[5] As each witness told the story of a specific place, they marked the courtroom map with its location, helping to create the complex maps of Xeni Gwet'in Land on which, in part, Justice Vickers based his decision about proven Title Land.[6] Where stories based on intimate experience of the Land had sufficed for millennia, cartographic technologies eventually produced paper and digital versions of a map with place names that had never been mapped in this way before, let alone in Tŝilhqot'in.

The world of Nen gagunlhchugh deni nidlin living all over the Land is rooted not only in different mapping traditions but also in different senses of place and time. It resists the stasis of what Gilbert Solomon, in exasperation, referred to as "these little polygon places," that is, the cartographer's representation of, for example, traditional uses in specific locations. It's not only people who "live all over" but the Land which is gagunlhchugh all over. Like water and animals, plants and people, the Nen is alive. To move on the Land is to feel that connection and see, among many other things, its material signs, whether in ʔEsggidam ancestor rock painting or recent Sweat House frames and salmon drying racks. A settler guide once commented to me disparagingly that Tŝilhqot'ins "leave their things all over and don't put them away," revealing in a flash the rift between settler law's domestication of the Land in terms of "property" that needs tidying and "putting away" (as in the Indian Act's language of fences and separate houses),[7] and, in contrast, Tŝilhqot'in practices of living all over the Land as home, intricately known and familiar. "We *are* the Land," as Chief Roger says. "Title is with me." Or, as the great Chickasaw poet, novelist, and Knowledge Holder Linda Hogan writes, "what happens to people and what happens to the land is the same thing."[8] The interconnecting and mutually reinforcing principles which are the groundwork of Dechen ts'edilhtan Tŝilhqot'in law are Dadaben Medicine for Land and Nenqayni People healing from genocide and growing strong again on the return home.

Nen The Land

Clearcuts

David Setah, Xeni Gwet'in

I was always a planner in Nemiah, and when I went to Stoney, I started seeing a lot more Forestry plans. For a lot of it, you wonder what they think. It's just like anything in industry anywhere, I guess – they don't consider anything out there. All they want to look at is the trees and how much money they can make. They don't take the environment into consideration. We raised all the things that are in the Forest Practices Code right now when I was working at Stoney with late Chief Tony Myers, Lloyd Myers, Dave Quilt, and all the Elders. In the Forest Practices Code nowadays, they gotta borderline the fish-bearing creeks and fish-bearing lakes. That's everything we brought up and they implemented it.

One thing about them is they actually did sit and listen to us. We got them to identify through us all the deer's winter ranges. Deer migrate into the mountains and they migrate back out. There's places they hang out in the winter, places they hang out in the summer, and there's the migration route between the two. All the Elders know about those things. They've lived off the Land long enough that they know every migration route out there and every winter range. And in a lot of the meetings, that's what we brought up – we don't touch those areas where deer winter range because there's a really big difference between how warm it is and how cold it is if you're out in the open, and if you're in the forest, especially if the north winds are blowing. If you're in the middle of a field and the north wind's blowing, that's *cold*. And if you just walk into the trees, it's warm. Deer need that. All the wildlife out there need that.

We talked about all the plans that were coming in. There was no technology back then. They just brought out maps, outlined an area, painted it in different colours, and said, "Well, what do you want to do?" I didn't like seeing those clearcuts being way too big, plus they were borderline close to creeks, lakes, and everything. I remember even prior to that, the first time I went to Vancouver for a meeting. I was flying and as we were getting closer to Vancouver and reducing altitude, I could see really steep slopes logged right to the lake. You look at that and you know that's no good. A big rain's gonna bring all that down and muddy the lake. And once you muddy the lake, then you affect the fishes spawning and all that. That's common sense to me, so I started to wonder is it common sense to those guys? So that was my first impression of industries. They don't care. We battled them lots.

The first time my mom saw the clearcuts, she was looking, wondering what had happened. She thought maybe somebody had thrown a bomb and devastated the whole area. I told her, I think what's going on is they're actually logging it but different from what they used to. I'd seen practices like that before, around Stoney. I rode lots around there. That's one other thing I like doing, is riding a lot of horses. When I was riding, I saw the logging practices that happened around there. They had a sawmill and they got everything in, but they didn't leave a big clearcut. They left a lotta trees standing and they had skid trails and they brought it all in. Six and eight, those are the ones that got shipped out. When you ride through that today, it looks nice and open, and the trees are coming back nice. Lotsa grass. But the first time they looked at that kind of clearcut, automatically our people thought about the squirrels. They talk about the squirrel lots. That's how our lawyer [Jack Woodward] got his name, Dlig, 'cause he talked about the squirrels. Put yourself in the squirrel's little paws and look at all the hard work they're doing, just getting ready for winter. And then after they're done, they're relaxing and this machine comes and takes everything away. Do you think that squirrel's gonna make it through the winter? I don't think so.

It's really, really hard to understand why they don't understand it. I think we've gotta get them out on the Land and know everything that's out there. Then at least they've got a connection to the Land. Once you've got that connection and you know everything about the Land out there, what the animals live off, everything, then you've got more respect for the Land. I think what's happening nowadays is that a lotta people are losing that connection to the Land. And when you don't have that connection, you don't see animals, you don't see fish. You get your food at Save-On, Safeway, Walmart all the time and you don't know what's out there. If you live in big cities, you're always walking on concrete, your feet don't touch the ground, and you don't know what's out there. And that's what we're losing. A lotta people are not spending time in the forest, so they don't have the same respect we do, the same understanding. What does the wildlife need?

Respect

David Setah, Xeni Gwet'in

One thing my mom and dad really taught me to understand is respect. Once you start respecting one thing, then automatically you've gotta respect other things. And as you grow, you start to respect everything, from people to the Land to the lakes to things you live off – deer, moose. You don't go out there and just shoot everything in sight and bring it home. You take what you need. You only need this for the winter and you take it and dry some and cook some. And you always do that, you always have that respect and there's no way you're gonna wreck the Land, no way you're gonna wreck your own future.

Mom used to always talk about respecting people and the Land. I was laughing at someone, 'cause of what they did when they were not themselves, when they drank alcohol, and my mom just sat me down and told me, "Go ahead, keep laughing at them, 'cause if you keep doing that, you're gonna be there." So from then on, I stopped laughing at them doing that. She made sure I understood every single thing about respect in all different areas, and after that she wasn't worried about whether I was gonna respect and pass it on, 'cause she'd done her job, what was taught to her and how it was taught to her. She was carrying all that on.

Why?

Gilbert Solomon, Xeni Gwet'in

The time I said to the lawyer, "Why are they still logging?"

He said, "Well, you have to have Title first before they stop."

So we beat them in court, and they're still logging. We have Title, okay. Why are they still logging?

And they said, "If you got Title, you could get compensated. Royalties. Like, retroactive kinda thing."

We have Title and we're not getting compensated. I said "Now there's no more moose. We're not getting moose every year now."

"Why does Redstone wanna keep logging over there?"

Whatever.

"How come Xeni's not logging?"

I dunno.

They asked me in court.

For Harry Setah xinli[9]

Trina Setah, Xeni Gwet'in

For him, horseback riding was *really* important. He was a big believer in gettin' out on the Land by horseback. I'm so glad that I got to travel on the Land with him by horseback and see as much as I could with him. That's how I was able to stay out of trouble. He made sure to pick me up every Friday after school and bring me back every Sunday until the bus was made available for students to be picked up at Lee's Corner and dropped off at Lee's Corner, and then catch the other bus. I didn't really like relyin' on him to bring me all the way back to Williams Lake and then come back and go to work the next day, but he would have. He was there for us 100 percent. I could've been one of those that was partyin' every weekend, but no, it was horses for me. And the culture of horses is so strong in the community – everybody is with horses. That's what makes us so special, I guess.

He knew the Land like the back of his hand. I remember goin' up with him in the mountains, but he used to scare me sometimes. He would tell me stories. "You gotta be careful. You gotta stay right behind me. Make sure your horse is right behind me" – 'cause some of these places are really dangerous. I remember gettin' to the top, and we were gettin' ready to go over the mountain. Your horse is standing on a ledge and you're looking down and it's like all shale and rock and at the bottom there's a glacier. I was thinkin' horses do not have fear. As long as you don't have fear, they don't have fear, but I remember bein' scared outta my little –. He had no problem goin' down that mountain, and he knew that trail. It was nothing new to him, but every time I went up, it was always something new for me. A lotta people went up with him to the mountains, so they got to learn these trails, and they are not forgotten. I'm hopin' that they will continue to use those trails and keep them open.

Walking in the Forest

Lennie Solomon, Xeni Gwet'in

When I walk in the forest, I'm not afraid. I don't bring a gun. I'm not different from the trees and the animals. I pass through without being noticed. I'm the same as the forest.[10]

Nendidah gatŝ'i gan, gu deni helin han[11]
Everything is like a spirit

Ivor Deneway Myers xinli, Yuneŝit'in

Nendidah gatŝ'i gan, gu deni helin han.
Gwi tl'ugh ghenelhyax ?eyi gant'i, nengwi ?elagi ghenelhyax
?el ghenelhyax.
Gangu deni gant'ih han.

Nengwi tu ?eguwh nilin, ?eyi da nexwa tu helin
?Eyi chu gant'en gats'iŝen
Nengwi yagh bighadinjish nengu tel?ihi
?Eyi chu deni tŝ'ilh?in ?an.

Nenguyi nilhtŝ'i dish ?eguh telgih, nilhtŝ'i dish ?eyi deni
tsin, deni tsin helin.
Gwech'a ?eguh natelgish.

Nengu yagh sa ghadenug ?i
?Eyi chu gangu deni ts'ilh?in gant'ih.
Ghalhyiz, sanlhyiz gwelish ?aldzi gha?ash
Gwech'ez deni ?aldzi ch'ed ŝedex ts'edenish.
?Aldzi chugh helish ?egu deni, deni ch'ed ŝedex
?egu deni del diżben jid tŝ'eguzih.
Sitaweht'i chuh denish jiyelhdenish.

Nendidah gatŝ'i betsin gulin nunh.
Gwi yagh ?asdinlh gadant'i, ?et'an gadant'i, tŝi gadant'i.
Didagatŝ'i gangu deni gajint'ih.
Nenqay gagulhchugh deni hant'ih.
Gangu ne?inkwel gant'ih han.

Everything is like a spirit
Grass, flower, leaf, they are all like a spirit.

The river that flows, our water, is a spirit.
The air that we breathe, that is a spirit too.

The tornado is a spirit.
That's why it goes wandering by.

The sun that comes up,
Night when it's dark,
The moon coming out.

When there's a full moon with a person sitting on it,
When a person's blood is full,
They say the moon says,
Think of me in a good way.

Everything has a spirit –
Ants, leaves, rock.
Everything is like a human spirit.

The whole universe is like your mother.

Teẑtan Biny Fish Lake

Ivor Deneway Myers xinli, Yuneŝit'in

Those waters are just like spirits – alive. Those plants, different plants, are like human beings. They breathe. Those marine resources that are in the lakes, in the rivers, they're all just like human beings, trying to keep themselves alive.

When they're gonna put a pipeline through British Columbia, Tŝilhqot'ins have gotta be involved, because all those fish that come from the sea not only belong to the Tŝilhqot'in Nation. They belong to the other Nations that utilize those marine resources. So that whole ocean should belong to the Nation of British Columbia, because our marine resources come from there.

Fracking is another distortion in itself, especially when you're tampering with the ground. When you're drilling the ground, it destroys a lot of areas where there might be oil comin' out, and there might be some other resources which we don't know about.

Money is just like gold. It makes a person go crazy. And water, it's like gold and it's makin' people realize how precious these waters are. The whole world will be contaminated when they extract resources and destroy British Columbia, Canada, North America, South America, the other side of the continent.

When you extract natural resources, you create a path with a negative charge, and wherever there was a body of oil or gas that's been siphoned out, there's gonna be a large body of water in the future. Earth just goes [sound of earth collapsing]. And that might trigger volcanic eruptions that spout lava again. Where there was no Land before, there might be one day. There might be Land in the ocean and it will be huge, and the whole world, wherever cities rise, will be underwater. When they extract the oil or gas, what they're doin' is creatin' a vacuum under the earth. Then one day when that gives in, it's gonna create a big chaos there. If a light just hits that, boom. That's my vision.

It links to who we are. It links to how the earth evolved. It links to how the sun and the moon and the stars coincide in this earth. And some of us people in the world are going crazy over spoils that are in the earth, over shiny objects – silver, gold. What are they doing that for? Are they trying to find out if they can go to the other side of the sun? They want to go to Mars, and from there they could study some other planet somewhere else and find out if there's living beings on those other planets. But in the Tŝilhqot'in concept, leave things as is. Maybe take out a few things here and there, but not too much. Leave it as is.

Every year our animals are being depleted by the hunters. A lot of our game has been stolen through their [midugh] system. There goes our Aboriginal Rights.

There should be a big price tag on that one in return, especially for our trees and our waters and our marine resources. Every time the government makes mistakes, we should fine them, 'cause it's not their Land to begin with. If they're gonna destroy water, they're gonna destroy all the marine resources – all the different species that spawn up the river. And if there's an accident with a train and some of that spills into the river, or if there's a big truck transportin' liquid gas, fuel oil, diesel, whatever it be, and if it spills in the waters, they should be sued and assessed hefty fines. All our water that goes through the Chilcotin River meets the Fraser River right down to the ocean, and that belongs to the First Nations people that live along each side of the river.

Nen

Elder Marvin William xinli, Xeni Gwet'in

There's snow way up there, all [over the] mountain. High mountain.
With snowshoes, walk around, you know. Yeah.
Fish in the ice for a while.
Do that down there too [Xeni Biny]. Whitefish, get whitefish. Trout.
Smoke 'em. Make smoke offa that! [laughs]

There was trout a *long* time [ago]. Whole heap, big snow! [laughing] Sleigh.
Caught a moose somewhere in the bush. Elk way up the mountain.
The guys call [that] my base out there. [laughs] Red Mountain.

Sometime lotsa bear. Grizzly. Moose, not that much. Don't see elk. Just one.
They get grizzly.
Grizzly, they kill people.

Here

Gilbert Solomon, Xeni Gwet'in[12]

Dewhirst said, "Look, here's this river here. You see it? And here, this is where *you* live. Right here, this is your area where you from. Right here, this is where *you* live."

And I said, "Dewhirst, no, that's wrong. We don't live here, here. If we just live right here, we'll *die*. We need to go down the river or across the river. We need to go up this mountain. And we need to go way over there in the woods, and we need to go into that lake over there." I was goin' like that, you know.

And I said, "I dunno about you and what you're doin'. You're making a mini court case, and you're just writing, and you're not listening to all of this." I said no. *No.* I got mad at him. You know, like the other people – lawyers and, like, Dewhirst, he's just saying this, la la la la, and he doesn't know we have to go across a river and we need to go up this mountain, or we need to go to the woods or over here to get these berries.

Uh uh uh! Wuh! Huh! Could you see that, lawyers? Could you see it? [angrily] I said why is he doing that? I said why is this pelican here? Wake up, pelican.

And he kinda "Ohhh! Over in this camp." I said, "Yeah, we know. This camp is where we sleep. Go over this way, you know. You gotta take a pee over there." They got to go over there [themselves, not just look at maps]. I dunno.

How to Read a Map

David Williams[13]

In 2000 we were in this meeting and I remember a mapper from one of the ministries said there was trouble getting the Elders to understand how they could set aside areas. And she said, "Well, can't you just show them on the map that – you know, here's a, say, a CMT" – a culturally modified tree, which you really don't have. Trees don't last that long. It's not like the Coast. "Show them on the map and we can draw a line around it and save it." The postage-stamp idea, if you like. And I thought this woman just doesn't understand. These are Elders that don't speak English. They know where all these places are because that's where they've made their living, out there in the Brittany Triangle Tachelach'ed, the Place between the Waters, their hunting territory for thousands of years. And she said, "We could give them a course in how to read a map." And the first thought I had was maybe, lady, you should go out with them for a week on a trapline, and they could give *you* a course on what it's like to be out there at minus 30 or minus 40 and understand their lives a little bit and where they're coming from! You don't just protect one area – say, a beaver dam and a pond where you can trap beaver. It's the whole watershed you have to protect.

Directionals

Eila Quilt, Xeni Gwet'in

In the language [Tŝilhqot'in], it's so – I dunno if it's accurate or very detailed. You know how in English you can say "Go over there"? In Tŝilhqot'in it's not like that. I remember when we were younger, this plane flew in to Twin Lakes, and I guess his cargo area opened up and he lost his sleeping bags and all that stuff, and he told my dad about it. He told my dad what general area it was, and us kids were – you know, we don't know any better, but we know the Land. The next day he told us to saddle up the horses. He says, "You're gonna go here, you'll reach it by this time, the sun will be sitting here, and this is the kind of vegetation that will be there. You'll get a certain smell" – and it's just like watching a movie, you know. And the very idea we'd get to ride horses for the day, that was pay enough. We went and found that very spot, that very area, and we combed it and we didn't find [the stuff] there. So my dad asked the guy was the wind blowing that day and had us go to another area. [The language is] very descriptive. And it doesn't leave room for error.

I taught Tŝilhqot'in language in the high schools for quite a while, and kids were learning the oral part of it. Towards the end of May, I brought in a box full of different things. The language changes for how you pick up the object and how you put it down. "We can't learn that!"

A River of Fish

Ivor Deneway Myers xinli, Yuneŝit'in

It goes down to the ocean. It comes back. It goes down. It comes back. A whole river of fish. They're just like humans – they have spirits.

They [midugh] destroy them through an agreement with government where they transport oil or gas across the sea. You can't make profit like that – destroy the marine resources, destroy the waters.

That's everything I know, right. Everybody who was alive was killed.

Seʔintsu My Grandmother (Part 2)[14]

Elder Henry Solomon xinli, Xeni Gwet'in

In the second part of "Seʔintsu My Grandmother," Elder Henry Solomon xinli tells of how he was brought up on the Land by his grandmother Galín and of her life going from Tl'esqox to Xeni and back, hunting, fishing, and harvesting food and medicines for the winter. The same format has been used here as for part 1, beginning with an edited translation.

—LORRAINE WEIR

She raised me … at Tl'esqox. We picked saskatoon berries there. As we travelled around, she told me stories while we gathered fish. Long ago there was no moose on the Land around here. All over this Land there was only elk, she said. Over there where the people died in the south, this is where the elk were. People went to get them. Elk and caribou also used to be over there, where people had died. They travelled past where the ducks were dead and where the people had died on the mountain. They crossed over where one comes to get caribou and wild potatoes sunt'iny are harvested and beartooth ʔesghunsh in the south and people get saskatoon berries dig.

There long ago the people picking saskatoon berries found that person who had died where the saskatoons grow in the south. People did not want to bury him there where the saskatoons grow. People made a kind of stretcher, and four people carried him over. A long time ago, they brought him over the mountain top. For three days they must have done that. That person was Nikw'elid. He died where the saskatoon berries grow. They carried him over the mountain to where the people had died, and they buried him there. They did not want to bury him outside there. All his siblings carried him there and buried him in the place where people had died. I usually went in that direction from Tl'esqox then and went all over the mountain. Sometimes I went to Xeni. I usually visited Achig. He hunted over there on the mountain and I travelled there with him. All over Xeni and Chinaẑch'ez I harvested wild potato. Then I went back to Tl'esqox, she said. Achig was a good man, she said. He was with me, said

my grandmother. Then I made lots of dried meat and I brought it east [home].
They travelled only by horse, not wagon.

This is what she used to tell me about how it was.

?Eguh yax   Tl'esqox   ŝidah
Then over there   Tl'esqox   I lived
Then I lived at Tl'esqox.

?egu ?eyen senilhyan, xaginih.   ?Eguh yax   dɨg
then that person she raised me it was. Then over there saskatoon berries
She raised me at Tl'esqox. We picked saskatoon berries there.

hubah   te?at'ih. ?Egu yax   lhuy boxa?at'in ?eguh
we picked   we did.   Then over there   fish   we gathered there
We gathered fish.

gagunlhchugh selh   nagwelnig   yax   nat'as   ?eguh.
all over   with me she told stories over there we (two) travelled then.
As we travelled around, she told me stories.

?Eguh yax   yedanx ?egu yuguh   lha mus   chuh gulah
Then over there long ago over there   not moose too   there was
Long ago there was no moose

nenduwh   nench'ed. ?Eguh guyi   denichugh gadant'i
around here on this Land. Then   that thing elk,   that type
on the Land around here.

?eyi dzanh   nenduwh yax   nench'ed   gunlin   hagughint'i,
that one only around   over there on the Land   it existed   it was,
All over this Land, there was only elk

nih ghini,   yax   nenduwh   nench'ed   gagunlhchugh,
she said it was, over here around here on the Land all over.
she said.

?Eguh hink'an yax   yaneŝ   deni diẑtŝan, ?egu
Then and over there north (towards the mountains), people dead, there
Over there, towards the mountains, where the people died,

denichugh ʔeyi   gant'i   gunlin, ʔegunah   denichugh
elk   that one that type it existed over there   elk
that is where the elk were.

qanats'iyidilh.   Denichugh hink'an bedzish chuh
people went to get them. Elk   and   caribou also
People went to get them. Elk and caribou also

gunlin   hagughint'i, yax   deni diẑtŝan ʔeguh.
it existed it used to be, over there person they died there.
used to be over there [where] people died.

Yuguh   tunulh diẑtŝan   ʔeguh gweghats'edilh,
Over there ducks they are dead there people travelled by,
They travelled past where the ducks were dead

ʔegun yax   deni diẑtŝan dẑelh   ch'its'idilh,
then over there people dead mountain they travelled over
and where the people had died on the mountain they crossed over

ʔegu bedzish xats'iyidilh.   Hink'an ʔeguh
there caribou many would travel (to get). And   there
where one comes to get caribou and

sunt'iny   ts'esen,   ʔegu ʔesghunsh tah,   ʔegun yaneŝ
wild potatoes one uprooted there, beartooth that type there that direction
wild potatoes are harvested and beartooth in the south,

dig   gunlin tah   dig   xanats'iyidilh.   ʔEgun
saskatoon berries there that type saskatoons people got that there. There
and people get saskatoon berries. There

yedanx yax   dig   xats'iyidilh deni ʔinlhanx
long ago over there saskatoons got that   person one
long ago people getting saskatoons found that person who had died

ch'adejagh yaneŝ dig   gunlin ʔegun.
he died   south saskatoon berries it exists there.
[where the saskatoons grow] in the south.

?Eguh hink'an guyen deni   ?eyen lha ?eyed dig   gunlin
Then   and   that   person him   not there saskatoon berries it exists
People did not want to bury him there where the saskatoon berries grow.

guts'ulhtilh ts'egut'in.   ?Eguh guyi bid-deni-naqex
he is buried people did. Then want that thing with stretcher
People made a kind of stretcher

gant'i   ba?ats'inlagh,   deni   diny   yalhtilh.
that kind   people made for him, people four   they carry him
and four people carried him.

Lha ?aguŝed sink'an   ?egun dẑelh   teŝ
quite long   it must have been there   mountain over top
A long time ago they brought him over the mountain top.

najiyetilhtin,   tad dzin   tesajat'in.
they brought him   three days   they must have done that.
For three days they must have done that.

?Eyen deni ?eyen Nikw'elid ts'edinh xanih. Yax   dig   gunlin
That person him Nikw'elid called it was. Over there saskatoons they existed
His name was Nikw'elid. He died where the saskatoon berries grow.

ch'adejagh. Gun   ?inlhes gugun   dẑelh   towh
he died.   That person really   over there mountain among it
They carried him over the mountain

najeyetilhtin   yax   deni   diẑtŝan
they carried him over there people dead
to where the people had died

jinats'aghinlhtin   ?eyed hink'an guts?aghinlhtin.
some people carried him into there and   they buried him.
and they buried him there.

Lha gu?anz ŵelhti ts'ut'in,   guyen deni   ?eyen.
Not outside he lies, they wanted him that   person him.
They did not want to bury him outside there.

Gwaneŝ   guyen   jeyelh   ghedex gatŝ'in   yax
Because of it that person with him siblings all of them over there
All his siblings

najiyenilhtin   ?egun deni   diẑtŝan
they carried him there   people   died
carried him there and buried him [in the place where] people had died.

gujiyaghinlhtin. ?Eguh yax   Tl'esqoz xanadash   ?egu
they buried him. Then over there Tl'esqox we came from then
I [Galín] usually went in that direction from Tl'esqox

gagunlhchugh dẑelhch'ed nasash,   gwatish   yugun
all over   mountain I usually go there sometimes over that direction
and went all over the mountain.

Xeni ?egun chuh nasash.   ?Eguh guyen   yagh ?Achig
Xeni there too   I usually travel. Then that person um   ?Achig
Sometimes I went to Xeni. Then

ts'edinh   ?eyen bets'en   nanasdash.   ?Egu nulh
he is called him   toward him   I usually visited. Then animals
I usually visited ?Achig.

sahutsax, yax   dẑelh   towh   ?egu belh   nas?ish.
he shot,   over there mountain among it there with him I travelled.
He hunted over there on the mountain, and I travelled there with him.

Xeni gagunlhchugh yax   Chinaẑch'ez tah   ?egu
Xeni all over   over there Chinaẑch'ez that type there
All over Xeni and Chunoẑ Ch'ed

sunt'iny   tah   ?anasdlish. ?Eguh yadah Tl'esqoz
wild potato that type I handle.   There East   Tl'esqox
I harvested wild potato. Then I went back east to Tl'esqox, she said.

natesdash xaghest'in selh   denish.   Guyen   ʔAchig
I go there I did that   with me she said. That person ʔAchig
ʔAchig was with me.

ʔeyen deni   nezun   xaghet'in selh   denish   xaghint'i.
that person   he is nice   he was   with me she said   it was.
He was a good man, she said.

Denish   guyen   seʔintsu   ʔeyen.   ʔEgu ʔetŝen-ŝegen
She said that person my grandmother that person. Then dry meat
said my grandmother. Then I made lots of dry meat,

lhan ʔasʔinsh ʔegu yadah   natesggish   xanih.
many I made   then East   I brought them   it was.
and I brought it east [home].

Naŝlhiny dzanh bid   ʔeguh   nats'edilh   lha waghigen
Horse   only   with it around   they travelled not wagon
They travelled only by horse, not wagon.

chuh gulah hagughint'i. ʔEgu gwaselh   nagwelnish xaghint'ih.
too   it was it used to be. That she told me about it   it was.
That is what she told me about how it used to be.

Salmon Boy

Nits'ilʔin Russell Myers Ross, Yuneŝit'in

In [chapters 2 and 3 of Nits'ilʔin Ross's graphic novel "Deyenz Lhuy Belh Nand-lagh: A Story of Transformations"[15]], I was tryin' to move in the same direction that Salmon Boy went from his home, being cast away in a sense, and then me, living in Victoria for a number of years and eventually returning home. We're always having that yearning to return home. But it's basically the narrative of that stay, and then – but it was neat because I met my auntie Linda [R. Smith]. I got to know her a lot better as she was in Victoria, and I got to actually see the three boys grow up in Victoria and visit them regularly. I still remember even when Jeffan returned home, I remember one night he was having dinner and he was like, "Yuck, salmon's disgusting!" I had an image in my graphic novel where I had the same sentiment when I was a kid and then I ate a bit and then I wouldn't eat it. But then I went and told him, "Jeffan, you know how far that comes? You've lived in Victoria. Think about how far you've travelled from Victoria all the way back here. That's as far as that salmon's gone just to be on your plate so you can eat it." He just, like, looked – "Oh! I didn't know that!" He ate it all up.

Nenqayni deni The People

Suwh-ts'eghedudinh Self-Care

Lorraine Weir

Tŝilhqot'in scholar Linda R. Smith writes that the principle of suwh-ts'eghedudinh, meaning "preserving oneself, self-care," teaches "care of the physical self, [care of] others, the handling of food resources, and keeping resources and lands pure." She explains that the

> ancient Tŝilhqot'in perspective has been that the earth is too sacred to inflict with negative impacts and other contaminants in the form of negative energy or chemicals ... As Tŝilhqot'in, one's connectedness comes through the ancient stories, influencing one's interactions with others in the community, respect for ancestors, and sustainable interaction with the environment.[16]

By affirming the people's jurisdiction over their Land, the Title case victory began the decolonial process of healing and restoring the ancient balance of Land and people, rooting hope for the future in the wisdom of the ʔEsggidam Ancestors.

The Land Is Our Backbone

Ivor Deneway Myers xinli, Yuneŝit'in

The Land is our backbone and we defended it. That's who we are. We are nothing without the Land. The Land is nothing without the People – Nenqayni. Nen means Earth. Qay means surface. Ni means people. Nenqayni deni: the Tŝilh-qot'in People of the Earth.

We are the true owners. Given to us by the Creator. That's why I always say the colonizers, they don't have jurisdiction. Yet they steal.

Tŝilhqot'in National Government? It's named after this river here. We're the river people. But we're also the earth's people. Nenqayni deni government. That's how I would like to have done it.

So.

All over This Land

Elder Mabel Solomon xinli with Dinah Lulua, Xeni Gwet'in[17]

From left, Dinah Lulua with her mother, Elder Mabel Solomon xinli, looking at qatŝ'ay. Photo by Lorraine Weir

Before my time, people lived underground in pithouses. They would dig a hole into the ground and build an underground lodge.

Before my time, there was no horses. You used your own two legs to get around. They trapped for many fur-bearing animals like beaver or muskrat and I don't know how to say some of the names she said. All kinds of animals – squirrels she said. They sold it to fur traders to buy food. Long before me. I just hear stories.

Back in the day, there was no [store-bought] clothing. You had to make your clothing from the fur that you got. People were very poor back in those days.

Back in the day, I was always by my father's [Sambulyan's] side, helping out in everything that he did. When the residential school started happening, my mom and dad hid me from goin' there. That's why today I don't speak the [English] language.

If you weren't lazy in those days, you wouldn't starve. They would go way out on Tŝilhqox Biny Chilko Lake to Tutl'az Franklin Arm. They'd make dugout canoes and they'd go across there and hunt. The late Donald Myers and his wife Helena (who was Sambulyan's daughter), they came way back into Tutl'az Franklin Arm with us in a dugout canoe to trap and preserve meat for winter.

Back in those days, they didn't have the iron traps that they use[d later]. They built a wood structure. The animal would go into the wood structure where they put a bait, a piece of meat inside, and when it's knockin' at the meat, it would collapse the whole thing over top of it to kill it. She [Mabel] helped her dad when he was settin' up traps like that. They dried meat from the deer and the goats – mountain goats.

She says sometimes they would be cooking dried meat over a fire and they used this grass that they use for drying sopalallie [soapberries] – the type of grass they use for that. They cook it with meat and they tie this grass to nearby bushes and that and the fur-bearin' animals, sometimes the weasels and martens would smell that and come. And they would kill it.

The men were hunters. They went into the bushes to find food. Like they hunted for food. They trapped for fur, and they skinned the fur and stretch them out and sold it to fur traders, and it was mainly the men that did all that part of skinning and stuff. Stretching the fur out for trade.

Back in the day, they would buy lots of fur, but they don't do that anymore. Even coyotes, she said, they would buy its fur. Squirrels and sesjiz, martens. Nambay, weasels. She said I set out traps for coyotes. I'd catch a coyote now and then and also lynx. Women didn't do this very much – it was mainly men. The women prepared the deer hide and moose hide and tanned it. They made moccasins and jackets and anything that you needed – gloves.

They started buying whiteman food by Stoney there, Lee's Corner. They had fur traders at Lee's Corner and close to Stoney there, at Chilco Ranch. A white guy named Guli with his wife, Mrs. Guli [skunk]! [laughs]

Oh, Mrs. Lee! Oh, okay. Mr. Lee, that's what she meant. Norman Lee. He threw a big wad of chewing tobacco. His wife was a white person too. He was a fur trader. She thinks that maybe her name was Agnes. After they got older, they passed on. Their store burned down. People from Stoney always went there. Norman Lee would buy all the fur that was trapped in the winter fur trapping. They buy all kinds of animal fur.

I was born here and raised here in Xeni in the field near old Sil Canim's house. My daughters and my sons were raised there. I was born behind there, January 19, 1923, in the wintertime in a tent. I was born on this Land.

We travel all over this Land of Xeni, travelling on horses. I always went with my dad, trappin' all over this Land. We had to do the hunting for the winter. We dried lots of meat, lots of meat. And we saved all the fat from the meat. You picked your teas and your berries and dried your fish and dried your meats. In the late fall, chase cattle to Williams Lake. We dried so much meat that we'd tie it up in the fur of the deerskin and her dad would load it by the cross and put it away for winter. She'd put deermeat in a big soup pot and cook it up and drain the fat and let it sit till it got hard, and then she'd put that away for winter use. The kids liked to eat the cracklings after the fat was drained off.

You'll never run out of food if you prepare your fish and your dry meat, and you'll always have food aplenty.

Tu Water

Lorraine Weir

As Ivor Myers xinli said with reference to Teẑtan Biny Fish Lake, "Those waters are just like spirits – alive." When an open-pit gold and copper mine was proposed by Taseko Mines Limited for this lake and the surrounding area, teachings about Tu water were mobilized for presentation by community members at panel hearings conducted by the Canadian Environmental Assessment Agency (CEAA) in 2010 and 2013. In the next two chapters, we will focus on those teachings in detail, but it's also important to include Tu water in the context of teachings about the Nen Land in order to understand these keystone principles of Tŝilhqot'in epistemology in relation to each other. Tu water is sacred and, as Chief Roger says, "We always talk to the water and tell the water why we need it." Inside the womb, the child listens to the parents speaking and emerges into a language, culture, and people already familiar to them. Thinking about the sacred connection between women and water, Marilyn Baptiste later talks about the need for women "to stand up and start coming together in ceremony with our drums for the water, for Mother Earth, and taking back our responsibility in doing that." During the 2013 CEAA panel hearing at Teẑtan Biny Fish Lake, Cecil Grinder performed ceremony, praying "to this water to look after me, my body, wherever I'm hurting ... When I go in this water like this, it's a prayer for me." As Elder Dinah Billyboy xinli told the CEAA panelists, "We are the River People and the river knows that ... The river is our life."[18]

One of the most powerful recent statements about Tu is ʔElhdaqox Dechen ts'edilhtan ʔEsdilagh Sturgeon River Law, adopted by the ʔEsdilagh First Nation Chief and Council in May 2020. This law is a response to the catastrophic rupture of the tailings pond at Imperial Metals' Mount Polley mine in 2014, releasing twenty-four million cubic metres of contaminated water into ʔElhdaqox the Fraser River. An eloquent statement of Tŝilhqot'in values and principles concerning Tu Water, this law states that the river must be respected and is "a gift, not a resource." In the context of Imperial Metals' actions, "There are consequences for mistreating ʔElhdaqox. ʔElhdaqox is powerful and any mistreatment of it can have dire foreseen and unforeseen consequences for the next generations." Tu Water is a spiritual being interconnected with the beings of the river people. As ʔElhdaqox Dechen ts'edilhtan states, "People, animals, fish, plants, the Nen, and the tu have Rights in the decisions about their care and use that must be considered and respected."[19]

Nenqayni ch'ih The People's Way (The Tŝilhqot'in Language)

Black Memory

Marilyn Baptiste, Xeni Gwet'in

One of the things that we are still trying to work on is reviving our ceremonies and different aspects of our culture. Our old Tŝilhqot'in language is being lost. Some people don't even know what I'm saying when I say that. Many of our ceremonies are in what they call black memory because of the traumas in residential school. That's how one of my friends, Valerie Setah, explained it to me. There is this place of great trauma that our people went through. They put these memories and traumas into this place of black memory when they don't want to see them or feel them ever again. They want to be able to survive, so they create a wall or black memory so they can continue through life.

Hanging onto My Voice

Lois Williams, Xeni Gwet'in

My matrilineal grandmother, Nelly Lulua, was a very stubborn and a very intelligent person. She learned to do a lotta things on her own. She lived off the Land and knew how to take care of cattle and horses and how to hunt. And that's how I was able to hang onto my voice and know how to speak Tŝilhqot'in and learn. That's how my mom [Elder Maria Williams] was able to hang onto her language as well. She only spoke Tŝilhqot'in, and that's how I grew up. My grandmother Nelly hid my mother Maria in the mountains when the police came to pick up children for the residential school in Williams Lake.

I learned English in school and I picked it up so fast and so easily that I almost forgot how to speak Tŝilhqot'in, but I really tried to hang onto it. I had people mocking me and calling me stupid because I didn't know how to speak Tŝilhqot'in. Like, a lot of that type of verbal abuse. There's still that cycle of abuse that got carried on from the impacts of residential school, and everybody needs to do their own healin' work and to be able to develop a new healthier pattern. So.

I've been able to do work on myself, work on my own trauma, and come back a softer person. I guess more compassionate, the way we're supposed to be, you know, with our Tŝilhqot'in teaching, with our values. Our teachings are lha hunilt'i, which means: "Don't think or act like you're better than anyone else." And nen deni hunint'in, meaning "love" – like "Love your community, love your family, be loving toward other people." So those are some of the teachings that our Elders keep telling us. My mom used to say, "Watch your big mouth!" [laughing] She used to always say that. She knew some English words. She knew that words could be quite hurtful, and she'd always be looking out for us and teaching us. And within those teachings we learned our Tŝilhqot'in laws, our rituals, how each person grows up.

It's all to do with action. If you're doin' activities on the Land, that's how you learn your language. It's all activity-based. And through your actions, how you live your life, how you hunt or fish or how you make a fishnet or how you make a baby basket. It's all connected because we're taught since we're little, and the baby could hear you when they're in your stomach. When they're born, they turn their head 'cause they recognize your voice. They start learning the language from the womb.

It's the same with laws and rituals. Each stage of your life, you're taught different things. Not to do certain things, not to eat certain food. When I was pregnant, my mom made sure to really teach my husband that as well. He was not allowed to go to funerals while I was pregnant. And I wasn't allowed to go to funerals. My mom was very, very firm. Kept us in line and told me I wasn't allowed to eat berries. I was supposed to listen with all my children, but with the last one, I ate berries, and sure enough, [when] she was born, she had blueberry marks on her lower back and strawberry marks on the back of her head. So I was like, "Oh my gosh, my mom's gonna get mad at me!" I was thinking, you know, when she was born. I think my mom was just relieved that we were both okay and we came home safely, but she looked at me and she said, "I know what you were eating when you were pregnant." You can get blueberry and strawberry marks on the baby's face and skin, and that's always what you would like to avoid. They're just very, very strict on what you eat and what you do. And at each stage of my life, I have to learn things and I have to teach my own kids as well. Which is quite the challenge because we don't live in the Territory. I'm still teaching them the laws and rituals, so when we come back here, it's an easier transition for them.

Body Language

Maryann Solomon, Xeni Gwet'in

Some people are more spiritual. They can see things. They can sense it. Some people probably have that gift. It's like yourself, I'm sure sometimes you can know almost right away what somebody is like or what kind of person they are.

Animals sense what kind of person you are. Like in my book,[20] I found where these guys were joking around, making fun of the bear, and the bear came in and killed 'em all. There's lots of stories on that. Animals know what kind of person you are, whether you're a good person, a bad person, what you did in life, what you think about. They sense all of it. They sense dangerous energy, so they'll attack. That's what the Elders told me. By the energy rays, body language, they know what sort of person you are. If I saw a bear, I'd tell my mom [Elder Mabel Solomon xinli] that the bear just looked at me and kept on walking, and she always said, "'Cause he doesn't wanna see you or he doesn't like you!" Once in a while, I'll see a bear and he'll look at me and keep walking, and I'm like, "Well, I guess he likes me!"

I really believe the stories the Elders tell about the animals. They're tough because of something in that person's life. They know when you talk about them. My mum always said when I was younger, "Don't talk about the bear 'cause they can hear you. They're gonna come!" We weren't supposed to talk about them when we were camping. It's almost like our life is different animals, you know, thinking how they move.

Ch'ih gudzɨsh[21] Place Names

Beginnings

Ivor Deneway Myers xinli, Yuneŝit'in

Tŝilhqot'in culture goes way back and we go back. When you're first born, you look at the sky, the moon, the time of year. Where you're born could be beside a rock, could be along the river, could be on the Land somewhere. And that's how you were named. They give you a name when you're first born. Sit'ax was born beside a rock. Tŝi is rock and t'ax is beside. That's why he got his name. Like place names, it was the same thing for a human being, especially First Nations.

So that's your first given name, and they nurture you, they feed you, and they also take care of your ts'iny [umbilical cord]. With the ts'iny, they'll wait for a while till the child grows up to maybe five, six, seven. I learned why they place it under an animal track – could be a deer, moose, or whatever. For girls, they sometimes put it under a deer track or a raspberry bush or some type of berry bush. If the ts'iny was placed under the track of whatever animal, then you become almost like that, so if it's a deer, you can jump like a deer – fast, fast on its feet. It jumps over a fence with no problem. But if it's under a berry bush, you become a berry picker, like a harvester in the summer. A lotta berries ripen in the country. My mum did that for me. I'm not sure where she placed it. Probably underneath a deer track.

Place Names

Ivor Deneway Myers xinli, Yuneŝit'in

Place names are crucially important. They tell how Tŝilhqot'in people used to live in this area a long time prior to contact, when Tŝilhqot'ins called their

Territory Nenqayni Nen. During the time of the Big Flood, somebody on that boat with Deneway and his people said let's call this river whatever, and place names came to be. Place names are our identity. The earth is our body and the body that's in us is like the earth. That's what we call Title and we're born from that. That's who we are. It's like a mirror – our body's from the earth, and we're like a Title in itself.

The most important part of recording is place names, especially when Elders are talking about a certain area and they talk about the history and have a story about that area. A lot of people don't know about history and when we record that information, it becomes the public domain of the society and [can be] used in teaching, whether elementary, high school, or postsecondary education. There's a lot of hearsay stories from European people about how we got here in North America, but place names give an example of how the people utilized an area, lived in that area, and tell of actual events and other names that were given in the past.

Today I think our people are traumatized and still breaking out. There's some good people out there that have good knowledge. Just have to fit them together. It's not gonna be easy unless we have some of those recordings of those place names – history of that area. That's the most important. Without that we're nothing, we're gone.

There's some other place names that have never been revealed because they're – I dunno – not ready yet, I guess. Or I dunno what they're afraid of. They should be upfront and get some of those Elders to be recorded, you know, without being angry or jealous or whatever. They could approach Elders just to do that. Otherwise this is gonna be history [i.e., gone] and we've got nothing on the other side. That needs to be done ASAP. It's gonna fade away, this history. And nobody will know.

When the first European people came in the country, they began to name areas after people, like Anahim Lake, Anaham Reserve, Toosey, Nemiah, Alexis Creek. They named our river here the Fraser River, but we had a name prior to that, and it didn't look right to them. We still call it ʔEsda, ʔElhdaqox, and it means Dirty River. That was told to me by one Elder, and other Elders say the same thing. When our people used to live along the river, Fraser River, they used to call it ʔEsdaqoxt'in. Place names for the rivers are related to the continuous flow of the area. For example, ʔEsdaqox, Sturgeon River. Sturgeons used to go up the river. They still do. That's why they call it Sturgeon River.

Kappan Lake is another one that was named after the fact, and Kappan was finally acknowledged. Kappan was a Tŝilhqot'in Warrior, a Tŝilhqot'in leader, who was proudly chosen to be the leader after they killed their noble leader.

He was the last Tŝilhqot'in leader over there. I dunno that other person's name who was a very noble leader there and they killed him. So.

The area of the Xeni Gwet'in court case is just a small area that was given [by the Plaintiff] as an example. At the beginning, I guess they just wanted to give an example of where the Title area is, and there was no discrepancy by affirmation. And they had to utilize that one as an example and it became the Nation's Title area, but it was also being said that there's other areas on the outside of the so-called Claim Area, and those other Lands still had to be ratified. The truth is that the Elders that still speak the language were trying to reveal something in the Xeni Gwet'in court case, but they were told no, that's all they could do. They wanted to reveal some of this information but they couldn't at that time. They couldn't further expand on some place names and how some Tŝilhqot'in people utilized those areas at one time. They could only go so far.

Place names get you somewhere if you know your oral history. You have to find out how long they used that area at one time, prior to smallpox. Some archeological evidence might be that there were wars here and there. There were some bodies on the ground. They were trying to retaliate and they got killed. Things like that. Some of our arrowheads were found somewhere else, somewhere far because we went and helped out. Some of our arrowheads went there. Just like that, you know. You have to know the actual story behind a place name.

Colour, Name, and Design

Rita Lulua Meldrum, Xeni Gwet'in

Back in the day, each family had their own design, baskets, colours, clothing, how it's done. So when other people saw you, they knew which family you were from. That's lost. That's what Grandma [Elder Inez Lulua xinli] told me, and I don't hear anybody else saying that.

How Grandma told me how people were named was you got four names in your whole life. Your kid name – how you behave when you're a kid. And when you became a youth, you got another name because you behave a certain way. And then you become an adult and you get another one. And then at the very end, you get another name. There's a certain name that follows all the way through but that also identified which family you're from and who your grandparents are. And so people would find out which family you're from according to colour, name, and design.

Names and Regalia

Rita Lulua Meldrum, Xeni Gwet'in

It was lost. We don't even know what kind of regalia – I don't know if you call it clothing – we wore back then. Nobody has pictures and nobody really knows. So most of these [contemporary] regalia or uniforms are probably a vision that came to them. What to make and what to use. Mostly it's visions that individuals get to create their uniforms. In Coastal cultures they understand what the uniform stands for and why it's made that way in that style. And a song goes with that uniform. And the name. We had all that, but it's not there [anymore]. My grandmother used to tell me about how that was done but forgotten about. I was ten when she died, so she taught me when I was like eight, nine, ten – and there's only certain things that really imprinted in my mind.

Dadaben Medicine

Ceremony

Rita Lulua Meldrum, Xeni Gwet'in

I got my niece to do all the artwork on my drum. All the time she was doing that, she was thinking of her mom, and her mom is my sister who passed away. The drum represents the cedar from Mother Earth. We use that as a frame. And we use the skin from the deer or the moose or whatever to make a drum. We also use it to make purses, bags, stuff to store stuff in that we use for clothing. We also make moccasins out of deer hide. We use the wood to make rattles so we can sing and meditate to the sound. This rattle is made out of wood with seeds in it, I think. And this other rattle is also made out of hide and wood, and when we clap them, we have to do it in thanks and in honour of Mother Earth. And I have sinew there which is also made from deer. So this is what we use. [shaking the rattle]

This is medicine that we collect. We also use sage and other medicines to calm us down and to balance us. I've also got pitch that I made. My grandmother taught me and my cousin Joyce [Charleyboy] reminded me how to make it. It's really good for burns. (My grandmother adopted Joyce's mum.) We also use cedar boughs or any kind of boughs. A friend of mine in Kincolith made this basket for me. Like all Nations everywhere, they use bark, leaves, or whatever to make baskets.

We collect our food, so I made you Indian tea, Labrador tea, from back home. And I also made you spring salmon with bread to let you know that we use the river. We need clean water to survive, so we can feed ourselves, nourish our body. So these are all the things that we use to clothe ourselves and to keep ourselves balanced.

Learning from My Grandmother

Rita Lulua Meldrum, Xeni Gwet'in

I learned from my grandmother [Elder Inez Lulua xinli], which is totally different than adopting from other Nations. My grandmother just used sweats for healing, like spiritual healing. And she used to get me to help her build the fire, and ever since I was about five years old, she would get me up at five o'clock every morning to go swimming. It didn't matter if it was winter, spring, summer, fall. My dad told me it was spiritual teaching to get me to be a healer or to help other people. I know one day I was just crying to my dad, saying, "I don't like doing things like this." Ever since I was eight or nine, I would see spirits and see things before they happen. It's a little scary to me 'cause Grandma died quite young, so I never got the full teaching. I probably got half a teaching and then she passed away.

When I was a teenager, most of the adults that were around were alcoholics. So I moved to the city to get away from all the alcohol and family violence and all that. All the dysfunction that comes with drinking. I moved away from home to get away from something I didn't understand. I moved to the city and started my healing journey. And I've been here since. Not to say that I'm done my healing journey. I'm still working on it, too.

Now, We're Healing

Gilbert Solomon, Xeni Gwet'in

Now, we're healing. While we're healing, we're gonna heal other people on the outside. We need to learn how to live off the earth, 'cause there's gonna be no power. So you guys could teach us how to do that, live off the earth. This whole place could become a picture of the world – to teach them how we treat everything on the water. Everything has spirit – it's all spiritual. So when we're healing, the economic side goes to healing, not to forestry or mining or whatever we're looking [at] out there. People can get money here as we heal them in different ways. We're healing each other. We're not healing ourselves from the outside. We're healing from the outside in. We have this country intact to prove to them that there's a heaven here on Earth if we could just keep going the good way, that way we gotta go from here on or else the earth is gonna get

RID of us! Like, they've done that before a few times. The earth just says, "ACH! Don't do that! ACHH!"

Elder as Encyclopedia, Elder as Healer

Gilbert Solomon, Xeni Gwet'in

A professor is an archeologist. That's what I said to the lawyers. I said, "An Elder is like a professor. I dunno how you say it. A walking book." And then I said, "Encyclopedia – this one person right here." She'd answer you, like, *now!* She's not gonna think about it. Like, "Oh!" Yeah.

Dad [Elder Henry Solomon xinli] was like that, too. If you'd go over there angry – "Whaddya doin' with that, yeah, yeah, yeah, yeah, yeah – this person givin' me a hard time!" And then he'd say something like I'd be ashamed of what I just did. [laughing] I'll be like "No!" "Holy *smoke*," he'd say. [in a quiet voice] He said no more.

I was so ashamed that I had brought this up to my dad. He took me out of this. He put me in the [other] guy's shoes when I wasn't looking after myself. He said a few words and it'd make you see the whole picture right *now*. You'll be looking back at yourself and the *whole* thing happening right there. When I wasn't [breathing heavily] no more, he said, "*WUH!*"

What do you call that? Humble? No. Different than humble. Fix me and cure me *now*. You know. A few words. Like, *ahhh!*

The Medicine Drive

Lorraine Weir

When I was invited to go on a medicine drive with the Elders, I was too busy to use my digital recorder. "Here's a shovel," said Betty Lulua, "and this is how you dig xilhdilh." She plunged her shovel into the ground and began to dig up a green leafy plant, taking care to keep the roots intact. All around me in the forest, the Elders were digging xilhdilh Indian hellebore and picking bedzish ts'ediyan Labrador tea and bending down to carefully examine leaves and shoots. A young man with a rifle walked the perimeter in case of grizzlies.

I went around and took pictures before I tried to dig. Digging proved to be very hard work, but in spite of the fact that I was an inept novice, the Elders smiled kindly and encouraged my efforts. On the way back, I got to sit in the passenger seat of the van and get some advice from expert driver Laura Setah. A helpful midugh had told me to avoid driving through enormous deep puddles on gravel roads by putting two wheels on the shoulder. Laura was appalled, but she didn't show it other than to say, "That way you go straight down if the shoulder's soft." To my right, the shoulder plunged down an embankment into the forest. "Puddles always have bottoms," she said.

Xilhdilh is made into a salve and used for arthritis. Bedzish ts'ediyan is dried and enjoyed as a tea.

Betty Lulua holding xilhdilh Indian hellebore while Elder Eileen Sammy William looks on. Photo by Lorraine Weir

Drumming and Singing

Marilyn Baptiste, Xeni Gwet'in

One of the visions I had was to be able to bring back the strength and honour of our drumming and singing. One of my first and greatest witnessings of this was when I travelled to the St'at'imc Territory gathering in May 2008 with Roger when he was going to do a presentation on the Title and Rights case there. I almost did not go but was so thankful I went. While we were waiting for the gathering to begin, it was announced that the runners were coming in from all of the St'at'imc communities, notifying them all of the gathering. When they were getting near, everyone went out to receive them. We lined up on both sides of the gathering grounds and they ran into the centre while we were all drumming and singing. It was such an honour to witness my vision of Elders, leaders, youth, and children drumming and singing with honour and pride. It was amazing and so beautiful to be part of this and witness the support they showed when anyone spoke. They were respectful and kind, drumming to acknowledge everyone's words.

Throughout my leadership we always welcomed and encouraged our youth and young ones to come and join in the singing and drumming. We have had so many young girls and women singing and drumming. It is very powerful. When my first granddaughter Madisyn was little, before she could talk, she would pick me out of the lineup of speakers to come to me with her mom and my late niece Marie. Madisyn was so amazing and would come to me when [I was] drumming, singing, and speaking. I am so proud of her and her amazing strength. I have been learning our Tŝilhqot'in drumming and songs with our family from Yuneŝit'in, including the late Madeline Myers Ross, Maria Myers, Helen Haig-Brown, Linda Haig-Brown, and others who used to come together and practise at different homes and have potluck-style meals together. We need to keep this practice going.

A lot of our communities which are on the BC Hydro grid have been doubly impacted, not just by residential school but by the luxury of the hydro. A lot has been lost in that. We are very fortunate as Xeni Gwet'in, because we're off the hydro grid and our community has a lot of gatherings. We're extremely busy and we have to continue in our way and continue on the Land and water.

Our drum and our song are very important as part of our spirituality as a people. I think it was not long after I became Chief, my nephew Dalton [Baptiste] was at a powwow and he showed me a couple of drums that were going in to raffle. One had a hummingbird on it, and I wanted that one, but he won the other one. He gave me that drum and I have carried it throughout our whole fight, throughout my leadership, and encouraged our young people and all of our people to get up and come and join in drumming and singing. Drum and sing and learn *our* songs, our Tŝilhqot'in songs, so my people, my children, can be a part of this and bring out the strength of our spirituality and our culture.

Energy

Maryann Solomon, Xeni Gwet'in

There's a certain energy, and when you have this energy, you have to respect it and use it properly, 'cause if you don't, then it touches something there. It's not exactly negative energy. You call it bad luck or you touch a plant when you're on your time and it kills the plant. You can't touch people's hair – your husband's or your kids' – and if you touch them when you're on your time, then they have to have somebody fix their hair for them. Their hair would turn grey faster because they have this energy. It's almost the same thing when somebody touches a gun and they're not allowed to hunt for a year, they can't carry babies, they can't go fishing. When you go to a lake, the fish sense the energy and they go out. The fish won't come inland again. That's why they use twins, because twins have special powers. If somebody catches a fish when they have this energy, then they get a twin and they fish along the shore. The fish will come in again. If they're gathering medicines, there's something they have to do, and they have that knowledge. You know, when they're gathering medicine, they always have that knowledge of why they're sending prayers up to almost like the spirit of the plant. Sending prayers to it and thanking it while you're gathering and you're doing medicines and healing.[22]

Deyen Healer

Ivor Deneway Myers xinli, Yuneŝit'in

Songs are you – your own identity. You don't reveal to no one. You sing yourself. Belongs to you, no one else. It's up to him, up there in the sky. You're not supposed to share it with anyone. Only time you'll ever sing to a person is when you're healing them, putting their spirit back in them sometime. Or you can use it wherever you have to go for communicating with those spirits.

Somebody in the sky somewhere would bring you that song. You have to sing that song. They'll become your power. After each fast. It could be maybe ten days after you finish the first fast, whatever. If there are five more days, they could give you another power. And so on. It's like that. Sit'ax had many songs, my great-great-grandfather. He used to cast out evil spirits.

Whoever gives it to you through the sky, the great spirit, they tell you how to sing a song and how to heal people. That's how it was. If somebody asked you to dance, you couldn't help but dance right in front of them. If somebody asked you to heal this child, you gotta go over there and do it, and you don't ask for any money. You don't ask for nothing but do a good deed for that person.

I hear people. I'll hear the spirit of a person. That spirit. I do that. I'm supposed to. Say somebody touched a person here, and it hurts. I just take it right off. I'm not strong like those other people, though.

See, that's the reason why you go fast in the mountains for a long time, like Deneway did, the way Moses did, the way Jesus did, the way Noah did. That's how they got their power. They fasted.

*   *   *

One thing I wanted to tell you that I heard from my grandfather George [Myers]. Says long long ago, a lot of people were starving, and I know there was no horses in this Land at that time. None whatsoever. People used to travel by foot. And they had dogs during those days and they used dogs as packers to transport some things. And the bow and arrow also originated long ago.

It has been told by another Elder that one time there was a Medicine Man who was starving. He was gaunt, with nothing in his stomach. So this deyen man dreamed about how to make a bow and arrow and how to use it to kill animals. And in his dream it came to him, how to make this bow. And how to make the strings. And how to make the arrowheads. And how to make the arrow stop.

In his dream that's what was told to him, so he made one. And in his dream, he also probably had the power of that bow. Only a deyen person that has a power of that bow could use the bow to his gain. A person just like yourself or anybody else tryin' to stretch that bow, you cannot with your hands, even with your two feet and two hands – you can only stretch it so far. But when that Medicine Man comes around and grabs his bow, he stretches it arm's length. [making the sound of an arrow shooting through the air] That's how powerful that bow is.

My grandfather told me about that one there.

Gwenig Stories

What Is a "Legend-Story"? A Conversation

Chief Roger William and Lorraine Weir

Roger: To you what is a legend? It's a myth, right? To me, legend, I understand it to be a creation. Things change in this world. For us in our Territory, our animals are us too, and I believe the stories really happened. What if you open up a dictionary? When we say "legend," it's probably not even close to what the dictionary says.

Lorraine: Made-up story. Fiction.[23]

Roger: Made-up story, fiction, yeah. And to us, no, it's not. And that's what that lawyer for BC asked me: "Is that a myth?" He was really trying to understand me, and I said no, and he said, "Oh," so he thought about it. We could say creation story, but creation could mean we created something that's a myth. So what is the right word in English to say what Lhin Desch'osh is? We just say Lhin Desch'osh – that means this is what it is, that's the closest. Lhin Desch'osh is a story, that's what happened – creation, beginning of time. So.

Gwenig means story, stories being told. Sadanx gwenig means way back in historic times and that could be Lhin Desch'osh, Datsan Raven, Tseman Salmon Boy, all those different stories.

Sadanx is when the Land was created – the time of creation. if we're talking about creation story, I could say sadanx gwenig. Sadanx is before yedanx, long ago. Digudanx is more recent than yedanx.

Digudanx is during that time of contact when non–First Nations – midugh – started coming in. Starting to see these people and there's something happening. This is probably not yet the time of smallpox, but there's contact.

Lorraine: So gwenɨg is story? Not legend?

Roger: I'm just thinking, if I were to go by what the dictionary is saying about legend [fiction, made-up story], I don't think we have legend stories. We've got actually happened, like we're talking about gwenɨg is story. When I was testifyin' in court, we were talkin' about a "legend story." "Did that really happen?" they asked me. I really believe it happened. It wasn't a "legend story." It really happened. I don't even know – story. Like, history maybe.

No matter what you say or do, you're not gonna change my mind. This is what I believe. That's a sadanx gwenɨg story. The story is what Tŝ'ilʔos did to people who try to do things. I talked about the Chilco Ranch when they tried to bring their cattle up.[24] That's a yedanx gwenɨg story.

Time

Ivor Deneway Myers xinli, Yuneŝit'in

Sadanx is old, very old, long ago, during the time of the legends, during the times of the stories being told by our people. Long, long ago. How the earth evolved. How the animals became to be. How the chipmunks became to be. How Lhin Desch'osh was running after an animal and he grabbed the top of that animal and made that mark, and to this day they call that a chipmunk. Rocks froze. Those four rocks froze – Alexis Creek. Only three of them are left there. They were tryin' to build a road there and they disturbed that ground. One rock is missing. Without lettin' us know. And there's another rock, and it's more southwest of Alexis Creek. There was a woman who was not allowed to see any man. There was a man that was following her, I guess, and she stepped on a pebble. She turned around. Froze. Dead. Turned into that rock.

Words for Time

Elder Minnie Charleyboy, Tŝideldel[25]

k'andzin	today
k'anits'alilh	when you're young
xeldanx	yesterday
ʔilhed xi ghili	"a year or so"

digudanx	"a year or so"
yedanx	a long time ago ("there seems to be no time limit when you say yedanx")
yedanx denilin	"long time ago people"
ʔEsggidam yedanx denilin	"longer ago than yedanx denilin"
sadanx	"when our Ancestors were like animals," "long ago time stories"[26]

Reading between the Lines

Annie C. Williams, from the trial transcript

When Tŝilhqot'ins speak their language, you got to kind of read between the lines. They … never really finish a story. They want you to finish the story. They want you to think about what it is that you are doing or what it is that was happening at that time, and from that you learn.[27]

In the Dark Time

Elder Eileen Sammy William and April William xinli, Xeni Gwet'in

Elder Eileen: Me, I didn' testify. I was goin' to, and then the lawyer went to Redstone instead! He said he'd be here tomorrow! [laughs] I [was going to] tell the stories. Just, like, the legends from way back. There's a lot. Like when we were in Mission, I'd tell the story.

It have to be night time before I talk about *old*, old legends. They're always told in the dark time. 'Cause you go blind, some of them. You'll go blind [if you tell them in the daytime].

They teach quite a bit. They teach the young ones things that they don't even know.

April William xinli: They teach them respect for the Land. [The stories] from way back remind us what they used to think, 'cause it didn't just begin from today.

Getting the Kids Settled Down

Rita Lulua Meldrum, Xeni Gwet'in

Grandma [Elder Inez Lulua xinli] always told us stories around the campfire. When it got dark, she would tell us stories from long time ago. But during the day, we had to work or do whatever – play, help with the farm work, or whatever. We were busy during the day, so we couldn't get interrupted by talking. So I have a feeling that they tell you things like, "It's done at this time" because the underlying thing is, "Okay, if we say this, then the kids'll believe us." It's like, oh, we can't talk during the day because you have to work between daylight and evening. Then it's time to relax and to listen. That's when you're tired, and you can just sit there and listen to Elders tell stories, but if they did it during the day, you know, it would interrupt the work.

Also, we tell kids not to swing at night or run around at night because you'll run into spirit. We tell kids that so they won't run around, because we want them to settle down and listen to the stories that are being told. If you swing too fast, you run into spirit and you get thrown off balance and you won't have focus. You get Indian sickness. And if kids run around, the same thing. If they run into spirit, then they get Indian sickness. Then you need a spiritual healer to balance them and get rid of whatever they ran into. Ghosts, whether bad or good.

Knowing the Animals

Lois Williams, Xeni Gwet'in

When I was a kid, my sisters, my brothers, and the kids in the neighbourhood all ran up and down that road by Konni Lake. We'd start in the mornings and maybe we'd get to the opposite end. Maybe we'd get as far as Chilko Lake. Back and forth, that's how we spent every day throughout the summer.

Children are taught the stories so they'll know the animals. We didn't fear the bears, cougars, bobcats, wolves, horses, other animals, and all living creatures native to the Tŝilhqot'in Territory. The stories tell us who the animals are.

I remember playing outdoors from the sunrise to the sunset as a child. My siblings, cousins, and I knew where to drink fresh water and where to pick berries. We were never taught to fear the animals.

Horses on the Nemaiah Valley Road. Photo by Chief Roger William

Lha yudit'ih We Always Find a Way

Dechen ts'edilhtan Tŝilhqot'in Law

Traditional Law

Maryann Solomon, Xeni Gwet'in

Dechen ts'edilhtan is traditional law. Literally, it means laying a stick, but forget about the stick! [i.e., it's a metaphor] It means this is how the law is. This is the law. Back then, this was our culture, our way of life, the way we were raised since we were born. Like how the baby had to be handled, what the mother had to do, everything. Today people don't know that. We go to the hospital, but back then, this was their life. Today we call it a ritual, but it was just their way of life. For example, how a woman had to take care of herself at the beginning of her pregnancy. There were certain foods she had to eat, certain foods she couldn't eat. Certain things she couldn't do and some things she had to do. When the baby was born, there were certain things that had to be done. It goes on and on. Throughout a person's life, there's different stages until that person's old, and there was a lotta stuff people had to follow. Otherwise, certain things would happen to them, and maybe they would suffer. You know, they had to be aware of that.

Some people still practise the traditional laws, but not everybody's been teaching their children. Our kids today don't listen. They think we're just making up these stories, but there are some people who will start sharing the old ways with me. I know because my mom [Elder Mabel Solomon xinli] taught me and my dad [Elder Henry Solomon xinli] always made sure we knew – always talking, constantly reminding us. You know, there were many of us, so I think he did a lotta talking!

Well, I lost two brothers, but I have two sisters and I have three brothers and three that are half-brothers. Yeah, I had eight brothers. We were a huge family. My mom's family was another huge family. Their dad was called Sammy, but that was changed to William.

In Our Time

Marilyn Baptiste, Xeni Gwet'in

[Dechen ts'edilhtan is about] how we gather on the Land and practise our culture. We need to continue to pass on our culture and the laws of the Land. Many people don't actually understand that the way we hunt and the way we respect the animals are all a part of the laws of the Land, and that's how we protect our future generations. A lot of the time, it's hard for people to put that into words or explain it, because in our time, before European contact, we practised those things, we *lived* those things. We didn't have to say it and teach it in a classroom or a court or in meetings.

Logging Nemiah

Joyce Charleyboy, Tŝideldel

I remember William Setah looking at me, and he said, "It's not gonna happen. I don' know why they keep comin' back." He said, "You look at the whole Territory" – 'cause I believe they had 'em on a flight a few times. "Everywhere they've taken and taken, and there's just this little area where we're livin' right now is all that's protected." So I tried to be there as much as I could, and then when I left the community, I went home because my grandmother Nellie needed me. I ended up getting in leadership and served eight years in my community. Because of the ties I had with Nemiah and because that's where my mom's from, and being there in that community, it was always something that I believed – you know, my kids and my grandkids are gonna see the pristineness of it because our Territory [Tŝideldel] was almost gone at that point in time. And I was getting lost in my own Territory because of all the roads that had been put in.

From the time that I left to when I came back, it was just gone. There's nothing really left. And Dad takin' me out there and sayin', you know, is *this* what they want? And if we continue, he said, we're gonna have nowhere else to go for hunting. What're we gonna do? And a few of the other Elders that had a hand in raising me were in negotiations, I believe, with Riverside (which is Tolko today) at the time. One of the Elders said, it takes how much water, you know, for one tree to grow? And he said, When they're cutting all of this, all our waters are drying up. There's no natural springs anymore. All the ponds are gone. Can't they see what they're doing?

Earth's Protocol

Gilbert Solomon, Xeni Gwet'in

How are we gonna follow the protocol from here? We have right now a protocol for the Land, the earth, all the elements that's in there, where they tell us stuff – what to do and where to go. We know the material-world way is destructive of the only Earth that we live on today. We need to follow the real protocol and start listening to how we need to go as humans on the only Earth that we share with everybody. We don't have any other Earth that we can go to. We're all on this same earth shootin' across the cosmos at some three hundred thousand miles an hour. And we need to and we want to know who's drivin' it, you know. [laughter] So I think it's drivin' itself, and we just need to listen to it and to learn what we need to do. We say we don't worry about who's driving the earth. We just gotta worry about what *we* need to do while we're on it.

We need to keep honouring all the elements. Like the water, the most powerful medicine we have, so we need to keep that intact and not contaminated in any way. Nowadays we need to zero in on the curriculum for our children. We teach them from when they're born, and we need to teach 'em a good way, 'cause we know there are prophecies saying that the grandchildren that are born nowadays are the Ancestors coming back to show us the real way, so we're gonna be learning from our grandchildren. They're gonna teach us. We think we know stuff now, but we just know a little bit. The grandchildren will fill that in about how to *really* go, 'cause now we're confused, wondering where to go, you know. We're probably thinking it's the same as the material world where we only need to make money somehow, but it's not sustainable. It doesn't last, it just peters out. In the earth protocol, we'll have a job forever – the feelings that we give to the earth and the ceremonies that we do and the teachings that we do with the children and the rest of the children of the world. We need to tell 'em, Yo, we gotta go *this* way now! We can't go this other way, 'cause we're all together, you know. We've got blankets on our heads, and we're confused, and we need to say, Whoa! Hello! Over here! We know what we need to do and we need to follow Earth's protocol.

Now we're programmed to the max, and we're working on the deprogram part of ourselves so we can teach our children, our grandchildren, this good way that we know about. It's been known for thousands of years, all these things that work. Medicines out there that we need to acknowledge and consume and know that, 'cause it's there. It's not in a store or in a grocery store or wherever. It's right there in the woods.

Approaching with the Positive

Gilbert Solomon, Xeni Gwet'in

Mount Polley:[28] well, that part where that comes in, we need to check ourselves with that negative part. We need to not go there, 'cause we been there too long, and nowadays in the prophecies, they're saying that this negative thing is disappearing, dissipating, it's not gonna work no more. Positive is gonna take over, so we need to maintain positive. Let's say when we're fighting for our life – in the court case or whatever. We need to approach it with positive, not negative. We approach them with that. We need to learn how to work that positive. That's the one we need to hold onto. You can't just show you're harder [tougher], you know. You need to hold onto that. You can't fight it or anything, that feeling that we have. Like we've been doing it for so long. And the negative part that's been the material world, we call that negative soul. So we need to somehow gradually deprogram from that negative, go into positive, 'cause if we stay in the negative, Elders long time ago told us stories. When I was a little boy, they told us there'd come a time where the negative is not gonna work no more, and you're gonna go crazy if you stay negative. Your mind, your whole system won't be able to take it and you'll go completely *crazy* – so crazy that if there's a big fire over there, you'll run right into the fire, that's how crazy you'll become. So you don' wanna be negative. You wanna be positive, even towards anything that's a danger to our life, like all the chemicals, toxic anything.

Whatever your intention is, that feeling that you're going towards something, probably you don't put the feeling out there. Kinda like if you approach an angry crowd, and you have a good feeling. That crowd can't see you. You walk right through them. They didn't see you, they didn't notice you or anything. But if you get angry, they'll see you. It's like somebody looking for trouble, wanting to fight somebody, and going through the crowd, and just looking for that challenge from somebody. But if you don't go there, they can't see you, they just walk right by you, look at your eye and go by you and don't see you, you know.

We go way back into when they were creating. Kaboom! All that information comes from the sun, so the sun knows. Gonna take that information back. You guys don' know how to use that information, abusing it. Gonna utilize anything that's on the earth – ocean, the whole earth. So we're gonna learn how to focus, how to help the sun utilize that, with positive. 'Cause if it's a negative, it's gonna pull us into a negative. So even when something heavy like that [Mount Polley] comes around, we need to stay positive. All this time in all this negative world that we were living in, there's all the time we were in positive. If you go to Mexico, you'll notice all the people out there who are suppressed but they're positive there. Somehow, that positive's staying there. You know, it don' wanna leave them, and they have it, like "*Oh!*" So when we talk about negative things happening on the earth, we need to not go crazy about it and lose our mind, you know. [laughs] We need to stay positive so we could help that river, we could help that whole area, with this positive, saying we need to listen to the silence. The earth's talking to us. The sun's talking to us, the stars, everything's talking to us. Sometimes we think we're just thinking it in our mind – it's somebody telling you stuff. Like, let's say you're having an accident. You're going sideways in your truck. Listen to yourself. Something, somebody's gonna tell you what to do in a split second, like *this*. You gotta listen to *that*.

We want to teach the rest of the earth's children how it should go. I think nowadays the teenagers know this material world part, so they need to learn like a protocol that we are all sacred and our spirits are like powerful beings, and we need to keep being powerful as humans that live on the earth that's shooting across the cosmos and circling round the sun, and that keeps going for a while, you know. We don't want the earth somehow to go off course and go into the meteor belt and do a number on us, you know! [laughter]

The feeling that we need to give to the earth – it wants positive, not the negative things. Earth's got spirit like us, the same spirit. We have the same spirit as that tree over there. And the water. All this. Our spirit when we pass over, we'll know. We'll say, "Yeah, I remember, we were on the earth," you know, like that. So. We just need to learn Earth's protocol. How are we gonna live for the rest of our on and on? The earth's not gonna stop [laughs], right away! It's gonna go for a while. So we just need to learn how to listen. Like some people say, you can hear silence but when you hear something in your mind, it's not silence. That's somebody telling you stuff.

The People That Didn't Listen

Joyce Charleyboy, Tŝideldel

There's a story about Miner Lake and the people that didn't listen. We used to camp at Miner Lake all the time, at the end of the lake. I was goin' in there and I had to question my grandmother.

I said, "Did you know I heard really strange noises when I was at Miner Lake?"

And she said, "Where at? I want you to show me. What kind of noise?"

"Sometimes I almost feel like I hear children, but I don't know what it is, you know."

And so we went up there.

She said, "This is an old camp. People died here that didn't listen to how deep the snow was gonna get, how hard times were gonna be. They didn't harvest as much as they were supposed to, and they starved. They cremated them here. That's why you're hearing their unsettledness. Somebody needs to come in and show them that they need to move on. They're stuck here because of the way they died. These are people that didn't listen to the laws, they didn't listen to the way we were. That's why they all died."

Working towards Healing

Elder Catherine Haller, Xeni Gwet'in

I've been a healer since I was ten years old. I lost it when I started drinkin'. I got it back in '91–'93. I got everything back – it took me a long time. It was a gift that I got, and it was so valuable to me. I had a choice knowin' how I can get it back. I was up in the mountain. In '94, I made a choice to go up there to the mountain for one week. I stayed up there – I walked up there, on the other side. I stayed up in the mountain for one week cleansing myself. Nothing to eat, just a little water, that's all I brought. I was survivin' from that. By the time five days had passed, I was hearing lotsa voices. People were cheering me on. "You made good choice. Don't fall and lose it." That's what I heard. That sounds like Amanda or Eswily talkin' to me all the time. And Leenie. So I thought I'm being watched. And I took it from there. I got everything back, and I'm still experiencing being a traditional person.

I can't drink any more. I used to be abused. I was raped. I was a punching bag. They broke my teeth. They broke my nose. They fractured my head. They punched my glasses right into my eyes and cut inside my eyes and I had to go to the hospital. I think I have been through enough damage and enough shame. Satan came with a good strong voice and I listened to them. Now I think, no, I won't listen to it. I wanna be who I am. I wanna be a healthy person. I wanna be givin' support to that person that needs my support. I will give that to them. All that stuff that I did, I didn't really see with the clear vision that I have now. It was always blurry. It happened to me because I wasn't really lookin' at the earth and the Land. I lost a lot of things because of alcohol. I know we're gonna have to work towards our life balance and open our vision to go forward and never be blind. We work towards our healing.

ʔEtsu tadalh ʔalh Grandma in a Circle of Light

Elder Catherine Haller, Xeni Gwet'in

Long time ago, there was ʔEsggidam ʔEtsu (ancestor grandma) and there was another lady that was havin' problems. There was a lake as big as Konni Lake here. ʔEtsu told her to start walkin' at midnight around the lake, slowly. "After each mile, if you're tired, sit down. It's your choice. You sit down to prepare to pray from your own heart, talkin' to Creator. They're gonna be watchin' you." That grandma that sent this woman was a healer. This woman was havin' a lot of problems with her mind and her spirit not understanding other people. So ʔEtsu told her, "Every time you stop, count. Count how many times you stop." She kept goin' and every time she stopped, there were different prayers to be said, words from that grandma I'm talkin' about. And she went right round the lake.

She was going blind, too. When she went round the lake, ʔEtsu told her, "When you get up there, I want you to wipe your hands on one of the trees and close your eyes at midnight. And I want you to cover your eyes, both sides. Lie down under a tree. And if you fall asleep, stay that way. Don't wake up until the sun's up." So she woke up with the sunrise, and her vision had come back to her. She was so happy she was crying, because she could see a long distance.

Then ʔEtsu told her to go up on the mountain and stay there for three days. She gave her three days because when the woman went around, there was no food there and she made it in four days. So another three days up on the mountain. That was hard. It's just like punishing yourself and giving back to the person that you made mistakes with, saying, "I'm sorry this happened to me. It was all my fault. It was all my stuff I was getting punished for, and now I'm gonna have to learn how to walk around the water to give myself back to the earth and be grounded again."

That was all. And the mountain was where she was doing the fasting and brushin' off and purifyin' herself to the rocks. Up there is purifying, because she was using juniper bush to brush herself off. And when she finished, she came home. Guess what ʔEtsu told her? She had to go around the lake again. That was a rosary. That was the medicine way. She made it. And when she came home, she gave that old lady an offering. She started cryin'. She felt really good about what she didn't feel and punished for what she did. She took herself back and gave back, saying, "I'm sorry, 'cause I done –. I know you were lookin' and I was doin' this and that. It wasn't right for me." So, my body and my life in town. Somebody could get me to go across but I didn't want to. But ʔEtsu guided her around the lake with the words she used and she called it nen nadeẑiyah. It means you made it around the circle without lookin' back, and you're strong. That's what ʔEtsu was telling her. And she felt it in her own experience, she did what she could. Right to the end, she was conscious that this was happening, somebody was talkin' to her. And she stopped right there. ʔEtsu kinda sent powers to that lady when she stopped. That old lady knew where she was and told her, "Don't come back to where I am, go up in the mountain again from there." So she did three more days up there.

There's no cups up there, just a little water you can drink and wet your mouth for three days. And, you know, you do cleansing – woman's process in traditional ways. And you talk about the things that you wanna be and confess the stuff that hurts you. Walk the path for your health to the earth and water. That's what ʔEtsu meant, that healing. And when that old lady slept on it and turned the lights on for her, she started walking back at night. ʔEtsu had sent her message up and that lady understood. And when she was comin' back, that old lady prepared a Sweat Lodge. That's our church, long time ago. So ʔEtsu built a Sweat Lodge out of moss, and it was like a dome tent for only two people. So that got prepared, but that lady had no clothes, so she just found – what did she find? Moss – sorta like moss that she tore out and put together with, I dunno, with sticks she bent. She covered her private area, and she came back. And when she went under in the Sweat Lodge, she had to release everything. She told Grandma. "I'm gonna flush myself out. If you don't mind." "That's your choice," ʔEtsu told her. So when she got under there, they started four rounds. Each round means something. So she prayed four rounds. At the end, someone came with a traditional buckskin dress for her. The grandpa brought it. She started really crying. She felt good. She knew where she belonged, but she was falling down, up and down, like being through and going on.

What did we call this story? ʔEsggidam tadalh ʔalh [Ancestor in traditional light] or something like that they call her, because it's very old – it's a really old story. Beyond my past and your past! Really far away, but it might be true, because she was blind and she got her vision back. And she was a healer. When she was goin' around the lake and said that was a rosary, that's what they call the medicine wheel in Tŝilhqot'in. Just by listenin' to the story and closin' my eyes, it comes back to me how it's been told. But this is long ago. My grandma used to talk about it. Back then when they would talk about something, you'd kinda experience what was there, what they were talking about. My grandma's voice and grampa's voice and my mum's voice, it kinda cuts into every story I tell. It's just the way you tell the story, what it stands for. Like this lady was gettin' blind because she was losin' all her abilities. And at the end she got happy because she said, "I can communicate with people now." She started to hear in a good way who she's lookin' at. At first, she didn't really wanna communicate with anybody. She was grumpy and sick and everything. She had grown up all tired. So. I think about that lake, too, when that story comes to me. We'll call it Grandma – ʔEtsu tadalh ʔalh means Grandma Sittin' In Traditional Light – in a circle of traditional light.

So this is what they did for support in very traditional ways. We need our people to have treatment, and this is what we could bring back. I think about that a lot, but it's really hard to get it back. I have a Sweat Lodge. But that lady was strong enough to walk up a mountain no matter how sick she was. And that's what I did, too. I was thinkin' of that story when I did that. I felt stronger than when I came back from treatment. I learned lots of communication skills in treatment, but I learned a lot of my traditional skills through the healing up on the mountain for four days. I didn't come back until the fifth day, because what I got into to go up there was to understand myself in a traditional way so I could go on and go back to my own traditional living. How to live off the earth – which I didn't know I'd lost. So those experiences, that story, went back into me, and I went back up there. And if I hadn't, I would have fallen off the wagon.

That healing option is still sittin' there and waitin' for us. I did part of it. That's how we used to heal long, long ago. That's the ʔEsggidam way of doing it. Like the ʔEsggidam clothes I'm talkin' about, the moss. Imagine how strong we can be.

Water and Fire

Elder Catherine Haller, Xeni Gwet'in

We used to go through here [Henry's Crossing] by wagon. Each day we travelled to where[ver] just by wagon. We were still happy. We were healthy. We were always smiling. We had no guns, just our hands and a slingshot and an arrow, maybe, and maybe a thrower, a thrower and stick. Mum used to teach us a lot of things. Our protection was that there was nothing we couldn't push away, but Mum led us in our journeys where we respect and communicate with Elders around us but not to ask questions in a certain way – the question should be asked and, "No, don't go there." That's what we were taught. Never let, you know, [the idea enter] your mind that you are unhealthy. And always have a smile. No matter how unhealthy you are, just give that smile. A person might be sick and you might lift them up with that smile and your energy and the way you pray.

Have a healthy life, you know. You have to really have open eyes and open heart to everybody no matter what kinda person they are. No matter if they're not smiling, just keep on smiling. One smile is not gonna hurt you! And when you cry, there's water comin' out, and if you're hurt, don't be afraid for the tears to come out. When you load it in, you're like a lock – you're lockin' everything in and you don't communicate well, especially when you're in an office and there comes the water from tension if you're not healthy. If you're not drinkin' enough water, your body's kinda running out. That's disrespect. You're water inside.

Water, we use it in a lotta ways. We use it to baptise our babies, and us women, we take a bath in it during the full moon. In the Sweat Lodge, we use it for a blessing for our lava rocks. You can go a week without water, live without water – I bet you we'd all go to sleep!

Last year I was thinkin' about fire. Fire is a blessing. Fire is sacred for us, but in a way for the [whole] world. Most of us are not treating each other right. Maybe something went wrong there. Tears of the earth. It's sad.

Do you have an altar? I always pray to my altar. Any time I feel that way, I always pray for the earth and everybody – the food, people, water, wind, camp. People are campin' in the [smoky] air, you know.[29]

Where do we go? We go back to our first place. A few more years to keep us goin', because we're not the same [as when we're younger]. Our hair goes grey. More stress with that. Our eyes start to shut off. Our voices. Our brains can't keep [on]. Our heart starts to give up.

That's the way we were taught.

Baskets Are ʔEsggidam Ancestors

"Taken"

Lorraine Weir

When I asked Elder Mabel Solomon xinli about qatŝ'ay spruceroot baskets, she told me, "They've all gone." Then she explained that decades earlier, midugh had come through the community and offered ten dollars a basket. As Mabel put it, baskets were "taken." I was familiar with qatŝ'ay from the large collection at the Museum of Anthropology (MOA) near my office at the University of British Columbia, and I began to wonder how they'd gotten there. Thus began a path of research which led to Mabel and a group of Elders visiting their Tŝilhqot'in belongings at the Museum in September 2016. The question of how the baskets had come to be so far from home can be framed in many ways and includes the larger question of stolen Indigenous cultural heritage worldwide.[30] But first I wanted to see if I could track down some local answers in response to Mabel's words. Here is some of what I found.

The first detailed discussion of qatŝ'ay in English was published by James Teit in 1904 as the conclusion to his study of "The Shuswap" in the second volume of Franz Boas's Jesup Expedition's Memoir.[31] The study was based on two weeks Teit had spent in the Tŝilhqot'in four years earlier and includes detailed descriptions and drawings of how the coiled baskets were woven and the designs characteristic of them. Teit had an extensive personal collection of Nlaka'pamux baskets and was also involved in collecting baskets for a wealthy associate of Boas's, Homer Sargent, who funded Teit's research and donated Tŝilhqot'in baskets collected by Teit to Chicago's Field Museum of Natural History. Historian Wendy Wickwire credits Sargent's interest in baskets to the "basket-collecting movement that was sweeping across the southwestern United States" at the turn of the twentieth century.[32] Sargent made many gifts of baskets to the Field Museum over the years, including thirteen baskets purchased from dealers in Seattle and Vancouver and donated in 1920. The popularity of Tŝilh-qot'in belongings was so great between 1904 and 1920 that the Field Museum received five more collections, including baskets collected between 1903 and 1904 by "C.F. Newcombe, a major supplier of northwest coast material culture to the museum in the early years of the 20th century."[33] The museum paid $54 for the 1904 shipment and $45 for a larger shipment in 1907. Near the end of his life, Teit was forced to sell his baskets to pay for his cancer treatment, and the Ethnology collection of the Canadian Museum of History in Ottawa acquired some of his collection.

Like the Field Museum in Chicago, MOA has also received most of its extensive collection of qatŝ'ay from settlers who gifted their collections to the Museum. Almost half of the fifty-nine baskets and related items at MOA comes from the collection of Alfred John Buttimer, described as "a pioneer of the British Columbia salmon canning industry"[34] and founder of the Brunswick Cannery Company. Buttimer was born in Bathurst, Nova Scotia, arrived on the West Coast in 1890, and "entered the cannery business in the north and also on the Fraser River."[35] After BC Packers took over his company in 1925, he went into the real-estate business in Vancouver. MOA doesn't provide details of how he acquired the baskets in his collection, but perhaps Buttimer's wife was a collector like Mrs. A.J. Beecher, who donated most of the other half of MOA's collection of qatŝ'ay to the Museum.

Perhaps C.F. Newcombe was the dealer Elder Mabel Solomon xinli and Elder Cecile William xinli are referring to when they speak of qatŝ'ay being taken. In 1911, Newcombe was hired by the British Columbia Provincial Museum in Victoria as agent and "for four years he travelled throughout the province, compiling a major collection of artifacts"[36] so they could be preserved for "posterity." Testament to the predatory zeal of Newcombe and other buyers and collectors, qatŝ'ay are in museums all over the world. In Haida Gwaii, Newcombe was also involved in grave robbing to secure "artifacts" for sale, including human bones. Justice may have prevailed in the end as he died of a "cold" (perhaps pneumonia) after a buying trip to 'Yalis Alert Bay in 1924.

Tenelh Birchbark Basket

Elder Marvin William xinli, Xeni Gwet'in

Tenelh the basket is called. Tenelh. That's long time ago.

Tenelh passed away. My mum passed away, too. She had old basket. We put 'em on trailer somewhere.

I know a lot of people who made basket down here. Elders made baskets out here. There's still a few. I don't know why they stop.

Doing it by the fires, they make this up, make baskets. Big baskets too. It's like [in] Anaham, old people made baskets. Old women. Young people [didn't].

Yeah, a long time ago, old people. Just practise with those baskets. Those people made those baskets real nice.

My mum made baskets, round baskets.

Old people all gone. It's like we're stuck.

On Qatŝ'ay Spruceroot Baskets[37]

Elder Mabel Solomon xinli with Dinah Lulua, Xeni Gwet'in

1. Burke Museum of Natural History and Culture, catalogue number 1–1058, Chilcotin Basket. Tatla Lake, BC. Source: Robert Lane[38]

This spruceroot basket was made by Nenqayni. Sil Canim's wife, the late Jeanie, used to make many baskets like these. Sil Canim was a good Chief and they killed him. She made baskets with animals and birds around it in circles. You use it when picking berries, like soapberries and saskatoons. You beat soapberry branches over it, allowing the berries to fall into it. What is called grass for soapberries – pine grass – is placed at the bottom [on a berry rack] and you pour the boiled berries onto it. When it is dry, they put a cup or plate over the cooked berries and press it flat. It dries like that.

The late Jeanie made all sorts of baskets like these with all kinds of animal designs on them. Those are spruceroots. They find them among spruce stands. They dig into the ground and see them and dig them up. Jeanie Canim made baskets out of those. I didn't do that. Only Mom did that. They made them a different colour with dye – something with a red bark.

I wonder what the late Sil did with the ones made by Jeanie. She made a variety of different baskets. Some of them (above) were this large [gesturing] and they bent something for its top. And they made nice lips on the edges of the tops so it doesn't fall apart. This one is like that. She made lots of those. She made some with geese around them. This one is like that at the bottom. This basket has that at its edges. It was made nice and someone wrapped it.

2. Burke Museum of Natural History and Culture, catalogue number 2001-82/1, Chilcotin Burden Basket. Source: James K. Caldwell, Marilyn Caldwell

This one (above) has geese and that's deer with the short tail. Using an awl, they put holes in it and pushed the spruceroots through. You can use a spruceroot basket to pick any kind of berries. My late father used to prop sticks up against the saskatoon bushes. Jeanie gave Mom some of these baskets and she picked berries with them like Saskatoon berries. My dad Sammy [Sambulyan] would pack them.

Lha yudit'ih We Always Find a Way

3. Burke Museum of Natural History and Culture, catalogue number 1–1244, Chilcotin Basket. Purchased from the Alaska Fur Company

Nenqayni made this (above) too. They were probably from that area just travelling around here buying nuSay [pails] and things like hides. They used to make baskets like those long ago. There are diamonds on there (above) on the bottom. Many people must have made these. If you tried to make them today, you could make them. You have to dig the roots. They're all over the place. Spruceroots are used to put them [baskets] together. They find them among spruce stands. They dig into the ground and see them and dig them up.

There were many other ones [baskets] and many of them which Nenqayni made around here were left in the distant east in places [museums] for them. Just the women made these baskets. The men were hunters. They hunted for food and they trapped for fur. They skinned the animal and stretched out [the pelt] and sold it to fur traders. It was mainly the men that did all that skinning and stuff. Stretching the fur out for trade. The women prepared the deer hide and moose hide and tanned it. They made moccasins and jackets and anything that you needed – gloves.

Making Qatŝ'ay Spruceroot Baskets[39]

Elder Cecile William xinli with Dorrine Lulua, Xeni Gwet'in

You use an awl to weave the basket and continue on in the same way. That's how you do it. You weave it around and around like that. It gets bigger as you weave.

There are probably different ways of doing it. She [Cecile] used an awl to weave it in and out, especially where it was loose. That is how it is done. When you put the root through, that is what it looks like. Towards the end [of making the basket], she did it differently. (She probably did that one that way.) I just tied it. It is probably alder. There is lots down there. The white grass is called common reed grass. It doesn't grow around here. It grows in front of Alexis Creek. That is the only place it grows. It is white and it grows there. There is some west of Alexis Creek below the road, too. They use it so the basket will be white. They used that [spines from feathers] to strengthen the top part.

We used [the basket] to pick raspberries. You wash it until it gets really damp. Water won't be able to drip through it. You get it really wet. Soak it. I remember we picked raspberries in it. They made them for picking berries. You can pick sopalallie in it. Long time ago people used it. That was when there wasn't anything else to use. They used a different kind, too, but I don't have one of those. There was a tree for it. It is called birch. You could probably use it to sew anything. Raymond xinli [Cecile's brother] had one. Someone gave it to my mom, and Raymond had it. People used to like picking berries. Long time ago we didn't have much. Mostly berries.

Birchbark was used also. They probably soaked it to soften it and used it for weaving. They used it to pick berries, too. There's probably some east of here across the lake [Xeni Biny], over there where Fos Fey used to live. You probably have to cut it up. If you rip it, you will have to sew it. You can make it soft by using hot water. There is some at Sheep Creek.

[I picked this] west of Alexis Creek at a place called Old Dungeon. You had to walk way up there to get on top. There is probably lots of raspberries up there. We used to walk up there with this. You can probably pick with this one, too. The birch is light. This one [qatŝ'ay] is heavy when it's wet. They probably used to pick sopalallie in it long ago, too. They probably used the basket made of birch mostly. There's probably going to be some sopalallie growing. There is already some sopalallie east of here. If it rains a lot, then it will grow.

Before [i.e., years ago], some of these [baskets] were taken from me. I did not want to give them these ones. They took the nice ones. The ones with tough wood. Cottonwood.

People had no money, [so] I trapped squirrels. There seem to be lots of squirrels now. We used to trap squirrels all winter. We used to check it [the trapline] every two nights. We used to set about twenty traps. We used to do that all winter. It was forty cents a squirrel. We used to make quite a bit. We had money all summer long. We started in the fall. The first of November we would start, when trapping started.

They [midugh buyers] probably buy it [the fur] in Anahim Lake. They treated us bad out there. They [midugh] go trapping, too. There is probably muskrat over there. Around here there is really no place to trap squirrels. I tried it. It's too hilly. That person they used to call Edith Inscho had nice land in the east called New Meadow. She said she used to shoot lots. You could shoot lots, but in February they sleep in their nests. You chase them out. Sometimes there is lots in their nests. Edith Inscho had nice land. She did that long ago. Around here you can't do that, because it's too hilly.

Dorrine Lulua: You caught fish too?

Cecile William: Yes, all the time. That is how we ate good. There should [still] be some whitefish, but nobody sets net anymore. There wasn't much deer back then around here. We used to mainly eat fish. The moose are probably getting healthy now. I used to work with hides, but it got too hard for me. I can't work with hides anymore. I made lots, but I couldn't sell them.

Elder Cecile William xinli with one of the qatŝ'ay she made. Photo by Lorraine Weir

Chapter 9: Nen gagunlhchugh deni nidlin We live all over this land   283

Gan ʔeguh tsox, tsox ʔant'i beghadantŝi. ʔEguh xi beqex naghilht'ih ʔeguh gats'elhʔinh hats'elhinsh. Guʔen ʔelhinaghinqalh.

You use an awl to weave the basket and continue on in the same way.

ʔEguh gats'elhʔinsh ʔan. Nenduwh guʔanwh nadenaghinqalh. ʔEgun guʔanwh nadenaghinqalh galhlhʔin. ʔEsdan nenchagh ghelilh ʔanh.

That's how you do it. You weave it around and around like that. It gets bigger as you weave.

ʔEgu gwelanwh sinsh xeʔats'elhʔinsh sant'i ʔeyi chuh. Tsox bid xayebeʔelhyilh layelhʔinsh ʔan. Gangu ʔeguh lha nit'i lant'ih ʔeguh, guyi bech'ed lhet'es ʔeyi.

There are probably different ways of doing it. She [Cecile xinli] used an awl to weave it in and out, especially where it was loose.

Gan gats'elhʔin. Belh gugheʔinlht'ish. ʔEgu ʔeguh gant'ih helish. ʔEch'ilʔaz ʔeguh ʔeyuwh gayelhʔin. ʔEyagh gaghinlhʔin sant'i. Gan jidaŝilhʔun ʔan.

That is how it is done. When you put the root through, that is what it looks like. Towards the end she [Cecile xinli] did it differently. She [Cecile xinli] probably did that one that way. I [Cecile xinli] just tied it.

Ch'es tesant'i. Gutŝunh la gant'i gulin.

[The black material] is probably alder. There is lots down there.

Tl'ekw'a ts'edenish. ʔEyi lha nenduwh nench'ed gant'i, yadah Alexis Creek gwenes ʔeyed dzanh gant'i gulin, lhek'el nadadilʔah.

[The white material] is called common reed grass. It doesn't grow around here. It grows in front of Alexis Creek. That is the only place it grows. It is white and it grows there.

Alexis Creek gunish chuh gant'i ʔeten gutsonz ghinli. ʔEyi gan lhek'el ŵelax qa gu gats'elhʔinsh sant'i.

There is some west of Alexis Creek below the road, too. They use it so the basket will be white.

ʔEyi gan bedex gweduts'igh qa yilagh sant'i.

They used that to strengthen the top part.

Bid ʔughiban ghinli, texaltsel.

We used it to pick raspberries.

Tinaŝinʔan. ʔInlhes naninidinsh. Lhajid tu badulged gulah hat'insh.

You wash it until it gets really damp. Water won't be able to drip through it.

ʔInlhes nasilhtsel, tughilhʔa.

You get it really wet. Soak it.

Bid texaltsel hughinban yeneŝinsh. Bid ?ets'uba la gwe?ats'elh?insh ghan.

I remember we picked raspberries in it. They made them for picking berries.

Bid nuŵish nanentaghalhghelh. Yedanx deni gant'i bid ?anajeŝt'in. Lha gwetah gwegulih ?eguh. Guyi ?eyuy chuh ?ats'aghinlh?in. Sid ?egu lha gant'i nanses?ah.

You can pick sopalallie in it. Long time ago people used it. That was when there wasn't anything else to use. They used a different kind, too, but I don't have one of those.

Dechen gha gulin. Dechen ch'i ts'edenish gant'i. ?Eyi gan did binanentaghanqalh saghint'i.

There was a tree for it. It is called birch. You could probably use it to sew anything.

Raymond dzanh gant'i. Yagh ?Inkel gant'i bats'eni?an, gant'i na?ah ghinli.

Raymond xinli [Cecile's brother] had one. Someone gave it to my mom, and Raymond had it.

Dechen t'uz ch'i ts'edinh ts'uzih. ?Eyi chuh tu ?itats'edelhtinsh detli helish sant'i. Nats'eneqash sanh. ?Eyi chuh bid ?ets'ughinban.

Birchbark was used also. They probably soaked it to soften it and used it for weaving. They used it to pick berries too.

Yadad gant'i gulin sagunt'i yad. Yadad gunez ts'en.

There's probably some east of here across the lake.

Guyed Tiŝandanx ts'egwedinh la. ?Eguh gwenuwh gwetowh gant'i gulin jedenish.

Over there where Fos Fey used to live.

Xats'elht'ish sant'i. Xaghingganz ?eguh nanentaghanqalh sant'i.

You probably have to cut it up. If you rip it, you will have to sew it.

Detli ts'elhtsish sant'i tu-niẑel bid.

You can make it soft by using hot water.

Sheep Creek la gant'i gulin.

There is some at Sheep Creek.

[Dorrine Lulua:] Nendid nenduwh bid ?unaghinban? Nents'in?

Where did you pick with this? Where?

?Eyad Alexis Creek gunish Old Dungeon ts'egwedinh ?eyed texaltsel yadish. Yadish tenexaŝinlgay texaltsel lhan sagunt'i. ?Egun nanaxeghidansh ghinli nendid chuh nat'ah.

West of Alexis Creek at a place called Old Dungeon. You had to walk way up there to get on top. There is probably lots of raspberries up there. We used to walk up there with this.

Nendid chuh gateghanlh?ilh sant'i.

You can probably pick with this one too.

Guyi ch'i lhesnih ?eyi nend̂zay hat'insh ?an nendid ?eyi selhtsel guntsel jid nendaẑ sanh.

The birch is light. This one is heavy when it's wet.

Nuŵish chula binats'enaghilhghelh sant'i yedanx.

They probably used to pick sopalallie in it long ago, too.

Nenguyi ch'iyelhenish ?eyi su.

They probably used the basket made of birch mostly.

Nuŵish nanentat'inlh sagunt'i.

There's probably going to be some sopalallie growing.

Gwatish yedanx nuŵish xanih gudah.

There is already some sopalallie east of here.

Nenk'ed gwechugh nagwaghinlhtan gagwetanilh.

If it rains a lot, then it will grow.

On Baskets: Elder Mabel Williams xinli

Lorraine Weir

Elder Mabel Williams xinli with her daughter June Williams. Photo by Lorraine Weir

Lha yudit'ih We Always Find a Way

Elder Cecile William xinli's eldest sister, Elder Mabel Williams xinli, remembered that her mother used to make round qatŝ'ay. "Long ago, people used them for storage," she said, and they also put them on either side of a horse to carry things like fish. People "used to put hot rocks and water in the basket and that's how they would do [cook] the fish." They used the same method to heat water and wash clothes in the baskets. Not only the roots but also the tree bark was used, and nothing was wasted. "Tree bark [was used] for medicine [and] there was this one child that lost a lotta weight and they gave him the juice from the cambium and he was able to be better and he put on a lotta weight."[40]

Making a Ch'i Baby Basket

Elder Eileen Sammy William, Xeni Gwet'in

Elder Mabel Solomon xinli's sister, Elder Eileen Sammy William, makes ch'i baby baskets as well as coats, vests, moccasins, and other useful items from buckskin which she tans herself and then adorns with embroidery or beadwork. This is how she makes a ch'i baby basket.—Lorraine Weir

1. Elder Eileen William prepares willows for making a ch'i baby basket.
Photo by Chief Roger William

It takes me a long time, like one day and then tomorrow day and then tomorrow I finish it [the basket]. [laughs]

2. Helped by granddaughter Chiʔela William and great-grandson Lucian William, Elder Eileen puts the assembled basket frame on a cooler.
Photo by Chief Roger William

My mum Annie Sammy William used to make these. [She] teach me. These, the outside frame, it's a different kind of wood, like fir tree, the skinny fir tree or pine tree. And these skinny ones like the small one at the bottom, that's k'ezen willow. You could make a small one, bigger size, medium size, and large one.[41]

You have to put really boiling water on the edge so when you bend it, it don't break. And you could steep it. You could let it stand overnight. I'm not that fast anyway! [laughs]

3. Chiʔela William pours boiling water on the willow frame while Eileen and her daughter Agnes look on.
Photo by Chief Roger William

You put some kind of a string like this, tie it on the front like this, and over. You make that side taller and this side not as tall. I could tie to frame, too, like the bottom frame. And this one here. If you don't tie it, it'll go sideways.

4. Elder Eileen ties the willows to the weighted frame while daughter Agnes and son Roger look on. Photo by Chiʔela William

You put rocks in there so it could stay on one side and not go up. We do the bottom and top frame first. Then when that's dry, we use willows, tie up all around.

5. The ch'i weighted with rocks and bricks. Photo by Chief Roger William

My mom make me do everything. Yeah. Teach me everything – how it's done. I had to hay and as soon as I stopped hayin' there'd always be something for me to do. [laughs] Mom never treated [spoiled] me! [laughter] "You just have to stand in one place, Eileen!" Yeah, yeah! [laughs]

6. Deer hide is sewn on the outside of the weighted ch'i frame. Photo by Chief Roger William

I'm the youngest one! [laughs] And I'm the *last*!! [laughs]. I dunno who's gonna learn from me. Probably April xinli or Marion is one of them. The rest, they don't mind – they don't want to. They kinda have a hard time with it.

7. Elder Eileen smiles at the completed ch'i with colourful cotton fabric sewn to the frame and a handle and interior restraints put in place to keep the baby safe and snug during their first year. Photo by Chief Roger William

Then you find pinecone and you tie 'em all around. [chuckles] Maybe once you know how to do it, it would be easy when you put your mind to it. You could try, too!

They're [baskets] easy to handle them when they're [babies] small. Otherwise, you might hurt them or whatever. Even on horseback, you could carry them. With this, put 'em on your back. Had a long string to carry them, and you could tie 'em around yourself so it won't bounce off! [laughs] Used to be neat when you see people long time ago, it was neat. [laughs] It moves with your body. Yeah.

Going Visiting

Lorraine Weir

In September 2016, a group of fifteen Elders and their helpers came to visit their Tŝilhqot'in belongings at MOA.[42] Elders Mabel Solomon xinli, Cecile William xinli, and Eileen Sammy William were in the group and shared their knowledge as they examined the baskets closely, peering inside and sometimes happily catching a whiff of tea leaves or dried fish. Elder Eileen carefully examined a ch'i baby basket and said that ch'i should only be used for one baby and then placed in a tree so the baby will have good luck. If you don't do this, Eileen said the baby would grow up not knowing much. She also recorded a list of words for different parts of a ch'i.

Elders and helpers with qatŝ'ay in the Textile Research Room, MOA. From left, Maria William, Cecile Williams xinli, Maryann Solomon, Mabel Solomon xinli, Laura Setah, Christine Lulua, Lorraine Weir (standing, holding digital recorder), Doris William, Juliana Lulua, Eila Quilt (standing), Annie C. Williams, Loretta Williams, and Eileen Sammy William. Standing, from left, Frank Purjue xinli, Payel Laceese, and Gerald Lawson. Seated are Benny William and Ubill Lulua xinli.
Photo by Linda R. Smith (Yuneŝit'in)

Words for Ch'i [43]

Elder Eileen Sammy William, Xeni Gwet'in

ch'i bets'anx diztan	bottom of the basket
ch'i bedex	top part of the basket
ch'i betsanx ʔedelʔash	head of the basket
ch'i bedanaŝiwed	the bend in the head of the basket
ch'i binats'iyaqax	carry with this
binaldzed	the straps tied to the fabric so you can pack (carry) the baby in the basket
ch'i layan bighużni	the fabric that covers the basket and the straps used to tie the baby down with the strings
ch'i ʔezez bighużezni	you wrap the hide over the basket

Remembering

Lorraine Weir

When the Elders went back to see more of their Tŝilhqot'in belongings, they remembered that bark baskets were used to store leaves for tea, including denish kinnikinnick leaves and bedzish ts'ediyan Labrador tea. These baskets were hung from the ceiling and kept the leaves dry. Qatŝ'ay spruceroot baskets cause condensation, so leaves were never stored in them, but bear grease Ses tlagh was. Pitch ointment Chen dzax tlagh was also stored in bark baskets, and larger baskets were used to heat water and make soup and stew. [44]

After their recording sessions, the Elders laughed and laughed and walked around MOA enjoying themselves, even though they'd arrived at the hotel late the night before. Some had been perplexed that they were given cards instead of keys to their rooms and that the cards made the elevator work, too. At midnight after their late arrival, Elder Susil (Cecile) xinli had gone up and down in the elevator, crowing with amusement and getting out in the foyer only to climb in the elevator again and go for another ride!

Over the nine years since recording for this book began, three of the Elders who shared their knowledge about baskets have gone to the spirit world. We honour the lives and teachings of Elder Mabel Solomon xinli, Elder Cecile William xinli, and Elder Mabel Williams xinli.

Elder Eileen has now retired from the arduous work of tanning hides and making baskets. You can see her art in the form of gloves, vests, jackets, and baby baskets throughout this book. Sadly, her granddaughter April William xinli did not live to fully develop her gifts as an artist and is in the spirit world now, too. Chief Roger's daughter Chiʔela makes beautiful things with the skills she learned from her ʔEtsu Eileen.

From left, Laura Setah, Doris William, Eileen Sammy William, Susie Lulua, Juliana Lulua, and Eila Quilt at MOA, UBC, Vancouver. Photo by Lorraine Weir

CHAPTER 9 ENDNOTES

1   James Lulua Sr. remembered these words from his grandmother Emily Ekks Lulua xinli. Transcribed and translated by Maryann Solomon and adapted by Lorraine Weir.

2   For an introduction from the perspective of legal practice, see Alan Hanna, "Going Circular: Indigenous Legal Research Methodology as Legal Practice," *McGill Law Journal / Revue de droit de McGill* 65, no. 4 (June 2020): 671–709, lawjournal.mcgill.ca/article /going-circular-indigenous-legal-research-methodology-as-legal-practice/. See also: Val Napoleon, "Tsilhqot'in Law of Consent: International Indigenous Trickster Court," *UBC Law Review* 48 (2015): 873, heinonline.org/HOL/LandingPage?handle=hein.journals /ubclr48&div=29&id=&page=; Alan Hanna, "Dechen ts'edilhtan: Implementing Tsilhqot'in Law for Watershed Governance" (Ph.D. diss., University of Victoria, 2020), hdl.handle .net/1828/11933; and Lorraine Weir, "'Oral Tradition' as Legal Fiction: The Challenge of Dechen Ts'edilhtan in *Tsilhqot'in Nation v British Columbia*," *International Journal for the Semiotics of Law / Revue internationale de Sémiotique juridique* 29 (2016): 159–189, doi .org/10.1007/s11196-015-9419-8.

3   See Crystal Verhaeghe, Emma Feltes, and Jocelyn Stacey, *Nagwediẑk'an gwaneŝ gangu ch'inidẑed ganexwilagh / The Fires Awakened Us*, report (Williams Lake, BC: Tŝilhqot'in National Government, 2017), www.tsilhqotin.ca/wp-content/uploads/2020/12/the-fires -awakened-us.pdf.

4   Words spoken during the Free, Prior, and Informed Consent forum, held May 19–29, 2015, in Ottawa. See Chief Roger William, "Title Is with Me," *Northern Public Affairs* 4, no. 2 (May 2016): 27–31, whatis.fpic.info/files/npa_right_to_fpic.pdf.

5   As Justice Vickers put it, "As the evidence unfolded it became apparent that in order to assert his claim, the plaintiff had to conform to the Eurocentric need to define boundaries. Traditional boundaries, surveyed with proper metes and bounds were not a possibility; some boundaries simply had to be found" (*Tsilhqot'in Nation v. British Columbia*, 2007 BCSC 1700, 645).

6   See expert witness Ken Brealey's PowerPoint, *Mapping Aboriginal Title: Tsilhqot'in v. British Columbia* (iddpnql.ca/wp-content/uploads/2019/02/02_Ken-Brealy_Planiterre -April-19-and-20_EN.pdf), which includes examples of the composite maps he prepared based on Tŝilhqot'in witnesses' testimonies in court. In the early days of what became the Title case, anthropologist David Dinwoodie suggested that place names are stories that can be expanded to cover a map without divulging sacred information which the Elders were concerned to protect. The late Keith Basso pioneered this approach in his seminal book, *Wisdom Sits in Places: Landscape and Language among the Western Apache* (Albuquerque: University of New Mexico Press, 1996).

7   For example, the Act's section 81(1): "The council of an Indian band may make by-laws not inconsistent with this Act or with any regulation made by the Governor in Council or the Minister, for any or all of the following purposes, namely ... (f) the construction and maintenances of ... fences; (j) the destruction and control of noxious weeds; (k) the regulation of bee-keeping and poultry raising," and so on. See Bill Henderson's "annotated

Indian Act": "The *Indian Act*, R.S.C. 1985, c. I-5 (Annotated)" (web page), last modified January 15, 1996, www.bloorstreet.com/200block/sindact.htm. Louise Mandell provides this summary: "In successive revisions to the *Indian Act*, meagre reserves were established for Indigenous Peoples who, by a miracle, survived introduced diseases. There was a prohibition against the Potlatch and the Sundance. Cultural destruction was legalized. Ceremonial regalia were confiscated. Indigenous people could not leave the reserves without a permit. Some Elders today recall a time when they could not congregate unless reading a Bible or singing hymns. Access to justice was foreclosed. The *Indian Act* made it illegal to raise money to go to court to fight the land question or to hire lawyers to assist. This legal barrier remained in place for the next quarter of a century. Eventually, residential schools carried out this policy of cultural eradication. Genocide was the midwife to Canada's birth" (Louise Mandell, "Tracking Justice: The Constitution Express to Shared Sovereignty," *BC Studies* 212 [Winter 2021/2022]: 72, doi.org/10.14288/bcs.no212.195688).

8   Linda Hogan, *Dwellings: A Spiritual History of the Living World* (New York: Simon & Schuster, 1995), 89.

9   Harry Setah xinli testified at trial for six days and was the first Tŝ'il?os Park ranger and ?Elegesi Qayus Wild Horse ranger from 1993 to 2009. He suffered a stroke while testifying in Xeni before a government panel which determined compensation for abuses suffered in residential school. Harry Setah died on October 1, 2009. Trina Setah is his daughter.

10 Transcribed by Lorraine Weir from memory on June 3, 2015.

11 Transcribed and translated by Maryann Solomon (Xeni Gwet'in).

12 Gilbert Solomon worked as a translator and cultural interpreter for the Plaintiff's lawyers during the initial interviews with the Elders and was himself a witness at the Title case trial, as was anthropologist John Dewhirst whose genealogies of Xeni Gwet'in families provided crucial evidence of the time depth of the people on the Land. Here Gilbert remembers what he saw as Dewhirst struggled with Tŝilhqot'in concepts of place names and mapping based on experiential knowledge rather than printed representations.

13 David Williams is co-founder and president of Friends of the Nemaiah Valley. He was involved for many years in ecological research, organizing and fundraising in support of the Title case, Tŝ'il?os Park, and the initial stage of Dasiqox Tribal Park (now Dasiqox-Nexwagwez?an).

14 See the source note for part 1 in the endnotes for chapter 2.

15 M.A. thesis, Indigenous Governance, University of Victoria, 2005, unpublished, web .archive.org/web/20180711170222/http://www.uvic.ca/hsd/igov/assets/docs/Russell_Ross _MA_2005.pdf.

16 Linda R. Smith, *Nabaŝ Oral Literature Documentation, October 17th, 2011–September 30th, 2012*, Final Report to Terralingua, a Collaboration Research Study with the Yunesit'in Government (Stone Band) and the Xeni Gwet'in Government (Nemiah Band), 12, terralingua.org/wp-content/uploads/2018/09/Nabas-Oral-Literature-Documentation -Report.pdf. See also Linda R. Smith, *Nabaŝ: CEAA Panel Submission 2013*, www.ceaa-acee .gc.ca/050/documents/p63928/93512E.pdf.

17 This recording with Elder Mabel Solomon xinli was facilitated by her daughter Dinah Lulua, who provided a running translation throughout the interview. That translation is given here in a slightly edited version that retains the occasional ambiguity of Mabel's voice being spoken through Dinah's in effortless collaboration.

18   Quoted in Smith, *Nabaŝ*, 27.

19   *ʔElhdaqox Dechen Tsʼedilhtan / ʔEsdilagh Sturgeon River Law*, May 27–28, 2020, www.esdilagh
     .com/PDF/Esdilagh%20Elhdaqox%20Law%20Final%20Version.pdf. "This law is the first we
     [the ʔEsdilagh First Nation] publicly share in a formal written format as part of our exercise
     of our caretaker role within the Tŝilhqotʼin Nation. We realize the contemporary necessity in
     recording our laws in English written form, even though many deeply embedded teachings
     are lost in translation" (3).

20   Maryann Solomon, *Xeni Gwetʼin Ancestral Laws and Customs / Xeni Gwetʼin ʔEsggidam
     Dechen Tsʼedilhtan* (Nemiah Valley, BC: Xeni Gwetʼin First Nation, 2012).

21   Literally, "named after something."

22   For more information on Tŝilhqotʼin concepts of energy, see Linda R. Smith, "*Súwh-
     tŝʼéghèdúdính*: The *Tsìnlhqútʼín Nímính* Spiritual Path" (M.A. thesis, University of Victoria,
     2008), hdl.handle.net/1828/934.

23   *Legend*: "A story from the past that is believed by many people but cannot be proved to be
     true" (*The Britannica Dictionary*, sense 1); "an unauthentic story handed down by tradition
     and popularly regarded as historical" (*Shorter Oxford English Dictionary*, sense 1). Compare
     Justice Vickers on "Creation stories. These are more in the nature of legends or a traditional
     story, explaining certain landmarks, i.e., a mountain, a landslide area, or a significant rock
     outcropping. Or they may be stories that explain the nature of particular animals and the
     relationship of the Tsilhqotʼin and Xeni Gwetʼin to those animals. The single consistent
     thread appears to be the spiritual dimension attached to each of these legends. In that regard
     they are not unlike the creation stories found in the Old Testament. One would not expect
     to find someone who witnessed the events in the Garden of Eden; nor is there a survivor
     to recount the events that gives rise to the story of Jonah and the whale or Noah and the
     ark. All of these stories have a spiritual dimension. If they were relevant to an issue before
     a court, hearsay evidence would be necessary because of the certain death of anyone who
     might have witnessed such events" (*William et al. v. British Columbia et al.*, 2004 BCSC
     148).

24   See chapter 12, "Tŝʼilʔos and ʔEniyud."

25   Elder Minnie Charleyboy testified at trial for twenty days.

26   *William v. British Columbia et al.*, proceedings at trial, day 83, March 1, 2004, para. 48, 1–2,
     trans. Agnes Haller.

27   Annie C. Williams, *William v. British Columbia et al.*, proceedings at trial, day 131,
     September 20, 2004, para. 63, 33–45.

28   On August 4, 2014, the dam ruptured on a tailings pond at Imperial Metals' Mount Polley
     copper mine, sending twenty-four million cubic metres of mining waste into Quesnel Lake
     and other waterways extending as far as ʔElhdaqox the Fraser River. This catastrophe and
     others like it disproportionally impact Indigenous Peoples and have been classified as acts
     of "environmental dispossession." See for example Janis Shandro, Mirko Winkler, Laura
     Jokinen, and Alison Stockwell, *Health Impact Assessment for the 2014 Mount Polley Mine
     Tailings Dam Breach: Screening and Scoping Phase Report*," January 2016, 22, www.fnha.ca
     /Documents/FNHA-Mount-Polley-Mine-HIA-SSP-Report.pdf.

29   This was recorded during the 2019 wildfire.

30   In a recent report, the Tŝilhqot'in National Government includes as a priority the sourcing and repatriation of Tŝilhqot'in baskets and other belongings now in international collections. See Tŝilhqot'in National Government, *Strategic Plan for the Management of Tŝilhqot'in Cultural Heritage*, 2022 report, www.tsilhqotin.ca/wp-content/uploads/2022/03/TNG _StrategicPlanTsilhqotinHeritage.pdf.

31   James Teit, *The Shuswap* (1909), in *The Jesup North Pacific Expedition*, vol. 2, part 7, and *Memoirs of the American Museum of Natural History*, vol. 4, part 7, ed. Franz Boas, hdl .handle.net/2246/38.

32   Wendy Wickwire, *At the Bridge: James Teit and an Anthropology of Belonging* (Vancouver: UBC Press, 2019), 133.

33   James W. VanStone, "Material Culture of the Chilcotin Athapaskans of West Central British Columbia: Collections in the Field Museum of Natural History," *Fieldiana. Anthropology* 20 (May 28, 1993): 4–5, www.jstor.org/stable/29782599. See also the Autry Museum of the American West's Collection Online, collection of Mr. Homer E. Sargent, collections.theautry .org/mwebcgi/mweb.exe?request=record;id=PE32747;type=701.

34   "Fred J. Buttimer Called by Death: Well-Known Canneryman Had Been Resident Here 44 Years," *Vancouver Province*, April 24, 1934, 2, quoted from *WestEndVancouver* (blog), "Buttimer, Alfred John (1867–1934)," westendvancouver.wordpress.com/biographies-a-m /biographies-b/buttimer-alfred-john-1867-1934/.

35   "Alfred J. Buttimer Dead," *Vancouver Sun*, April 25, 1934, 15, quoted from *WestEndVancouver* (blog).

36   Kevin Neary, "Newcombe, Charles Frederic," in *Dictionary of Canadian Biography*, vol. 15, *1921–1930*, online (Toronto: University of Toronto; Québec City: Université Laval, 2003), www.biographi.ca/en/bio/newcombe_charles_frederic_15E.html.

37   This version of Elder Mabel Solomon xinli's words is based on Dinah Lulua's translation during the recording and on Linda R. Smith and Maryann Solomon's partial transcription and translation.

38   Images courtesy of the Burke Museum of Natural History and Culture, Seattle. Robert B. Lane was an American anthropologist whose Ph.D. dissertation, "Cultural Relations of the Chilcotin Indians of West Central British Columbia" (University of Washington, 1953, www.proquest.com /openview/f69d0860c09cc06956e5a0026e2e69d2/1?pq-origsite=gscholar&cbl=18750& diss=y) was relied on by counsel for the Plaintiff and by the Court in the Title case.

39   This interview was facilitated by Dorrine Lulua whose voice is sometimes audible in the switches in and out of the third person. An adaptation in English by Lorraine Weir precedes a bilingual text of this interview that was transcribed and translated by June Williams (Xeni Gwet'in) with Lois Williams (Xeni Gwet'in).

40   This translation is based on June Williams's facilitation of the interview with her mother, Elder Mabel Williams xinli. For more details on the plants used in making qatŝ'ay, see Turner, *Ancient Pathways, Ancestral Knowledge* (2015).

41   Elder Eileen explained at MOA that "baby basket sizes are measured using the hands – three hands being a small basket (four, five hands …). The height of the basket is also measured by hand. The sides of the basket are made shorter for those who are breastfeeding" (from notes made by Linda R. Smith, September 2016).

42   We are grateful to all of the Elders who came to share their knowledge, and to all of the helpers, curators, and volunteers who made the visit possible, including Betty Lulua and Annie C. Williams who handled logistics for ʔEniyud Health Services in Xeni; Linda R. Smith our project translator; MOA Curators Pam Brown and Dr. Susan Rowley who graciously organized and facilitated the visit, sʔəyəɬəq Elder Larry Grant (xʷməθkʷəy̓əm) who welcomed the Elders, filmmaker Jeremy Williams who generously donated his time and expertise, and Zakir Jamal Suleman who was our student volunteer. We also gratefully acknowledge the support of MOA, the First Nations House of Learning at UBC, the Department of English Language and Literatures, the Institute for Critical Indigenous Studies, the Hampton Foundation, and the Xeni Gwet'in First Nation Government.

43   Recorded by Lorraine Weir. Transcribed and translated by Chief Roger William and Maryann Solomon.

44   From Linda R. Smith's notes made during the Elders' visit to the Museum of Anthropology, September 2016. My thanks to Linda for her notes and all her help during the Elders' visit. —Lorraine Weir

Teẑtan Biny Fish Lake and the (New) Prosperity Mine

Water Is Sacred

Chief Roger William

My auntie Madeline Setah xinli said that water was always sacred to us and that we always talk to the water and tell the water why we need it, just like when we talk to the animals or to the birds. In ʔEsggidam ancestor time, there were a lot of rituals for when we're inside the mother's womb – things the parents did or didn't do, things they ate or didn't eat. When a child is born, they're already familiar with the language, the culture, and the people. When they become an adult, they go out on their own to a place like Teẑtan Biny Fish Lake, and they get their spiritual power, which could be a bird, an animal, or a fish.

Harry Setah xinli called Teẑtan Biny Fish Lake a one-stop shop where you can almost live year-round because it's got everything – berries, medicines, fish, wild meat, moose, deer, wild horses. You can survive in a small area where there's everything you need. My uncle Eugene Sammy William xinli was born there because they went up the mountain to get away from the Big Flu in the valley. Lots of people died in the valley. One of our members, Catherine Haller, talks about my uncle, Jimmy Bulyan xinli, doin' a ceremony there. That's where he got his horse power, and that's where Catherine got her power. So it's a sacred place. On the island in the lake there's a big pithouse. In 2010, the archeologists couldn't see it, but our people could see timber in there but it's been years [since it was used]. You could see that it was a pithouse.

My connection to Teẑtan Biny Fish Lake is the uncle I was telling you about, Jimmy Bulyan xinli, who had the power of a horse. He used to live there, and our people still fish and range cattle there. It's moose habitat, too. But last year through the Tsilhqot'in Framework Agreement we found out there were 50 percent less moose than in the previous five years and 64 percent less calves. Teẑtan Biny is inside the court case area, in the proven Rights area but outside the Title Land.

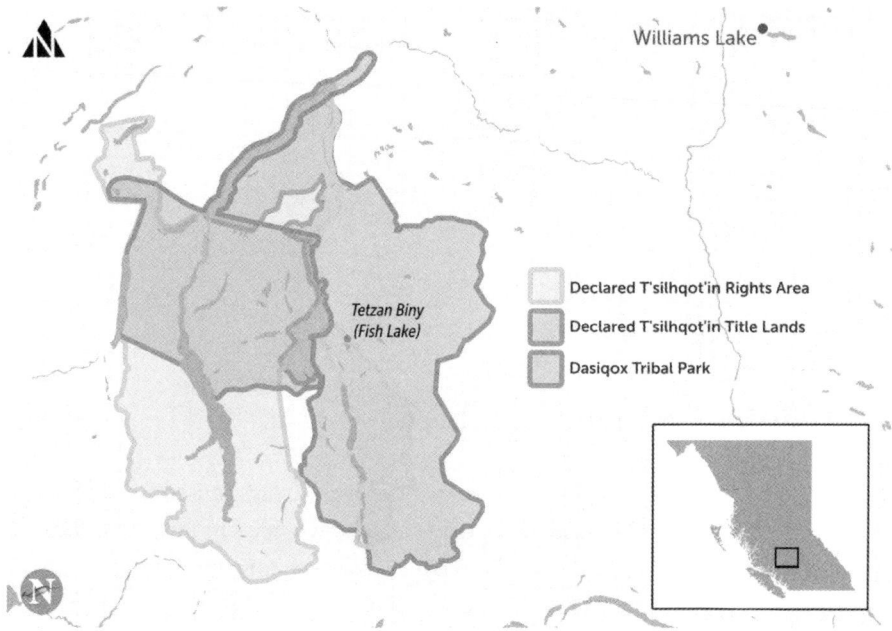

Map of Teẑtan Biny Fish Lake in context. Courtesy of Carol Linnitt / The Narwhal. A larger colour version of this map can be found on page I of the colour insert.

The Duty to Consult

Chief Roger William

The duty to consult wasn't well defined until cases like *Delgamuukw* (1997) and *Haida* (2004). In the late 1980s and 1990s when I was involved in leadership, consultation was loose in all ministries, especially the Ministry of Mines. Back then, that Ministry's legislation and policies were old, but they were making some changes. The Ministry of Forestry and other Ministries were more up to date. The Ministry of Mines was slower and still operating under legislation dating back to its beginnings in 1899. They have the power to buy you out whether you like it or not if a deposit is found under your property. You can negotiate a price, but you're probably not gonna get what you want. The Ministry felt that having to consult with anybody was moot, and they said that there's only a 2-percent chance of finding a mine when exploration is undertaken. That's the power of the Ministry of Mines in BC. There were referral letters that came from government saying somebody wants to log or to mine and they would give you fifteen days or thirty days to declare your interest. Many, many referrals came and went, and we'd try to go through the pile, but sometimes by the time we got to a referral, the project had already started. If you didn't respond, it went ahead. It had already been approved, because we'd missed the deadline. That was consultation in those days.

While we were negotiating the Brittany Lake Forest Management Plan, we were also dealing with Taseko Mines Limited. They had found a large gold and copper deposit at Teẑtan Biny Fish Lake, and they wanted to get it out. We had to find a way to get involved in this, but we were already doing everything we could to deal with all the referrals while we were going to court. We couldn't roadblock somebody who wanted to drill to find out more, so we got legal advice, talked with our Elders, and decided to have our people hired to do the drilling and help the company. We told our people very clearly that while they might have a job this summer or next summer, that didn't mean they would have a job all the time, because we might not agree with whatever this project came to be and might have to stop the drilling. Consultation is a big issue, and we wanted to make sure that we proceeded carefully.

We were creating a paper trail. You know, we couldn't prove that the drilling was gonna have enough impact to stop them. We could've roadblocked, but they probably would've taken us to court. There were so many things that we were dealing with at that time, and we had to choose our fights as Xeni Gwet'ins and as Tŝilhqot'ins, knowing that if we didn't roadblock and didn't get involved, the argument would be that we weren't doing anything. We'd already filed the 1990 Trapline case and received an out-of-court settlement in '91.

The Chilko Lake Study started in 1990 and dealt with Land that had been set aside between Tŝilhqox Chilko and Dasiqox Taseko and eventually became parts of Tŝ'il?os Park. At that time we were also dealing with the logging – Brittany Triangle – and we had the roadblock at Henry's Crossing in '92 for two months. We had a four-year planning project from 1993 to 1997. Then there was drilling at Fish Lake.

We didn't agree with commercial logging or mining, but we opened the door to look at the mine proposal. Sometimes if we just keep saying no, it's like giving a green light to a company to go ahead, because if we go to court based on that, the judge may say, "You didn't even try to work with the company. No matter what, you just kept on saying no, so we don't agree with your argument to shut this down." But if a judge looks at all the evidence we present that the environmental assessment missed certain things, and they see that we participated in a process and tried to create a picture, the result may be different. If the judge sees that every time we tried to create a picture, the company pushed their agenda, the province pushed their agenda, and the federal government turned it down, they may understand our case differently. If the court rules that we kept trying to be involved and we showed a paper trail proving that we tried to work with the company, but they never answered our questions, then they may rule in our favour and turn the mine down.

We figured Taseko was probably not gonna get that far and the deposit was probably not gonna be that big. We thought that legally it would be hard to prove that what they were doing was affecting our Aboriginal Rights and Title because they were drilling, making little holes. How did that affect our Rights? Our lawyers were saying that it's pretty hard to prove from the drilling that they were going to do anything that would have an impact and it would cost a lotta money to go to court. So we were wrestling with that and thought that maybe when they did more drilling, they'd find out it actually wasn't that much. Then, as time went on, we realized that there *was* a large gold and copper deposit and that they wanted to find a way to extract it.

On one hand, we were kinda choosing our fights, 'cause we didn't have money to fight everything. On the other hand, we were using our lawyers, getting advice, and sitting down with the company. We knew the cost of a legal battle from going to court on the Trapline case, but we chose to be involved with Taseko, and we made it very clear to them that our involvement didn't mean that we agreed with the proposed mine at Teẑtan Biny Fish Lake. The August 23, 1989, Declaration that our Elders had put forward with the leadership, Xeni Gwet'in members, and the people said that there should be no commercial logging, commercial mining, or exploration in our caretaker area. I got in as Councillor in 1988 and as Chief in 1991, so I was involved from the beginning, and nothing was to be done without our involvement. Taseko was saying there was a big deposit, so they needed to do more drilling, and they were interviewing and advertising through us to hire people. Some of our people built the cabins there and actually did some drilling, but we were very clear that we don't agree with open-pit mining. We told them if you guys can do something different, we'll look at it, but if you're gonna do open-pit mining, we don't agree with it. We wanna make sure we're involved in your interviewing, the hiring of experts. We wanna look at all your options. We know that an open-pit mine has the worst impact on the environment.

The Prosperity Mine Proposal

Chief Roger William

In the first proposal for what Taseko called the Prosperity mine, they said that the most environmentally sound and economical way to take that gold and copper out was to drain Teẑtan Biny Fish Lake, because it was gonna get damaged anyway. The company said they would look at options, because we'd said we wanted to be involved in interviewing for staff positions and in hiring experts. We wanted to look at all of the options with them, but none of these things happened. Initially they said there were nine options, and then they reduced them to three. The first option was to drain the lake. In the 2010 panel hearing, Taseko argued that they had chosen the best option, but we'd had no say in that.

Creating a Picture

Chief Roger William

By the late '90s, the price of gold and copper was really low, and Taseko Mines Limited threw up their hands and walked away. During that time, through the Nation and the Xeni Gwet'in leadership, we heard stories that they had tried to sell the deposit but couldn't, because it was a low-grade deposit. So they moved off between the early '90s and the end of that decade. We'd created a paper trail and tried to be involved with them, but we now know that the company was not really willing to work with us.

In 2000, the price of gold and copper started coming up, and there was a change of government federally as well as provincially. Taseko strategically called us and sent letters once a year until eventually their pace started to pick up more. We knew they were gonna come back, and in 2000 they started getting hold of us again and asking to work with us. In 2002–2003 they said officially that they wanted to meet with us, and in meetings they told us that they wouldn't go ahead if we didn't agree. If you look at the transcripts of the Canadian Environmental Assessment Agency's first [2010] and second [2013] panel hearings, you'll find our leaders talking about how Taseko was saying that they wanted a "social contract" with us before they started. In 2004–2005 we worked on the Memorandum of Understanding and the Letter of Agreement, and we signed in 2006, saying that we were gonna create a picture, show it to our people, and they would decide if they agreed with it.

We needed to create a picture before we decided. In that picture, we wanted to look at what this mine was going to be and at the impacts on the environment and the damage which the mine could do. We wanted to know what the footprint of the proposed mine would look like. Would the mine leak, and where would it leak? What kind of leak? We knew there was gonna be a leak – there's no such thing as a mine that doesn't leak. Once the picture was clear and we knew what the mine would look like, then our Nation and our community would be involved and decide. If the people voted in favour, then we'd need to know what the agreement would look like. What about impact benefits, royalties, jobs, and spinoffs? We told Taseko that it's up to you how much you wanna do this picture with us. If you keep muddling up this picture, it's gonna go against you. We're gonna try and create a picture with you, but if you leave the process and do things without our involvement, that's your problem, because the less we know, the more likely our people are gonna turn you down. They have questions, and you need to answer. We wanted to know exactly what the footprint of the mine was gonna be. We wanted to know, and then the people were gonna decide. To me, that didn't mean I agreed with the mine. That meant that we wanted to create a picture and there are letters and meetings where we said that entering into discussions does not mean we agree with the mine. The Letter of Understanding said this is without prejudice to our Rights and to our Title. Without prejudice doesn't mean that we agreed with the mine. We wanted to create a picture. That was the agreement, and everybody knew that. The Declaration says no mining, so between 2006 and 2008 we said let's look at the picture, but the discussions fell apart.

After the Rights Declaration (2007–2009)

Chief Roger William

When the decision in the Title case came down on November 20, 2007, things got interesting. The trial judge said we had 100 percent Rights to hunt, to trap, to trade, and also to catch and use wild horses. Our Rights area included Teẑtan Biny Fish Lake. The trial judge also said that we had met the test of Title to almost 50 percent of our declared area, but Fish Lake wasn't inside that proven Title area. So that's when Taseko started to push their weight around, but they had known right from the beginning that Teẑtan Biny Fish Lake is in the Title case, because it was in our Trapline case. In 2007, we were working on a process which would have federal government, provincial government, Taseko

Mines Limited, and the Tŝilhqot'in Nation working together. We agreed to be involved with what is called a Joint Review Panel hearing through the Canadian Environmental Assessment Agency (CEAA). Many people and groups were also involved, including Friends of the Nemaiah Valley, the David Suzuki Foundation, MiningWatch Canada, the Council of Canadians, and the Fish Lake Alliance. During that time, we knew that the federal Liberal government would not look at any project that included a lake with fish in it. The NDP government in BC also had many processes that the company had to deal with, so we felt that protected us.

We did a roadshow to all six Tŝilhqot'in communities, we met the people, we met the Elders, we met the General Assembly, went to the Nation Assembly, and then from there we were gonna work on the environmental assessment knowing all the questions and concerns that the people had. Taseko provided some funding to us at the TNG level to be involved, and we hired Loretta Williams as the liaison between the Chiefs and Taseko. We worked together so we'd know what the issues and concerns of the people were. By the time the joint panel hearing was over, we'd know all the answers, including exactly where the powerline was going to be, how they were gonna take the gold and copper out, what kind of road they were planning to build, and what kind of damage was gonna happen. Then the people would say yes or no in a referendum vote. The people would decide.

When the decision in the Environmental Assessment Process on Kemess North Mine came down on September 17, 2007, it was negative. They turned down the mine. So Taseko Mines Limited got scared and was adamant that changes be made to our joint review panel process. Then BC pulled out of the joint panel hearing, saying that we were too far apart. Taseko said they'd do their own environmental assessment, but we didn't trust them any more than we trusted BC. They weren't worried when we didn't agree because the Title decision had come down and they knew that Teẑtan Biny Fish Lake was outside the proven Title area. That's when we dug in our heels and said through the media that from here on, it's gonna be clear, we're gonna do everything we can to protect Teẑtan Biny Fish Lake. The Fish Lake mine is not gonna happen. Right from the beginning, we never did agree. The Declaration of August 23, 1989, said clearly no commercial mining, no commercial exploration, no commercial logging. They knew that. In 2008, we said that's it, there's no more. We pulled out of the Taseko agreement. There's money that we spent trying to help create that picture that Taseko hasn't paid us to this day [2015], but then they argued why they didn't owe us. On January 14, 2009, BC approved the Prosperity mine.

Jobs and Money

Chief Roger William

When we agreed to create a picture from 2006 to 2008, we knew that if we clearly told the company that at all costs we were gonna turn the mine down, it could be used against us in court. They could argue that we'd already made up our mind before the process started. So we told Taseko that if they wanted to create a good picture, they'd better do a good job and resource the process so we could make it clear. We went to the communities and we got a lot of resistance from the beginning. Some of the members got mad at Loretta [Williams] or at the Chiefs, saying, "You're selling us out. This mine is gonna kill us." Between 2006 and 2008, former leaders and Elders said, "What are you guys doing?" Our members didn't trust them and they were questioning me about why we'd been working on this together. We said that we'd been very clear from the beginning in my community and in the other five communities that we were gonna make an agreement with Taseko to create a picture, involve the people in it, and then members would decide whether or not they agreed with it. We went from 2006–2007 when we were working with Taseko pretty well to 2007–2008 when they were starting to push us.

By 2008, we were the only ones fighting the mine. Everybody else wanted the mine, including the City of Williams Lake, 100 Mile House, and Quesnel. Taseko started doing media about creating jobs. In their wisdom, Taseko took advantage of the mountain pine beetle epidemic, which was happening then. People were losing their jobs, and mills were shutting down. It was a tough time. They spent a lot of money on media, lobbying Ottawa and Victoria, and they did everything in their power to say that people needed jobs, and they would provide them. They didn't care about the mine's footprint or the leaks. Taseko had gotten everybody thinking jobs, and by the end of 2010, people started thinking maybe they were right.

We challenged them on that. We didn't think the City of Williams Lake was really gonna benefit. When you're going to mine, you want the best people. We might have gotten some jobs, but certainly not all of the seven hundred jobs that they said they were gonna create. The City of Williams Lake and us Tŝilhqot'ins would have been lucky to get two hundred of those jobs and the rest would have gone to outsiders. And then the company would probably have bypassed the City of Williams Lake and 100 Mile House and Quesnel to get their parts flown in from Vancouver. That's what we were arguing: Do you really think they're gonna hire you? We started circulating that question, and when Taseko's parent company bought the Gibraltar mine out, we asked whether they had an agreement with First Nations in the area. We wanted to see the agreement, but they never responded. That's when everything started falling apart. Taseko said they didn't agree with our media, but our two-year agreement with them about how each side would communicate with the media had stopped by that time. They said jobs and money, and we said no, our people won't get the jobs. They'll go to people from way out there, and Teẑtan Biny will be destroyed.

A Mistake

Gene Cooper, Xeni Gwet'in

I think our people just thought mining: devastation. That's the first thing. 'Cause there were recommendations from up north [Kemess North Mine] about how mining was going. There's information from the States about how mining has been going. A lot of times, mining runs everything, and that's a big concern. If Canada had environmental control of mining, and if mining could be a bit more respectful of the environment and figure out a way to work with the people, I think it'd be a lot easier. But for them to come in and just say, you know, "We're mining" and try a show of force, that's just not a way to go, and that's what Taseko did. That was a mistake. They think they can come in and railroad not only First Nations but also the public, the government, trying to sell the employment aspect of things so that the people would force the government to bend their laws a bit in order to allow mining through. It was good timing when this court case came. That really changed their [Taseko's] attitude, made them recognize that as First Nations, we do have Rights out there, and those Rights are what have enabled us to survive for thousands of years.

The court case laid the foundation of our expectations in regard to how things should be done in forestry and also in mining. Any natural resource has to have all our Rights and Title in line, and that didn't happen. So they set the foundation for filing the court case. It was good, 'cause nothing changed from the way they said things in the beginning right to the end. You know, the province tried tripping them up, but no one was speaking the truth. Their story'll never change. That's why it's all about survival.

The First CEAA Panel (2010)

Chief Roger William

In 2010 the Canadian Environmental Assessment Agency (CEAA) panel visited each Tŝilhqot'in community, and people testified about how Teẑtan Biny Fish Lake related to them and affected them. Elders, youth, kids, everyone from our communities said no to Prosperity mine because there would be too much damage. At the end of the 2010 panel hearing, we realized that the tide was turning and more people in our area were against the mine than for it. We weren't happy, but we also weren't surprised. For years, Taseko had shown that you can't trust them, and we made it very clear in our press releases. Even when we had an agreement between 2006 and 2008, our members didn't trust them. They were questioning me about why we'd been working on this with Taseko. So we felt that as long as strategically we'd done all our steps and been respectful and honourable, we'd have to hit this head on.

When the report came down from the CEAA panel in 2010, the decision was no.[1] They said that there would be a significant environmental impact on the fish, on the interests of Aboriginal people, and on the grizzlies, so they couldn't approve the project. But they left the door open, telling Taseko that they could do another proposal if they could find another way to mine the deposit, and the panel would look at it again. When Taseko saw the panel's decision, they weren't worried. They argued that they were going to win, because the proposed mine wasn't in the proven Title area. In the end, the panel agreed with us, and the federal government agreed with the panel, so we won.

Nabaŝ

Maryann Solomon, Xeni Gwet'in

The mine, the Elders opposed it all the time, but Taseko Mines kept pushing their way in. And they were trying to change people's minds, like at meetings. They promise you this and that, and nothing will happen. Making everything sound really good to the community, but that's not how it was. We had people that had mining in their community talk to us about what was happening with the loggers and everything. So the Elders were aware of that.

Taseko's been fighting for that for a long time. Even though our community kept saying no, we still had to go through the process of this drilling and stuff, and I thought it was gonna get worse. Chief and Council were told that they couldn't just go in there and stop it. We were wondering if we went in there, would they go ahead and start mining? We had to go through the process.

I lived up there not so long ago. My parents had rangeland for cattle up there. I think they [Taseko] call it Little Fish Lake. We call it Nabas̄. We used to stay there every summer, and there was winter camp. Bring cattle up there to prepare them. It was for the rangeland. Even now, that's where we have our camp up at Fish Lake Teẑtan Biny, that area.

New Prosperity (2013)

Chief Roger William

When Taseko came back in 2013 with the New Prosperity project, they went to option two in spite of the fact that during the panel hearing in 2010, they argued that option two was worse than option one! Option two was to mine the area near the lake and save the lake. They proposed an open-pit mine below the lake and a tailings pond above the lake, saying that they were gonna move the tailings pond a few kilometres up and have pumps, so that any contamination would be pumped back into the tailings pond. So in the second round, when they put the New Prosperity project forward, they themselves argued that their own first option wasn't good! To take one example: The 1994 plan shows underground flow under the lake, but they didn't even put that forward until July 25, the day the panel was approved to start. It was held back three different times from the report. There were other questions, too, including one about the drilling in 1994. All that time, they never responded until the second panel hearing process started in 2013.

I feel proud right now. I saw pride at the panel hearing here in Yuneŝit'in today [Aug. 13, 2013] and I saw it in Nemiah when the panel went there. I heard the panel for the last two weeks in Williams Lake. I think most of the people – First Nations or non–First Nations – have a lotta questions and issues about that new project. A lotta of them are pretty skeptical about the new project. What I really feel is that the company is not gonna be able to save Teẑtan Biny Fish Lake if this gets approved. Between years five and ten, they're gonna come back and say that can't afford to save Fish Lake, they've gotta do more pumping, more this and that, and there's no way they'll save it. They're gonna go in the hole saving it. This mine is gonna shut down, and they're gonna go into deficit. And they're gonna come back and get approval to drain Fish Lake and destroy it, like the first time. I've felt for a long time that the grade of the deposit's so low, they probably can't afford it, anyways. They're just gonna destroy, contaminate, do damage, and go in the hole. We'll be left with the damage.[2]

The "Moral Roadblock"[3]

Marilyn Baptiste, Xeni Gwet'in

Even before I ran for Chief, I was asking – and other people were asking – why we were signing exploration agreements *in the Declaration area* when the Declaration says no mining, no exploration. Why was that happening? I asked that question, and the answer was because Woodward and Company said if we don't make an agreement with them, they'll just go ahead without us. That's exactly what Jay Nelson says today [2015], and that's exactly what they said even when we were going through the fight with Taseko Mines Limited. In 2009, when Taseko Mines Limited was going in to do more exploration – supposedly for the sake of the [2010] panel hearing – the lawyers said we've gotta take the high road. We need to stand down and let them do their drilling and their exploration. And that was so hard.

The lawyers and everybody else agreed. Oh yeah, we should stand back, stand down. And so we had to sit back and watch this company go in and destroy our Land and drill how many places up in Nabaŝ? Alice William, who grew up at Yanah Biny Little Fish Lake and Nabaŝ, was travelling in and out of there, and she put up her own signs in there too. And Mabel Solomon and her family had utilized that area as well, for grazing cattle each year. It was like death by a thousand cuts for them to have to sit back and watch this happen. And we're supposed to "take the high road." What "high road," may I ask?

The lawyers advised to make that agreement with the exploration company, because previous to my being elected as Chief, the Chief and Council had signed agreements with two different exploration companies. One was a two-year agreement, and one was a one-year agreement. The one that was a one-year agreement came back in 2008 wanting another agreement, and Woodward and Company told me you can't refuse to sign this agreement, because the other company has a two-year agreement and they're still out there as well. I'm like –. So basically, I said I'm not willing to sign whatever agreement. And then I said fine, if you want to have a discussion for me to even think about any such thing, then they're gonna have to give to a scholarship fund that is no strings attached. I was looking at a hundred thousand dollars, but one of Woodward's junior lawyers said to me, "You guys have free education already. Why do you want to do this? Like, it's complicated."

I was so taken aback. I just couldn't believe my ears. But I didn't lose it, I didn't disrespect them. I could've told my people outright and shown them exactly what it is that we actually face in that, but I was trying to save face, not only for Woodward and Company but for my former Chief, because of the faith that he has in them. That is a slap in the face. I couldn't believe my ears, and I'm like, excuse me? And I talked to Jack about that and said that's unacceptable. Unfortunately, we settled on fifty thousand and it still sits in the trust [account] with them (2015), because we need to get our policies and stuff in place on it.

We went through panel hearings in 2010 and again in 2013. I have to say, one of the greatest honours was being able to be there at the panel process, even though we went into that federal assessment reluctantly, because at the end of the day, *they* made the decision. But we and the Nation went through the whole process, and being able to be at every single panel hearing was a very great honour. To hear the voices of our people, to stand by them and to hear their passion and their heart for protecting the Land and water. How many of our Elders wouldn't even come and talk to you, but they sat in front of that panel and did a submission?

After the first Canadian Environmental Assessment recommendations, and on the day of the federal government's very gracious decision and very smart decision to say no to the Prosperity project as proposed, they said yes to Mount Milligan. That was a blow, because I work with Anne Marie Sam of Nakazd'li, and I told the Minister that when he called. So we knew that the Prosperity issue would be back. They [Taseko Mines Limited] came back in 2011, and they were going in to do more exploratory work, supposedly for the sake of the second panel process. We fought, met with governments, met with the company, and it was such a waste of time. The alternative, number 2, had already been pushed in the first panel process, and it was agreed by the company, the government, and the panel that alternatives 1 and 2 were worse than the one that they denied in 2010. So, of course, when they decided they were gonna go and do more exploratory work, I said, I'm sorry but I cannot allow that. We will not allow that. That's not gonna happen. We cannot do this. And Jay Nelson the lawyer told me, "You cannot do that. If you block them, they're gonna get an injunction, and then they'll make you pay, and they'll do this and that and –. We've gotta take the high road." And I couldn't see any high road! The high road was right up over the top of the hill they were at before. I said, I don't care, I can't do it this time. I mean, we had the Declaration, we had the win in 2010. How was it possible that we were gonna step aside and let them do this? No way.

The weekend before that happened, the company had three rigs going out there. A couple of our people were out hunting and saw the trucks going by the 4500 Road, and they followed them down. They stopped them at the Taseko bridge when they were just going in to the Taseko Lake Road, and they said to wait there for the Chief to return. We don't have cellphones out here, so they had to get back to the community. They tracked me down and said that these people from the company were trying to go to Fish Lake, and they were waitin' for me at the bridge. I can't remember what [husband] Emery was doing, but he said phone my brother-in-law Edmund and sister Sharon, so Edmund came with me, and we went to the bridge. We parked and got out to talk to them, and it was hilarious. They just assumed my brother-in-law was Chief! Edmund said, "No, she's the Chief." Anyway, we chatted and had some good laughs but, "Yeah, you turn around and exit our Territory." They said, "We're supposed to be at work, and we don't have this permit," and I was, like, "No, we can't let you do that." So he said, "Well, I gotta phone my boss." He had a satellite phone. I said "Yeah, no problem, go phone your boss." They got me to talk to their boss on the phone, and they said, "Well, if we go back out, they're gonna turn around and come back next week." I said, "That's fine, we'll be waiting."

And so it just ended up being myself, my late niece [Marie Williams xinli], my hubby [Emery Phillips], and little Buddy the Pomeranian dog. We thought the others were out hunting, but they were in town! I phoned one of my members in town, and I said can you go and see if this rig is sittin' there? No, no vehicle. So I'm like, okay, they're comin'! We had this radio that we thought would help us, and we pulled up to the 4500 Road to sit and wait. The RCMP came along, and they said they were responding to a call from the Valley and that they were gonna sit there and have their lunch. We had a little bit of activity on our radio, but we couldn't hear it. Then the RCMP drove off. They didn't tell me anything, so I'm like, okay, let's go, follow them! So we followed them maybe two and a half kilometres or so down the road.

I didn't stop the company. The three of us didn't stop them. They were already stopped. The RCMP stopped them! I hopped out and went and started talking to the lead guy, Jeremy Crozier. He said he had a permit and was gonna have to do his work, and I said, "I'm sorry, you do not have authorization to be in our Territory." And he kept trying to get me to say whatever about a roadblock, and I kept telling 'em, "You do not have authorization. We have not been consulted. BC has no jurisdiction. We respectfully ask you to turn around and leave our Territory. We're not happy. Do you want me to tell you all over again?" Anyways, he was gonna attempt to pull away, and Emery backed up, so that meant he was right there with me. So after that, Emery just stepped out and had a cigarette, and then he asked Emery, "What are you doin' here?" "I'm just here supportin' the Chief!" So then we were back and forth, and I kept repeating. They had two security guys, and one of them said, "The RCMP is here. Why don't you go talk to them?" And then the Sergeant came and basically said they want you to stage a roadblock. They are willing to turn around, but they want you to stage a roadblock. Of course, with all their cameras and their videos they had full intention to go to injunction court, and so did we. I said they could back up and turn around. No, it might wreck their machines, and it would cost more money! I said, "Fine, if you go to the 4500 Road, then you can turn around." They all agreed, but they wanted us to stage a roadblock!

So I got back in the truck, and Emery backed up all the way to the 4500 Road, and I hopped out. Then, with Jeremy Crozier in the lead truck, the whole line of trucks came, and I stood on the road, 'cause Emery wasn't staging a roadblock! Crozier drove right up to me, and that's what you see in that photo.

Truck driver Jeremy Crozier and Chief Marilyn Baptiste in confrontation, 4500 Road, Xeni Gwet'in[4]

When Crozier got down, he said, "You're blocking the public road." I said, "You're in our Traditional Territory. You do not have authorization." I wish I could get it all on film now! Then Crozier was back at it again, and it was like, holy smoke! I said, "Did you forget what you were doing or something?" We were going through all this discussion over again, and I kept repeating what I had already said. In all of this, we had one small car come through and pass by – no problem, no roadblock. He finally decided to turn around, and they had how many crews all lined up there? I dunno how long it took them to turn around and head back out. One of their guys came over and said he wanted to go down to the Elkins Creek Ranch to let them know they were not coming, and I said, "No problem, we can do that for you," and off he went. After everything was all done, the RCMP came over, shook my hand, and I said, "Okay, good, I'll allow you to escort them out this time!" When the company went to injunction court, they named Emery Phillips and then my niece and myself. And the other three were phantoms! They were Lhatŝ'assʔin![5]

Taking Back Our Responsibility

Marilyn Baptiste, Xeni Gwet'in

Women need to stand up and start coming together in ceremony with our drums for the water, for Mother Earth, and taking back our responsibility in doing that. The message comes from the grandmothers, the Ancestors, that we need to do these things, and I believe that we have started, not just here with our people on a minimal basis, but also across Canada. It is our women who have constantly been impacted, but not only our women. It wasn't our way to treat our women that way. We need to really focus on that and help bring back the ceremonies that we need to do for the water, for the fish, in this situation with the [Mount Polley tailings] dam breach. There's a lotta that that needs to happen, and also a lot of healing that needs to take place in our women. Our Elders are a big part of that. But our men cannot be left behind because of the learned disrespect and the learned Western way that's been imposed upon our people. It needs to be healed, and we need to get back to our way. I think a big part of that is doing ceremonies to help give strength to the leaders in the work that they're doing. All women need to come together in giving thanks through prayer and ceremony. The grandmothers are calling on us, and we need to take action. I'm happy that so many people are realizing that and seeing that. Can you imagine if the lawyers had interviewed more women? They would've gotten a helluva lot more. A lot of our men are interviewed and the women are not for whatever reason, but the women also carry a lot of knowledge and teachings as well as the knowledge passed down from their husbands, too.

Matrilineal Culture

Lois Williams, Xeni Gwet'in

Our culture used to be matrilineal until the churches came in, the Catholic church, and everything became Catholicized so they looked at men as leaders when really it was the women. The women were there holding the communities up. And the men were the ones that were the last outer layer of the circle in the community, and they were the ones that were protectors and hunters. But we also had women that were hunters. They were Warriors as well. So there's no divide in between what men and women could do. Everybody was pretty much equal and that's how I was raised too.

"They Finally Heard Us"

Elder Mabel Solomon xinli with Dinah Lulua, Xeni Gwet'in

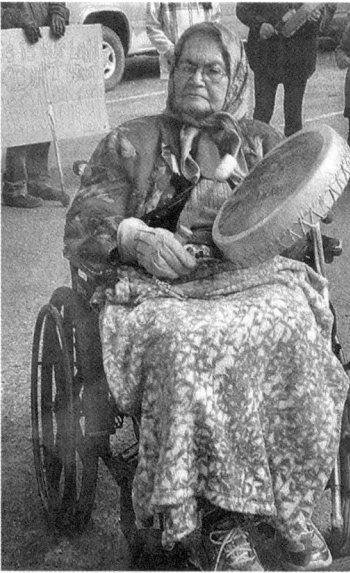

Elder Mabel Solomon xinli at a demonstration. Archival photo courtesy of Gilbert Solomon

She [Elder Mabel Solomon xinli] said we didn't like it, but they kept trying to mine Fish Lake and I talked about it lots of times to different people that came to interview me. If they were to mine it, they would've poisoned our deer, our moose, our wild chicken, our animals. I spoke to people about these things. They would've killed all our fish. They wanted to drain our lake, our Teẑtan Biny. We didn't want them to do that. They would've poisoned all our animals by blasting the rocks. They said that the contamination wouldn't leak, but I didn't want them to mine that place. If the contamination leaked into our rivers, it woulda killed all our fish, our salmon. They kept telling us that water wouldn't leak. We would contain it. [laughs] But I told them water seeps underground everywhere.

They had a roadblock, and there was many of us there, she said. I went with Maryann [Solomon]. Maryann asked me to come with her, so I went with her. She [Mabel] said I didn't have a shotgun, but I threatened to shoot the first shotgun![6] [laughter] They [Taseko Mines Ltd.] left the area.

She said, I dunno who said it, maybe it was a Chief. They didn't know about people on the Land. My mom always said they don't hear – no matter how much we talk, they don't hear us. And then [Chief] Marilyn [Baptiste], at the Assembly of First Nations, I think it was, she made a speech about my mom with her shotgun and then when she came back she said, "You know what I did?' She said, "I said that to them!" And my mom said, "They finally heard us, eh."

Conclusion of the 2013 CEAA Review Panel

The 2013 CEAA Review Panel concluded that the New Prosperity mine was likely to cause:

- significant adverse effects on water quality and fish and fish habitat;
- significant adverse effects on the current use of lands and resources for traditional purposes by certain Aboriginal groups, on their cultural heritage, and on their archeological and historical resources;
- significant adverse effects on wetland and riparian (interface between land and a river or stream) ecosystems; and
- significant adverse cumulative effects on the regional grizzly and moose populations, unless necessary mitigation measures are effectively implemented.[7]

A Rubber Stamp for Mining

Chief Roger William

We feel BC is pretty much a rubber stamp for mining. They'd approved the Prosperity mine proposal in 2010, and it was the federal government – the Conservative Party whom we have a lot of concerns about – that stopped the mine from going ahead. We know BC and Canada have the last say. We don't agree with it. We think it's *our* Rights and Title, but we gotta prove that we have Rights and Title. Where in the world do you have to do that? It's crazy. But what are we gonna do? So we gotta create a paper trail. We gotta create a picture, and if this picture is so good that we can agree with it, then people will approve it. And we'll have to make sure that all our Rights, our Title, our interests, our opportunities are protected if there's approval. But we can't even look at our Rights or royalties until we know that our environment, our culture, and all the sensitive issues around that are clear and our people have said yes and we can go with it. But if our people say no, then we have a paper trail.

What keeps Williams Lake going seems to be the mining, the logging, and the belief that the company is bringing hope back. Money, jobs, the mill industry, the loggin' industry. BC keeps approvin' the process – they approved the environmental assessment six years ago. So as long as Taseko's got money to keep fighting, they'll probably find different legal avenues against the decision, because you can only appeal so many times. They know that if this breaks through, there's gonna be a lotta other mines that'll break through. If they find a big pot of gold where they're drilling, if Fish Lake is approved, that door is wide open. The different mining exploration companies probably support Taseko's push, so that's probably where they're getting money. I wouldn't be surprised. And they're using Amarc – I think there's a lotta support from Amarc.

The Federal Decision: Minister Leona Aglukkak (2014)

Chief Roger William

Maybe at the beginning, Taseko Mines Limited was trying to find the best environmentally safe way to do the mine, but part way to the end, they went political and they went jobs, because in the 2000s when the [mountain pine] beetle epidemic came, a lotta jobs were lost in Williams Lake. So Taseko said, Well, we don't need First Nations, we'll just say here's a job opportunity. This mine is safe, we're gonna create seven hundred jobs. And they kind of stopped communicating with us or looking at the real scientific side of it and started focusing on the economic side. That's what we've been dealing with.

Taseko was not happy, so they were all over the media talking about it. They had a time limit to file a judicial review, so they went ahead with it, saying, It all depends on the federal decision. If it's in our favour, we'll drop it. We still had to wait for the federal decision on it, and we knew that back in 2010, the Minister of the Environment, Jim Prentice, had agreed with the panel. With Leona Aglukkak as Minister, we felt pretty confident, but we also knew that the Conservative government was resource-extraction oriented at all costs. With their roots in the Reform Party, the Conservatives rejected special Rights for Aboriginal peoples. They saw what was coming with more than 630 First Nations on our side and many non–First Nations groups, too. There was a lotta pressure on them. Aglukkak was one of many Ministers, and we knew she could be overridden, so we were confident, but at the same time, you never know. At the end of March 2014, we heard that the federal government had decided in our favour.

They Said No!

David Setah, Xeni Gwet'in

Prosperity mine surprised the hell out of me, even with the [2013 CEAA] panel hearing that said no. I said yeah, that's not bad, but it's not over. There's still the ministers. They'll listen to them, and they'll just go the other way. And the Minister [Aglukkak] said no. I was sitting there, I said holy moly! What's happening? They've never done this, not at that level. We've never gotten 'em to say no. And when they came back saying they were given evidence of why this should be looked at again, I thought the area's still gonna be wrecked. How do we know they're gonna go by all those things, and how do we know they're gonna make it better? All those are just words right now [2014]. They haven't proven nothing to us.

I tell 'em, They've [Taseko] got nothing, you guys. Why can't we just stomp it out, get it outta the way? But eventually, they came back. The second time, I was thinking it's a mistake in analysis, and I kept thinking to myself, maybe if I keep thinking the same way, they're gonna say yes this time. The panel did it again. Yeah! Maybe they're really starting to open their eyes now, but I was still thinking about the Minister, 'cause a majority of the government can say yes and there's nothing the other people can do. When they said no, I was on the floor, speechless! [laughs]

It Wasn't Over Yet

Chief Roger William

But it wasn't over yet, as Taseko Mines Limited filed two judicial reviews, one against the CEAA panel, and one against the federal government's decision. We weren't surprised that Taseko was unhappy, and we knew right away that they weren't gonna give up. We know that when they were an exploration company before they became Taseko Mines Limited, they tried to sell this project, and it got nowhere because other companies doubted the economics of it. So when the decision came down, it was another victory for us, and we felt the project's dead now, but we had to protect our interests, so we filed our arguments. Taseko wrote a letter to the Minister arguing that the wrong model had been used, and they explained that they were gonna put this material on the whole of the tailings pond so it wouldn't leak.

What's interesting about those arguments is that they were talking about the wrong model themselves. We heard and our experts heard Taseko themselves say that they would put this material *where needed* and not on the whole pit. In their letter to the Minister, they were telling a different story, but if you look at the panel report's description of what Taseko Mines Limited was saying, you'll find that they weren't gonna do the whole pit. We always argued that draining the lake is going to do too much damage and the New Prosperity version of the project saves the lake. We'd already questioned the economics of both the project and the possible damages. All along we felt and I still feel today [2017] that economically, the project can't happen. Never mind the impact of damages. With the amount of gold and copper compared to the amount of material they've gotta remove to get there, they'd probably go into deficit.

Taseko did all their due diligence in consultation. They offered us really good exploration opportunities, monitors, studies, jobs, revenue. They've been creating a paper trail, and they wanna tell the story that they've been working with these First Nations and look at all these agreements they proposed. "We're fightin' this court case. We're not givin' up. We wanna do it for you people." That's the story, so I think that, if they break through, it's gonna open up other mining, but if they don't win, they can still go after damages, because they spent all this money. To me, if they lose this one, they're gonna come back and ask for their money back from the Crown. They'll be saying, "You guys approved our mining claim, you approved our permit, but you won't let us mine. We're gonna take our money." And then the province can argue, "Well, you couldn't prove that you could do it safely, so we're not gonna pay you. You couldn't meet the test of safety and Aboriginal Rights." I'm sure there are gonna be all kinds of arguments.

There's only so much funding, but you've still got to fight this fight. To me, it's been amazing to be able, for the past twenty years, to sit in front of my members, who continue to say the same thing: We need control, this is our Land, we're not gonna agree to that type of activity, that's gonna destroy who we are and what we're doing. I'm not worried about Fish Lake and the amount of money that could come outta there. Who wouldn't want that kind of money, but our people say money isn't important, the Land is. The destruction that's gonna happen to Teẑtan Biny and the rest of us, that's worth more than money.

CHAPTER 10 ENDNOTES

1   See CEAA's *Report of the Federal Review Panel: Prosperity Gold-Copper Mine Project, Taseko Mines Ltd. British Columbia*, July 2, 2010, CEAA reference no. 09-05-44811, www .ceaa-acee.gc.ca/050/documents/46911/46911E.pdf.

2   On May 14, 2020, the Supreme Court of Canada rejected Taseko's application to appeal the federal government's 2013 decision to reject the proposed New Prosperity Mine following the 2013 CEAA panel's negative recommendation. For a detailed timeline, see Carol Linnitt, "A Timeline from Birth to Death of Taseko's Embattled New Prosperity Mine in B.C.," *Narwhal*, May 14, 2020, thenarwhal.ca/timeline-birth-to-death-tasekos-embattled-new -prosperity-mine-bc/. Susan Smitten's 2010 documentary film *Blue Gold: The Tsilhqot'in Fight for Teztan Biny (Fish Lake)* provides a powerful introduction: vimeo.com/9679174.

3   These are the judges' words in connection with Marilyn Baptiste's stand against the proposed (New) Prosperity Mine, for which she received the Goldman Environmental Prize in 2015. She was awarded the Eugene Rogers Environmental Award by the Wilderness Committee (2011) and the Council of Canadians Activist of the Year Award (2012). With the First Nations Women Advocating for Responsible Mining (FNWARM), she received the Boyle Initiative Award (2010).

4   Video screenshot courtesy of Goldman Environmental Prize, incorporating footage from Jeremy Crozier's truck camera. See the Goldman Environmental Prize's YouTube video "Marilyn Baptiste, 2015 Goldman Environmental Prize, Canada" at youtu.be/jOh6w14bl8g for the documentary that was shown when Chief Baptiste was awarded the Prize on April 20, 2015, in San Francisco.

5   Lhatŝ'asʔin means "we do not know his name." During the Tŝilhqot'in War, the great Warrior Chief Jinadlin was identified as Lhatŝ'asʔin to his captors.

6   There is a Solomon family story that when one of the members of a film crew filming at Ts'utanchuny Dadaben the Medicine Camp saw Elder Mabel sitting in her wheelchair, he wanted to take a photograph of her holding a rifle in her lap, but her son Gilbert Solomon felt that this could endanger her and he wouldn't allow the photograph.

7   Source: Minister of Environment and Climate Change, Impact Assessment Agency of Canada, "Backgrounder: Proposed New Prosperity Gold-Copper Mine Project," 2013, ceaa.gc.ca/050/evaluations/document/98460?culture=en-CA. For an analysis of mining regulations and settler colonialism in the context of the proposed (New) Prosperity Mines, see Dawn Hoogeveen, "Geographies of Settler Colonial Dispossession: Rejecting Gold and Prosperity on Tsilhqot'in Territory" (Ph.D. diss., University of British Columbia, 2016), hdl .handle.net/2429/57079.

CHAPTER 11

Lhin Desch'osh at Teẑtan Biny Fish Lake

You can't *own* the Land. You *are* the Land.

—CHIEF ROGER WILLIAM

Introduction

Lorraine Weir

On August 9, 2013, during the second environmental assessment of the proposed New Prosperity mine, the Canadian Environmental Assessment Agency panel did a site visit to Teẑtan Biny Fish Lake. This was an opportunity for Tŝilhqot'in Elders, knowledge keepers, leaders, and healers to impress on the panelists and Taseko Mines Limited representatives the sacred significance of the Land and waters which the proposed mine would obliterate. The storytellers and organizers sought to share an experience of the sacred by engaging visitors in a ceremony of words and actions, telling part of Lhin Desch'osh, the great sadanx gwenɨg story from the long-ago time, blessing with water from the lake, and encouraging people to immerse themselves in the lake at the end of the visit. If the extraordinary beauty of the place wasn't enough to persuade the panelists that a vast open-pit mine was unthinkable, then the voices of the ʔEsggidam Ancestors on the Land and in the ancient words of Lhin Desch'osh would teach them to understand the impact of "new prosperity" on the people and their way of life. Clear-cut logging had brought Xeni Gwet'ins to the brink, leaving no recourse but the monumental undertaking of the Title case. Now an open-pit mine threatened the Nen itself and would destroy the spiritual, cultural, and material heritage of the people in this place.

A long narrative comprised of linked stories, Lhin Desch'osh tells of how the Nen Land was created, how the watercourses came to be, and how a young woman came to be abandoned by her family and taught her sons to make most but not all of the animals safe. As Chief Roger explains, "Lhin is 'dog' and desch'osh is some kind of deyen healer, some kind of power, something great that nobody knows about, beyond what our Medicine people can do. Part of him was a dog and part a young man. That's why the story is called Lhin Desch'osh." A story which tells of how drumsongs and stories began, it teaches the sacredness of the Land and all beings who live as relations with it, as well as the consequences of not upholding obligations to each other.

The plan for the site visit was that Elders would each tell part of the story, but due to an unfortunate mix-up, most of them weren't able to be present, so Chief Roger and Linda R. Smith, a Yuneŝit'in linguist and knowledge keeper, told the story instead. The site visit also brought a change in CEAA's usual recording technology, which was not intended for mobile outdoor use. The CEAA technicians improvised with digital recorders, the sound quality is uneven, and the recording incomplete, so a transcript wasn't made, even though the audio file is in the public domain like all CEAA panel hearing records and available to anyone on request. So this chapter includes some improvisation too and excerpts from the audio file, which CEAA kindly provided, have been transcribed and included. However, the core of this chapter comes from the recording we made at Tl'esqox after the panel hearing in that community and several days after the site visit. As darkness fell, Chief Roger was inspired to tell the story of "Lhin Desch'osh" in much more detail than had been possible at Teẑtan Biny. Not wanting to lose Linda R. Smith's and Cecil Grinder's important contributions to the recorded site visit, we've included excerpts from their words as well. This chapter concludes with an excerpt from Union of BC Indian Chiefs (UBCIC) Grand Chief Stewart Philip's closing remarks at the event. By improvising in these ways and bridging worlds, we hope to share something of the power of that day and of Lhin Desch'osh, the creation story of the Tŝilhqot'in People.[1]

The Site Visit

Chief Roger William

I'll try to stick close to what we talked about last Friday, August 9, 2013, at Fish Lake Teẑtan Biny, Dasiqox Taseko for the joint panel hearing of the Canadian Environmental Assessment Agency. We had people from Taseko Mines Limited and the CEAA panel members. Many other people were out, including a lot of Xeni Gwet'ins and Tŝilhqot'ins. Chief Russell Myers Ross was there from Yuneŝit'in community who share the Caretaker area – Teẑtan Biny area, Dasiqox area – with us. Chief Joe Alphonse, Tribal Chair, also attended. I believe Chief Francis Laceese was there, and myself, both of my Councillors – Loretta Williams and former Chief, now Councillor, Marilyn Baptiste. City of Williams Lake Mayor Kerry Cook attended with Sue Zacharias, one of her Councillors. We had Union of BC Indian Chiefs President Grand Chief Stewart Phillip. We thanked everybody and explained our connection to Fish Lake and what we feel about Fish Lake.

We met at Taseko Lake Lodge and drove in. We went to a place that used to be a trail back in the day, going along the Taseko River to Gwetex Natel?as Red Mountain. It's an old 4 × 4 trail, an old wagon road, and you eventually branch off to Red Mountain and then back southeast to Yanah Biny Little Fish Lake and Wasp Lake in that area. Bisqox is an obsidian rock that our people made arrows out of, and it's the name of a creek in that area. That's the trail we were on, and there's a large bench there where you can see the lake and the river. We wanted to talk about Nadilin Yax, and that was the closest we could get to it.

What we wanted to do was get our Elders to line up and tell the Lhin Desch'osh story, but those Elders ended up not having the right equipment, and they couldn't make it. The other Elders that were there weren't comfortable talking. If the crowd had been smaller, they probably would have talked, but we had a large crowd. Cecil Grinder was there and did ceremony with us. Cecil is a former Chief who is retired from the RCMP and is now a councillor for Tl'etinqox Anaham. He's been doing medicines for quite some time now, following his late uncle Raymond Alphonse's teachings before he passed on that Cecil get back to his culture, drumming, and ceremony. Raymond taught Cecil when he was growing up. We used sage, a medicine that grows around here at Tl'esqox. We also used juniper, another medicine that we use for smudging. Sage and juniper are used to purify an area and to cleanse a person. You talk to the medicines, telling them what you're doing, just like Elder Gilbert Solomon talks about how his mom would talk to the fish or the animals or plants when working with them, acknowledging them, because they are living beings and are a society.

My auntie, the late Madeline Setah, and many of our Elders talk about the power of Tŝilhqox Biny Chilko Lake. It's a healing lake. You go into the lake and talk to it, tell it what you want to do, and it will help you. In our culture, the strongest time to cleanse and do many ceremonies and rituals is before the sun comes up, so people would go into the lake before sunrise and cleanse themselves, just as they would cleanse themselves with sage and juniper before sunrise. You can do these rituals at other times, too, but before sunrise is the strongest time. Elder Joseph William xinli told of using datsan k'achih, juniper, for healing when he was at Fish Lake many years ago. They used to travel on snowshoes in this area in the winter, and it was so bright from the snow and the clear sky that he was blinded. He got some juniper bush and smudged with it. He got his sight back.

Cecil [Grinder] used juniper and sage to smudge, and he went round with a feather to do it. He joined me, and we had water from Chilko Lake, and we cleansed ourselves. Then we did a drumsong, the Teẑtan Biny song. It was nine in the morning, and there were a lot of people. I went around like Cecil did, and I used a feather to bring the healing water to each person. We wanted to cleanse everybody, because we were going to tell the story of Lhin Desch'osh during the daytime.

Lhin Desch'osh is a sadanx gwenig ancient story which our Tŝilhqot'in people only tell in the evenings, so since we're close to seven in the evening [when this was recorded], I'm gonna talk a bit about it. There are many branches of this Lhin Desch'osh story and some that I don't know. I'm just gonna talk about what I know. When the panel hearing was at Fish Lake, it was daytime, so we didn't want the story to be too long. That's why I ended where the chipmunk almost got caught, when it got the marks on its back. Elders tell us that these stories are sacred and they are supposed to be told at night, so we smudged with sage and juniper to protect everyone when the story was told. We felt that if we used the sacred water, sage, and juniper, and all did this together with the same mind, the same thought, and for one reason only, that the panel and Taseko Mines would know what we were talking about on this site visit. So we cleansed everybody, including the Taseko people and our people, before we told the story. After I prayed and went around with the water, I explained that although some of the Elders couldn't be present, those who were there were listening and would let me know if I said something wrong, although they might not feel comfortable speaking in such a large group. Linda Smith also knows the story of Lhin Desch'osh, and we told it together.

Who Should Hear Sadanx Gwenig Ancient Stories?

Lorraine Weir with Ivor Deneway Myers xinli

When sadanx gwenig were offered as evidence by some of the Elders at trial, they were not only told in a public venue (though sometimes in the evening, depending on the story and the Elder telling it), but subsequently corroborated by Justice Vickers, who compared them with the written versions in English published in 1900 by Livingston Farrand. Although Farrand's sources and translators are unknown, Justice Vickers estimated a timeline for the stories, showing that they had been known by Tŝilhqot'ins since before the date of what the court called "sovereignty assertion," 1876.[2] In a sense, this was as close to "time immemorial" as Justice Vickers needed to get with reference to settler chronology, and he proceeded to compare versions of sadanx gwenig told by the Elders in court with the versions printed by Farrand. Both processes brought these stories decisively into the public realm, as did the telling of parts of Lhin Desch'osh at the 2013 CEAA site visit to Teẑtan Biny.

The late Ivor Myers, who spent much of his life recording the Elders' stories, explained the importance of sharing gwenig stories in broader terms. This is what he said when I asked him about publishing gwenig in this book:

> In today's society, it's no use to keep the stories to yourself. If you keep them to yourself and nobody knows, then you wouldn't know the essence of the stories behind them. Society out there might as well know today. It will give them the essence of who we are, how we got here in North America, how we were here in the time of the Big Flood that happened long, long ago. That way they wouldn't just talk, guessing where First Nations people come from. Not very many [Tŝilhqot'in] people talk in front of the public, and I've been trying my best to reveal this information in public, especially in meetings sometimes – that our Land doesn't just go right there, it's further than that. If you don't use those stories, that's history [i.e., gone]. No more. Therefore that information should be brought forward and brought to the public, so people will know what this person knows about those stories, especially the most important ones. I was in awe when I heard those stories which I'd never heard of before. And there are some Elders out there who still know those stories today. If society wants to really know about the

Tŝilhqot'in people, my advice is it's okay to bring this information forward, so people will know who we are as people and as the Tŝilhqot'in Nation.

These words and Ivor's teachings before he went to the spirit world have guided my (Weir's) practice with respect to sadanx gwenig throughout *Lha yudit'ih*.

Twins

Chief Roger William

When you're in the mother's womb, you're being taught a lot of things, including Lhin Desch'osh and the other stories, so when you're born into this world, you'll be familiar with the voices, the stories, and the drumming. In the womb, you're being fed Tŝilhqot'in culture, food, rituals, and beliefs, and you're comfortable with it all. You're not being moved, you're not being surprised, and you're learning it all. When you're born, you're taught many ritual beliefs, stories, and legends, and you're being prepared to be an adult. During the time before their baby is born, the parents, both female and male, can do certain things and not others. For example, they can't be closely involved with any death in the community, and they shouldn't be engaged in mourning or participate in celebrations that are rituals to deal with spirits. They have to step back and leave it to other people.

In our culture, twins are very powerful, and there's a process for twins. They say that the mother and the father have an energy because their children are twins. Twins can't look you in the eye for very long and they can't be angry and wish for something bad to happen to somebody, because it could come true. When any child is born, they already have power, but when a twin is born, their power is huge. You become an adult when you get your man's voice or when you're on your time if you're a woman. That's when twins get even more power, and that process continues throughout their lives. Right from the beginning, twins have powers, and they grow up being taught about mistakes and how to fix them. As children, they may make honest mistakes or do things that would hurt others. They're taught that what they did is not right and this is how you fix it through rituals. Once they become adults, they go through the same process as anyone who already has power, except that twins are probably gonna get more power and most of them feel that they're deyens (traditional healers) already.

They say when a young woman is first on her time, she is the most powerful, and each month it gets a little bit weaker until, as she gets older, the power is not as strong. Women on their time are not supposed to pick up a weapon or step over one. There are other things they can't do, and especially when a woman is young and transitioning from childhood to adulthood, she may make honest mistakes. Twins can fix those. Twins are raised more carefully, because they know how to fix stuff and do different types of rituals, including the use of sage, juniper, and water. So that's how we were brought up from Lhin Desch'osh, from the culture.

Lhin Desch'osh

Chief Roger William

Lhin Desch'osh goes *way* back, before contact, to the beginning, to the early time.

There was a village Nits'il?in (Chief) and his family, and they had a dog. Lhin was their dog. The Chief and his people all had pithouses, and they always gathered food. They camped out and brought food back to their cachepits.

The Chief's daughter had just become an adult – she went through her process. In those days, the parents arranged who you would be in a relationship with, and this young lady was waiting for this to happen. She knew about it, because she'd heard stories and been told ritual beliefs. Then at night when she was by herself in the pithouse, this young male would come. Now she was an adult, and this was the training process.

He came in probably like any other time and, you know, she knows these stories. Then they made love but she never knew who he was. She woke up in the morning, and he was gone. And she looked around the village and wondered, "Who is this person?" It happened several times, and she didn't know what to think, because there was supposed to be an arrangement. This must be the arrangement. She thought, "Maybe there's something else I don't know about?" because she was supposed to know all this, and she didn't want to ask her parents what's going on, because this is how things go.

She got some paint, because she wanted to know who she was making love to. We used different plants for paint like on the petroglyphs. When they were making love, she dipped her fingers into the paint and put her hand on his back. She knew he was gonna leave again. Next morning he left, and she was looking around the village and looking around and she couldn't find anyone. She was getting worried. She didn't know who was doing that with her. And she looked around, and she looked, and then she saw her old dog, and she saw the mark on his back. Then she got worried! She ain't gonna tell *nobody*!

Back in those days, creation time, everyone spoke Tŝilhqot'in – the people, the animals, the birds, the fish. Everyone spoke Tŝilhqot'in. There were stories that when a woman had a baby, she would die when the child was born. It was just like that. So women knew they were gonna die when they had a baby. During that time, different animals would kill people too. Eat people.

Raven and Magpie, there's many different stories about those two. In this case, Raven was only thinking of himself, but he knew the stories and the legends, and he knew the rules, so he always played within them. It was always for himself, never for the community, never for the people, never for his family. But Magpie was always looking after people – in this case, this young lady, the Chief's daughter. Magpie was probably suspicious, because the young lady was not talking to anybody. She was terrified about what she'd found out.

Time went on, and things happened. Time went on, and she was pregnant. She didn't let her parents know. She thought maybe she wasn't pregnant, because she wasn't showing too much. Dogs don't show much, right. That helped, but she was still worried, and Magpie was observing. Magpie knew people. She knew how people are and what they do, and she noticed the young lady wasn't the same. She was changing, and Magpie was watching. Magpie wanted to help, but she knew that the young woman didn't know. But Raven was suspicious. It's like he wanted to create chaos all the time. There are stories about that.

It came to the time when she was gonna have the babies. The way they say it in Tŝilhqot'in, she was so worried, and then when she had the babies, she had three little puppies. You can imagine what the leader, her father, the family – everybody just freaked right out! They were scared and they were angry, because they hadn't been told. "You need to talk to us. What's goin' on?" Magpie was trying to help out – "It's okay!" You know, trying to make her feel better. "I'm here for you." But the people, the animals all together, they were all angry. They were up in arms. "This is not right! This is totally off everything!' At that time, there were a lot of things that weren't good. Some animals hunted and ate people. So everything was already in chaos, and then this happened.

They. All. Left.

Magpie knew that the family were gonna leave. She heard stuff. It took a week for them to decide what to do. The young girl and her puppies could have perished, all of them. Punishment was severe in those days.

Magpie was putting stuff away for the young girl. She knew that the family was gonna move away and leave her. This is not normal. This is bad. If the young girl hadn't been the Chief's daughter, they would have dealt with her like that. Chased her out, on her own, or put her to death. But she was the Chief's daughter, so they all moved away.

Raven knew Magpie was putting stuff away, so he took some for himself and his family. That's just the way he is. There's good reasons and bad reasons for that, but it's a different story.

The young girl was hurt, angry, frustrated. She blamed herself for everything. I should've this, I should've that, you know. But Magpie kept checking on her, telling her there's fire here, there's food there. Making sure there *was* fire, because Magpie knew that Raven was going to snuff out all the fire when the family left. He wanted to make sure that the young girl didn't survive and neither did the old dog and the puppies. As far as Raven was concerned, the family was going to be gone, and the fire should be gone, too. So Magpie put stuff where Raven couldn't find it, and Raven took food and took fire and was making sure it was all gone. He felt that he'd done his job, taking everything, leaving the young girl with nothing. But Magpie knew.

As time went on, the young woman and the three puppies survived. The old dog got left behind, too, and the story is that he knew history and legends. As a human being, he was a young person, but in dog years, he was old. When he went hunting, he believed that the young woman was harvesting, but she made a straw dummy that looked like her. She put it way up in the field, because she wanted to know what was going on in the pithouse.

> The mother created this figure on the hill, and she made it look like a woman, dressed in women's clothes, and she had a spruceroot basket on her back, and she really looked like she was digging there. According to my grandfather, she was digging something called gwilet and it's not a plant that I know. I've asked some Elders, but they don't seem to know what it is, so we're still trying to find out about that plant. Anyway, this woman in the story, they called her Gullabi, some say Oolabee, that's what her name was, this created woman. She was created so that the mother could go and see what was happening in the house, so that her family would think she was still up on the hill. She's important to this place [Teẑtan Biny] because she came here. They all came to this place, to the lake up here.
>
> —LINDA R. SMITH, August 9, 2013[3]

She'd started really paying attention when she returned home and noticed that things were different. There were little footprints, baby footprints, and a man's footprints. "Hm," she thought. "Something's going on." She went out to harvest as usual, but she sneaked into the dummy she'd made to look like herself. When the puppies went out to look around, they went back in and told their father that she was working, harvesting over there.

She'd made a hole in the side of the pithouse so she could peek in and see what was going on. When she sneaked back to look, she saw them inside. They'd all taken off their hides. The old dog was a handsome strong young man who sang and danced around the fire with the three little boys. They sang Tŝilh-qot'in songs.

The young woman watched as they sang and danced. She planned a way to catch them and keep them human, so she would have her family. Then she rushed in and grabbed the puppies' hides. She threw the three hides into the fire but when she grabbed the old dog's hide, he jumped back in. They struggled, and when she tried to tear the hide off him, it ripped in half and she threw it in the fire. That's why he's called Lhin Desch'osh. Lhin is dog and desch'osh is some kind of deyen, some kind of power, something great that nobody knows about, beyond what our Medicine people can do. Part of him was a dog and part a young man. That's why the story is called Lhin Desch'osh.

Now it's summer. Fall time, harvesting. The old dog had lots of knowledge. He was smart. Because her father was a Chief and her grandparents knew stories about what the animals did, the young woman also knew those things. She knew about her culture and her language, and she also knew how things were on the Land, good things and bad things. And she knew about twins. She had not just twins, but triplets, and they were human now. She knew that's power. She knew about what animals did out there, but first she had to put food in her home.

According to Charlie Quilt, she didn't want to tell them the story about the animals until they were ready for their journey. She was abandoned and she survived. She taught her boys how to hunt. She made bows and arrows and she taught them how to hunt each animal ... In the meantime, the villagers who had left were starving. They were somewhere else and they were starving and Magpie came and checked on [the young woman and her family] and found that they had lots of meat and the houses were filled with meat. And Raven also came back and discovered that Magpie had got some fat and meat, and so he figured out that Magpie probably got it from this woman. Anyways, Raven went back, and so the villagers came back. She told them that they could come back.

It was that winter that she started telling them the stories about the animals, because their journey was to happen the following spring. They were going to journey among all the animals.

—LINDA R. SMITH, August 9, 2013

You know, puppies grow pretty big in a year and are already running around by then. Now these boys were growing so fast and their parents were teaching them the stories, the legends, and the rituals. She and her husband were moving around, going hunting, and she harvested medicines. She picked berries, wild potato, beartooth, all that stuff, and the boys did it all, too, and they also went hunting. They filled all their cachepits with meat. Around the fire at night, they talked about the country and the animals, and she started teaching them all the stories, legends, and rituals and about making changes. The dog knew the history, too, and he also taught the boys. "You boys are triplets. You've gotta be positive all the time."

Way back, her grandparents talked about different signs, something happening in the future when it was time to make changes and fix a lotta things. She knew that she was connected to that. She was the mother of triplets and her husband the father of triplets. He was desch'osh – he had extra power. From her parents, grandparents, their families, the young woman knew that she had to start taking steps. She knew that she *was* the change. She *was* that time. She had given birth to triplets and was still alive. She had to make it so other women didn't die after giving birth. There were animals that ate people, and they had to change that, too. Her whole community had been shocked and left when they saw that she was still alive and had the puppies. The whole thing was just totally wrong. But she had extra power, and now she could make change.

> They were gonna journey among all the animals. And Lhin Desch'osh had special powers. He was a very strong Medicine person and he had a Medicine staff. Lhin Desch'osh and the boys were travelling around finding different animals and they travelled to this lake [Teẑtan Biny].
>
> —LINDA R. SMITH, August 9, 2013

There are many stories that are part of Lhin Desch'osh. One of them is Salmon Boy. In this story, the triplets were inside the salmon, and they went down the river to the coast and came back four years later. Another story is about a very large beaver. Some say the beaver was as big as a cabin, and some say as big as a big moose. Something like that. The boys and their father were trying to deal with the beaver, but it went underground and made a tunnel. There was a fight, but the beaver ate people, and it swallowed Lhin Desch'osh and dragged the boys through the mud as they kept trying to catch up with it. They were digging, digging, trying to save Lhin Desch'osh, trying to catch the beaver as it tunnelled along. That's where the river is – Taseko Dasiqox, Nadilin Yax the mouth of the river, Chilko River, Tŝilhqox Biny. That's where the beaver was tunnelling, trying to kill Lhin Desch'osh, and that's where the boys were digging, creating the Tŝilhqot'in River, trying to save him. That's how the river was created. That's how the mountains and this Tŝilhqot'in Land came to be.

> They found the beaver, and I can't remember now what Lhin Desch'osh used to catch it, whether it was a spear or what, but he was actually pulled along on this beaver trail underground. He was pulled along there and disappeared. So the boys were pretty concerned about their father, so they were looking for him. So they dug along behind him, they dug the earth out, and they went all the way to the end of Chilko Lake, near Chilko Lake Lodge, and that's where they found him. He was already there. He was whistling there and gutting the beaver and skinning the beaver, and they came upon him. And there, my grandfather says, there's a really big beaver dam there and that was that beaver's house. And it's still there today. My grandfather also thought that there might have been some wood there that looked to be from that time period. And he saw the site. I haven't seen the site yet – I've been wanting to go and see it, but I haven't done that yet. So that's all I know about the beaver. They say that's why the Chilko River flows down the area that was dug. That's why. And they even say that this river comes down the same way, too, and all the rivers flow down the way they do today.
>
> —LINDA R. SMITH, August 9, 2013

Anyways, many things were happening then, and there's another story about the last animal that the mother, father, and the three boys dealt with. It's about the chipmunk. The mother was harvesting, and the boys were full of energy, challenging everything, and they were hunting. They wanted to fix everything. She had a story to tell them, but she forgot part of it. Then it was too late. She forgot to tell them that you're not supposed to fix chipmunks. By the time she realized what she'd done and had gone to find them, they'd almost caught the chipmunk. That's why it's called ts'egwelts'ansh in Tŝilhqot'in – you can see the three fingers of Lhin Desch'osh in the stripes on its back.

> And the woman at home remembered that there's one piece of information she forgot to tell them about, so she sent Oolabee up here to tell them. It was about the chipmunk. She forgot to tell them how the chipmunk killed people, and Lhin Desch'osh needed to know that information to be able to escape from being killed.

So they were up here when she caught up to them, Oolabee. She was a created person, and she came to life as a woman, and she was sent up here. So down here at the lake, she caught up to them, and she said, "I forgot to tell you something." And then after that, she couldn't speak. She went dumb. Lhin Desch'osh rubbed her mouth, thinking that he could help her speak, but she wasn't able to say any more. So according to Charlie, Lhin Desch'osh killed her there, and that's where she died, along the lake somewhere down here.

—LINDA R. SMITH, August 9, 2013

If you go down past Anaham to Alexis Creek and then you work your way back to the river from the highway, there's a place in the open where you can see one, two, three dogs, and the main dog, the boys and their father, Lhin Desch'osh. That's where they all turned to stone.

Transformation

Chief Roger William

I think the first transformation in our culture is the Lhin Desch'osh story and the twins, or triplets in this case, are a big part of that change. The old dog that was with the Chief in the village for all those years taught the young woman and their children when he became a young man – half-human, half-dog. And they saw the power. They were able to gather food and fill up the pithouses, the homes, the earthlodges. The Magpie was still able to communicate with the people. So was the Raven, who was always trying to do something, being able to bring all those people back home and their food and everything. No one had ever seen anything like that before. People knew about twins, about power, and about what they could and couldn't do, but here was Lhin Desch'osh, and he was the one who was making changes. These changes were so important and necessary because of the conflicts between humans and animals, birds, fish, and the Land. So Lhin Desch'osh had the triplets to fix things, but because the children didn't really listen to everything they were told, they turned to stone and never did finish their job, though things were a lot better than before they started. Lhin Desch'osh did a lot of work, but it was never really completed. That's what we have in front of us. From that time on, they no longer spoke one [i.e., the same] language. That all changed.

Nun Wolf

Chief Roger William

I keep thinking of what David Dinwoodie was asking when he was trying to understand the language. "Nun," he said, "how come these words have nun in them all the time?" Nunitsiny is grizzly, nundi chugh is cougar, nun is wolf, nudi dalmalh is bobcat. You know. Nundi is lynx. He was trying to understand how come. And those animals would eat people. It's probably from Lhin Desch'osh. My thought is that's probably what Lhin Desch'osh didn't get to. The whole Lhin Desch'osh story is about trying to change the Land, because there were animals that ate people. Some animals didn't get changed. One of the Elders was talking behind me, and she said they intended to go around the earth – Nenqay, Nen, meaning the world, the earth. She said they never did make it right 'round, and they turned to stone. That's what a lady, an Elder, told me just when I was starting to talk.

Why Did You Tell This Story to the CEAA Panel?

Chief Roger William

How I told Lhin Desch'osh would not be how an Elder would teach it. I told it by elaborating on each part. I told the story, and then I talked about history, about European contact and the three groups of people, and I kinda mixed it all up and tried to go back to Lhin Desch'osh. I went around it and back to it and backed it up with some information. And I included present understandings, too, the way we think today, the way the culture is today, European or BC Canada culture, and related that to what was happening back then. I was helping them figure it out. Healing is going back to our culture, learning those legends and stories.

We were teaching them our connection to the Land. We were teaching them that we knew there would be damage. They [Taseko Mines Limited] say there's no significant impact outside this watershed. "This is Fish Lake. The bowl is Fish Lake. Any damage stays here, it's not gonna leak out, there's no leaks in this footprint." And we don't agree with it. We asked questions. We've been at this for twenty years and we still have questions about a lotta things.

The Lhin Desch'osh story is probably a myth to them, but for us that story is part of the power, the energy of the triplets and how the Land was created. It's the story of Nadilin Yax and how the river was created by the beaver. It teaches that you don't need the police to discipline you or a park ranger to say you're hunting too much. Creator is looking over you and will affect your life depending on what you do on the Land. We told them that you've gotta be born into this story to understand it. You can't own the Land – you *are* the Land. You're part of the Land. Everybody spoke Tŝilhqot'in, including the animals and fish and birds. You have to be born into the Land and live it to really understand how this Land was created. I mentioned how punishments were severe, because you were born into it and you were taught. If you didn't follow your rituals, legends, and stories, you could be banned from your family and your community. You could be put to death. Your actions could affect everyone, not only yourself. Your family, community, even the Nation. There were no police, there was no ranger or doctor who gave you a pill to fix things or put you in jail or whatever. We knew the Creator was there, and me, I could do things when nobody saw me. I'd get away with it and nobody would ever know, but the Creator watches me and will create my path, and I would suffer for it. Usually the one who does whatever is the first one to suffer. If not, it would be somebody they love – their family. Depends on what they're doing – it could be their whole community, could be their Nation.

Since I was a kid, the way I've been taught, I'm scared to lie, to cheat, to take advantage because the Creator is looking at me and I've got my little girl, my older sons, my wife, my mom. I don't wanna be selfish and do something for myself so that they're going to suffer. Something's gonna happen to them, and I'm gonna lose something. I'm not worried about going to jail or being caught, I'm worried about what's gonna happen to my family. You know, me is one thing, I can live with that, but why should my son Linden suffer for what I'm doing? He's got his own life, and if I'm being selfish, I'm wrecking his life. He didn't do anything wrong, but he's suffering for it. That's what I worry about, and that's the training that's ingrained into us.

I also talked about the three groups of people: one group that loved both sides, one that stuck to the culture, and one that went a new way. Those gaps got wider as time went on. I talked about our medicines, our spirituality, and our deyen people (traditional medicine people). They were so powerful back then, because throughout the Tŝilhqot'in, every child was taught, believed in, spoke, and did the same rituals. So the rituals were powerful, and since the smallpox, the Tŝilhqot'in War, and residential school, they've been fractured. We've still got some deyens, but they're not as strong, and some of our deyens are a bit corrupted. I elaborated on some of that stuff at Fish Lake.

I elaborated on our belief that if we do everything in our power, prepare ourselves, and do everything the way we're taught as Tŝilhqot'ins, but things don't go right, or if I die or somebody dies because of my actions, then it's meant to be. You can't pass your time [to die]. No matter what, that's gonna happen, so you celebrate that person's life, because they lived in that honest way and worked hard and the Creator took them back. You would be cremated and there'd be dancing and celebration. There's a celebration for birth, there's a celebration for death, and that's why our Elders taught us that it's an honour to die. You're put on this Earth for a reason to do certain things, and there are ritual beliefs and stories about that. We're told the story of Lhin Desch'osh, and we learn from that. We prepare for everything that we do. To prepare for winter, we move all down this Land, preparing ourselves for what we want to do. But not everything is success. Not everything works well. Lhin Desch'osh talks about a lot of that.

Ceremony

Chief Roger William, with excerpts from the transcript, 2013 site visit of the CEAA panel

The morning portion of the panel hearing was at Taseko Lake Lodge. Then it took us all about forty-five minutes to get to Fish Lake. We had a feast and drumming and then ceremony. We did the water ceremony, the fish ceremony, and we went to the lake. Then we bathed. People took turns and cleansed themselves with the water, and some of the Taseko people participated in this.

We were drumming songs while all this was happening. Cecil [Grinder] danced holding a fish while we did a drumsong in a big circle around a medicine bundle. We had juniper and sage burning and water there. Cecil put the fish down and talked about doing this ceremony for Fish Lake and for the water, the sage, the juniper, and the fish. Then he talked about the different families who had used Fish Lake and the names of their descendants today. He thanked people for being present and invited them to go down to the lake, and he explained the ceremony that we were going to do.

> It's important that we come back and that we acknowledge the forest, the mountains, the air we breathe. That sun, that water, everything between grows.

It's important that we acknowledge Mother Earth. Sa, sun. Tu, water. What you hear out there. That's the powers in between that we have to control in a good way.

Mother Earth is looking after us, because we're looking after her.

Just listen to this water. Just like our Elders talk to us at nighttime. Close your eyes. Listen.

—CECIL GRINDER, August 9, 2013[4]

When we got to the lake, a young woman sang the Water song, singing it out into the lake, and then we started to drum. Cecil talked about the importance of the water, which is part of us, part of who we are, and part of everyone present. Water is important to everybody. Then as he began to cleanse himself and wash his hair, Cecil talked about cleansing and invited everyone to join him. After we were all done, he gave me the fish to feed our Ancestors. They're all here with us, he said, and he talked about all the people who are buried at Fish Lake. He talked about cremations which took place in the area and about the pithouses and graveyards on the island in Fish Lake.

Water is a living thing, just like me and you. Water's got a heart. It's got a place to live. If we contaminate this water, if I spit in this water, if I pee in this water, if I do that in someone else's water, I'm contaminating this water. My grandmother always said this water's going to be healing you when you walk into this water without shivering and you come back out. Because you can go into Taseko, Chilko, all these other different lakes, you can go in there. You can heal your body. You go in there, you come back out without shivering, you're ready for a lot of things. If you're shivering, you've got a lot of things to work on. This water here is important to our people. This water's important to us. This water here is a living thing.

I'm gonna pray to this water to look after me, my body, wherever I'm hurting, wherever my mind needs to go, my eyes, my nose, my mouth, wherever I need to say what needs to come out, whatever I need to eat that needs to go in. When I go in this water like this, it's a prayer for me. It's a ceremony.

—CECIL GRINDER, August 9, 2013

That morning Cecil went out on the lake in a canoe and did ceremony with sage, juniper and water on the island. He talked about that, and several people talked about the sacredness of the island. Then Cecil asked everybody to gather so we could go down by the river and invite the spirits to join us. The last thing to do was to put the fish in the fire, and Cecil told people not to look at the fish. In our culture, you don't look at people when they eat, you let them eat in peace. He put the fish in the fire to feed all the Ancestors that were there with us that day, and the youth sang a couple of drumsongs.

> This morning I went out, I went out in a canoe early this morning. And I went out and I seen things that I'd never seen before, I heard things that I never heard before. It's important. It's like what I was saying this morning down there when we listen to the water. Listen to that water.
>
> —CECIL GRINDER, August 9, 2013

We sang a competition song at the end with the women on one side and the men on the other, including people from the panel hearing and the CEAA secretariat, from Taseko, the mayor, Tŝilhqot'in women, and everyone. The competition was between the ladies and the men to see who was louder, and each side sang part of the song. As we sang, Cecil called out to us –"Louder! Closer! Keep coming!" When we got close enough, both sides sang together. I don't know whether everyone from Taseko was there, but some were. For sure all of them could hear it!

We wanted to affirm for Taseko and the panel that we have a culture, we have a language, and we don't agree with the Prosperity mine. It's gonna cause damage in many ways – environmentally, culturally, socially. Taseko keeps coming up with findings that the mine will have no impact. "We got the best experts in North America, Canada, BC. Fish Lake is a bowl and we're gonna protect Fish Lake." Actually, the damage is a lot more than in the 2010 proposal. They draw lines around things and say they're protecting the lakes. They talked about the fish-spawning area and enhancement, but the fish are gonna be fewer but bigger. There are gonna be youth programs [funded by Taseko Mines Ltd.], yeah. And compensation for Aboriginal Rights – that's the law of the Land now. They're gonna compensate for damages. Whatever.

Title Is Inherent

Grand Chief Stewart Philip (Union of BC Indian Chiefs)

This is not about gold, it's about water. This is not about copper, it's about fish. This is not about jobs, it's about the integrity of the environment.

We do not rely on the courts to decide whether or not we have Indigenous Land Rights. We believe our Indigenous Land Rights are conveyed to us through our Creator and our inherent nature. By inherent, I mean that our Title, our Indigenous Land Rights, are part of us. It's part of our DNA, and it's not something the Supreme Court or other courts have any sway or influence over determining whether that is or is not a fact. It is a fact.[5]

CHAPTER 11 ENDNOTES

1   Lhin Desch'osh was first published in 1900 as "ʟendix ̇tcux" by Livingston Farrand in a collection of thirty-two sadanx gwenig ancient stories titled *Traditions of the Chilcotin Indians* (collected in *The Jesup North Pacific Expedition*, vol. 2, part 1, *Ethnology and Archæology of Southern British Columbia and Washington*; *Memoirs of the American Museum of Natural History*, vol. 4, part 1, ed. Franz Boas, hdl.handle.net/2246/39). Justice Vickers relied on Farrand's version in his decision. Three versions of Lhin Desch'osh were told to the court (by Elders Minnie Charleyboy, Julie Quilt xinli, and Patricia Guichon xinli) and are available in the trial transcript, a public document. In addition, Doris Lulua xinli told the story in her affidavit. Lhin Desch'osh is part of perhaps the best known of all Dene story cycles, the dog stories, and extends across all of the Dene language groups and cultures. See for example George Blondin, *Yamoria the Lawmaker: Stories of the Dene*, Northwest Passages series (Edmonton: NeWest Press, 1997) and Alice Legat, *Walking the Land, Feeding the Fire: Knowledge and Stewardship among the Tlichǫ Dene*, First Peoples: New Directions in Indigenous Studies (Tucson: University of Arizona Press, 2012). For some coyote analogues, see Marianne Ignace and Ronald E. Ignace's *Secwépemc People, Land, and Laws / Yerí7 re Stsq̓eys̓-kucw*, McGill-Queen's Indigenous and Northern Studies (Montréal and Kingston: McGill-Queen's University Press, 2017).

2   See *Tsilhqot'in Nation v. British Columbia*, 2007 BCSC 1700, 585–602.

3   Transcribed from the Canadian Environmental Assessment Agency's audio file of the August 9, 2013 site visit to Teẑtan Biny Fish Lake. Courtesy of the Canadian Environmental Assessment Agency. Livingston Farrand in *Traditions of the Chilcotin Indians* spells Gullabi or Oolabee as K'olepi (14).

4   Transcribed from the CEAA audio file of the site visit, courtesy of the Canadian Environmental Assessment Agency.

5   Transcribed from the CEAA audio file of the site visit, courtesy of the Canadian Environmental Assessment Agency.

CHAPTER 12

Getting Our Sight Back

Imagine how strong we can be.

—ELDER CATHERINE HALLER (Xeni Gwet'in)

Introduction

Lorraine Weir

After the BC Court of Appeal decision on June 27, 2012, all parties were unhappy and sought leave to appeal to the Supreme Court of Canada. This chapter begins with Chief Roger's reflections in October 2013, anticipating the hearing in Ottawa and planning the Title Case Express[1] so the Elders could be present for the culmination of their work as witnesses and knowledge holders. After a whirlwind bus trip which brought the Elders to First Nations communities across Canada, they arrived in Ottawa for the hearing on November 2, 2013. The culmination of more than two decades of work in the courts and on the frontlines, that day proved to be a surprise as counsel for the defendants seemed to lose their way when the judges asked penetrating questions. By lunchtime, the Elders were feeling optimistic, and by suppertime everyone – Elders, Chiefs, lawyers, community members who had bussed across Canada for this day – was celebrating. It was not until June 26, 2014, that they heard the decision: victory at last. The Supreme Court of Canada made the first declaration of Aboriginal Rights and Title to a specific piece of Land in Canadian history, recognizing 1,750 square kilometres within the Xeni Gwet'in Caretaker area as Aboriginal Title Land. Using the traditional Dandzen Loon song as an image of the process of decolonization, Chief Roger thinks about the work ahead to restore Dechen ts'edilhtan Tŝilhqot'in law to Title Land and achieve a just settlement for damages dating back to the arrival of the first settlers at the beginning of the nineteenth century.

Since Time Immemorial

Chief Roger William

When you talk to any of our leaders and our people, they'll tell you this is our Land. We never gave it up. We have to go through this system in the Supreme Court of Canada to prove that we exist, to prove that we have Aboriginal Rights and Title, but we know we have it. Whatever decision comes, that's just another part of this process. We never gave up our Rights and Title. We never sold it, there was no agreement to give it up, we still have it. The Supreme Court of Canada ahead of us is very important, but it's not the end.

We've always said that we've lived here since time immemorial, since this Land was created through Lhin Desch'osh, and we know that from creation stories. *Delgamuukw* (1997) established that as long as we can prove that in 1846 we were living in a certain area with our own People and our own laws, protecting our boundaries, we can prove Title. We're here today because of cases like *Calder* (1973), *Sparrow* (1990), *Guerin* (1984), *Alphonse* (1993), and *Marshall* (1999) as well as *Delgamuukw*, cases that laid the foundation. Lobbying and direct action by First Nations going way back also got us here. The *Calder* decision said no government can extinguish our Rights and Title, and the Constitution Express (1980) laid out a lot of our Rights. Before *Delgamuukw*, you needed to have an "expert," someone who went to university and uses paper to tell our story to the judge. After *Delgamuukw*, our Elders could express themselves in court.[2]

The Title Case Express

Chief Roger William

I was talking to Dlig, Jack Woodward, and we were excited, because after twenty-four years of fighting, we'd been granted leave to go to the Supreme Court of Canada on November 7, 2013. What if we took the Elders to Ottawa and introduced them to First Nations people across the country? We started to plan the Title Case Express. The Elders deserved it. They see way back to the way we were before contact, to our economy and strength and pride in those days. We were totally in sync with the Land right from the creation stories to the time of contact. If they wanted to do one thing in their lives, it's to tell this country that this is our Land, this is who we are. *Delgamuukw* made that possible. The Elders said now we're free to say this is our country. Our Title Case Express came from the 1980 Constitution Express that went from BC across Canada to Ottawa.

So we want to recognize our witnesses who are still alive today and healthy enough to travel. We want to bring them on a bus trip across Canada and stop at First Nations communities in each province to introduce them to First Nations. There's an Elder in the group who doesn't know English – only knows Tŝilh-qot'in. First Nations will get to meet these individuals who testified and sacrificed to be where we are. We're leaving next week on October 30, before Halloween. We start in the morning and it'll be a seven-day trip, arriving on November 5. We're working with seventy First Nations to do a two-day assembly on the court case. We'll talk about court cases across BC and Canada, and we'll rally. Then on November 7, the hearing will last one day. So over three hundred days at trial to six days in BC Court of Appeal to one day in Supreme Court of Canada.

I decided that this year [2013] we'd celebrate, and it was my idea to bring people to Ottawa. While the lawyers were doing all their work, we wanted to get other First Nations on board politically, but we really didn't have to, because people were already aware of Taseko Mines Limited and the Prosperity mine project. I commend Taseko for preparing people, because First Nations already knew about us and the court case thanks to them.

I thought of the Elders who went back to our rituals when they said that as long as we're honest and telling the truth, the truth wins. They'd said that we might have to take this case all the way to the Supreme Court of Canada. I remembered the Elders who passed on their knowledge to us, and we learned from them, but they didn't make it to the trial because they were unable to travel or their hearing and memory were affected. I thought of their struggles and their fight. When Judge Vickers's decision came down in 2007, it was proof that those who were able to testify did a great job. By the time we were going to the Supreme Court of Canada, eight of those Elders were no longer with us out of the twenty-six who testified. Twenty-nine Elders submitted affidavits so, counting them, twelve were no longer with us by 2013. In July [2014], we lost Francis Setah, who testified in Nemiah. It's almost like he waited to experience and feel the Title.

The Elders on the way to Ottawa. First row from left: Dave Lulua, Juliana Lulua, Christine Cooper xinli, Minnie Charleyboy, and Delia William. Back row from left: Annie C. Williams, Norman George Setah xinli, Ubill Lulua xinli, David Setah, Chief Roger William, and Gilbert Solomon. Photo by Jeremy Williams

Sleepless Nights

Lorraine Weir with Elder Ubill Lulua xinli, Xeni Gwet'in

Elder Ubill Lulua xinli recalled the 1980 train trip in terms of sleepless nights on uncomfortable train seats as the prelude to Pierre Elliot Trudeau's dismissive behaviour: "He just got in the car and went somewhere else ... Trudeau didn't want to talk to anybody. He used to walk all over the Chiefs, too. He didn't wanna see Indians." As Elder Ubill summarized the White Paper, Trudeau "wanted Indians all to be white men [but] ... I don't wanna be a white man. I wanna live the way I am now ... That's why we are still Indian now. If we hadn't gone there, we would all be white men now."[3] Fortunately, the New Constitution Express [as the Title Case Express was sometimes called] in November 2013 was more comfortable: "Every time we got off, we stopped and slept!" [laughter]

Dlig

Chief Roger William

A little story about Dlig. We were at a meeting with the Ministry of Forests, who were talking about clear-cutting jackpine the way they do because of the low value. The wind blows it over if you log selectively. Jack Woodward was at that meeting in Nemiah, and he said, "How can you do that when there are so many squirrels? They've got a home. It takes them all year to harvest to get ready for winter, and when you cut their trees, they've all got a short time to find another home before winter, but it's some other squirrel's home. They have to fight for that home. That's not right, you know." So everybody started teasing him, calling him Dlig because he was protecting the squirrels. We call them dlig.

This Is How We Did It

Chief Roger William

We needed to fundraise to make the Title Case Express happen, so I brought the idea home to the TNG Chiefs and they approved. TNG Director Crystal Verhaeghe and I started working on it, and in Xeni we started fundraising, doing loonie and toonie auctions. We did presentations, and both First Nations and non–First Nations people donated, sponsored, or helped with the trip. That took the whole summer, and we started talking to the Elders and leaders, asking who's gonna go on this trip. I was excited to hear our Tŝilhqot'ins saying, "Hey, we're approved to go to Supreme Court of Canada! We all knew this day might come, and here it is at last!"

Everything fell into place. Crystal and her team at TNG went overtime and beyond the call of duty while they did their usual jobs at the same time, because we were intervening and our lawyers were working. Crystal's team organized our accommodations and connected with people in each community we visited as we drove to Ottawa. The AFN also did a great job. Chief Charlene Belleau at Esk'etemc did a lot of work organizing the trip for the AFN and National Chief Shawn A-in-chut Atleo was involved. Shawn had been the regional chief of the BCAFN for five terms. Doing all that at once, we made this trip possible. However, organizing was one thing, and actually going through with it was another. We forgot about the time changes along our route! Those are the things you learn from.

We left on October 30 and planned to be in Ottawa by November 6. The Northern Secwépemc gave us a send-off that morning in Williams Lake, and there were representatives from BC and from the City of Williams Lake City Council with the Mayor and the whole Council there. There were presentations about the trip and prayers, drumming, and some gifts. Then we left on the bus. I was the only Chief on the trip. The rest were too busy in their communities, or it was too much of a time commitment for them. They met us in Ottawa. Councillor Loretta Williams was with me, and Councillor Marilyn Baptiste was at home. We issued a press release saying that what we planned to do before Supreme Court of Canada was to introduce our Warriors, the Elders, and leaders who testified in court to the rest of Canada. We wanted to thank First Nations across Canada as well as non–First Nations by bringing these Warriors, and at the same time we wanted to acknowledge the sacrifices they had made and why we were giving them this trip. We were saying this is how we did it, this is how it started. This is how it feels. Some of the Elders had never left BC before and they were very excited.[4] You'd think with the time difference we would've been three hours early, but by the time we got to Ottawa, we ended up being late! It was quite a journey. After twenty-five years of work and fighting, just going on the Express was amazing. Just to see First Nations in each province being patient and excited when we arrived was amazing. There was ceremony, drumming, feasts, and gift exchanges as we were hosted by each community. Sometimes people ask whether the trip was hard on the Elders, but they were still awake at night in the bus while the younger people were sleeping, so I dunno who was more tired!

The Title Case Express was about Title Land. It was about ownership of Land, because we as First Nations, first people of this country, own this Land. It's our Title, our Rights, so this Express was to stop at First Nations communities in each province and say this is our Title. First Nations are following the foundation cases and all the leaders read up on them, so they know about our case. We travelled BC and Canada telling that story – the trial started in 2002, took five years, and the decision in 2007 said we met the test of Title from the *Delgamuukw* decision; we have Rights to 100 percent of the area, Title to almost 50. The story's already out there, and this trip was almost an updating, saying this is where we are, this is how we did it, and we wanna thank you for fighting for your Rights and Title on this Land. We got told stories of what they've done on their Land and the significance of actions they took that have kept who they are, what they've done, the benefits, everything. So we were learning from them, and they were learning from us. We all said we have Rights and Title. You know, it should be the provinces and territories proving *they* have Title. But this is what it is.

We stopped in AFN Chief Perry Bellegarde's community on the way to Ottawa and again on the way back. When we arrived at Fort William First Nation in Thunder Bay, Ontario, I dunno how many hours late we were, but Chief Georjann Morriseau and her people were still excited. They'd waited a long time, and we had a good feast there. In each community we stopped at, people knew about our court case. We told them stories, and they told us what they were going through. It was good to hear what the possibility of Title might mean to First Nations that already have Treaty and to hear what their issues are. They were pretty excited!

My second-oldest son Linden was on the trip with me. All my kids wanted to come, but they couldn't. We fundraised for all of the witnesses and their helpers, and there was a fee of over five hundred bucks for anyone else who came, like my son. We talked about the other kids coming, but they were in school, and my oldest son was working, so Linden joined us, and I think he'll probably remember it for a long time. He not only got to go across the country and stop in First Nations communities but also to know his Elders better. Jeremy Williams was hired to be a media person, and he was with us to video-record the trip.

The Elders talked to me on the trip, and some told me their concerns about what was happening on the Land or they told me stories. I was also on the phone a lot or dealing with email, because Council and staff at home were working and needed to communicate with me. But it was a trip where I was able to just jump into a bus and enjoy travelling all day, and I was with my son, so it was good. I had a great time. I wouldn't think twice about doing it again, but next time, there might be some stuff to fix, like calculating the time changes so we wouldn't be so late and could leave earlier in the morning!

Hoping for the Best (2014)

Shannon Stump, Xeni Gwet'in

We thought the Supreme Court of Canada decision was gonna come down in the fall. Our oldest son Linden and Roger were talking about it, and Linden's like, "ʔAba [Dad], what're you gonna do if you lose?" And Roger's like, "Well, if we lose, we'll work with it. You know, I gave it a 110 percent, and I'm gonna keep doing it. Just because there's one door closed doesn't mean I'm gonna give up and forget about life. I'm gonna still keep pushing for it. You know, this is for you guys, for your kids and for the next generations to come. I'm gonna keep fighting for it right until the very end, and someone's gonna hear me one day. Someone's gonna get tired of me yapping about all this, and they're gonna hear what I'm trying to do. I'm not gonna stop."

Somebody heard him! So it was just amazing. We knew this day was coming, but we didn't think it was actually gonna come, you know what I mean? This is all First Nations' goal, but to actually get there, to do the paperwork, to put the time and energy. People were like, "Hm, I dunno," and we did it. We sacrificed a lot, not just me being his wife and my kids, but the community. We sacrificed a lot. The community sacrificed a lot. They supported him, and we supported him. And the surrounding communities, too, they supported Roger, like the trip to Ottawa. When they bussed over, they went on no money. That was all fundraising and donations. People were like, "We have no money and you want how many people to go to Ottawa? Do you know how much it's gonna cost? Hotels and meals and you're gonna have to stop ten million times 'cause you're gonna have Elders. You can't just drive 24-7, you know." And he's like, no, we're gonna run with it, and they did it, and it was all by fundraising. I fundraised. Nemiah is really generous. You could have only thirty people there, and you'd still fundraise about nineteen hundred bucks in one night. We just ran with it and hoped for the best, and people wanted to be part of it.

Good News: Proposed New Prosperity Mine Rejected

Chief Roger William

We were on the bus in Regina, headed to First Nations University as part of our Title Case Express. It was Halloween, around four in the afternoon BC time, and I got a text from our lawyer. We won! The panel report had come down, and they found that the proposed New Prosperity mine would have a significant impact on Fish Lake.[5] It's the only time in this country that the same project has been looked at twice by the CEAA, and both times they found in our favour. We started celebrating on the bus! It was a good feeling knowing that the panel agreed with us that this proposed New Prosperity mine is gonna destroy the lake.

All summer, when we could've been fishing more, hunting more, we were doing the environmental assessment, dealing with the panel and meeting with Taseko Mines Limited. Everyone was involved – our Elders, youth, everyone – with questions and concerns about this New Prosperity mine. Each Tŝilhqot'in community had the panel in their community, and their people told the story of their concerns about this New Prosperity mine. It was a crazy summer. The proposal had gone from the Prosperity mine to New Prosperity and now they [Taseko Mines Limited] were gonna save Fish Lake, not drain it as they'd said in 2010! Here's the pit, here's the tailings pond, and right in the center is Teẑtan Biny Fish Lake. We knew there was underground water and there would be leakage. Within a matter of five years, if you're lucky, you'd be impacting the lake. It was all fresh in our minds while we were on that bus.

"We Have the Stuff"

Joyce Charleyboy, Tŝideldel

It was awesome, it was something that nothing could ever replace. Every morning at breakfast, we're listening to some of the stories. When they're together, things come out. Just listening to them [the Elders]. And my mum getting to spend time with her siblings she's never really had time with. I didn't think anything could ever change. I had gone through a health scare, and I had been back and forth to the doctor's in Richmond, you know, and I had been sick quite a few times on that trip and they *knew*.

One of the Elders said "How are you feeling today?" And somebody would come up with some kind of medicine, like Native medicine. [laughs] Like, where the heck are you guys keeping this stuff?! Roger laughed at me. We were in Sault Ste. Marie, and I was just nauseous. Probably six months before, I had gone through chemo, so I still was getting sick from that, and one of the Elders walks by, and she looks at me, and she said, "You're not eating?" "No, I can't eat, like I can't eat *anything*." And she said "Oh! just wait," and she left and came back, and she had this liquid stuff, and she said, "I want you to drink it all – *now*!!" And I'm like, "What is it?" and she said, "I'll tell you after you drink it all." And I drank that, and it was balsam. And she said, "You should be okay, probably better now. But you need to tell us if you're not feeling well. *We have the stuff.*"

Ottawa

Chief Roger William

We got to Ottawa. We had a few days before the hearing, and we had meetings with different political parties, the federal government, Amnesty International, and so on. People enjoyed their time while the Chiefs met and planned. We still had to wait for the federal decision on the mine, and we had meetings in Ottawa just like Taseko Mines Limited, the City of Williams Lake, and the Chamber of Commerce in Williams Lake, which all went and lobbied for the New Prosperity project. We went and lobbied to say no.

Amnesty International sponsored a public forum on the Title case in Ottawa on November 6, the day before our hearing at the Supreme Court of Canada. That organization is very important to us, because they're our link to the United Nations to say, in spite of what Canada says to the contrary, Canada isn't really looking after its First Peoples. They keep the government, whether BC or Canada, aware of that. Amnesty International is a big part of bringing UN rapporteur James Anaya to do, like, an audit of Canada, to actually check out Canada's treatment of First Nations with us. He met with us in Vancouver in October 2013 and listened to First Nations from across BC, so we were able to tell him our history from the Tŝilhqot'in War to smallpox, the Prosperity project and the Rights and Title case.[6]

At the Supreme Court of Canada

Chief Roger William

The song I sang in the morning outside the Supreme Court of Canada was Tŝ'ilʔos. Elder Catherine Haller had a drum made for me with the Xeni Gwet'in logo of Tŝ'ilʔos painted on it by Nelson William, and when she gave it to me in 2007, she said "In exchange, I want you to make a song about Tŝ'ilʔos." So that moment when I came up to do the drumsong, it was Tŝ'ilʔos. I'm singing about the whole story of Tŝ'ilʔos and his wife ʔEniyud and their kids. The moral of the story, the history, the meaning behind it, it's all one. To me, Tŝ'ilʔos is a leader who had a family, and this family separated, and so he looks after the Land and his people forever. When I sang that song, I was talking about right from who Tŝ'ilʔos and ʔEniyud are to the leaders to the Land to the animals to the fish to the waters to the Tŝilhqot'in tradition and to keeping it there. If you'd been there to see Tŝ'ilʔos and ʔEniyud before the Tŝilhqot'in War compared with today, it wouldn't look much different. There's no clearcuts, no mine. It's all pretty much intact. That song talks about all that. So Tŝ'ilʔos is protecting us.

Tŝ'ilʔos and ʔEniyud

Elder Minnie Charleyboy, Tŝideldel

Tŝ'ilʔos left his wife because Tŝ'ilʔos was too mean, that's why. Tŝ'ilʔos got three of the children and ʔEniyud got two. There's five kids involved. When ʔEniyud left Tŝ'ilʔos, she walked right past Chunoẑ Ch'ed Potato Mountain. As she was going back past that way, she was planting the beartooth and the [mountain] potatoes. Lower on Chunoẑ Ch'ed Potato Mountain, the last piece of the potatoes, she just shook it out of that gunny sack that she had, the last bit. As she kept on walking, when she finished planting the potatoes, she went across Tatlayoko and looked back towards Tŝ'ilʔos, and she was crying looking back, and that's when she turned to rock. If you leave your husband, this is what will happen. That's what she thought. And that's why she turned to rock. The children are sitting right beside her. Same with Tŝ'ilʔos. Tŝ'ilʔos is kind of mean, and if you point at it, that's how come you'll get caught in bad weather. If you don't get caught in bad weather at the time you did it, in the wintertime sometimes you might get caught, and you might even freeze to death.

—*William v. British Columbia et al.*, proceedings at trial, March 22, 2004, para. 25, 1–34.

On the steps of the Supreme Court of Canada, November 7, 2013. From left, Loretta Williams, Patrick Lulua, Geri Elkins, Joyce Charleyboy, Chio Setah Alphonse, Jasmine Quilt, Peyal Laceese, Chief Roger William, and Cecil Grinder. Photo by Jeremy Williams

"Tŝ'ilʔos Did It"

Chief Roger William

Since I was a child, I've always been told when something happens, "Tŝ'ilʔos did it." There's a story about way back, Chilco Ranch – the other side of Yuneŝit'in,

Stoney – they were in Xeni, and they chased cattle out there, and they were trying to set up in Nemiah. And this is in August – the grass was long. He left his cattle there in Nemiah, and they went back to get more. When they came back, it had just snowed –in the middle of August. Six feet of snow wiped out all their cattle. So they ended up where Chilco Ranch is. The intent of that rancher, what they wanted to do, was not good, so Tŝ'ilʔos snowed 'em out. Wiped out the cattle. So there's stories like that about Tŝ'ilʔos. ʔEniyud, the same. The Elders say Tŝ'ilʔos did it.

The Night before War

Chief Roger William

From the time a Warrior is in their mother's womb, they're being taught to honour the Land and the people, to protect the resources that come from the Land. You're trained to deal with the lack of food or its absence. No matter what level you're at, you still have this focus. So, for me, wearing all my mom's work, knowing the tradition, spending all those hours preparing for court and in court, in meetings and roadblocks, hunting and fishing, our life, everything – it's all right there. The night before war, Warriors danced around the fire.

The Elders Arrive at the Supreme Court of Canada

Joyce Charleyboy, Tŝideldel

That was funny! People who flew in didn't have a knife, but everybody that came on the bus had a knife. I dunno where we were stopped, but [Grand Chief] Stewart Phillip was laughing because we had dried fish [on the bus], and he said "Oh, if only we had a knife!" And I said, "Don't say that too loud! Somebody's gonna pull one out!" He said, "Are you serious?" And I said, "Yeah!" So I said to one of the Elders, "He needs a knife," and she pulls out her knife. He said, "You carry a knife?" [laughing]

Anyways, we were going into court, and the security kept looking around, and I'm thinking "What is he doing?" And he said, "Are you one of the coordinators?" And I said, "Yeah, I am." He said, "Can I talk to you for a minute?" I said,

"Yeah," but as I was goin' through, the darn thing went off – the beeper – and he said, "You're gonna have to leave your bag here." And I'm lookin' at him, like. "I just need to talk to you, but leave your bag here. There's somethin' in there." So I said, "Yeah, okay." So I went [to talk to him], and he's like, "I have all these knives!" [laughter] "This is from your Elders," he said, "and I need you to tell them that I'll give it back at the end of the day." He said, "This is the first time I've ever seen so many weapons! – Like, they're little old ladies!" And I said, "Oh, yeah, *they're* the ones that need the protection!"

So I went back [to the lineup], and Chief Joe [Alphonse] said, "What's goin' on? Like, why are they stopping them?" And I said, "Joe, we forgot to tell them to leave their knives." And he said, "Ohhh! Is that what they have?" And I said, "Yeah." So he said, "Then why are they gonna search your bag?" I said, "I'm not tellin' you." And he said, "I know why they're searchin' *your* bag!" I said "Never mind!" And so in front of all the Chiefs they pushed me forward. I could see Chief Percy [Guichon] looking at me like I don't know what they're doing. And I said, "Never mind!" and he said "We're gonna have to take stuff outta your purse, 'cause we need to know what's in there." Well, there was a knife in there. And he's like, "I hate to say this, but that's actually bigger than the ones that are in there!" The security guard laughs. He's like, "If you're the coordinator and you have the bigger knife, I don't think I'd wanna mess with any of you!" And then he laughed, and Joe was like, "How big is it? Does she have a bigger knife? Like, is that what you were talkin' to him about?" And I looked at the security guard and said, "Don't tell them anything!" And he's like, "Why is that?" And I said, "'Cause they're the Nation Chiefs, and I actually work with them!" [laughs] And so Percy gets me alone right away, and he said, "How many knives were there?" I said, "Every one of them had a knife. Every one of them!" He's like, "Are you sure?" And I said, "Yeah, you need to see this. When we're [back] down here, they're gonna give it back. Watch this, they're gonna all line up." And sure enough, at the end of the day, they're all lining up to get their knives! So Joe laughed and said, "I think I know where it came from." Joe's going around and saying, "You need to carry a knife with you when you go [to Ottawa]!" And I said, "No, I didn't! I didn't say a word!"

The Women's Hunting Knives

Chief Roger William

The women's hunting knives created a bit of a chaos. Our Director Crystal Verhaeghe was there, and the security guards had to keep everyone safe and get the Elders in. A lot of the knives that we use are the ones that you skin deer and moose with, and they're pretty easy to carry. You know, the blades are flexible. Some of these knives are a pretty good size, but they do the job. You can skin with them and work on the animal with them.

That night we had a supper sponsored by MiningWatch Canada, and we talked about what had happened during the day. It was pretty funny, because there's always jokes between the men and the women about who's the real Chief. With the women's knives gone, the men had felt pretty brave!

Justice Incoming: A Day in the Supreme Court of Canada

Chief Roger William

When I went into court, I was ready for whatever came up. I felt really confident that we'd done everything we could to be prepared. I was taught as I was growing up, from my mom, my grandparents, my uncles and aunts, Elders, that you treat everybody with respect, so in this whole twenty-five years we never disrespected government or companies. We treated them with respect, but we let them know where we stood, and we backed it up. And we prepared. When I was going to that court, there's nothing that I didn't do or we didn't do that we should've done. As I was growing up, I followed what I was told. If you did everything in your power to respect, to not take shortcuts, to work hard, and to treat people as you want to be treated, and whatever you're trying to do, you're well prepared and you're ready for it, then if it doesn't work, if it's not done, it's meant to be. There's a reason for that. So I felt going in that we'd done that. There's nothing else we shouldn't have done, nothing else we could've done. And here we are in court.

That day I prepared myself to the best of my ability. I was hearing the Elders from when I was young. Twenty-five years ago, I heard these stories and was told about being honest and being able to tell Canada that this is our Title, not yours.

Through all those years, my mom made me everything I was wearing that day. Not only the buckskin but the pants and the shirt. She made all that.

I had a drum made with the picture of our logo on there drawn by a Xeni Gwet'in. It's a creation story.

And I came to the highest court in this country fighting a battle from the time of the Tŝilhqot'in Warriors to today. Because of them, we were a Nation when we went through all this.

All rushing through me that day.

I didn't drink, I didn't eat. That whole day I didn't need to. I was just there.

And I was there with Title and that Title is what my mom made me.

I had Elders who testified in court, the Warriors I call them. I had our Tŝilh-qot'in leaders. I had a lot of other leaders that were interveners in our court case. They were all there.

I felt the sacrifices my wife's made in raising our children and supporting me and then doing her job. I felt how strong and powerful she is. And my mom, who humbly did everything she could to help me be where I am. And all the uncles, the aunts, my siblings.

It was a day to see justice incoming. It was a day when all the transformations from the Tŝilhqot'in War to now were present from moment to moment.

We have Title. This is our Title. These are our Rights. That's what every First Nations person wants to tell Canada.

I come from a strong foundation of language, culture, pride and a history that gives me confidence, and I've always felt this way, right up to that day and here it is. Five years of the trial, all the days that I testified – examination for discovery for four weeks and then examination in chief for over a month and cross examination over two weeks – and here it is.

That's what it took to get to that day. All the sacrifice, my wife's support, my mom's support. Anyone else might say I don't need to do this with my life. I should just take care of my family. I should just be home with my kids. But I still was home with the kids, with the family, and able to do what I'm doing with all that support.

I was thinking of the Tŝilhqot'in Warriors, the residential school, my mom being in the Mission, I was in the Mission. I see the impact on our kids, our future generations. My wife's been working with youth and children. She's got this connection that nobody can teach with them, and they're just drawn to her. My son was there. David Setah was there. He was a big part of my life, him and Gene [Cooper]. Together we went through stuff, and I learned from them when we were young. And the leaders. And all the Elders who testified were there. And the young generation was there too – my great-niece Chio Setah

Alphonse, Jasmine Quilt, Peyal Laceese. The lawyers. Jack Woodward – when former Chief Benny William introduced him to us to today, all the sacrifices he's made and all the things he's done. And the Friends of the Nemaiah Valley, David Suzuki Foundation, Lannan Foundation – all these groups.

That's what made it possible for me to sit there and hear the arguments and the statements of the interveners. And then the questions which the judges were asking. I wasn't too surprised by what BC and Canada were putting forward in their arguments. But then their lawyers were scrambling and trying to stick to their guns, and some of them were changing their arguments.

A Really Good Chance

David Setah, Xeni Gwet'in

The lawyers for the province and the federal lawyers were bringing up their cases, and one lawyer was just picking out one reason from 339 court days why we shouldn't have Title. One Judge [Madame Justice Rosalie Abella] just kept asking, "Out of 339 days, I'm pretty sure there was a lotta other evidence that was given about why they should have Title. So why are you picking out this one thing?" And then finally all the lawyers kept humming and hawing, jumping around the exact questions you're asking. And then they won't give you a real answer, they'll just dance around it 'till you're blue in the face. Finally, the Supreme Court of Canada judge [Chief Justice Beverley McLachlin] said, "You're talking single tree leaves now over the whole court case?" [laughs] That was awesome to hear. And another lawyer comes up giving his evidence on the opposition side, and one of the other judges asked him, "Why is it so hard for you guys for a First Nation to have Title? All of the evidence is given in front of you, and you still deny it. Why is it you guys fight so hard against them having Title?" After all that, I was thinking we had a really good chance! [laughs]

The Water Song

Joyce Charleyboy, Tŝideldel

Amnesty Canada had their rally. They had songs on, and I looked at my sister Geraldine, and I said, "I think we need to be drumming." And she said, "What are you gonna do?" And I said, "I'm gonna go tell them." She said, "That's being disrespectful. It's their – they're –." And I said, "No, but they're rallying for us, and we need to –." She's just like, "I have nothing to do with this! I'm not even related to you!" [laughs] So I walked up, and I said, "Excuse me, can we just drum? Can you turn the music off? I think it would mean more if we drum. At least, for me it would." He said, "Oh, no, no, no, that's fine." So we did all the drumming during the rally. And it was funny, 'cause we were up there, and my uncle Patrick [Lulua] said, "Joyce, I want you to do the Water song," thinking that our grandmother Emily's Water song was gonna come out. It wasn't, it was my grandmother Nellie's Carrier Water song that came out. And they're all kinda looking. You could see them drumming – all of a sudden, everybody kinda stops. Like, what the heck are you singing? [laughs] But yeah, it was good. And then Chief Percy [Guichon] said, "You know, I was late" – he had to go get something and come back, and because of the traffic he had to be let off a couple of streets away. He said, "I could hear you girls singing. Boy, that did something to me. How powerful things can be."

Shen Song

Lorraine Weir

As it happened, Chief Percy and I met by chance at a red light shortly after he jumped out of that cab. Above the sounds of traffic all around us, a voice rose in the cold air and we were carried towards it. It was Joyce singing the Water song. Later that day, at the buffet supper offered by MiningWatch, Joyce sang again, this time the women's mourning song from Elizabeth Jeff. When I first crossed the Davidson Bridge into Xeni, I stopped midway to listen to the river, Dasiqox, rushing past. It was as though I was commanded by the river. That is what it felt like to hear Joyce singing that day on the steps of the Supreme Court of Canada.

Two Warriors

Lorraine Weir

It was in the middle of the day during the recess, and Chief Joe Alphonse was agitated when he spoke to me. I'd asked him if he'd gotten one of the few available seats in the courtroom, and he said no. "I refuse to go. I will *not* go into that room." When I asked why not, Chief Joe raised his arms and gestured angrily – "I will not go in to Canada. I will not. It's a matter of principle as a Tŝilhqot'in person. The Warriors are my Ancestors." Then he told me that he is a direct descendant of Anaham, the Grand Chief of the Tŝilhqot'in Nation during the Tŝilhqot'in War. Chief Joe serves as Tribal Chief of the Tŝilhqot'in National Government and has also been Chief of the Tl'etinqox-t'in Government since 2009. He sat with the Elders watching the hearing on large-screen TVs set up in the Grand Entrance Hall on either side of the classical double staircase leading up to the courtroom. I sat on the other side with journalists and other spectators. The Grand Entrance Hall creates a visual image of the posture of supplication which the appellants are presumably expected to adopt, going up the double stairway to the courtroom visible as a grand doorway at the top of the stairs. Invisible from the foyer, the judges enter the courtroom from inner chambers. When the court rises, the doors open high above the foyer, and appellants and counsel emerge to a rush of emotion from those gathered below.

Three Groups

Chief Roger William

That's the feeling. Being Chair of a country, feeling your Title and Rights. Going in to listen to someone else determine your Rights and Title or hearing the arguments of others about what is yours. It was a very strong principle that Chief Joe [Alphonse] had, and it makes a lotta sense, because Tŝilhqot'in Warriors were hung. They were tricked into peace-treaty talks, because there's no way the colonists could have caught those Warriors. The colonists' head man was killed, and they lied, they committed treason. Then the Warriors, our leaders, were tried in an unfair process, and they hung them. And the Supreme Court of Canada was gonna hear arguments about all that. Being the Chair, Chief Joe was setting an example that we don't recognize Canada, we don't trust Canada. What Canada did is wrong. It's a message that's gonna be very strong in the future, because that's a principle that a Nation with Title has. We stuck to it, and now we have Title back. We already knew we have Title. Now it's being recognized.

I can understand where Chief Joe's coming from. Many of the Elders who have talked to me have always said the truth wins. Don't worry about what to say. As long as you tell the truth, you don't need to remember anything. Tell the truth, and go through the court. To me, this is the modern Warrior. A Warrior that's coming from their Elders, a Warrior that's not a slave of alcohol or drugs, not a slave of the system that's been put in front of us from residential school to how they wanna impact our Land for the almighty dollar. So I see a Warrior who uses their own ammunition, their own system, their own way, and beats them. I totally respect and understand and agree with what Chief Joe did.

This story shows two Warriors coming from what happened in history, from the Tŝilhqot'in War, and no matter how you tell it, it makes a lot of sense. It's a story that says that we have Title. One Warrior says, "We'll prove it in your system, in your courts, your highest court." And the other Warrior says, "We don't recognize that system." So that's the two systems coming together. I talked about the three groups we were divided into from the smallpox to the Tŝilhqot'in War. Even though we were three groups, we were able to go through the Tŝilhqot'in War and then from the hanging of our Warrior Chiefs to the residential school to the Declarations of 1983 and 1998 by the Nation, to the 1989 Declaration of Xeni Gwet'in right to the roadblocks, to direct actions. Being a Nation and sticking together regardless of the fact that we were divided into these three groups. Here's a situation where one leader said, "I don't recognize your system, I'm not going in." And another leader said, "We'll beat you at your own game."

For Protection

Elder Eileen Sammy William and April William xinli

Elder Eileen William: Yeah, he [Chief Roger] did really good. All the people helped with all the stories he needed.

April William xinli: Roger was powerful to have his mother's support. Just like when he goes mountainracing, she smudges him and the horse with juniper. A brush[ing-off], and then you do the watering. Before he goes on the mountainrace. She does that to him and his horse.

Elder Eileen William: For protection.

April William xinli: For protection, so they don't get hurt.

The Hummingbird's Work

Chief Roger William

The story that was passed down to me is that at Chunoẑ Ch'ed Potato Mountain, there were women – some say seven and some say nine – picking wild potato. There was a little boy with them. At nightfall, the women decided to sleep there, and they slept together side by side. The little boy decided to sleep further down in the bush. At dawn he saw the Qajus, and they put a log across the women's necks because they were all in a row, and choked them to death. The little boy watched all this, and he took off running and got back to his people. Right away, the medicine person who had a hummingbird power sent his power out, and the hummingbird caught up with the Qajus. The hummingbird flew in a circle, and as they watched, he pooped on them. They wondered what was happening, and then they all fell asleep. It was the medicine person's power that put them to sleep. Because of that power, the Warriors knew where the Qajus were and caught them. They killed them all except for one, and they let him go. He jumped in the river and got away, and when he got home, he told the story of what had happened. They say that the blood poured out of him, and then he died.[7]

So that's the story that was told to me. In a lot of stories, Tŝilhqot'ins let one or two people go so the message gets back when they fear the neighbours will try to attack them again. That's what will happen to them if they do it again. I always heard stories about that when I was growing up.

They Come from the Coast

Elder Martin Quilt xinli, Xeni Gwet'in

Potato Mountain.
Lotsa women and children got killed over there by another tribe from way far out.
Tŝilhqot'ins caught up to 'em before they reach the ocean.
Nobody survive that one. They kill 'em all.
They jump in that swift water that swept to shore.
Run a spear through them.
That river, just straight up goin' down.
That's 1864 it happened.

Yeah, they were always on the lookout for people like that sneakin' round.

They come from the coast. Fifty miles to the coast from here.
They walked it in one day.
Over the mountain, cross the rivers.
Massacre Canyon, that's where it happened.

How the Lawyers Fell Asleep

Chief Roger William

To me and to our people, to our leaders, these lawyers weren't prepared, and they fell asleep. BC was the first to go through and then Canada. Our lawyers said that Canada changed their argument a bit based on what they were seeing, but they didn't really have much time to change and couldn't have taken BC's position without being ridiculed by the judges. I don't think they really thought about what the judges were gonna ask them. The judges were asking questions about the recognition of Title and Rights. And the lawyers were stumbling around trying to stick to their argument, but then another judge would ask a question. They still tried to stick to their guns that they agreed with the Appeal Court there is Title, but it might be small spot, postage-stamp style, and that would be good for First Nations. But the judges were questioning [trial judge] Vickers's decision and the Appeal decision, and I think the lawyers weren't really expecting so many questions. They were a bit thrown off. I think Canada had no choice but to make some changes to their argument, and that impacted them more. The argument they made in BC Court of Appeal and the trial was gone by the time of Supreme Court of Canada. Title is where we hunted, where we fished, where we survive off the Land, not just what we extensively use. It's more than that. I can go to a spot in my Territory, in Xeni or in the Tŝilhqot'in, where hardly anyone has been or no one at all, but they still call it BC.

Our people were blown away, saying there's all of Canada and *they* don't have small-spot Title. There are places hardly anyone uses or has ever even touched, but it's still Canada. Do they have to extensively use that mountain to have Title? No. Not according to Canada. But they try to make *us* do that. So I think the [Supreme Court] judges thought the same thing and recognized that their arguments didn't make any sense. You can have Title to big areas where you can gather and survive from them, not just from small spots. The argument about small-spot Title doesn't make sense. So it was like they were bewitched and staggering around thanks to the hummingbird. It blinded the lawyers and put them to sleep. They didn't do their homework. They were messing up. They didn't have a plan B or anything. They've been arguing this colonial argument since the *Calder* case, since *Delgamuukw*, all these other cases. That's two times three. We say two times three, that's the hummingbird's work. He put 'em to sleep and then our Warriors caught them up and took 'em out. That's what happened to those lawyers. They're highly paid, top-notch, otherwise BC and Canada wouldn't have them, and they're arguing the third most important case of their history to the Supreme Court of Canada, and they fell asleep!

Coming back, I think everybody was feeling good and everything that we had to do was done. We saw the judges question what BC and Canada had kept on saying for years. There were only two things we had to wait for. One was the federal government decision on the CEAA panel report, and the second was the Supreme Court of Canada's decision on Title. No matter which way it went, we knew we had always had Aboriginal Rights and Title. We just had to keep going towards the next step, an international process. At the end of March, we heard that the federal government had decided in our favour about the proposed New Prosperity mine, but it wasn't over yet, as Taseko Mines Limited filed two judicial reviews, one against the CEAA panel and one against the federal government's decision.

Volunteers

Lorraine Weir

Among the many organizations which contributed to the Title case over the years, FONV (Friends of the Nemaiah Valley) stands out as a group of volunteers who worked tirelessly in support of the case and of counsel Jack Woodward, as well as working in defence of Teẑtan Biny Fish Lake when first the Prosperity mine was proposed and then the New Prosperity mine. Over the quarter-century of the Title case, the contribution of volunteers from outside the community is not to be underestimated, whether in terms of fundraising, doing research ranging from archival to ecological and almost everything in between, or assisting the legal team with a myriad of details and tasks. Because this work often happened behind the scenes, it's worth highlighting the magnitude of the contribution of one of the many groups which helped to make the Title case possible.[8] Here is a brief history by David Williams and Pat Swift, co-founders of FONV, of some of the most important work undertaken by that organization.

The Friends of the Nemaiah Valley (FONV)

David Williams and Pat Swift

The Friends of the Nemaiah Valley (FONV) was formed as a society on December 1, 2000, and played an important role for the next fifteen years, first supporting the court case by raising $10,000 from the McLean Foundation for bear biologists Wayne McCrory and Marty Williams to do a wildlife inventory for Tachelach'ed the Brittany triangle. McCrory was amazed that wild horses should be present with all the other predators – cougar, grey wolves, lynx, bobcat, and, of course, black bears and grizzly bears – and he began to study them in some detail. In his report he concludes that they exist there in their natural habitat ... [and] this place is so special because you don't have a mix of animals like this anywhere else.

On June 6, 2002, we sat down with Roger and with Council at that time – David Setah and Gilbert Solomon – and put the idea to them that we create a Wild Horse Preserve in the Brittany Triangle. Declare it that and use the horse as an iconic animal to protect it. Roger came up with the idea of calling it the ʔElegesi Qiyus Wild Horse Preserve and making it the same size as the Aboriginal Wilderness Preserve. This work fed into the court case because, in the final judgment of Justice David Vickers, he said that one of the rights he found was the right to manage and use wild horses for their [Xeni Gwet'in] own use, which they had traditionally done, [and which had become] part of the culture, the northernmost horse culture in North America. It still is that. In her 2004 film *Wild Horses, Unconquered People*, documentary filmmaker Susan Smitten recorded the community gathering at which the actual declaration was made. Her film was made to create public awareness of Xeni Gwet'in and the Wild Horse Preserve. The Wild Horse Ranger project was subsequently developed in an effort to have a presence out on the Land and, over ten years, FONV probably raised a quarter of a million dollars for that program, which was co-managed by BC Parks. The program supported the late Harry Setah as the first Wild Horse Ranger, followed by David Setah.

The Dasiqox Tribal Park [now called Dasiqox-Nexwagwezʔan] had its origins in 2007. Creating a conservancy was essentially Wayne McCrory's idea and mine. I sat down with Roger and his Council, and Councillor Marilyn [Baptiste] put forward the idea that a conservancy be created. Wayne said a conservancy's the best way of protecting [the Land] because it's not a BC park, and a conservancy allows for more of the traditional activities that First Nations were practising there. We commissioned a study on the best form of protection.

We looked at tribal parks, we looked at conservancies, we looked at Class A provincial parks, and presented those as options to Marilyn [who was elected Chief in 2008] and Council. And we prepared a brochure. But we began to think about the tribal park as a concept that might work, so we commissioned a report by biologist Maggie Paquet. Part of what we are doing is providing the background science. We've always seen that the First Nations would claim the park and be the managers.

In 2007, Wayne McCrory and I decided that we needed to look at the Upper Taseko area and the whole southern rim of Xeni Gwet'in Territory. We'd use the same device that I originally used for the Brittany Triangle to determine the grizzly habitat values as a threatened species, essentially, and to use that as an argument against the mine but also in favour of the preservation of a much larger area. So we commissioned Wayne and Lance Craighead of the Craighead Environmental Institute in Montana to do that study, and Wayne started out with the concept that the area is equivalent to the Greater Yellowstone Ecosystem – two and a half million hectares. So McCrory and Craighead produced a report over a number of years which identified it as a significant area which should be protected. We used that in the argument against Prosperity Mine.

We took a *very* active role in the fight against Prosperity Mine. In 2008, we began a campaign against it. We weren't sure which way the community was gonna go on Prosperity Mine. We heard talk against it, but we didn't hear strong opposition, and that's when we asked Amy Crook [from the Fair Mining Collaborative] to come and speak to the community. She came with Anne Marie Sam [Nak'azdli Whu'ten]. Amy spoke and Anne Marie Sam spoke and talked about what mining [the Mt. Milligan mine] had done to her community in the Peace River. The community decided that they were going to go against this mine. I made a couple of presentations, and we hired Wayne McCrory to develop a report and to make presentations to the [CEAA] hearings as well. Wayne and I both made presentations in the [Nemiah] Valley at the first set of hearings. Then at the technical hearings at the end, we also both made presentations. I focused on the socio-cultural aspects of the mine, the impacts with that, and the economic impacts. FONV was the largest non-Aboriginal intervener, in terms of funding, in that first set of mining hearings. We hired Martin Schaefer, an economist, to analyze the potential costs, benefits, and losses of the mine. His was a significant report that had considerable impact. Prosperity Mine was defeated.

Last year [2013], we had seven different presentations to the New Prosperity mine hearings. We again got funding through CEAA, and again we were the largest non–First Nations group to receive funding. It was not enough to do what we needed to do, but various foundations have supported us over the years. We spoke with the Wilburforce Foundation and received a grant from them for $19,000 in the first year. To us, it was like a million dollars! So we hired a coordinator and director and developed programs. This started at the same time as the hearings for the New Prosperity mine. So we participated in the New Prosperity mine hearings at the same time that this program started to create the tribal park. We hired John Lerner to do a report on the alternative economy that the Xeni Gwet'in would like to develop. We hired Marc Pinkoski to do presentations and to manage the grant that we got. We hired one of our Directors at that time, Karen Hurley, to make a presentation on cumulative effects. We hired Wayne McCrory to do more research, and I did fieldwork with him. We hired Jonaki Bhattacharyya [to research the "Cultural and Social-Ecological Significance of the Region Surrounding Teztan Biny"[9]]. We hired Don MacKinnon, a professional engineer, to do an analysis of the added highway cost that the province would have to bear as a result of the mine. Road costs, maintenance, and upgrading, trucks – adding, over fifteen to twenty-one years, forty-two million dollars for the province to operate it [the infrastructure] excluding building a new bridge, which it *will* have to do over the Chilcotin River. So all this we put into the mix. Seven different presentations.[10] I did a presentation as well. And then we had closing remarks. So we're a significant player in the fight against New Prosperity mine. And again, we won that one.

I was one of the founding directors of RAVEN. Lynn Hunter was the other. It was Jack Woodward's idea and, of course, I gave up my retirement to follow his ideas and implement them just as a volunteer! [laughing] RAVEN is a charitable NGO which was created to support Jack's Beaver Lake Cree litigation, and that is one of RAVEN's mandates now with Robert Janes. And Grassy Narrows. But also now the four Nations fighting the Enbridge Alliance. We do that in partnership with other NGO's, but we are the funnel for all the money that's raised. RAVEN is also fulfilling the mandate to raise funds for the [Tŝilhqot'in] court case. We raised the funds at RAVEN to get the [Title Case Express] bus to Ottawa and home. We paid all of the associated costs. Seventy thousand bucks. The judicial review of [New Prosperity] cost seventy thousand bucks, and RAVEN's just finished raising that amount. RAVEN has become phenomenally successful. We have a multi-million dollar budget.

The Decision's Coming Down (June 26, 2014)

Chief Roger William

The summer went on, and we were still fundraising for our wagon trip, which was in its sixth year, started by Jimmy Lulua and June Cahoose Lulua. To me, they're Warriors. They're all about who we are and how we should be. Every year, we're getting tighter for funds. It was Friday, June 19, and we were gonna get ready for the trip, and I got a text that morning from a lawyer saying that the Supreme Court of Canada decision's gonna come down on June 26th. I was pretty excited already, and I put it on Facebook so everybody would know the decision's coming down. I was talking to people while we were getting ready to go, telling them. When we start off on the wagon trip, we do prayers and drumming, and I did an update about what was going to happen and that I'd be going to Vancouver for the decision. So we were all celebrating when we left on the wagon trip, and we were pretty excited knowing that the decision was coming down soon.

The night before, I was thinking about the BC Appeal court decision coming down exactly two years before, on June 27, 2012. It was a bittersweet victory, winning Rights and being awarded small-spot, postage-stamp-style Title. I didn't sleep too well that night. I was excited and nervous. Twenty-five years and all this. The next morning at 6 a.m., we were gonna meet at the office of UBCIC in Vancouver. They'd been with us since day one, and BCAFN, AFN, and the BC Summit were all gonna be there. This is a moment of truth, a moment of reconciliation. The last time there was a Supreme Court of Canada decision on Rights and Title was on December 11, 1997 [Supreme Court of Canada decision in *Delgamuukw*]. The day before, we'd strategized three versions of a press release with the Chiefs and the legal team – for a big win, a partial win, or no win. So we were prepared for whatever, but we didn't know what to think that morning. They had breakfast for us, but I just had coffee and didn't eat.

Jay Nelson[11] was the first to get the decision on email, and as he was reading through it, he was talking to us about it, and so we knew within minutes that we'd won Aboriginal Title. First ever in BC or Canada. And it was like, "Oh, we're celebrating!" Wow! I was just sitting there, and I had my phone and had already written down my thoughts. I took pictures of people there, and I had pictures of the wagon trip, pictures of my family, the Express. I was ready to go, and all I had to do was write, "We won Title!" So that was how I told people on Facebook.

The statement I made to the media came from my heart, from everything that I've been involved in from the beginning, what I felt and what I wanted. Every day on the wagon trip I thought about it, and the night before, I didn't sleep. So it was all ready in my mind when I spoke. What I said is now the law is back in place. We fought very hard for our traditional law [Dechen ts'edilhtan]. It's the law of our Ancestors that we've been using all of our lives being Tŝilhqot'in. This is Tŝilhqot'in Title. This is our Title. Dechen ts'edilhtan [literally] means placing a stick to mark that this is where it is – now the law is in place. Tŝilhqot'in Title. Now that's the law. The Supreme Court of Canada put the law in place, back to Tŝilhqot'in Title. Tŝilhqot'in Title has always been there, but since contact, it's never been recognized. We didn't go to war and lose or negotiate Title away. That never happened. That Title has always been there, and now the law's in place. We've got Title. Even the highest Court in its own country recognized Tŝilhqot'in Title. When I say Dechen ts'edilhtan, I'm thinking here is a Title we never gave up. We got it back. Now we're gonna move forward and address that Title Land. We're gonna use that to negotiate the whole Tŝilhqot'in, and if that doesn't work, we'll be going for all the [non-Indigenous] families in the court case area.

Supreme Court hands vast swath of B.C. to First Nation in 'game-changer' decision

Unanimous ruling grants aboriginal title over 1,750 square kilometres of sparse territory

PETER O'NEIL

requirement that land use must be consistent with the needs and interests not only of current but also future

'ABORIGINAL TITLE CONFERS THE RIGHT TO USE AND CONTROL THE LAND AND TO REAP THE BENEFITS FLOWING FROM IT'

SUPREME COURT: Ruling is a judgment for the ages. » B1

BUSINESS: Impact worries B.C. firms. » B4

VAUGHN PALMER: Welcome to the new B.C. It's their land. » B1

EDITORIAL: Land title rights clarified. » B6

THE VANCOUVER SUN

Headlines, the *Vancouver Sun*, June 27, 2014. Courtesy of PostMedia

Today it's not the way it was when we were all born into it. We were trained right from the womb to the day when we leave this Earth. And to get back to that, we have to go back to that process and talk about the next generation of parents who have to instill all those laws and teachings into their babies. Those parents have to start teaching that and living that. And my understanding from my upbringing is outta that comes respect and beliefs that are based on spirituality, because life is a celebration for many different things, including when you leave this Earth. You're cremated so that you're set free. And then you're fed, because we're taught that through fire or through wildlife, we feed our Ancestors to keep them strong to look after us, so we'll look after them. Because if they're hungry, they're weak. Then they're gonna be fighting each other for what they find. When the spirits are not healthy, we're not taken care of, and that could be used by other First Nations, our neighbours, to impact us. So we were very disciplined, and that discipline was so strong that if we intentionally went against it, our father – our leader – would take us out. They would get rid of you, either by banning you, depending on the situation, or actually killing you.

So that's how serious the laws were back then, because you're born, you're trained, and there's no excuse for you not to know these ritual beliefs. There's no forgetting. It's *in* you, born into you, and you go out and do something bad. You had bad intentions, and there's gonna be repercussions – your life is gonna be at stake here. That's how bad it was, so we were very, very disciplined. That's what I was taught when I was growing up. You know Creator's watching you. Like, I was told, that person's watching you –"If I don't see you doing something bad, he'll find it, and you're gonna pay for it, and somebody you love – it could be me, I'll be impacted because of you. Could be something you love – your animal, your horse – and he will pay. Creator's gonna make that happen." So that was how it was, and that's how Tŝilhqot'ins were. What I'm saying is that the law is back, Title is back. We've always had it, and now the highest court in this country recognizes it though in their terms, not ours [i.e., settler law, not Dechen ts'edilhtan].

There are laws in our Tŝilhqot'in that you probably couldn't make in Canada. They'd be against the law. Canadian law doesn't include a lot of the detail that's present in different laws and ritual beliefs that we had. For instance, our ritual belief that there's a Creator out there. We pray to the Creator, that's where we go, and our Creator's looking after what we're doing. We're trained to go by our rituals, and if we don't go by them, it will impact what we love, who we love, or our own lives. People will know that, because we're struggling. Canada's gotta hire RCMP and hire judges to make sure we're obeying the law, but for us, it's spiritual. When you were in the womb, you were taught our system and you lived and breathed it. When you're born into it, it's your law, and if you wanna take shortcuts, you wanna be bad, your intentions aren't good, then you're gonna pay.

Tsilhqot'in Nation v. British Columbia, 2014 SCC 44: Summary

The court:

- granted a declaration of Aboriginal Title (to 1,750 square kilometres of land) for the first time in Canadian history;
- affirmed the territorial nature of Aboriginal Title and rejected the "postage stamp" theory of site-specific occupation;
- granted a declaration that British Columbia breached its duty to consult the Tŝilhqot'in with regard to its forestry authorizations;
- clarified and affirmed the Delgamuukw test for proof of Aboriginal Title, underscoring the three criteria of occupation: sufficiency, continuity, exclusivity;
- affirmed the importance of the "Aboriginal perspective" (as well as the common law perspective) on Title.

What rights does Aboriginal Title confer?

- the right of enjoyment and occupancy of Title land;
- the right to possess Title land;
- the right to decide how the land will be used;
- the right to economic benefits of the land;
- the right to proactively use and manage the land.

Consent

- "The right to control the land conferred by Aboriginal title means that governments and others seeking to use the land must obtain the consent of the Aboriginal title holders."
- If consent is not provided, the "government's only recourse is to establish that the proposed incursion on the land is justified under s. 35 of the *Constitution Act, 1982*."

Justification

- The Supreme Court of Canada concluded that the guarantee of Aboriginal Rights in s. 35 of the *Constitution Act, 1982* operates as a limit on both federal and provincial legislative powers. Therefore the proper way to curtail interferences with Aboriginal Rights and to ensure respect from Crown governments is to require that all infringements, both federal and provincial, are justified.[12]

Honour

Gene Cooper, Xeni Gwet'in

The Supreme Court decision – you know, that was really breathtaking to hear the unanimous decision of the eight judges, with not one judge against the decision. We felt it honoured our Elders who have passed during the time since this court case was started. A lot of our Elders have passed along the way, and some passed after they gave evidence.

When this decision came down, we felt a lot of emotions, deep emotions, because we felt that decision did justice, did honour, to our Elders who stood up and gave evidence on the truth, so I felt the decision was good and I was glad it came out that way, as well. It makes it easier, 'cause we've been saying for so long, "This needs to change, that needs to change. You guys need to make sure that these waterways –." They're always forever trying to get into areas we don't want 'em in. Trying to use another economic excuse. This court case kinda puts a grip on things so we can move forward, and I think the province right now is struggling to interpret this, how they're gonna deal with this Title case. So it's a good time for First Nations to step forward and figure out their plan right now and move with it.

I think they've [the people] heard it [the case, SCC decision] well enough and a lot of the youth, I think, got on board. The reasons for the fight have always been told to them and so they have an understanding. And our Elders also have an understanding of it 'cause we keep interpreting too.

Dandzen The Loon

Chief Roger William

A lot of our creation stories talk about how things change and different things happen. The legend stories talk about different marks on the animals and birds, and if you hear these stories in your upbringing and you look at a certain bird or animal, you see streaks or marks and say, "Oh, okay, that's why they've got that mark." Lhin Desch'osh is about shape-shifting to the way we are now and about how as animals, birds, and fish, we all spoke Tŝilhqot'in. In the story about Lhin Desch'osh – half human, half dog – all that changed.

Dandzen is one of the many birds and animals that are in our creation stories, in the different legends that our Elders have passed down to the younger generation. Dandzen is the loon, and the drumsong known as the Dandzen song goes back before my time, before European contact, and is still being sung, connecting what happened long ago to today. This drumsong is about a Warrior who is also a hunter. He had lost his sight and was frustrated when he came upon a lake in the Tŝilhqot'in. He needed to provide for and protect his family, his people, but he couldn't see. Dandzen was in the lake, and he was watching the Warrior. He saw the Warrior's frustration and noticed the beautiful necklace on him. Dandzen said, "I'll make you a deal. In exchange for your beautiful necklace, I'll give you back your sight." When we won Aboriginal Title in Supreme Court of Canada, this necklace was given to the loon, and we got our sight back. If you see Dandzen today, you'll see the beautiful necklace on him. That's what this drumsong is about.

I've been singing the Loon Song to celebrate the Supreme Court of Canada decision, which came down on June 26, 2014, recognizing Tŝilhqot'in Title and bringing our sight back. What we saw the day before the decision was years and years of impact, including court cases, lobbying, meetings, decisions, and negotiations. There was no certainty during the hundred and fifty years of contact. It felt like it blinded our people. People in my community in BC, and Aboriginal people all over Canada, are blinded, because we're put in a situation where some of us have treaties, some of us don't, but there's no real good intent either way. The system is broken. It just keeps on taking. I think of the impact of the smallpox epidemic of 1862 to the Tŝilhqot'in War to residential school: we got blinded by this whole process. Some of us lost not only our language but our beliefs, our rituals, our being as Tŝilhqot'in people.

Among the three groups I talk about – the real traditionalists, the new Tŝilhqot'ins, and the ones who are in the middle and go both ways – each group impacts the others. They help each other, they survive with each other, and they impact each other and learn with the new system of European governance, the European lifestyle or the Western lifestyle, if you wanna call it that. So those of us who are traditionalists, those of us who are taking in the new, and those of us who are going back and forth – we somehow hung onto each other. We found a way, because our tradition is the same, and we share the reality that these impacts are not good for our culture, our Land, and our resources. One group is saying this is a good way – education, business, jobs jobs jobs. And another group is doing both tradition and jobs. We're all kinda each other.

So it's like we're blind. Some of us forget that the Creator is looking at us. Some of us are thinking that because no one can prove we had bad intent, no one can prove that we're hurting, and we're taking shortcuts so we can get away with it. We learned that in the residential school. We learned that in the small-pox epidemic. That's the survival instinct of any human being. And we learned it because at least 80 percent of our people perished. Lost. If we lose 1 percent who are close to us, that hurts us so much. Imagine 80 percent. That alone is gonna blind and hurt us. It makes us numb. We're going into the courtroom as three groups that are numb to this whole process. Our trust issues are strong, not only in relation to governments, non–First Nations people and business, but to each other. After years of mistrust among ourselves, now we're starting to connect. Think of this Prosperity mine proposed by Taseko Mines Limited, beginning in the 1990s to now [2016]. The three groups – the traditionalists, the ones who favour the new, and the ones in between – will be destroyed if this mine goes ahead and it impacts our river. We're river people.

The Dandzen song brings all that together. It's a traditional song that's been drummed from before contact to today and the Warrior-hunter is us. Dandzen the loon is our whole being – the lake, the water, the Land, the moving forward and exchanging. That song was sung to make that happen. This rift that's happened since 1862, 1864, the residential school, all these struggles we've had, it's all *now*. What I see is that on June 25, there is all this uncertainty, still being blind. Dandzen is still in the water watching, listening, feeling, smelling. The Warrior's on the shore, frustrated, struggling.

From 1862 to 2014, we were on the lake with the loon and the Warrior-hunter. The song was drummed to keep them there at the lake so Dandzen could make that deal and the Warrior get his sight back. The song was able to do that. When I sing that song, in my mind that's what I see happening in front of us. For a hundred and fifty years we were Dandzen on the lake, and the hunter-Warrior was on the shore struggling. And now on June 26, Dandzen made a deal with the Warrior-hunter and our blinders are off. Now we're gonna move forward. I see this song as the past and the future and getting our sight back.

Lhin Desch'osh did a lot of work, but it was never really completed. That's what we have in front of us. From that time on, people and animals no longer spoke one language. That all changed. Dandzen comes from before that time, and communication between the loon and the hunter-Warrior was still happening in the old way. They're still there, trying to make that deal to get the beautiful necklace and the Warrior's sight back. Before June 26th we went to court, we roadblocked, we got Tŝilhqot'in language in the school. We're drumming again, we're powwowing, we're bringing the Elders and youth back out onto the Land, we're doing the wagon trip. I see Dandzen and the Warrior-hunter trying to make that deal. That's what a lot of the things we've been doing are to me. That's what I saw on June 26th. So *now*, now that sight is there, and we can try to move forward from that. It's a Title decision that we can make decisions on and decisions from. It's an opportunity to use that win to try and get real, meaningful control for the whole Tŝilhqot'in. So right now, we're coming from reserves, trying to protect our Lands and resources, making different kinds of agreements, having roadblocks, going to court. Now we have a good stick and the Warrior's got his sight back. Now he's gonna go hunt, go to war, try and provide for and protect his people. Now we have Title Land. We gotta use that in a way that's gonna work for us.

My thought is we don't wanna go back to what Europeans did to us during contact. That lifestyle and that form of governance are not working. Our governance, our system worked. We want to get back to that, but how do we do that? Now, here's the Title Land and here's our Warrior. He's got a tool now to provide, to protect, and to move forward. So we are the hunters, we are the Warriors now, moving forward with this Title Land to develop a full process which will enable us to continue to hunt and protect our people and everyone in our Territory.

Recognizing Rights and Title

Chief Roger William

As time went on, our Declaration in 1989 and the Nemiah Aboriginal Preserve started pushing the envelope. What governments and companies were doing was going to have to change in relation to our Aboriginal Rights and Title, our Lands and resources. With the Constitutional Express in 1980 and section 35 of the Constitution in 1982, Aboriginal Title became a big issue, and the decision in our case made us the only First Nation in BC and in Canada to have a Declaration of Rights to 100 percent of an area. In spite of that, the BC government understood our rights to hunt and fish very loosely, and when push came to shove, they liked to say they were confused and didn't know whose Rights and Title we were referring to. Tŝilhqot'in? Shuswap Secwépemc? Carrier Dakelh? They preferred to use question marks, because for the first time ever, they had to come to grips with a large piece of Land with clear Tŝilhqot'in Aboriginal Rights. Nobody else's rights, just Tŝilhqot'in.

BC tried to buy time, afraid that recognizing the Title would stop economic development – pipelines, mining, LNG [liquefied natural gas]. In September 2014, they spoke of each First Nation being "unique" –"We wanna sit down with you in your unique way and negotiate an agreement." But they said they couldn't agree that we had Aboriginal Title and they wanted to sit down with each community and Nation to discuss that. So during that first meeting, everyone was excited but also angry because of BC's refusal to recognize Aboriginal Rights and Title. On one hand, they were telling First Nations, "We'll deal with you, we'll work with you at your pace whether you wanna be a community or a Nation" and, on the other hand, telling First Nations, "We can't recognize Title yet but will do that during negotiations." They were avoiding saying, "You'll have to go back to court and prove Title the way Tŝilhqot'in did." Recognition of Title continued to be a sticking point for them, and they wouldn't negotiate.

Xeni Biny. Photo by Lorraine Weir

Lha yudit'ih We Always Find a Way

Christy Clark and the
Letter of Understanding (2014)

Chief Roger William

For the first time in this country, an Aboriginal group has beaten the colonial government at their own game. They have all their policies and legislation that took over Aboriginal Lands, but even those policies and that legislation didn't help them in this case. So we wanted to meet the Premier of BC and then to meet Canada. Premier Christy Clark responded first. I have to commend her for actually stepping up to the plate, visiting Xeni on September 10, 2014, and signing a Letter of Understanding (LOU)[13] to move forward. We know what the history of BC is, so we were saying, "Well, *we* always knew this is all our Title and Rights, but now *your* country has recognized it, so here's some earth. This is Tŝilhqot'in Aboriginal Title earth." The Premier knows that they fought, they didn't agree, they did everything they could to say we didn't have any Rights, we didn't have any Title. So now we've proven our culture and our Title, and we're giving her a buckskin bag, embroidered by my mom, and filled with earth from Xeni, Title Land.

The bag was made by a Tŝilhqot'in Elder, my mom [Elder Eileen Sammy William], and it was done respectfully, positively. It didn't come with a negative overtone like, "See, this is our Land, we're gonna do this!" No, this bag was made in a positive way and a cultural way, and if you know my mom at all, you'll know that. The bag is made of buckskin which she tanned herself, and it's embroidered on one side with a map of Title Land and on the other side with Tŝ'ilʔos representing Xeni Gwet'in. The earth is Tŝilhqot'in Title earth. The earth was no different on June 26 than on June 25, but now that earth comes from Title Land and their own highest court says that, and it's in evidence. That beautiful bag made by an Elder was presented to the Premier to say, "Here's a gift from our Land, our culture, and we wanna move forward now." Now we've proven our culture and our Title, and in giving this bag to Christy Clark, we're saying "This is Title Land, protected by our culture and tradition."

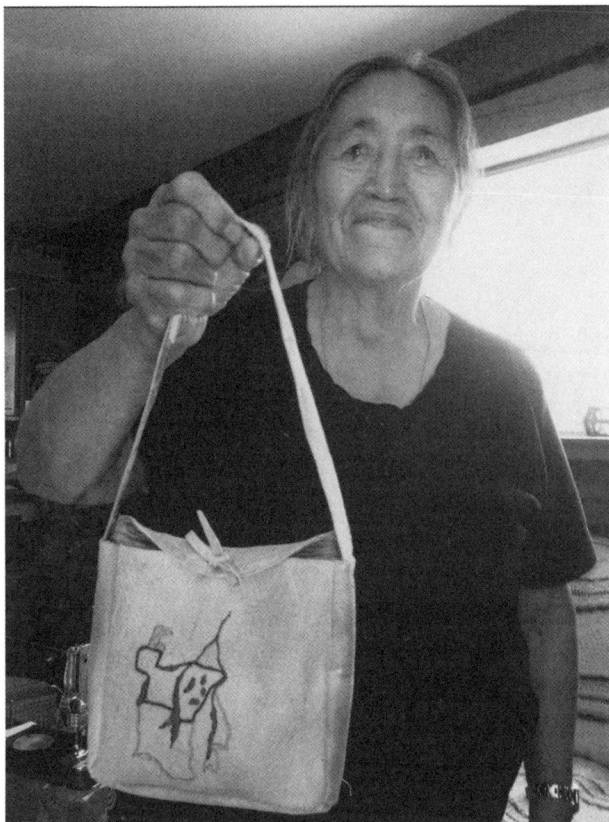

Elder Eileen Sammy William holding the tanned buckskin bag with embroidered map of Title Land, which she made for presentation to BC Premier Christy Clark. Photo by Chief Roger William

The First Six Months

Chief Roger William

That six-month agreement (the Letter of Understanding of September 10, 2014) was a bit of a victory. Without the Title win, I think we would've been looking at an 80 percent cut in timber and probably a 0 percent agreement on revenue sharing on the old mine at ʔEsdilagh that was renewing its thirty-year license. BC gave us $800,000 for six months so that we'd have capacity to deal with negotiations. Part of that LOU agreement was also to negotiate a negotiating process and deal with some pressing issues, including questions about the maintenance of roads and responsibility in emergency situations like a flood or a fire on Title Land. BC said they'd continue dealing with those situations if they arose. So with that money, we were able to sit down with our communities and give them an update of what happened in terms of timber, minerals, and capacity funding to negotiate. All of that was in the first six months after Title declaration.

Lha yudit'ih We Always Find a Way

The LOU Agreement with BC allowed us, with the approval of the TNG Chiefs, to fund phase one and phase two of the Wild Horses Program in Xeni. We also signed a five-year Forest and Range Opportunity (FRO) Agreement, which promised thirty cubic meters of timber per person. Five hundred dollars a person, I think. The communities have been getting this every year. We ended up getting almost $200,000 a year for Xeni, and Stoney (Yuneŝit'in) gets almost the same. Anaham (Tl'etinqox) gets almost $700,000. So when the decision came down in June, the FRO was in its fifth year, and we were gonna renew it, but our five years had gone by already by April. So we didn't sign the agreement. It's revenue based on how much timber is actually harvested from your area and what the timber is worth. So when we calculated, it brought our number way down, and we didn't sign. And then the court case win came in. BC came in September and said they'd keep giving us an FRO rather than a Forest Consultation and Revenue Sharing Agreement. But because of the Title win, they've been giving us the FRO, five hundred dollars per person, thirty cubic metres a person. Let's say down the road, if we win in court and negotiate how much timber damage there was, that'd just come off the top. It doesn't replace what we could get in negotiations or in court. So this legal agreement is goin' towards any revenue in the future, whether negotiated or in any court case. Our communities don't get very much money, so that helps. It doesn't answer the whole problem, but it's better than nothing.

Like other First Nations, we felt that wasn't enough, and the next agreement was for revenue sharing based on the amount and value of the timber. However, when you calculate the value of the timber for the mills in the Tŝilhqot'in, the result was that we lost 80 percent of our funding. You'd think a revenue sharing agreement would go up, not down! So when negotiating the LOU, we said we didn't agree with the new revenue sharing on timber, and they agreed to stick with the FRO, and that remained. This LOU agreement was still based on five hundred dollars and thirty cubic meters of timber per person, and that's how much the Nation will get per capita. We also agreed that for every new mine, there would be a revenue-sharing agreement for First Nations. BC agreed to provide half a million dollars for the Gibraltar mine at ʔEsdilagh for that first year.

We also dealt with BC Hydro during that time, making an agreement that they would continue to maintain their poles on the northern tip of Title Land, and we will negotiate damages out of that in the future. We said that we wanted to continue managing local operators like ranchers, tourism operators, and residents so they could continue, and we wanted to make a smooth transition. We agreed with a guide to continue their guiding on Title Land, but we didn't approve of hunting at all, because in the Tŝilhqot'in, the moose numbers are

50 percent less for the last five to ten years, so no hunting for now in Title Land by non–First Nations people.

When we started strategizing our next step, we asked why don't we just finish this whole court case off? Let's go back to court and go after damages for Title Land. We talked about it and decided to try and negotiate. BC and Canada have always preferred negotiation to court, and they've been saying that for years, but consider that the BC Treaty process has only resulted in eight signing on since 1990,[14] while the rest are still in limbo. But now for the first time, there was a First Nation that's gonna negotiate with BC and Canada on the basis of a huge win. A lotta First Nations wanted to work with us and had ideas about how we should negotiate or what we should do. So we, the Tŝilhqot'in leadership, were going around the province and Canada updating people on the Title win and thanking them. We were also working with different academics and we still are today (2017). In our own communities, we were updating members about the Title win and talking about the next steps. We met with local non–First Nations operators as well. So there was a lot to do, and we needed to keep focused.

During the six-month period after the Title win, we also hammered out a lotta language about the negotiations process and how many years it would take. We talked to our people, and it was decided that we'd look at the whole Tŝilhqot'in. The Title win itself is not negotiable, but we will negotiate with BC on what they can do on Title Land. We talked about our vision for the other five Tŝilhqot'in communities. All of the Tŝilhqot'in leaders and people felt that we should be involved in decision-making about all of the Tŝilhqot'in Territory and be able to get revenue from it. In 2014, that was all still ahead of us. We also wanted to look beyond Rights, Title Lands, and resources. Priorities are education, housing, health, culture, and language. To do that, we need the federal government to be involved, and we wanna meet as soon as we sign an agreement with BC and look at damages. What kind of damages to our Rights and Title happened on Title Land? What kind of revenue did BC collect, and what kind of revenue did people take out of our area and benefit from it? Discussions weren't done by March 2015, and the process was ongoing.

Then BC Treaty Commissioner Sophie Pierre resigned, and the province rescinded approval of the newly appointed Commissioner, saying that they knew First Nations weren't happy with the process, and the province wasn't either. At that point, we needed time to get back to our people and tell them about the five-year agreement we were going to sign and about the economic venture we were considering. That venture was River West Mill, which is owned by four communities – Tŝideldel, Tl'etinqox, Tl'esqox, and Yuneŝit'in. ʔEsdilagh and Xeni aren't part of that. During the three-month transition process, we wanted

BC to focus with us on the long-term viability of River West Mill and the cost of getting it running again. It had created over fifty jobs and was an opportunity for our people.

Meeting the Feds (2014)

Chief Roger William

You know, for all these years they've been in denial. Their legal argument has no real truth to it. And they know they've tried to throw a lotta roadblocks at all First Nations that are trying to expose the truth. Roadblocks like not negotiating in good faith, making it harder so when you go to court, it's gonna cost you money. Roadblocks like arguing little things that they've been arguing for years, so you'd almost think you were looking at *Delgamuukw* (1997) or *Calder* (1973) when you see their arguments in court or our information. All the resistance we faced from BC was almost the same as the resistance from the federal government, and our lawyers could pretty much see the arguments coming. The feds are gonna continue what they've been doing for all these years – cutting programs.

For six months before we met in December 2014, the Minister of Aboriginal Affairs, Bernard Valcourt, had no intention of dealing with us. When we talked to him, he said that whatever deal they made with us, they'd also have to make with the other First Nations, but he said he thought his programs and services were good. Meanwhile, he was making everyone accountable so he could prove to the general public that he was putting out a certain amount of money. He wanted to know the Chiefs' wages, he wanted to know the Councillors' wages. Where was the money going? He told us he's a lawyer, and when we came in, he said, "Oh, we're not that rich. You look at the walls, you can tell we're not that rich." That was his first comment to us. We were in his office, and he said that! I remember that. I know that. And his other comment that I remember is, "Since the '50s, my programs have been working. We're doing a lotta things. Anything we do with you has to be done with the rest." He didn't offer ideas, didn't suggest other ministers who could assist, he didn't offer anything. That's okay. I'm not surprised. We'll see what happens in the federal election in October 2015.[15]

Signing the First Law of Title Land in the Band office, Xeni, May 14, 2017. Kneeling in front, Gilbert Solomon pointing toward his mother, Elder Mabel Solomon xinli. Front row from left, Annie C. Williams, Elder Juliana Lulua, Elder Ubill Lulua xinli, Elder Cecile William xinli, Elder Margaret Quilt, Elder Joseph William xinli, Elder Delia William, and Elder Eileen Sammy William. Second row from left, Chief Roger William, Chief Bernie Elkins Mack, Alex Lulua, Chief Francis Laceese, Chief Russell Myers Ross, Elder Marvin William xinli, Loretta Williams, and Elder Norman Williams. Archival photo, Xeni Gwet'in First Nation

Xeni ʔeguh jid Nitsʼegugheniʔan
The First Law of Title Land

Chief Roger William

On March 20, 2015, after more than twenty-five years in court, the Chiefs enacted the Declaration as the First Law of Title Land. The only change that the Chiefs made in the Declaration was to leave the door open a bit so if the Nation wants to do something in Title Land and it's not within the Declaration law, they need Xeni Gwet'in approval, and if Xeni Gwet'in wants to do something in Title Land that's not within the Declaration law, we need the Nation's approval. This give-and-take made the Declaration into the first Tŝilhqot'in Law. So anything that's against the Declaration – it could be mining or commercial logging – requires both approvals. In future, way down the road past my time, there could be a type of commercial harvesting or a type of mining that could protect the environment, culture, and language so you could log or mine in a way that's safe. This allows that process to be looked at, but the people's approval from both Xeni and the Nation would be necessary to do that. So that was the First Law.[16]

The Nenqay Deni Accord (2016), Summary

Lorraine Weir

Signed by the Tŝilhqot'in National Government, the six Chiefs, and the Province of BC on February 11, 2016, the Nenqay Deni Accord is clear from the beginning that "the Tsilhqot'in vision is to fully restore their Nation to the power of the ʔEsggidam. They enter reconciliation negotiations as one step on that path ... [to] sharing fully in the wealth and benefits" of British Columbia.

The ʔEsggidam were "healthy and strong – as individuals, families, communities, and as a Nation. They had a rich culture and deep spiritual connection with the Lands and resources that sustained their people." Acknowledging the impacts of smallpox, the Tŝilhqot'in War, "the taking of their Lands, the devastating impacts of the residential school system, the imposition of the Indian Act, and mass apprehension of their children," the preamble affirms the resilience and strength of Nenqayni Deni the Tŝilhqot'in people and interprets Premier Christy Clark's visit to Xeni on October 23, 2014, as an act of "redress." The five-year Accord is described as "a reconciliation framework agreement to define the next phase of negotiations which will address the interests of both parties in Tsilhqot'in Territory and help bring the court decision to life."

The agreement defines "a role for Canada in the reconciliation process and commits both parties to engaging the federal government in this important work." Priority areas for discussion are "governance, economic development, justice, health, education, social issues, and land and resource management." These areas became the five "sub-tables" – Governance and Economic Development; Social, Cultural, Education, and Justice; Lands and Resources; and Declared Title Area Implementation. Tŝilhqot'in language and culture are strongly affirmed throughout the Accord as core principles with goals of fluency and pride; public awareness, appreciation and understanding of Tŝilhqot'in culture, history, and heritage; and the "recording and preservation of Tŝilhqot'in language, beliefs, oral histories including legends, and cultural knowledge for the benefit of future generations." Funding of more than ten million dollars was committed by the provincial government over the next three years (2016–2019).[17]

What's Next?

Chief Roger William

Everyone's saying what is Tŝilhqot'in gonna do now that we've got Title? There are options, and to me, they have to be housed up in a political, legal plan. Nenqay Deni Accord is part of that. There are other parts to it where there are damages on Title Land and we need to go after those damages too. There's Tŝilhqot'in Territory that's bein' damaged today, so that's another strategy to create. Nenqay Deni Accord is looking at all that provincially and there's also a federal process. We know how BC has been negotiating in the BC treaty process. We know how Canada has treated the provinces and territories and how First Nations with treaty have been treated. So we can't just continue to negotiate. We've gotta have a legal strategy too. I don't think there's any case anywhere in the world where a First Nation has won Aboriginal Title *in their own laws.* This is not our law. This is not our legislation. *They* created Canada and we beat them in their own court. We won but we weren't party to legislation that was put in place over us. But we used that to win Title.

The Nenqay Deni Accord is a tool that's gonna start in year two of the five-year agreement (Tŝilhqot'in Strategic Engagement Agreement, 2017). It's a grassroots-driven process. We need to really educate our people about exactly what these five tables are and we need to establish realistic goals because I know that our people's expectations are probably way up there in terms of what we're gonna negotiate compared to what we might be able to get. So if we spend some time telling our people: Okay, you all want self-government, right? You all want to make decisions on your land. You wanna be able to have opportunities and jobs, you wanna get educated and healthy, you wanna live a healthy lifestyle. I want you to know who pays for the programs and services we get. When you go to the hospital, who pays for that? When you get travel money, who pays for that? When you go see an eye doctor and get glasses, who pays for that? What about the road we travel on? Who pays for that road? I think once our people know those details, they can say: Okay, what kind of agreement do we want that's gonna work? I think that might come a little easier than not goin' through the details and people's expectations are like, we're gonna get a brand new house, we're gonna get all this stuff and we're not gonna work for it. No, no, no! We want our people to hustle. We want them to speak the language. We want them to know our culture and that nothing gets handed to them, but they'll have opportunities. We wanna give them opportunities for all that. Before contact, if you didn't get up and do it, you didn't survive so now we want to create a place where when they want to get up and do it, they can. I think that's the language that we need to understand when we're negotiating.

This Nenqay Deni Accord is gonna need to look at ʔEsggidam ancestors and how do we try to get back to ʔEsggidam. ʔEsggidam are Tŝilhqot'in people before European contact. In 1862 before the first Europeans arrived, ʔEsggidam had all their language and stories, totally without the influence of Euro contact. ʔEsggidam never had to deal with money. ʔEsggidam never had to deal with budgets. Before 1862 we were influenced by the land and we learned from it but Euro contact influenced us in different ways, confusing us, probably due to not understanding the English language. Maybe there's always gonna be that Euro influence even though we still believe in our ʔEsggidam.

Any money that we get out of Title Land and our negotiations has gotta go towards ʔEsggidam to get us back to that place. ʔEsgiddam who got educated, and got university and hustlin' skills. Deyen people should be there, spiritual power should be there. You know, Catholicism is there but it'll probably get slowly phased out in a respectful, honourable way. Not being called down, not being sworn at but slowly, slowly gone. And our spirituality will be comin' in in a respectful way. There's no hostile kicking out the Catholics – screw them, they screwed us. No, we're gonna do it in a way that's healthy for anybody who's ready for it. But if our parenting skills, our cultural skills, our language skills, our land skills are not there, we're gonna keep doin' what the government's been doin' to our land. But it will be us doin' it to ourselves.

You know, we've got people in our communities that think Tŝilhqot'in Nation is gonna be its own country with our own rules, our own laws, everything. And then we gotta make enough money in the Tŝilhqot'in to have a hospital, a school, roads, welfare if they need welfare, education dollars if they need them. How are we gonna make all that money? Right now, we need to be able to not give up our land. We're not gonna give up any Title to our land, we're not gonna give up any Rights to our land. We may loan it to BC and Canada, from parts of it to a lot of it, but they gotta pay us for it and the deal has to be for a certain number of years. Our people might be goin' back to healing for another fifty years – learning their language, understanding the residential school impacts, getting their parenting skills back, all that stuff. Let's say we get to a place where we are all healed. We've been impacted. We learned drugs and alcohol. In twenty years the Nation will still be here but the old lifestyle will have changed with everybody speaking Tŝilhqot'in and going to university, and hustling and going to work. And then we'll slowly develop from our traditional laws, rituals, beliefs, and spirituality to the new, modern decision-making and to budgets and money.

We talk about no logging, no mining and still making ends meet so there's gonna be stuff about tax. If I ever say you gotta pay tax, our people'll go crazy. Why do we have to pay tax? So we need to entertain that. We need to open up that Title Land and other Tŝilhqot'in reserves and their Title Land so that people can get a loan at a bank. How do you do that? Well, the bank ain't gonna loan to a reserve because they got no jurisdiction. There's no means of them getting their money back but there is legislation and policies that've been made between governments and First Nations like Westbank, Kamloops, and Osoyoos where there's reserve land subject to subdivision, and subject to business. If any of those fail, the bank takes over. They own it and they sell it to anybody in Canada. But whoever buys that place is under the rules of Westbank or Kamloops, and they pay taxes to Westbank or Kamloops.

We can't just say there's a boundary around Tŝilhqot'in and then have a bank or a hospital because it's not big enough to create that. But we can open up the door to the rest of Canada and say okay, here's Title Land, here's reserve land. Let's do business. It's gotta be done in a certain way. You can't clearcut. You can't mine. That's gonna do damage to the water and our culture and way of life. If you can live with that, you've got opportunity in this land. We'll give you a lease. We could even give you private land that you could buy and sell in the future but it would be under our rules, under our laws, and we'd benefit from whatever happens there.

Damages (2017)

Chief Roger William

They never wanted to give us Title. They thought they might give us postage-stamp-style Title but at the end of the day, the decision says we have Title to a large area and to me that has never been done before in Canadian history.[18] We know the history of how BC and Canada negotiate with First Nations but now there's a court case that has resulted in Title.

We're not done with Title yet. There's still a hundred and fifty years of BC and Canada running that Title Land and we're gonna go after those damages and all the revenues. Whatever they got out of that area we're gonna go after. We're gonna negotiate it, yes, but if those negotiations continue the way they have been, we're just gonna say let's go back to court. One example is that here in the trapline area there are several areas that were harvested in the '70s and the "80s – Gwedzin and Telhiqox (Cochin and Tatlayoko they call it in English).

We had an expert forester look at that and they testified at trial that the damage on that alone is a hundred million dollars. So if we hadn't won this case and BC had kept on negotiating the way they have been, there would've been no real repercussions because we still had to prove Title. Now we have Title.

Judge Vickers found in his decision in 2007 that there is a hundred million dollars of damage just on harvesting alone. So we can go a little further than that and think about private lands on Title Land. For all the years that the private landowner has held that land, there are damages. When the government created private land out of prime land that *we* use, our Rights and Title were impacted. The landowner paid tax to the government all those years and whether it's Williams Lake or Vancouver or wherever, whoever went there and lived there paid taxes. That's the revenue that BC and Canada have had for a hundred and fifty years. We want that revenue that was never shared with us. So whether taxpayers got paid by others who went there for an experience or simply paid taxes themselves, if that private land hadn't been there, tax would never have been owing. So let's say damages on that. And then on top of that, they've used the trails, the cattle have used the grass and the land, people have camped, and revenue came out of all those uses and all that damage. Revenue came out of giving people an experience or having cattle there, and the government taxed that revenue. So there's private land itself and there's the land that the private land use owner used and paid the Crown for a provincial license. It's so complex that we need experts to calculate how much damage, how much revenue on those Title Lands over a period of a hundred and fifty years, and so on. We want to negotiate our share of that because it was on our Title Land.

I think right now [2017] Title Land is a tool that we can use to negotiate not only the Title Land but the Rights Land which is twice as big as Title Land. Then the Tŝilhqot'in territory. So if we don't feel negotiations are working, we're gonna go after damages. That's gonna cost you money. Remember, we lost Title Land and we lost our Rights. If BC and Canada want to take a shortcut, they might want to negotiate in good faith the whole Tŝilhqot'in. Whatever that's gonna look like. We Tŝilhqot'in wanna have a say in Tŝilhqot'in Title Land and have a say in any revenue or any opportunity for more land. That's what we want out of the Tŝilhqot'in. Whatever that's gonna look like, I wouldn't know but now we have a tool and we will go back to court if we don't feel that BC and Canada are willing to go as far as we want them to. We have Title Land and there's a hundred and fifty years of damages and revenues and everything owing. We're gonna go after all that in court if they choose not to negotiate with us for the whole territory. So, yeah, BC and Canada don't have that issue with other First Nations. They have that issue with us.

Land and Inherent Governance

Chief Roger William

There was some language that BC had fun with then and continues to today (2017). For example, first BC said they couldn't give what was called "Title-like Land" back to the other five communities, but then they changed their mind. Some of the Chiefs wanted to specify a certain size, but BC said they couldn't do that, either. We wanted to negotiate it, but they were reluctant to. Another sticking point was language around inherent governance. Before Canada came to be, before contact, we had governance, so we wanted to specify inherent governance, but they were scared of that language. They felt that if they recognized inherent governance, they'd be giving up everything that follows from that recognition – giving up their point before they'd even entered negotiations. There's a lot at stake for them economically, including timber and mineral interests and the tax revenues associated with those kinds of interests. So we agreed that language around Land would be negotiated and that while we would continue to use the phrase "inherent governance," we would lay out the type of governance we wanted over the course of the negotiations. Since there was no agreement on the five-year process by the time March 2015 came, we extended the six-month agreement for another three months. They gave another eight hundred thousand dollars, another FRO-type (Forest and Range Opportunity) agreement, and another revenue-sharing agreement for minerals at the mine at Gibraltar. So now we had three months to try and deal with some of these hardline concerns.

In these negotiations with the province, we have our own negotiation support team, and BC has a support team as well. The two teams got together to work out agreements and understandings of the type of agreement, and the process was led by a Tŝilhqot'in, so everything we wanted came from us and we drafted the agreement. The draft goes from the team to their Ministers and then to the lawyers, and it's at that last stage that some things are taken off the agreement. June 26, 2015, the anniversary of the Title win, was the deadline, but the lawyers were trying to take stuff off the table. We'd been negotiating with BC since the LOU agreement on September 10, 2014, followed by the first gathering of the BC cabinet with First Nations. The second such meeting was in September 2015, and they wanted us to sign just before the gathering. We said no, since they'd been dragging their feet for months, and we decided to wait until after the gathering before we came up with an agreement. As Grand Chief Stewart Phillip put it, the BC government's reconciliation efforts were at "strike two," and they had one more year or "it will be back to the courts and pretty much back to the barricades."

To me, this process exposes that even after you win Title, this is the type of government you're dealing with. So let's say if we go back to court, we could go international, and we have options we can look at and that we've tried in terms of negotiations, but this is what we end up with. I feel that we're doing everything we can, but I'm not surprised where we're at. A lotta the language in the five-year agreement is pretty good, there's a lot of good intent, but I'm sure that BC could roadblock that too. There's only two things that we couldn't really come to agreement on in terms of language – inherent governance and Lands – so we're saying those things a different way in the agreement. The end result is we're not up front saying we have inherent governance, but at some point during the five years, we may say that. Similarly with language around Lands. At the end of the day, it may work. We don't know. So I feel pretty optimistic. Even if those don't work, we've still got the court process, we've still got Title, we still have options that we could use to continue with what we wanna do, where we wanna go.

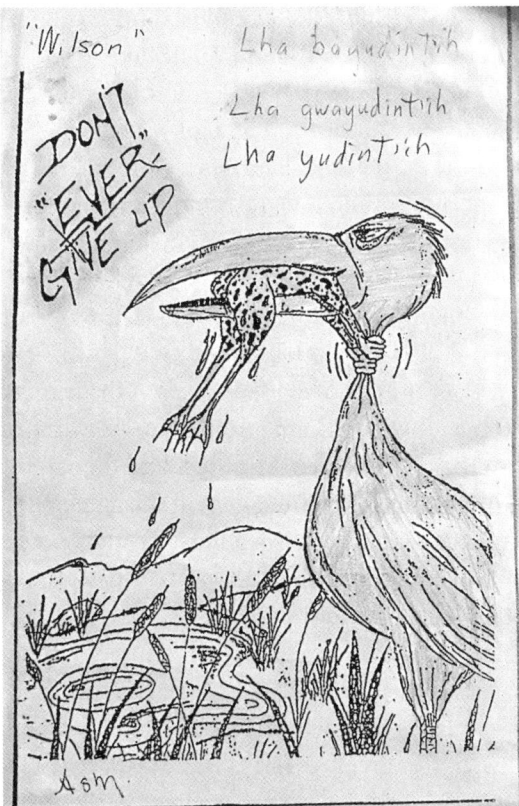

"Lha bayudint'ih / Lha gwayudint'ih / Lha yudint'ih / DON'T *EVER* GIVE UP." Chief Roger took this photo of a cartoon on the office wall of the great linguist and Knowledge Keeper William Myers xinli (Yuneŝit'in). A Gahan Wilson cartoon has been transformed into a Tŝilhqot'in Warrior poster featuring Heron (looking more like Crane) the Bad Luck Bird and Frog, refusing to be eaten.

The Tsilhqot'in Strategic Engagement Agreement (2017)

Chief Roger William

BC is gonna try and look at the decision and downplay what we should get out of it and whether we should negotiate or go back to court. They may gamble more by going back to court, because it takes longer and costs more money. So that's why we're looking at negotiations, because when we go to court, we wanna say we actually sat down with BC, we tried to sit down with Canada, but this is what we're facing, this is the wall. So if another judge is listening to this again after twenty-five years, they're gonna recognize that we tried to negotiate, we did our due diligence, and the court will have to decide if the parties are unwilling to do so themselves. That's why we're here [Vancouver, 2017] negotiating with the province, but we may go back to court on damages on Title Land regardless of whether we're negotiating or not. In the first five months of this five-year agreement, we need to have a pretty good idea of what the offer is from BC, but we're gonna lead with our statement of damages and the revenue they made for all these years. That's what we want. And they're gonna say yes or no, they're gonna counter-offer, and then we'll have a pretty good idea of whether or not we're wasting our time negotiating and should just go back to court for damages. We've gotta measure the cost of hiring lawyers and going back to court and what we might get out of it against how close we are in negotiations.

I don't put all my eggs in one basket. I'm not gonna live and die on this agreement. Whatever we do, we're not gonna sign an agreement to give up our Rights and our Title to the Tŝilhqot'in Xeni Gwet'in Lands and resources. We're willing to negotiate a process on how we're gonna be involved, as long as we're not giving up Rights and Title. We're dealing with a government that's resistant, scared, and gonna hang on as long as they can, but I'm really not very worried about BC and Canada. We know who they are. We know that they're gonna try and find every loophole they can get away with. But if we fall apart and BC and Canada take advantage of that, it's our fault. Like Chief Joe Alphonse always says, the only people I'm worried about is us.

Voting a Process

Chief Roger William

Since I've been in leadership, we've been saying what if we win Title? What's gonna happen? We know that there's gonna be elections. We know that if there's any revenues that come out of this Title, we want to use them for language, for getting back out on the Land, for respecting and honouring parenting, and for bringing all the healing back, our cultural ways, our spiritual ways. And somebody's gonna come and say, "Oh no no no no no! If I get in [as] Chief, I want to give you the money. You deserve the money, because you suffered. Your mom was in residential school, your dad was, you didn't have a good chance. I'll give you the money. You vote me in." So I'm thinking about this Nenqay Deni Accord and that people are gonna have to vote a process. That's what this Negotiations Charter is, and we're gonna have to create some policies and legislation and people that'll vote all that in. So whoever gets in [as] Chief, if they wanna change that, they'll need the people's approval.

Why Xeni?

Chief Roger William

I think since the Title win, there's been quite an excitement, but some of the people are having a tough time understanding why Xeni and why Tŝilhqot'in National Government and why the other communities are involved. "How come the Nation is involved? We won Title. We went to court and we didn't get any money from them to help us and now they're involved. Why?" So I always say that we have families from Xeni that are in other Tŝilhqot'in communities, and there's families from other Tŝilhqot'in communities that are in Xeni. And then I say that the majority who testified in court were from Xeni, but the rest were from the other communities in the Tŝilhqot'in.

The eight judges didn't say this is Xeni Gwet'in Aboriginal Title Land or the Roger William Title Win. No, they said this is Tŝilhqot'in Title Land and the Tŝilhqot'in Title win. So that means when I go to try and protect this Title Land, I'm sayin' well, my name is Roger William, I'm a Tŝilhqot'in, I wanna deal with this. They'll say oh, okay, Roger William, you're a Tŝilhqot'in person. But you know what, Chief Ervin [Charleyboy] says this. Chief Joe [Alphonse] says that. Who's the real Tŝilhqot'in person here? BC and Canada are gonna kind of have fun with us, eh? So that's what I tell my people. I say look at it as a Nation win. This is powerful. If there's any opportunity in our time, this is it. We get together as a Nation and expose what BC and Canada are about, because I don't think they're gonna agree with everything.

What BC and Canada were hoping we'd say is that it's Xeni Gwet'in Title. Then the judge would have said Xeni Gwet'in's only one Band out of six and he probably wouldn't have given us Title. But Judge Vickers decided that there was proven Title that was also outside the court case area. He drew a line saying it's not in the court case area, but you have proved Title over there, too. BC and Canada were arguin' that it's only Xeni Gwet'in, and Xeni Gwet'in are just one Band, an Indian Act Band. They're not the Nation. They don't have Title. But Judge Vickers wouldn't back that up. So that pretty much housed up everybody with us. I tell my people that, because some say, "Well, why don't *they* go to court in their area, and we'll support them?" We've got a template for winning here, so it probably wouldn't take as long as this case did, but it's gonna cost money. But really we don't have money right now, so we don't wanna do that. You know, we were able to get court case costs here. Are we gonna get court case costs for all the other Tŝilhqot'in communities? I dunno.

Each Tŝilhqot'in leader in leadership right now has their own pressures from their communities. They've got their own wants and needs. And they have a tough time feeling that Xeni should be gettin' all these different things. Chiefs don't mind seeing us really succeeding in our Title Land win but then when they go home, I think their people are like "What about *us*? What are you guys doin' for *us*?" It's an intricate process that we're dealing with, almost like an art. It's dealing with my family, my community, and with the Nation that's still healing. We're still powerful. We're still amazingly strong together as a Nation. Us Chiefs, we talk about how we fought Fish Lake together, we fought Aboriginal Rights and we stood behind each other. Now we've won and we're gonna try and figure out how we make it work. BC and Canada are not gonna say, "Okay, we'll give you everything in this whole Territory and you guys make it work." They're like "Oh, we'll fund your Title Land and we'll fund over here and a little bit over there." And then we're thinking if we're looking at a political and legal strategy, we need to make sure that there's wins for all of us. For BC, they need wins so their general public can see that this Title negotiation's actually workin', but our people they need to see things on the ground.

Lha yudit'ih We Always Find a Way

Nation to Nation (2017)

Chief Roger William

Chief Joe Alphonse says, "This case was not about separating from Canada. This case was about being recognized in a meaningful way within the society of Canada. We want to be a part of that society."[19] When Chief Joe says that, it's about us wanting to be recognized. We are Indigenous people and this is our Title and Rights. If you recognize us, that recognition is a *big* word. We're saying this is our Territory. Anything that happens in here needs our consent. That's what Chief Joe said. That's how you recognize us as Tŝilhqot'in people. To me, when Chief Joe says we want to be part of Canada, we're not even Canadians. Ervin Charleyboy says we weren't allowed to vote until the '60s, '70s, and then we weren't even sworn in as Canadians, that's what he said. I can see the analogy with what Joe thinks and even what I think. It's that you guys recognize this is our Land. You guys used it. We won part of it, we proved it in court. We can keep goin' back to court, but we're open to talking with you. We wanna be in Canada on *our* terms. This is part of Canada.

Let's use the analogy of a hotel room like the one where we're recording now. Here's Title Land – here's a whole room of Title. We think it's Title Land, and BC and Canada are not gonna give us everything that we want. So we gotta have a political legal strategy. So there's gonna be court cases for that hat, maybe. Maybe for that lamp over there. Maybe part of the bed, you know. How are you gonna use that bed? How are you gonna sleep here? Whose gonna pay what? You need our consent. That could almost mean anything, because if you recognize this is my room, you're not gonna just take stuff outta here without asking, and there's gonna be some agreements when you take my hat and go out that door with it. What kind of agreement does that? But we're gonna try and negotiate. BC and Canada are gonna resist a lotta things on this whole hotel room. So I think that a lot of these cases are probably just gonna push BC and Canada to do the right thing. Well, that's what it has to be. Otherwise, why wouldn't we go back to court, right? Because if negotiations ain't goin' good, we gotta go back to court in some cases. So I tell my people that right now, BC and Canada are probably still surprised. The big surprise is that we won Title to this place. They're probably surprised that we're [all six Tŝilhqot'in communities] still together. They're probably hoping that it's only Xeni Gwet'in that's gonna negotiate this little piece of Land.

What is "Nation to Nation"? Here's Tŝilhqot'in people who speak one language and are living in one geographic area. That's a Nation. There's no other

Tŝilhqot'in-speaking people outside of that Nation. There could be Dakelh Southern Carrier, who've got almost the same dialect and they're Athabaskans like us, but they're not Tŝilhqot'in, they're Carriers. When we speak together, we are Tŝilhqot'in, and they are Carrier. So Nation to Nation is probably what Canada should come to the table with.

We want to be in Canada. We're not in Canada yet. You guys took our hats. You guys wrecked our beds and you destroyed our bathrooms and you told us to stay *here*, right *here*, like that. "We don't want you going to that bed, to that bathroom. We want you to stay *here*. You're gonna go under Canadian rules." So we still have to figure out how this is gonna be Canada in here. So far, you guys have been taking and doing stuff to that bed without our consent. What I see is that you put us here, and you've been using the rest of this place without our consent. We said we want to be in Canada, but you need our consent. We want to rebuild that relationship. It's not gonna be the way it used to be.

You know, the decision is really interesting, because BC and Canada can override Title, but they gotta compensate, and they can't affect our Rights. That's what the decision says. So how are you gonna affect this little chair? Are you gonna pay us for it? You wiped out all the moose, whatever. You wanna take over Title Land. You pay us everything and the eight judges said: Okay, you can override Title and you gotta compensate but *you can't affect Rights*. Would BC and Canada waste their time on paying for this little chair here without affecting our Rights? That wouldn't make them much money. Why would BC and Canada wanna override Tŝilhqot'in Title when they can't impact our hunting and our traditional ways in Title Land? They might try mining – that makes a lot of money. Or logging – that makes money. But they both impact our Rights. So, okay, you can't do that. What can you do on Title Land that's not gonna impact our Rights? Really, the eight judges are saying you can't impact Tŝilhqot'in Land. They said we've got Aboriginal Title. They said we can make exclusive decisions as long as these decisions don't affect our Rights. We're saying we wanna be part of Canada, but it's gotta be on our terms. We're gonna be Canadians, but on *our* terms.

I'm thinkin' of Ivor Myers xinli. He said in our meeting, "They use our Land, they gotta pay for that. They wanna keep using it in the future, they better pay for it." So my thought is, politically, from this point forward, we need to be recognized as Tŝilhqot'ins. If you've been using this Land, you're gonna have to make a deal with us. We're willing to talk to you about how you're gonna catch up, because you used the smallpox on us, you used the Indian Act on us, you used the residential school on us. So let's fix that. We're not gonna say you guys owe us this much for one hundred and fifty years. We're gonna say well, let's get our homes fixed up, let's get our language, let's get our culture. We wanna be able to use the Land again. I've got Elders and members here that know how to do that. Let's resource those Elders and members and let's rebuild this country here. Let's get recognized. So we wanna create a better Canada by having you recognize *us*. We've proven in your own [settler] system under your own rules that we've got Aboriginal Rights and Title, but we haven't been sworn in as Canadians.

We're all at different levels and all catching up, but there's gonna be a time when we're all gonna point a certain way to that place over there. So Xeni Gwet'in might get there before everyone else, but that doesn't mean everyone won't get there. Some communities might get there faster than Xeni in different areas. Xeni might get there on culture and language, maybe. Who knows? We're all Tŝilhqot'in, and everybody who lives under the process will understand it and be happy with it. But right now, we're all over like this. Even in our own community, we're all over. To me, we want to get to this level here. Tourism operators, Xeni Gwet'in, Tŝilhqot'in, and these five tables [in the Nenqay Deni Accord process] gotta work at creating this understanding and this law to help us do that.

Creating Something New (2018)

Nits'il?in Russell Myers Ross, Yuneŝit'in

I think of the moments of being really stuck and always having to think through them, think how are we going to get around these moments, because for us it's crazy in a sense. It's always been our Land. We're trying to raise our families and move forward and then we still have obstacles about silly jurisdictional things. Even during the first engagements with the province, they basically gave us a blank slate, but we didn't know where to start. "You start it for us." In a province [without] a memory or history of what happened, they were like, "You fill it in, because we don't know." We thought the province had this clear picture in mind when they were defending themselves with their court case, but really there's nobody at the steering wheel that understands the history other than their position on who has jurisdiction. They don't really have a clear memory of what happened or how to rectify or re-engage issues of injustice. So early on in the engagement, it was clear where the province was. It still seems like a learning process trying to understand that part of it. What Roger had to go through must've been such a cat and mouse game, using the law to deny and try to deflect, while not being able to do stuff that he could otherwise have done. Even with the negotiations, being criticized for not being there [at home in Xeni] but still making sure things are moving ahead on some level. Even myself, what do we do if we have to go to court with the [Teẑtan Biny Fish Lake] mining stuff?

You know, when I think of the Elders on our side, they're predominantly people that didn't speak a word of English. What effect does it have on you as a society when you have a group of people who don't speak a word of English come and [talk to] to a judge? What effect does it have on you when you're trying to claim that it's your Land, even though you've never been there to know what languages they spoke in that place for thousands of years? We've been incorporated into a system that we never agreed with. How are you, settler society, going to support us to get through these hurdles, to try to recreate something that we actually *do* want? I think that's the ask more than anything, but it's hard on both sides. I think of the inertia of how the Crown functions, how government functions, and even the inertia of how we've been transformed. How to even reconcile the administrative side of the government system compared to one that is rooted more in our oral and relational presence on the Land? I say that because I know a lot of our governing is really that spiritual and mental connection to the Land and the things on the Land and with each other. So I don't even know what the real balancing act would be. I might say things about how to juggle it, but, to be honest, I don't know if it's really that clear for myself, for anyone. Sometimes I just go back to okay, where do we want to put our energy? Why don't we do more language revitalization? You know, a lot of my time is focused on Land disputes, and I'd rather be putting most of my energy into early childhood education. We don't have that much space to just stop and reflect and reorient ourselves. There's so many times when we end up making the same pathway over again! [laughing]

I hear Roger saying that on a per capita basis, we should all be on a level playing field, we should be allowed to catch up. I get that, and I'm not really against that, but there's more strategic elements, like how much Crown involvement do you want in your life? How much autonomy do you want to have? There's things like taxes where I don't know if I really want to be involved with it. I don't mind having it be part of revenue, but I don't want be *doing* taxes and creating law around taxation. [laughs] There's certain things that I don't think the Nation really wants that badly.

As Chiefs, we're no longer in a position of just advocating for our people and pushing policy and political directions for people higher up. Now we're positioning ourselves into becoming a governing body throughout our Territory, so that requires a different tactic and strategy. It's not a huge leap to say let's have each community participate in our whole governing Council, but until you start actually destroying pieces of it [colonial governance] and putting new stuff in, it's hard [to see how it will all work]. To me, a governing body has to grow. If we're ever truly going to look for legitimacy from people, we have to slow down, go back, and grow out of being a governing Council. I think it's important that we dismantle or disburse power and see how it emerges, but I don't have a very focused, clear direction on it. I'm just making these pragmatic stabs at trying to diffuse power so that we can create something new.

What about "Aboriginal Perspective"?

Nits'il?in Russell Myers Ross, Yuneŝit'in

All we really got out of the court's concept of "Aboriginal perspective"[20] is an acknowledgment of Tŝilhqot'in governance and maybe a level of consent. I think that was difficult, but it did produce an opportunity to see their concept of "Aboriginal perspective" in lieu of our traditional forms of Tŝilhqot'in governance and law Dechen ts'edilhtan. To take things a step further, there's going to have to be another First Nations group that comes to say there's this inherent Right, or something like that, around governance.

Healing Coming Back

Chief Roger William

We were born into Dechen ts'edilhtan Tŝilhqot'in law and we were trained in it and lived it. War is an aspect of our traditional law. Today, we're at war within, trying to get back not only our Lands and resources, but that feeling and understanding of being part of the Nen Land and moving forward from that. So that's the war we're fighting now. For me and my children, the war is getting back to the language and ritual beliefs, but there's a new process – computers, vehicles, that world of technology. We need to be able to come from and use our Dechen ts'edilhtan while moving forward and adjusting to this Western world that keeps changing. A lot of our young people don't know what we went through. We protected them from that so they didn't have to deal with it, but now we need to say this is what it was, this is who we were. They need to be able to feel, know, and understand what it was before contact. They need to understand that history so we can move forward. So the war now includes Aboriginal Rights and Title, the Land question, healing from the damages done to us for generations, and healing our young people and the next generation.

A hundred and fifty years ago, we lost Warriors and there was a big sacrifice here. All these years our people have died from abuse, drugs, alcohol. Now that's got to change, and the healing will come back. Moving forward, there's still gonna be people dying, but here's an opportunity to change that spread of pain. During the hundred and fifty years, we protected our caretaker area and we struggled and advanced, but we couldn't have a say.

If other communities had felt like us and agreed with us, probably we would've done more, but no, they didn't, and I gotta respect them and their leaders. This case is forcing people to look at what's going on, whether you're an Elder or a young person. When we negotiate, all that's gonna come up. Because of the five tables, the Nenqay Deni Accord is forcing people to look at the big picture. We're gonna educate. What are we trying to do here? Look at what we have. Right now, we have welfare. Right now, you can get your glasses paid for, but they're probably cheap. Roads are being made – you get a rough road. Who grades it? Sure, Xeni Gwet'in Enterprises grades it but we certainly don't have the money to pay Xeni Gwet'in Enterprises to do it. So let's go look at those details. But there's always gonna be someone says hey, look at that [Tŝilhqot'in] basket! Oh, we need to bring that back. Kids in school, they're seeing this. I'm thinking out loud about our Title win, the reconciliation – residential school – it's slowly gonna be filtered into the schools from kindergarten to grade twelve, and not only First Nations but everybody's gonna learn about it.

I'd like to build a program about our own people. A one- or two-year program that you take before we give you postsecondary education dollars. You learn about all the Tŝilhqot'in Bands. You learn about the Indian Act. How many Bands in Canada? How many languages spoken in Canada? How much Land do we have? What are the programs and services? What about the residential school? I want them to have some main things to learn about. What is the Title case? What is the reserve? It's global – Canadian, First Nations. What is that story? What is that history? What about the smallpox? What did that do? We gotta have people to teach that. We gotta have curriculum so they can do it. And as the program is gradually integrated into elementary and high-school curriculum, the need for it will decrease, so that by the time students are in grade twelve, maybe they'll already know the material. Then they'll be in the colleges and universities. That's already happening now.

When I was growing up, the Tŝilhqot'in language was the dominant language. Everybody knew it. As time has gone on, our Tŝilhqot'in language immersion program and our daycare entirely in the language have become more and more important. Today, some of our youth wish they could speak Tŝilhqot'in, and they envy our Elders who don't speak English. They wish for that, but how things change. We've heard about royalties being given in other First Nations to people at age nineteen and then they go buy something and it has such a bad impact on them that sometimes they may even lose their life. So we talked about handing out such a royalty a little bit at a time starting with high school graduation, then going to college, speaking Tŝilhqot'in, being out on the Land – milestones. It's still ahead of us to figure out how to calculate it, but if there is such a royalty, it should go to someone that's getting educated or using their education more through the language and the Land. I don't even know if there's gonna be a royalty scheme. Here's some ideas about incentives – we can fix all the details later. If there is a royalty scheme, it shouldn't be just because you're nineteen years old. We wanna award people for the right reasons. What if we tell the parents that if you find a way to teach your child how to speak Tŝilhqot'in before they go to school, there'll be bonuses? If the grandparents speak Tŝilhqot'in, those parents will bring the child to the grandparents and that will help out the grandparents and they'll all learn. And whatever the grandparents need, the parents will help them, because they wanna help their child to learn.

If a person learns a language and a culture, that money'll be well spent, and it'll be used in a better way. We've been impacted so much that we need to find ways to get our language alive again. When a parent is tryin' to find a way to teach their child Tŝilhqot'in, they'll learn too. And they'll learn our culture and our ways. You're not just payin' a parent to teach the child how to speak the language, but you're teaching that parent how to be a Tŝilhqot'in. You'll think Tŝilhqot'in. You're on the Land Tŝilhqot'in. You're usin' traditional ways, because you're tryin' to teach your child Tŝilhqot'in. Without technology! We have First Voices, that's the resource.[21] Parents can practise with their kids and learn with them.

We've gotta develop our curriculum. Right now, curriculum development is all based on proposals, and everybody's tryin' to make it work, but there's no one person hired to collaborate with all the Tŝilhqot'in language teachers and put it all together. So we develop this curriculum using First Voices or another program. Maybe there could be a CD or a flashdrive that people can plug into their computer to help the parents help the kids to learn. Curriculum that includes legends, stories, history, hunting, fishing. Parents want their kids to learn and now there's an incentive for them – not a million-dollar incentive but it helps, right. What I'm sayin' is why don't we think of now as a moment to get our language alive again? And the best way to start is when the baby's young and they're learning to speak.

It's Our Land (2017)

Chief Roger William

Our people in Xeni and in the Tŝilhqot'in are all at different levels. Some of them have been involved in systemic abuse for years. Even their parents were abused, so there's a bit of dysfunction in our communities. Some of these people are smart enough and manipulative enough to become leaders. For example, I've got people in my community that are sayin', you know, "This is *my* family Land." That's thinkin' the midugh way. In our culture, before contact, we didn't say, "That's *my* Land." We said, "It's *our* Land. We've gotta look after it. It's there for us because of Creator. We all gotta use it." So that's what we need to get back to. And if we're gonna use Land for our home, that'll be respected. For sacred ceremonies, that'll be respected and honoured. But as soon as you're gonna use the Land to put money in your wallet, then you need to pay a fee. That's what we call tax. And that money goes back in the system to keep generatin' more dollars for the Land, for the people, for our way, for the culture.

So you'll need to do a business plan to buy a property for commercial use, and that will be zoned out. That property'll be subject to Canada under our rules, and if you mess up and go in the hole, then either the bank owns it and takes it over, or we do. Whoever takes it over pays taxes. They do all the things they gotta do back to the Nation, back to Xeni. So anything to do with culture and language – if you're out on the Land, you should be able to do it freely. You wanna hunt, you wanna fish, you wanna do ceremony – free. But as soon as you start makin' money and doin' commercial use, then you're gonna have to pay. And that money is gonna go back to the people, back to the Land. If you're gonna be open to BC and Canada and the bank's gonna give the person a loan, there's gotta be some kinda rules. We might give better deals or worse deals in other areas. And some areas are worth more than others. But our story will be huge, and you may make lots of money, but you will pay tax on that too. We're the first to win Title. We've got all these Rights. And we're healing as a community, and we're gonna get bigger. As we grow bigger and stronger, there's gotta be standards so that this place reflects what we want it to be and we keep it pristine.

If a person builds a house to make a living and to stay there, that's their Land, that's their culture. But as soon as that person wants to do business, then we'd have to create a place and a property for that. That place and property'll be subject to taxes and all that. Your tax'll be subject to how much you make a year, just like your income tax. So if it's a young person that's hirin' people and they're making lots, then there's gotta be a point on a grid somewhere where tax

Lha yudit'ih We Always Find a Way

kicks in. For example, takin' a tourist out for a hike and all that. Maybe there could be no taxes for that, but if they hit a certain number of tourists, then we may want to start assessing tax. But to me, the tax is not for money. The tax is for control to maintain the place as pristine, so we might set a limit on the number of people and over that number, the place is no longer pristine. How do we deal with more people? Tax will help us control how much a person charges, but we still need to figure out when tax should kick in. If we want full control of ourselves, then that means no more funding from DIA,[22] so we're gonna have to keep ourselves going.

We want Xeni to stay Xeni and not become overpopulated, but what if everybody wants to come back? On all the reserves, people want to come back when there are more jobs. Then pretty soon the number of people impacts tourism, impacts the experience, impacts the culture – the hunting, fishing, trapping, whatever. There's gonna be a point in time when we hurt each other because when everybody's doing the same thing, prices drop. But the money is there to keep everything managed and pristine because taxes and all that are gonna contribute to running our community and our Title Land. It costs money to keep it at a certain level, right?

In two years, in the federal process we'll be dealing with genocide, the impact of the Tŝilhqot'in War, the impact of smallpox. The residential school impact: How do we get resources to heal from that and to get our culture and language back and find all the money to hire our own people to bring that language and culture back strong? We'll be lookin' at all that. We've got lots of work to do, but we have such an opportunity now, and we really have to control that opportunity and try to do it right.

Change (2017)

Chief Roger William

Today we've got different groups who don't agree with Chief and Council. There are people who are older than me who call themselves hereditary chiefs as opposed to elected Chiefs. There's the younger generation who don't trust leaders, because there's destruction in general in BC and Canada. And there are people who feel that we should be able to use the Title case to get a stronger agreement. All of us want Title, whether young people or old. All First Nations throughout BC and Canada want what we had before contact – Title. But there are some things that I saw a long time ago that are beginning to happen today.

Because of the court case, our people feel that we should have control of the whole of the Tŝilhqot'in. They're learning more about other First Nations that have overlaps and how the government is using that to do what they want to do.

There are so many things happening today (2017) compared to when I first got in as Chief. Youth gangs, drugs, and alcohol are in our communities. Two or three families in one house plus drugs, alcohol, and unemployment: that's what we're dealing with. When liquor stores and bars are close to communities, I see damage upon damage. In Xeni, we're far away, but alcohol and drugs still get into our community, and some people can do them almost all the time. I think percentage-wise it's a lot less in Xeni than in the other communities. When alcohol and drugs are right across the river or across the road, the damage happens faster. I always think of how our Elders say it takes a community to raise a child. It takes one individual to turn a community around.

Voter turnout in Xeni is about 71 percent, but in other communities, you're lucky to get 30 to 40 percent, and 50 percent is really good. So you've got anywhere from 50 to 70 percent of people who don't really care what goes on. Maybe they're doing drugs, cheating other people to get money, throwing stuff on the ground, trying to get jobs. It's all about money. I see lots of bright young people coming up, but I also see a split between generations, with a majority of people my age and older wanting to do the right thing and a minority trying to cheat and do whatever. Among people my age and younger, I see a majority that don't care and want to do the wrong thing and a minority that want to do the right thing. I see some pretty good leaders in our communities, people who could do a good job, but there's pressure.

Every day I hear my own Xeni Gwet'in people sayin', "Oh, this is *my* family Land. You, Chief and Council, got no say in" – that's the kinda stuff that's happenin'. And you've got some leaders who are like, "How come Xeni Gwet'in's gettin' all these other little benefits and gettin' ranger money and we're still struggling?" That's all legitimate, all trust issues. You can't blame our people for not trustin', because you look at what happened to us for all these years – we've been lied to, tricked. Before my time, during my time, some Chiefs and Councillors hurt their own people. But there is also what my wife went through, what I went through, what my family went through. I think right now we're still struggling, and at the end of the day, I know I could've, I should've done some things differently with my family, like stop doing rodeo, but my wife liked it. Mountainracing I probably could've stopped long ago, and I probably could've spent more time at home. It would've been a lot easier, and my wife would probably still be working in Xeni. But as I said, the Elders always taught me that if I did everything in my power to be honest, to work hard, and things didn't work

Lha yudit'ih We Always Find a Way

out, it's meant to be. That's when things go sideways: I should've said this, I should've phoned this, I should've done that, I should've, should've, should've. There are still some should'ves in there, but not enough to affect my thoughts and what I'm trying to do. If there were a lot of times where I should've done something else, I think I wouldn't be able to enjoy my work for my people and enjoy my family. I know there are people out there who don't agree with me and say I've messed up big time, maybe because of jealousy, but maybe for good reasons. But I feel it's kinda meant to be, because I think I did the most in my power to do the best thing I could. At the same time, I also know that there are two other Councillors who could make a decision against me, and it will affect what happens. Majority decision-making in today's world sometimes doesn't line up with my views, right. I would prefer a majority decision that's behind me, but I also know that there was a majority decision that went ahead which I was against. But at the end of the day, that was probably the best decision.

The old way of making decisions is really interesting. When you were born a Tŝilhqot'in, you came into this world knowing what was right from what your father thought and said and what your mother thought and said while you were in her womb. You knew the ritual beliefs of the Tŝilhqot'in way of life coming from the legends and creation stories from way back. You learned how to live off the Land, know the place names, honour and respect the Land and the resources given by the Creator. If there was a leader who knew all these things, when they made a decision, nobody questioned it. Whatever that leader said was honoured as the best decision, even if a person didn't agree with it. Nobody argued it.

Today we live with the history of smallpox in 1862, the Tŝilhqot'in War in 1864–1865, and residential school. The world around us is democratic now. I know where we were back in the day, but if I were to make decisions like that now, without talking to my people, a lotta people wouldn't agree. Probably many don't know our history and sadanx gwenig ancient stories the way others in my age group and older do. Some young people know a lot about it, but fewer than among the older generations. Those are the three groups of Tŝilhqot'ins I mentioned, and we're trying to bring those groups together now. If I followed our traditional way of decision-making, I don't think I'd be here. If people feel you've done a good-enough job, they vote you in – or not – every five years. But it's probably not that cut and dried, because if I had a Council where people were all in my age group, we could probably make decisions simultaneously, the way I described with David [Setah] and Gene [Cooper]. After five years, people might be happy with that, even though they might not have been involved in decision-making as much as they wanted. It's a bit different if you've got a Council with some people who are younger and know the culture but not the way I do. They've seen destruction in leadership in the past, and they see destruction today in politics, whether in First Nations politics or provincial and federal. They don't see me as any different from that. Back when I was getting into leadership, the big picture was always what happened to us back then and what we wanna do with it tomorrow. I think that's what kept me going.

You know, I think about what Gilbert [Solomon] was telling me. Lots of times he said, "When I was listening to you way back, when you first started, we were asking you, and I was wonderin' what you were gonna say, and you didn't even stop, you didn't even think, you just said it. And the same thing – they asked you, are you going to court? You think you're gonna win? You said 'Yup, yup, we're gonna win.'" He said, "You didn't even stop and think about it and mumble around. No, you just said it right out." But if I'd kept leaping ahead, nothing would've happened. People would've said "Oh, he's always like that." But actually, those things I've been talking about *are* happening. Like, "holy shit! I remember him saying that five years ago!" Then people start thinking and, like, "*Oh.*" "I do ceremony for you guys all the time," Gilbert said. "That's why you guys are winning." I believe that. I feel that the Creator is looking after us, because we're making sacrifices to try and protect what we have, protect the Land and the Water.

Tonight we're talking about a dream, we're talking about an idea. You gotta have a goal, right? I mean, how could I argue with my own people saying why is TNG involved in this? How come we're not negotiating ourselves? Why am I arguing with 'em? 'Cause I'm saying it's a Nation win, it's a Nation process. BC and Canada will divide and conquer if we do it separately, and when I speak tonight about taxes, about all these ideas, I'm looking at the whole Tŝilhqot'in. I'm not just looking at Xeni. I'm past Xeni. Xeni is the vehicle that got us here with all the support and all the cases across this country to this point that got us the win. So we need to have this vision and create opportunities for it. This is my dream.

Prophecy

Gilbert Solomon, Xeni Gwet'in

You know what Uncle Eugene [Sammy William] did to me? I seen it in here [pointing to his forehead]. All those Elders, they came to make us see earth shakin', disaster, things happenin', all kinds of chaos. Like, the story's in there [in your mind]. He said, "That's gonna happen." He gave us heads-up where *all* of the things were gonna happen. 'Cause everything's gonna fall in positive space. A positive story's still here. You wanna keep fightin' for your negative here, but if it's [the negative] too powerful, you go in here, and you just go NUTS! Crazy! And you'll run into the fire – big fire happening over there and you, "Aiii!" and you run right into it, go crazy.

The head couldn' take that no more. You need to shift to the positive. Just negative, no world no more. If you put that negative in here, you just go nuts, say, "The end of the world!" But that's the end of negative, that's all that was. Tryin' to scare people – "Oh, the end is comin'! Oooohh!" You know. They try to scare you, it's like that. That's how you might even borrow lots of money, 'cause it's just gonna be the end, you know. Turn out the jaybird. You know. But the negative think like that. "Oh, I'm gonna get the band to play that! The end is coming!"

I think of my life, you know. It's a bit like I'm on a walk with my muddy boots and I walk right up and open your front door. My friends are, "Aaa, what are you doing?" "Makin' myself at home in your house!" And I might find other things that I wanna steal while I'm here, like your boots, you know, and I'll take them. Yeah. And now they started coming in, getting information now. Always to make some more money out of what little bit we got, and they come in and get that, too, and before we know it, there's court cases and people bein' compensated in some way, whatever loss they claim. And that's not there. We even went through court to say that we need this Title. Still, they're logging over there as you go outta town, you see all these logging trucks – still going in and out of that place.

We live off all this area, not just this little Title area. We can't survive on this little Title area, this little polygon place.[23] We need the whole ocean, the river all the way to the ocean. You know how the ocean is bein' contaminated? We're gonna sue the whole – like Russia, Canada, the United States, Europe – all those for damagin' our Earth. They're gonna pay, and then we're gonna teach them how to treat it right.

There's a whole lotta shakin' goin' on, and people are gonna be afraid that they're sick and they're dyin'.[24] Where do you think they're gonna go? Who do you think they're gonna go to? You heard of West Coast tsunami? It'll bring understanding of how we should treat the earth. And then money wouldn't mean *anything*, you know. You wouldn' be thinking about money. Since they hung the Chiefs, [they've been] exploiting the Land, but it's not their Land. So now you exploited the whole Land, and you make millions upon millions. And you thought you wiped out all the First Nations, but we exist now. The salmon's been going up and down the river forever, and we're just like the salmon, still there, kinda swimming along. The court says, "Yo, hello, you got Title." You know, they could just shoot us in the open, 'cause all the trees are down and we're *in the open*. You know, hunting season! We're like a sitting duck. No, I was just kiddin' ...

Moose becoming extinct. Yeah. Slowly becoming extinct. Buffalo, the same. When they first arrived over there, 17-what, fishing the buffalo. They say Oh, we could use the buffalo, and then those guys take the Land. We don' need their money. It's just gonna pay their debt in karma. The earth's gonna shake, and some of us maybe gonna be dead. Maybe some of us gonna go to some astral land somewhere else like in the stars. Some ships'll come here. They gonna take us all up, take us away. Yeah. So. "Ah, good, you guys. These guys, no, you're not gonna want them there. Here, take those ones. We'll bring you back, though." After all this is done, all that shakin' goin' on, spontaneous tsunami, except now, this whole place will be sacred. All the oceans, sacred. The whole Land, really sacred. When they say "holy," you know in that language, "very holy," it's gonna come like that. We see heaven, you know.

Yeah, they sowed the stories in our minds already. These Elders, they're telling prophecies to us – what's gonna happen, what you gonna see next. They just tell us, "That's gonna happen." And then we see it in our mind, just sorta this in our mind. We see it like a DVD, sort of. They were in our minds, yeah, we see it [but] not written down. It's like, "Ohhh."

In school they taught us Catholicism, and you know, I've been on this [journey]. Jesus told you what's gonna happen, and that's that. You know, are we gonna die, or what? And the shipwreck, nobody understands how that's positive, that part. We had negative already. Gone. Right now, we're in the positive. That negative is still there. Probably we need to change. Our Elders say, "You need to shift. If you don't shift, you go nuts! You need to shift in order to go ahead. You know, we gonna continue here. Right here. Shift *now*! If you don't shift, you go crazy." So if we as people here on earth, if we don't go positive, we just go nuts. And we wouldn't know how to listen to where to go. We'll be like a raindrop next time. Cleansed. We gonna get paid, but not in money. It's gonna be spiritual. There might be a fire that keeps somebody warm, you know.

In the court case, how we won was truth. Everything was true. From our hearts. And in there, I didn't have no enemy. I just made somebody learn how to understand us. Tell that story. Let the lawyers and the judge say, "Oh, yeah! I caught on! You know, I *heard*!" And I'm like, "Wow! I totally see you!" [gasps] And they're like, "I could feel and see that cowboy hat you got on there, yeah. Wow! You know, 'cause it *exists*."

The lawyers, the province, and them [the federal government] changed. They were healed. They positive-healed. They hear from just us. That's what they said. They're not working for no government, they said, those lawyers that were on the province and federal [sides]. They're not working for the province no more. They go and work for other First Nations. Some said they were working for the wrong side.

But me, right now I'm not trying to make no enemy. I'm not trying to create any kind of negative. This is all gonna be positive, done spiritually, and if somebody says the word "negative" behind us, they have something come to them – karma. That'll scare 'em out of that negative mode [so it won't] come back in our face again. So we try to maintain that positive. That's how we go now. No negative. No, Mom's not gonna carry no cyclone in her bag, no. No. Not allowed! Positive. Not warlike or nothing. We're gonna pray, we're gonna go into the spirit world in a good way. We're gonna hold our heads up high, and when we meet our Ancestors on the other side, "Yo." Proud.

CHAPTER 12 ENDNOTES

1   Sometimes called the Indigenous Land Title Express and the New Constitution Express.

2   Kent McNeil writes that, in *Delgamuukw*, "The Court made it easier for Aboriginal Title and other Aboriginal Rights to be proven by relaxing the rules of evidence to admit Indigenous Oral Histories and give them as much weight as written histories" (Kent McNeil, "Has Constitutionalizing Aboriginal and Treaty Rights Made a Difference?" – an excellent overview of Aboriginal Title and Rights in Canadian law).

3   "In 1969, Prime Minister Pierre Trudeau and his Minister of Indian Affairs, Jean Chrétien, unveiled a policy paper that proposed ending the special legal relationship between Aboriginal peoples and the Canadian state and dismantling the Indian Act. This white paper was met with forceful opposition from Aboriginal leaders across the country and sparked a new era of Indigenous political organizing in Canada. The federal government's intention, as described in the white paper, was to achieve equality among all Canadians by eliminating *Indian* as a distinct legal status and by regarding Aboriginal peoples simply as citizens with the same rights, opportunities and responsibilities as other Canadians." See Indigenous Foundations, "The White Paper, 1969," indigenousfoundations.arts.ubc.ca/the_white_paper_1969/. Pierre Trudeau's dismissive position towards Indigenous Peoples is well illustrated in the late Justice Thomas Berger's memory of him speaking in Vancouver on August 8, 1969, and arguing that "We can't recognize Aboriginal rights because no society can be built on historical 'might-have-beens'" (*One Man's Justice: A Life in the Law* [Vancouver: Douglas & McIntyre, 2002], 114). For a groundbreaking history of the Express and its continuing impacts, see Emma Feltes's doctoral dissertation, *"We Don't Need Your Constitution": Patriation and Indigenous Self-Determination in British Columbia* (Ph.D. diss., UBC, 2021), hdl.handle .net/2429/80484.

4   See Jeremy Williams's documentaries, *Tsilhqot'in Journey for Justice*, parts 1, 2, and 3, on Exhibits U of T (University of Toronto Libraries) and YouTube: exhibits.library.utoronto. ca/items/show/2496 and youtu.be/QbjIPGqOaMs.

5   See the CEAA *Report of the Federal Review Panel: New Prosperity Gold-Copper Mine Project, Taseko Mine Ltd., British Columbia*, October 31, 2013, CEAA reference no. 63928, www.ceaa-acee.gc.ca/050/documents/p63928/95631E.pdf.

6   See James Anaya, "Statement upon Conclusion of the Visit to Canada" (blog entry), October 15, 2013, unsr.jamesanaya.org/?p=1035.

7   Elder Francis Sammy William explained at trial that, "when that person [the Qaju] died, the power comes back to the one that had put that power on the person [the Tŝilhqot'in deyen healer]. It's just like your vision, the power that you have. Wherever your power goes, you see what's happening. Because his power's on the Qaju, when he's telling the story, he's actually seeing him [the Qaju] tell the story. Then when he finished, that's when he [the Tŝilhqot'in deyen healer] kill him; his power come back" (*William v. British Columbia et al.*, proceedings at trial, day 118, May 26, 2004, para. 22, 28–31; trans. Agnes Haller). *Qaju* is the Tŝilhqot'in term for Xwémalhkwu (Homalco) and Kwakiutl people.

8   Cindy English mentions the involvement of several other groups and individuals, as well as her own work and the crucial networking and liaising work which Jack Woodward undertook in order to make the Title case possible.

9   Jonaki Bhattacharyya, *Cultural and Social-Ecological Significance of the Region Surrounding Teztan Biny (Fish Lake) to the Xeni Gwet'in and other Tsilhqot'in Nations Relevant to Environmental Impacts of the Proposed "New Prosperity" Mine*, report submitted for the August 1, 2013, CEAA Review hearings, July 24, 2013, iaac-aeic.gc.ca/050/documents /p63928/91955E.pdf.

10   These presentations are available at Friends of the Nemaiah Valley, "Research and Readings," fonv.ca/fishlake/researchandreadings/.

11   Working with Woodward and Company, Jay Nelson served as Co-Counsel for the Plaintiff at trial and in the appeals argued before the BC Court of Appeal and the Supreme Court of Canada. He has served more recently as General Counsel to the Tŝilhqot'in National Government.

12   Mandell Pinder LLP, "Tsilhqot'in Nation v. British Columbia 2014 SCC 44 – Case Summary," June 27, 2014, www.mandellpinder.com/tsilhqotin-nation-v-british-columbia-2014-scc-44 -case-summary/. Quoted with permission.

13   Online: www2.gov.bc.ca/assets/gov/environment/natural-resource-stewardship/consulting -with-first-nations/agreements/lou_tsilhqotin_xenigwetin.pdf.

14   The eight signatory First Nations are: the Nisgaʼa, sc̓əwaθən məsteyəxʷ (Tsawwassen First Nation), ɬaʔəmɛn (Tlaʼamin) Nation, Huuʕiiʔatḥ (Huu-ay-aht) First Nations, Ka:ʼyu:ʼk't'h'/ Che:k'tles7et'h' (Kyuquot/Checleseht) First Nations, ƛukʷaaʔatḥ (Toquaht) Nation, Ḥuučuqƛisʔatḥ (Uchucklesaht) Tribe, and Yuułuʔiłʔatḥ Government (Ucluelet First Nation).

15   On October 19, 2015, the Conservatives were defeated, the Liberals won, and Justin Trudeau became Prime Minister.

16   See Tŝilhqot'in National Government, "Xeni ʔeguh jid Nitŝegugheniʔan," www.tsilhqotin .ca/wp-content/uploads/2020/11/Nemiah_Declaration_Tsilhqotin.pdf.

17   For the full text of the "Nenqay Deni Accord: The People's Accord," see Tŝilhqot'in National Government, www.tsilhqotin.ca/wp-content/uploads/2021/01/Nenqay_Deni_Accord.pdf.

18   Here is Chief Justice McLachlin's wording: "50. The claimant group bears the onus of establishing Aboriginal title. The task is to identify how pre-sovereignty rights and interests can properly find expression in modern common law terms. In asking whether Aboriginal title is established, the general requirements are: (1) 'sufficient occupation' of the land claimed to establish title at the time of assertion of European sovereignty; (2) continuity of occupation where present occupation is relied on; and (3) exclusive historic occupation. In determining what constitutes sufficient occupation, one looks to the Aboriginal culture and practices, and compares them in a culturally sensitive way with what was required at common law to establish title on the basis of occupation. Occupation sufficient to ground Aboriginal title is not confined to specific sites of settlement but extends to tracts of land that were regularly used for hunting, fishing or otherwise exploiting resources and over which the group exercised effective control at the time of assertion of European sovereignty ... 88. In summary, Aboriginal title confers on the group that holds it the exclusive right to decide how the land is used and the right to benefit from those uses, subject to one carve-out – that the uses must be consistent with the group nature of the interest and the enjoyment of the land by future generations. Government incursions not consented to by the title-holding

group must be undertaken in accordance with the Crown's procedural duty to consult and must also be justified on the basis of a compelling and substantial public interest, and must be consistent with the Crown's fiduciary duty to the Aboriginal group" (*Tsilhqot'in Nation v. British Columbia*, 2014 SCC 44, 50 and 88).

19 "Tsilhqot'in Case Is Not a Template for Resolving All First Nations Land Disputes," Business in Vancouver (website), July 7, 2014, biv.com/article/2014/07/tsilhqotin-case-is-not-a-template-for-resolving-al.

20 Writing for the Court, Chief Justice McLachlin stated that, "In my view, the concepts of sufficiency, continuity and exclusivity provide useful lenses through which to view the question of Aboriginal title. This said, the court must be careful not to lose or distort the Aboriginal perspective by forcing ancestral practices into the square boxes of common law concepts, thus frustrating the goal of faithfully translating pre-sovereignty Aboriginal interests into equivalent modern legal rights. Sufficiency, continuity and exclusivity are not ends in themselves, but inquiries that shed light on whether Aboriginal title is established" (*Tsilhqot'in Nation v. British Columbia*, 2014 SCC 44, 32).

21 First Voices (www.firstvoices.com) is "an online space for Indigenous communities to share and promote their language, oral culture, and linguistic history. Language teams work with Elders to curate and upload audio recordings, dictionaries, stories, and songs." Tŝilhqot'in is represented by the Xeni Gwet'in language app and is the work of linguist June Williams (Xeni Gwet'in) with the Jeni Huten Language Committee. The app, along with many other Indigenous linguistic apps, is published by the First Peoples' Heritage Language and Culture Council.

22 The federal Department of Indian Affairs and Northern Development (DIA) was restructured in 2017, becoming in 2019 two new departments: Indigenous Services Canada and Crown-Indigenous Relations and Northern Affairs Canada.

23 Alluding to the plastic polygons used to mark maps on the courtroom wall during the Title case trial.

24 Gilbert's reference to the classic song "Whole Lotta Shakin' Goin' On" incorporates his years as a musician into this ecological prophecy.

ʔElheh ʔadidinsh

We are telling the truth

Acknowledgments

Lorraine Weir

I am grateful to have had the opportunity to work with Ivor Myers during the last year of his life. Through his six recordings for this book, he left precious gifts and resources for the future. A brilliant and deeply learned Knowledge Holder, Ivor was also a poet at heart and he spoke with passion and eloquence. Witnessing Ivor's last journey, hearing him sing his song "Yatu" in ceremony, and listening to his words, including the Tŝilhqot'in saying which became the title of this book, changed my life forever. *Lha yudit'ih* is dedicated to Ivor's memory with love and gratitude.

In the early days of what became this project, I turned to my hən̓q̓əmin̓əm̓ teacher, sʔəyəɬəq Elder Larry Grant (xʷməθkʷəy̓əm), for advice. I had taken his traditional Salish teachings to heart and knew, as sʔəyəɬəq had often said, that when you get in a canoe, you have to paddle in the same direction as everyone else. I wasn't at all sure that it was appropriate for me to get in the canoe, let alone paddle, and I half expected to be told to wait on shore. Instead I heard him say, "We need all the help we can get. Do what it's in your heart to do." And so I did, though not without trepidation. The journey has been a long one and I have not returned to the place I left. Larry was the first to see some of what was ahead and to hold the canoe steady as I got in. Thank you, sʔəyəɬəq, for your faith in me. I hope I have lived up to your expectations.

For allowing me to be on the Xeni Gwet'in wagon trip, at Henry's Crossing every year, and present for events in Xeni, I'm grateful to Chief Roger and to Nits'ilʔin Jimmy Lulua (in office from February 2018 to February 2023) and to everyone in the community. To all of the people who made recordings for this book, I'm honoured and grateful to have had the opportunity to work with you. Your memories and stories, your courage and your eloquence are the heart of *Lha yudit'ih* and I hope you feel that I've taken good care of what you shared. Your words truly have the power to change the world and I'm humbled by your wisdom and eloquence. Over the decade of this project, many participants went to the spirit world and I want to acknowledge them and their families here: Elder Ubill Lulua xinli, Elder Martin Quilt xinli, Elder Mabel Solomon xinli,

April William xinli, Elder Cecile William xinli, Elder Marvin William xinli, Elder Mabel Williams xinli. May their words in this book be a blessing for their families and community.

Thanks to Jim and Dinah Lulua for always making me feel at home in Xeni and to Elder Mabel Solomon xinli for being the strongest and most courageous of role models. Dinah's patience and friendship made all the difference on many long days and I'm grateful for her insight and humour. Thank you to Roland, Udette, and Jesaja Class for your hospitality at the beginning of the journey.

Thank you to Maria Myers for the gift of working on the translation of Elder Henry Solomon's smallpox story Se ʔintsu, which is at the centre of this book, and for heartfelt words about languages and worlds in collision. Thank you to Dr. Patricia Shaw, Director of the BC Breath of Life Archival Institute for Indigenous Language Revitalization, for making Maria's week at the University of British Columbia possible. Thank you to Ben Chung, Karen Ng, and Zakir Jamal Suleman for helping. I'm grateful to all of the community linguists and translators who contributed to this project: Dinah Lulua, Dorrine Lulua, Margaret Lulua, Maria Myers, Linda R. Smith, Maryann Solomon, June Williams, Lois Williams. Thank you for your patience, hard work, and dedication to the language. This project would not have been possible without you. Special thanks to Maryann Solomon for going above and beyond at the end of the project and for dealing with endless "picky" questions!

To all the Tŝilhqot'in women who explained things to me, my thanks: Dinah Lulua, Catherine Haller, Betty Lulua, Rita Lulua Meldrum, Eila Quilt, Linda R. Smith, Shannon Stump, April William xinli, and Lois Williams. I'm grateful to Jay Nelson for many conversations about work over the years. Over the course of many collegial lunches, Tom Swanky shared with me his vast knowledge of Tŝilhqot'in history, and I'm grateful for his contributions to this book and for his support from the beginning. I regret that my colleague Wes Pue didn't live to see this book, which he encouraged from its initial stages. Thank you to the late Alasdair Bradley for believing, to the late Connie Fife for opening a door, to Robin for teaching courage, and to Sean Whonnock for humour and good advice. Thank you to my colleague Leslie Robertson for telling me to read Keith Basso and for always supporting this project.

I'm grateful to all of the individuals and families who have given us permission to include photographs of themselves and their relatives. Thanks to all the photographers who've allowed us to use their beautiful images here: Roland Class, Jesaja Class, Laureen Carruthers, Maryann Solomon, Chiʔela William, and Jeremy Williams. I'm grateful to Jeremy Williams for generously donating his time and skills to record the Elders' visit to MOA (the Museum of Anthropology at UBC) in September 2016 and for allowing us to use some of his Title case archive photos in this book. Thank you to Jesaja Class for restoring life to archival photographs and creating beautiful new ones. Thank you to Betty Lulua and Sage Birchwater for archival photos. And thank you to the Burke Museum of Natural History and Culture, Seattle, for permission to include the images of baskets which I showed to the Elders in Xeni. Thanks to Shawn Swanky for permission to use his smallpox map, to Friends of the Nemaiah Valley for their map of Title Land, and to Carol Linnitt and the *Narwhal* for their map of Teẑtan Biny.

I'm grateful to Carolyn Sadowska for permission to reproduce her painting of the temporary courtroom in Xeni. For permission to reprint and translate Elder Henry Solomon xinli's story Se ʔintsu, I'm indebted to Dinah Lulua for the Solomon family. For permission to reprint his morphological translation of Nenduwh jid guẑit'in the Declaration, I'm grateful to Dr. David Dinwoodie.

I want to acknowledge grants from the Hampton Foundation, UBC Arts HSS, SSHRC, and UBC's Office of the Vice-President, Research and Innovation in support of travel, equipment, and translation costs. This book would not have been possible without the support we received. For support for the visit of Xeni Gwet'in Elders to MOA in September 2016, I'm grateful to Dr. Susan Rowley, Pam Brown, and Gerald Lawson at MOA, Dr. Daniel Heath Justice and the Institute for Critical Indigenous Studies at UBC, Dr. Linc Kesler and the First Nations House of Learning at UBC, and Dr. Siân Echard and the UBC Department of English Language and Literatures. This project was conducted with certification from the UBC Behavioural Research Ethics Board.

To the people who read *Lha yudit'ih* in draft, thank you for your time, comments, and encouragement. I am indebted to Sage Birchwater, Gene Cooper, Cindy English, Alex Leslie, Meredith Quartermain, Nits'ilʔin Russell Myers Ross, and David Williams. Sage transformed the draft into a conversation on Messenger and made it real for the first time. Later he helped with innumerable details. Gene also helped with details as well as liaising with people. Cindy wrote pages of analysis, catching mistakes and drawing on her own detailed memories of events she'd been part of. David's comments arrived like an unexpected gift at

Christmas, and Meredith brought both legal and poetic skills to a careful read of the whole manuscript, sending me reports of her experience and inspiring renewed confidence. Russ struggled with an impossible schedule so he could make good on his promise years earlier to read the whole draft. Tom Swanky provided generous and detailed assistance with the history of smallpox in the Tŝilhqot'in and with the Tŝilhqot'in War. Gary Geddes helped with residential school history. Later in the process, editors Charles Simard and Catriona Strang brought meticulous attention to every detail of the book, editor Alicia Hibbert (Métis) helped to fine-tune the whole manuscript, and Erin Kirsh helped with illustrations and captions. From the moment I first presented the project to our publisher, Kevin Williams of Talonbooks, he supported it wholeheartedly and has been a model of patience and commitment through the many years of preparation of the book. It took one village to create *Lha yudit'ih* as an oral history and another one to transform it into this book. Making a decade-long journey from one to the other has been my great privilege and I thank everyone who has been involved in it.

Special thanks to my collaborator, Chief Roger William, whose patience and good humour were sometimes sorely tried by the vagaries of dealing with writing and publishing but whose energy never failed. We survived challenges which neither of us could have foreseen in 2012 when we first discussed this project – from wildfire to significant changes in the political climate in the Tŝilhqot'in to the impact of the pandemic on communities and on this project. Thankfully, neither of us wavered in our sense of the importance of the Title case, of this book, and of all the stories shared with us. It has been an honour, a profound learning experience, and a gift to create this book with Roger.

Thank you to the late Caterina Geuer and to Sage Birchwater for debriefing with me in Williams Lake and supporting my work from the beginning. At crucial moments, Sage reminded me that my urban academic background made some things more difficult, and he was right. I will miss Caterina's stalwart commitment to this project and her gentle understanding. Thank you to Alex Leslie for listening to thousands of stories, surviving lonely weeks and months, and navigating the huge changes which this project brought to our lives. Our dogs over the years – Adrian, Roo, Momo, Lucas, and Patrick – kept me company while I worked late into the night. In Xeni, Susie and Dennis Lulua's dog Shredder welcomed and looked after me every summer. Thank you to my sister Lorna Weir for endless confidence in my ability to change fields and undertake this project and for providing a quiet refuge to complete the editing. For support during the last months of the project, I am indebted to Jodey Castricano, Jason Chang, Joe Hetherington, Brandy Kawulka, Marieke Leliveld, Ellen McGinn, Nelia Tierney, Peter and Meredith Quartermain, and Lorna Weir. First and last, to my students over many years, thank you for inspiring hope in dark times and in bright ones.

Chief Roger William

There are so many people I would like to thank for making this all work. First and foremost, I want to thank my mother, Eileen Sammy William, my wife Shannon, my sons Colten (and his daughter Reyna Seniya, my grandbaby), Linden (his partner Lyndsay and their two boys and a girl, my grandbabies) and Liam, my daughter Chiʔela (Sierra), my father, the late Walter Stobie (his children and grandchildren, my brother and nieces and nephews), my auntie/mother, Madeline Setah (who delivered me with the help of grandfather Sambulyan) and all her children, whom I consider my siblings, my uncle Wilfred William xinli (and his children, grandchildren, and great-grandchildren), my brother Harry Setah xinli and Laura Setah (their children, grandchildren, and great-grandchildren – my nieces and nephews, including great-nieces and great-nephews), my brother Martin Sammy William xinli, my sister Agnes William (her children and grandchildren – my nieces and nephews), my sister Phyllis William (her children and grandbaby – my nieces and nephews and great-niece), my brother Gene Cooper (his children and grandchildren – my nieces and nephews), my brother David Setah (his children and grandchildren – my nieces and nephews and great-nieces and great-nephews), my brother Gerald Royce William (his son Malachi), my auntie Lucy (Sammy William) Lulua and her children Francy and Lillian, who stayed with us, helping my mom look after their parents and the ranch, and who are like family – my sisters and mom.

Others who have been a big part of my life or have influenced me include the Tŝilhqot'in Warriors, my great-great-grandfather Qaq'ez (older brother of my great-great-uncle Lhatŝ'assʔin), my grandparents Sambulyan (Sammy William and Annie Sammy William), my great-uncle Eagle Lake Henry xinli (ʔElegesi), great-uncle Billy Dag xinli, and uncles and aunts. I remember the families around me during my upbringing, helping my mom and auntie Lucy xinli with my grandparents and the ranch, like Uncle William Setah xinli (former Councillor) and Auntie Madeline (Sammy William) Setah xinli, their children Uncle Henry xinli (former Chief) and Mabel Solomon xinli, and their children Uncle Eddie Sr. xinli and Auntie Eliza (Sammy William) Quilt xinli, their children Uncle Eugene xinli and Auntie Mabel Williams xinli and their children, Uncle William (former Councillor) and Cecile xinli, Uncle Danny xinli (former Chief) and Cecile William xinli, Auntie Theresa, Uncle Donald xinli and Auntie Helena Myers xinli and children, and all my uncles and aunts, including Uncle Jimmy (former Councillor) xinli and Emilia Sammy William xinli and children, grandchildren, and great-grandchildren, Francis Sammy William and children, grandchildren, and great-grandchildren. There are also my uncles' and aunties' children or grandchildren like Madeline Myers xinli, Mary (Sammy William) Alphonse, Doris William (sons Blaine and Willard), Norman William, Juliana Lulua (her son Stanley Lulua), Francis Myers xinli, William Isnardy, Ivan Solomon xinli, Ronnie Solomon, Raymond Lulua (William and Cecile's son) xinli, Ivor Myers (former Chief) xinli, Rocky Quilt, Larry Quilt, and others like Christopher Haller xinli who lived with us, helping us out with ranching. Almost the whole community are my family one way or another, including traditional adoptions.

My sister Agnes inspired me, working for Xeni Gwet'in First Nations Government going on thirty-two years as education administrator. My sister Phyllis was our manager for more than twenty years and worked in finance in the Xeni Gwet'in First Nations Government for ten years. She also worked in our Tourism and Projects Centre. Both of my sisters are fluent in Tŝilhqot'in. My younger brother Gerald Royce William also inspires me, as he does all the hunting and fishing for our family, and he worked for TNG Fisheries for at least ten years. James and Dinah Lulua (our BC Elders Gathering King and Queen, 2016) were a big part of my upbringing, helping us out and taking us to hockey and rodeo. Thank you to Dennis and Susie Lulua for always helping. Susie got her early childhood education training and taught Tŝilhqot'in immersion in our Charlene William Daycare, where no English is spoken at all. She and her sister Selina Myers took the children out on the Land camping and learning how we used the Land.

My late brother Harry Setah and his wife Laura Setah used to help me with rodeo and hockey. My whole upbringing was hanging out with and learning from my brothers Gene Cooper and David Setah, and I thank them for that. I learned a lot with them, and they kept me from being bullied when I was a child. Gene was the youngest to get on Council at nineteen years old, while still in high school. He was back on Council with me as Chief, and then left to work with the Cariboo-Chilcotin Justice Inquiry and Commissioner Anthony Sarich.

He was then hired at Tŝilhqot'in National Government, dealing with forestry. A lot of Gene's work was part of our evidence at trial. David was a long-time Councillor, working with me for fifteen years on the Brittany Triangle forest management plan and Natasewed Forest Products, experience which was part of his testimony at trial. David also worked as our Tŝ'ilʔos Parks Ranger and ʔElegesi Qayus Wild Horse Ranger, and he was a long-time Councillor. Thank you to former Councillors Gilbert Solomon, Robin Lulua, and Alex Lulua, who were on Council with me prior to filing our Title and Rights case and going to court and with Gene and David contributed to the filing and the five-year trial.

Thank you to my brother Harry Setah xinli, who was our first Tŝ'ilʔos Parks Ranger and ʔElegesi Qayus Wild Horse Ranger, working with residents, lodges, guiding outfits, trappers, and tenure holders. A lot of Harry's work was part of his testimony in court for the Title case. Gilbert Solomon got our Ts'utanchuny Dadabeni Medicine Camp going with Edmund Faubert, David Faubert, and Juanita Cervantes. They built a Lhiz qwen yex Tŝilhqot'in earthlodge (pithouse). Gilbert testified about the Medicine Camp in court. We also did a lot of ceremonies for our legal fight there.

I would like to thank Patrick Lulua, who is fluent in Tŝilhqot'in language, culture, ceremonies, and drumming. I rodeoed with him in his later years, and he was the one who turned me around in riding/bucking/cow riding which translated into my being a good bull rider for fifteen years. Thank you to Annie S. William, who is like my sister, as her mom Madeline Setah xinli delivered me with the help of her father Sambulyan when my mom went into labour while raking hay with team horses. Annie worked with me during my leadership, doing reception and finance, and then in finance at CCATEC (Cariboo Chilcotin Aboriginal Training Employment Centre) during my time as board member and president.

In my role as Chief and leader, I want to thank all our past Chiefs and Councillors in Xeni Gwet'in and our managers and staff. Thank you to our former Chief Marvin Baptiste xinli for meeting with the trappers and amalgamating our Xeni Gwet'in Trapline. Without that, our Trapline Case and our Aboriginal Title and Rights case and trial would never have started. He also got the school – now known as Naghataneqed School – started in Xeni. This is what saved me from a fourth year in residential school. I was schooled in Xeni from grade four to grade nine. What a blessing!

Chief Marvin also brought in George Colgate, first as long-time manager for the Nemiah Valley Indian Band (Xeni Gwet'in First Nations Government), then to start our Xeni Gwet'in Enterprise, and now as our consultant finishing off what we had him start in Green Energy. Thank you George Colgate for getting XGE (Xeni Gwet'in Enterprise) going strong, maintaining roads, water (water line to the west end of Nemiah Valley), electrifying Tl'ebayi community, being hands-on in getting underground wire to the west end, and eventually powering us all up across Nemiah Valley. All of this work was part of our win.

Thank you to former Chief Adam William, as he led the charge from Xeni Gwet'in to Ottawa, along with Indigenous Nations across Canada, to bring our Aboriginal Rights and Title into the Constitution of Canada, and for helping us bring forward the Nemiah Aboriginal Preserve for our people. Thank you to former Chief Benny William, who ensured that our people were heard about not wanting BC Hydro. Benny brought many homes to our community, working with our portable sawmill and bringing fuel and groceries to our people. He and former Chief Adam William started the building housing our community offices and hall and had it up and running by 1984.

Thank you to Annie C. Williams, who was Councillor before being our first woman Chief and was on Council again after her Chieftainship. Together with former Chief Adam William and myself as Councillor, she started the Nenduwh jid guẑit'in Nemiah Valley Aboriginal Preserve Declaration (August 23, 1989) at the direction of the Elders. She has also been our Xeni Gwet'in First Nations Government Manager, Xeni Gwet'in Enterprise Manager, TNG Executive Director, and our present ʔEniyud Health Service Director.

Thank you to Marilyn Baptiste, our first second-generation Chief (her father was Chief Marvin Baptiste xinli) and our second woman Chief. With her partner Emery Phillips and niece Marie Williams xinli, she stopped Taseko Mines Ltd. (TML) from drilling at Teẑtan Biny, forcing them to work with us. Through our legal team, we forced TML to provide funding to our Nation as part of our costs in the CEAA Panel Hearings in 2010 (when she was Chief) and 2013 (when she was a Councillor).

Thank you to former Councillors Lois Williams, Chris Williams, and Loretta Williams, who were in leadership after our five-year trial win. We were still in negotiations and doing appeal cases during their leadership, and they were part of all that.

Thank you to Cindy English, who started Friends of Nemiah Valley to fundraise for us, worked with our Xeni Gwet'in Elders and members doing traditional-use and Land-use studies, including a traditional-use study on Teẑtan Biny Fish Lake, and testified at the CEAA hearings in 2010 and 2013 to protect Teẑtan Biny. She also connected us with Assembly of First Nations (AFN) Chief Ovide Mercredi, who funded us to force Carrier Lumber to make an out-of-court settlement where they stayed out of our trapline for five years.

Thank you to David Williams, who took over FONV and helped us fundraise for the Title case, protect Teẑtan Biny, and get Dasiqox Nexwagweẑʔan Tribal Park going. David also fundraised for the ʔElegesi Qayus Wild Horse Preserve. I also want to thank all the Indigenous Peoples, communities, Nations, and organizations like the Union of BC Indian Chiefs (UBCIC), the AFN, the BCAFN, and the BC First Nations Summit for all your lobbying, direct actions, meetings, and negotiations and for intervening in our Supreme Court of Canada hearing in Ottawa on November 7, 2013.

Thank you to the Western Canada Wilderness Committee, the Lannan Foundation, and the David Suzuki Foundation for support in funding and media. Thank you to the Council of Canadians and the Chilko Resorts and Community Association for their work as interveners in our Supreme Court of Canada hearing.

Thank you to Woodward & Company and Jack Woodward. Jack sacrificed a lot when our Xeni Gwet'in community couldn't afford payments for long stretches at a time. Thank you to his team, including Murray Browne, Gary Campo, Patricia Hutchings, Heather Mahony, Drew Mildon, Jay Nelson (who also took on our Teẑtan Biny case pro bono and worked as our lead negotiator at the TNG level), Sean Nixon, Dominique Nouvet, David M. Robbins, Renee Racette, and David Rosenberg and Paul Rosenberg of Rosenberg & Rosenberg.

Thank you to all our expert witnesses, including Dr. David Dinwoodie, who stayed in our community for a couple of years doing fieldwork for his Ph.D. dissertation in anthropology; to ethnobotanist Dr. Nancy Turner for her testimony at trial and all her work in support of the protection of Teẑtan Biny Fish Lake; and to Dr. Jonaki Bhattacharyya for her work with FONV, her dissertation on our Qayus wild horses, and her work on the Dasiqox Nexwagweẑʔan team.

Thank you to TNG Executive Director and Tribal Chair Joe Alphonse of Tl'etinqox, who stood behind us in Xeni Gwet'in, getting TNG Chiefs onside to support us. He was a big part of my getting hired as TNG Tŝilhqot'in Stewardship Director to deal with the 2007 decision in the Title case, the 2008 negotiations, and the 2009 TNG Consultation Framework Agreement that eventually became the Stewardship Agreement. He also helped deal with the protection of Teẑtan Biny. I want to thank former TNG Tribal Chair Chief Ervin Charleyboy and Chief Percy Guichon of Tŝideldel; Chief Thomas Billyboy, Doris Baptiste and Chief Bernie Elkins Mack of ʔEsdilagh; Councillors Leslie Stump and Cecil Grinder of Tl'etinqox; Chief Lloyd Myers, who testified at trial, and Chief Ivor Myers xinli of Yuneŝit'in; and Warren Houde and Chief Francis Laceese of Tl'esqox for his leadership and support on the Tŝilhqot'in Title win journey. Chief Francis was Chief during our Henry's Crossing roadblock, the trial, the appeals, and the win at the Supreme Court of Canada. The Tŝilhqot'in National Government has given him the title of International Chief since the Title case win, and Chief Francis continues to do a lot of international work. Thanks also to former TNG Executive Director Crystal Verhaeghe for the hard work, planning, and organizing throughout and for the Title Lands win. Thank you to J.P. Laplante for technical support, planning, meetings, and organizing, including protection of Teẑtan Biny.

Thank you to Ray Hance, former Chief of Tl'esqox, who was our TNG Executive Director and TNG Vice-Chief leading up to the Title case, and for his support technically and politically in our two-month roadblock in 1991, the Chilko Study that eventually became Tŝ'ilʔos Parks, and the fight to protect Teẑtan Biny during the early stages in the 1990s. Thanks also to the late Brian Mayne, who was Ray Hance's writer and had strong writing skills. Thank you to former Chief Tony Myers of Yuneŝit'in who was instrumental in having us use his TNG TUS (Traditional-use study) in the Supreme Court of BC. Thanks to writer and editor Don Wise for *Wolf Howls: Tŝilhqot'in Nation Journal*, a newspaper which circulated for many years and covered the Henry's Crossing roadblock and the beginning of protecting Teẑtan Biny.

Thank you to our Xeni Gwet'in leadership between February 2018 and February 2023: Chief Jimmy Lulua, Councillor James Lulua Jr., and Councillor Margaret Lulua. Thank you to former Chief Russell Myers Ross, who got his M.A. and became Chief of Yuneŝit'in during the Title trial. After our Title win, he was the Technical Chief with our negotiators and technical team, working closely on negotiations agreements that lead up to the Nenqay Deni Accord Agreement with BC. Chief Russ, along with me and former Chief Marilyn Baptiste, was a big part of getting Dasiqox Nexwagweẑʔan (Dasiqox Tribal Park) going.

Last but not least, thank you to Dr. Lorraine Weir, UBC professor (now emeritus professor), who has done amazing work on this book. I am very impressed with what she has put together. Lorraine has studied our Title case and knows it well. I met her at Lee's Corner in 2012 when Pam Quilt introduced us. I was a Councillor at that time and Marilyn Baptiste was Chief. Marilyn invited Lorraine to come out to our Xeni Gwet'in office a couple of days later, and during our meeting, Marilyn mentioned that I had always wanted to write a book about the Title case. Lorraine gave us her background of the Nation she comes from (fifth-generation Irish Canadian) and the colonial history there. We decided to work together on this project.

Lorraine interviewed me about the Title case over several years, starting in June 2013 during the Canadian Environmental Assessment Agency's review panel hearing on Teẑtan Biny Fish Lake. A year or so later, I asked her to interview Xeni Gwet'ins and Tŝilhqot'in Elders, People, and Leaders of our Title case journey. Wow, it's now going on ten years, and Lorraine has finished *Lha yudit'ih* after three years of pandemic. That could have been a blessing in disguise, as it kept her home working on the book! We are very different people, and we debated a lot during our interviews. She was able to get very good information from the people she interviewed. I read the whole draft several times, and some of what our people shared surprised me – very powerful and sometimes sacred information about what we as Tŝilhqot'ins have gone through and are still going through. It is important that all of these stories and this information be written down for future generations, especially as many of the people who contributed to this book are now in the spirit world.

I hope that *Lha yudit'ih* will spark more stories and inspire more Indigenous Peoples and Nations to have hope and move forward on their journeys towards recognition and strengthening their cultures. And I hope that non-Indigenous people who read this book will learn from our stories of what we have been through and be inspired by our fight for our Aboriginal Rights and Title and for our Lands, water, and resources.

Neither Chief Roger William nor Lorraine Weir received any remuneration for their contributions to this book. All royalties from the sale of this book will be donated to Lha yudit'ih Seniya Tŝilhqot'in Ch'ish Yats'elhtig Qa The Lha Yudit'ih Fund for Tŝilhqot'in Language, Xeni Gwet'in First Nation.

Chronology

1846
Oregon Boundary Treaty, accepted by the Court in *Tsilhqot'in Nation v. British Columbia* as the date of British "sovereignty assertion" in British Columbia.

June 1862 to January 1863
Over 70 percent of all Tŝilhqot'ins died of smallpox.

1864
The Tŝilhqot'in War.

October 26, 1864
Head War Chief Lhatŝ'assʔin, Chief Biyil, Chief Tilaghed, Chief Taqed, and Chief Chayses executed.

July 18, 1865
Chief Ahan executed.

May 2, 1984
A Declaration of Sovereignty (General Assembly of the Chilcotin Nation).

August 23, 1989
Nenduwh jid guẑit'in Nemiah Declaration.

April 18, 1990
Nemiah Trapline Action commenced.

May 7, 1992
Henry's Crossing Roadblock commenced.

December 11, 1997
Delgamuukw v. British Columbia (3 SCR 1010).

December 18, 1998
Brittany Triangle (Tachelach'ed) Action commenced. The Trapline case.

November 18, 2002, to April 7, 2007
William v. British Columbia et al. 339-day trial commenced in Victoria and five weeks in 2003 at the Naghataneqed Elementary School at Tl'ebayi in Xeni.

December 11, 2003
Deadline for First Nations to file Title case writs per *Delgamuukw*.

November 20, 2007
Justice David Vickers delivers his decision (*Tsilhqot'in Nation v. British Columbia*, 2007 BCSC 1700).

November 15–22, 2010
BC Court of Appeal hearing, Vancouver.

July 2, 2010
Report of the Federal Review Panel, Prosperity Gold-Copper Mine Project.

June 27, 2012
BC Court of Appeal decision (*William v. British Columbia*, 2012 BCCA 285).

October 31, 2013
Report of the Federal Review Panel, New Prosperity Gold-Copper Mine Project.

October 30 to November 6, 2013
Title Case Express, Williams Lake to Ottawa.

November 7, 2013
Supreme Court of Canada hearing.*

June 26, 2014
Supreme Court of Canada decision (*Tsilhqot'in Nation v. British Columbia*, 2014 SCC 44).

September 10, 2014
Letter of Understanding to achieve reconciliation.

October 23, 2014
Apology by BC Premier Christy Clark for the wrongful hanging of the Tŝilhqot'in War Chiefs and exoneration of them.

February 11, 2016
Nenqay Deni Accord signed.

November 2, 2018
Prime Minister Justin Trudeau's exoneration of the Tŝilhqot'in War Chiefs unjustly hanged in 1864.

---

* Webcast of the hearing available on the Supreme Court of Canada website: www.scc-csc .ca/case-dossier/info/webcastview-webdiffusionvue-eng.aspx?cas=34986&id=2013/2013 -11-07--34986&date=2013-11-07&fp=n&audio=n.

The Twenty-Nine Tŝilhqot'in Witnesses at Trial

An asterisk denotes the name of a witness who is now in the spirit world.

Witnesses

Thomas Billyboy (ʔEsdilagh)

Chief Ervin Charleyboy (Tŝideldel)

Minnie Charleyboy (Tŝideldel)

*Christine Cooper (Tl'etinqox)

*Patricia Guichon (Tŝideldel)

*Ubill Hunlin (Xeni Gwet'in)

*Elizabeth Jeff (Tŝideldel)

David Lulua (Xeni Gwet'in)

*Doris Lulua (Xeni Gwet'in)

*Theophile Ubill Lulua xinli (Xeni Gwet'in)

Lloyd Myers (Yuneŝit'in)

*Cecelia Quilt (Yuneŝit'in)

*Julie Quilt (Yuneŝit'in)

*Martin Quilt (Xeni Gwet'in)

David Setah (Xeni Gwet'in)

*Francis Setah (Xeni Gwet'in)

*Harry Setah (Xeni Gwet'in)

*Norman George Setah (Yuneŝit'in)

Gilbert Solomon (Xeni Gwet'in)

*Francis Sammy William (Xeni Gwet'in)

*Joseph William (Xeni Gwet'in)

*Mabel William (Xeni Gwet'in)

Chief Roger William (Xeni Gwet'in)

Annie C. Williams (Xeni Gwet'in)

Affidavits

*Patrick Alphonse (Tl'esqox)

*Amelia Hunlin (Xeni Gwet'in)

*Agnes Pigeon (Tl'etinqox)

*William Setah (Xeni Gwet'in)

*Eliza William (Tŝideldel)

List of Interviewees for *Lha yudit'ih*

Unless otherwise noted, each interviewee and/or their representative gave consent for publication of edited excerpts from their interview(s) in *Lha yudit'ih*. The number of interviews given by each person is listed after their name. If materials were not used from interviews and consent was not requested, the names of those interviewees are preceded by the sign •.

Tŝilhqot'ins

- • Wesley Alphonse (Tl'etinqox) – 1

Marilyn Baptiste (Xeni Gwet'in) – 2

Joyce Charleyboy (Tsideldel) – 1

Gene Cooper (Xeni Gwet'in) – 1

Catherine Haller (Xeni Gwet'in) – 2

Betty Lulua (Xeni Gwet'in) – 1

Dinah Lulua (Xeni Gwet'in) – 2

James Lulua Sr. (Xeni Gwet'in) – 2

Patrick Lulua (Xeni Gwet'in) – 1

Susie Lulua (Xeni Gwet'in) – 1

Elder Ubill Lulua xinli with Margaret Lulua (Xeni Gwet'in) – 1

- • Chief Bernie Elkins Mack (ʔEsdilagh) – 1

Rita Lulua Meldrum (Xeni Gwet'in) – 2

Ivor Deneway Myers xinli (Yuneŝit'in) – 6

Maria Myers (Yuneŝit'in) – 5-day workshop

Eila Quilt (Xeni Gwet'in) – 2

Martin Quilt xinli (Xeni Gwet'in) – 1

Nits'ilʔin Russell Myers Ross (Yuneŝit'in) – 1

Laura Setah (Xeni Gwet'in) – 1

Trina Setah (Xeni Gwet'in) – 1

David Setah (Xeni Gwet'in) – 1

Gilbert Solomon (Xeni Gwet'in) – 3

Elder Mabel Solomon xinli with Dinah Lulua (Xeni Gwet'in) – 2

Maryann Solomon (Xeni Gwet'in) – 2

Ronnie Solomon (Xeni Gwet'in) – 1

Shannon Stump (Xeni Gwet'in) – 1

Benny William (Xeni Gwet'in) – 1

Elder Cecile William xinli with Dorrine Lulua (Xeni Gwet'in) – 1

Elder Eileen Sammy William with April William xinli (Xeni Gwet'in) – 1

Elder Marvin William xinli (Xeni Gwet'in) – 1

Lois Williams (Xeni Gwet'in) – 2

Elder Mabel Williams xinli with June Williams (Xeni Gwet'in) – 1

Allies

George and Marg Colgate – 1

Cindy English – 1

David Williams and Pat Swift – 1

Table of Contents by Name

Table of Contents by Name 429

Bibliography

LEGAL CASES

Carrier Lumber Ltd. v. British Columbia, (1999) 18 B.C.T.C. 241 (SC)

Delgamuukw v. British Columbia, (1997) 3 S.C.R. 1010

Tsilhqot'in Nation v. British Columbia, 2007 BCSC 1700

Tsilhqot'in Nation v. British Columbia, 2014 SCC 44

William et al. v. British Columbia et al., 2004 BCSC 148

William v. British Columbia et al., Proceedings at Trial, 2004–2005

William v. British Columbia, 2012 BCCA 285

DECHEN TS'EDILHTAN TŜILHQOT'IN LAW

General Assembly of the Chilcotin Nation. *A Declaration of Sovereignty.* May 2, 1984. www
.tsilhqotin.ca/wp-content/uploads/2020/12/1983_Agreement_GeneralAsseblyofTN
_DeclarationSovereignty.pdf. Revised in 1992: see *Wolf Howls: The Tsilhqot'in Nation Journal*,
October 1997, sisis.nativeweb.org/tsilhqotin/oct97dec.html.

Tŝilhqot'in Nation. *Nenduwh Jid Guzitin Declaration: Nemiah Aboriginal Wilderness Preserve.*
Friends of the Nemaiah Valley. www.fonv.ca/nemaiahvalley/nenduwhjidguzitindeclaration/.

———. *ʔElhdaqox Dechen Ts'edilhtan / ʔEsdilagh Sturgeon River Law.* May 27–28, 2020. www
.esdilagh.com/PDF/Esdilagh%20Elhdaqox%20Law%20Final%20Version.pdf.

Tŝilhqot'in National Government. *Nenqay Deni Accord: The People's Accord.* February 11, 2016.
www.tsilhqotin.ca/wp-content/uploads/2021/01/Nenqay_Deni_Accord.pdf.

———. *Xeni ʔeguh jid Nits'egugheniʔan.* March 19, 2015. www.tsilhqotin.ca/wp-content
/uploads/2020/11/Nemiah_Declaration_Tsilhqotin.pdf.

OTHER REFERENCES

Abley. Mark. *Conversations with a Dead Man: The Legacy of Duncan Campbell Scott.* Vancouver:
Douglas & McIntyre, 2013.

Alphonse, Chief Joe. "When He Exonerated Six Tsilhqot'in War Chiefs, the Prime Minister
Recognized Our Truth." *McLean's*, November 14, 2018. macleans.ca/opinion/when-he
-exonerated-six-tsilhqotin-war-chiefs-the-prime-minister-recognized-our-truth/.

Anaya, James. "Statement upon Conclusion of the Visit to Canada." Personal blog entry, October 15, 2013. unsr.jamesanaya.org/?p=1035.

Archibald, Jo-ann, Q'um Q'um Xiiem. *Indigenous Storywork: Educating the Heart, Mind, Body, and Spirit.* Vancouver: UBC Press, 2008.

Basso, Keith. *Wisdom Sits in Places: Landscape and Language among the Western Apache.* Albuquerque: University of New Mexicow Press, 1996.

Berger, Thomas. *One Man's Justice: A Life in the Law.* Vancouver: Douglas & McIntyre, 2002.

Bhattacharyya, Jonaki. "Knowing *Naŝliny* (Horse), Understanding the Land: Free-Roaming Horses in the Culture and Ecology of the Brittany Triangle and Nemiah Valley." Ph.D. diss., University of Waterloo, 2012. hdl.handle.net/10012/6521.

Blondin, George. *Yamoria the Lawmaker: Stories of the Dene.* Northwest Passages series. Edmonton: NeWest Press, 1997.

Borrows, John. *Freedom and Indigenous Constitutionalism.* Toronto: University of Toronto Press, 2016.

———. *Law's Indigenous Ethics.* Toronto: University of Toronto Press, 2019.

Boyd, Robert. "Smallpox in the Pacific Northwest: The First Epidemics." *Anthropology Faculty Publications and Presentations* 141 (Spring 1994): 6–7. pdxscholar.library.pdx.edu/anth_fac/141.

———. *The Coming of the Spirit of Pestilence: Introduced Infectious Diseases and Population Decline among Northwest Coast Indians, 1774–1874.* Seattle: University of Washington Press with UBC Press, 1999.

Brealey, Ken. *Mapping Aboriginal Title: Tsilhqot'in v. British Columbia.* Slides presented at the PlaniTerre Conference in Mashteuiatsh, QC, April 19–20, 2017. First Nations of Quebec and Labrador Sustainable Development Institute (FNQLSDI) / Institut de développement durable des Premières Nations du Québec et du Labrador (IDDPNQL) (website). iddpnql.ca/wp-content/uploads/2019/02/02_Ken-Brealy_Planiterre-April-19-and-20_EN.pdf.

Brown, R.C. Lundin. *Klatsassan, and Other Reminiscences of Missionary Life in British Columbia.* London: Society for Promoting Christian Knowledge, 1873. doi.org/10.14288/1.0056091.

Business in Vancouver. "Tsilhqot'in Case Is Not a Template for Resolving All First Nations Land Disputes." July 7, 2014. biv.com/article/2014/07/tsilhqotin-case-is-not-a-template-for-resolving-al.

The Canadian Encyclopedia. "Timeline: Residential Schools." www.thecanadianencyclopedia.ca/en/timeline/residential-schools.

Canadian Environmental Assessment Agency (CEAA). *Report of the Federal Review Panel: New Prosperity Gold-Copper Mine Project, Taseko Mine Ltd., British Columbia.* October 31, 2013. CEAA reference no. 63928. www.ceaa-acee.gc.ca/050/documents/p63928/95631E.pdf.

———. *Report of the Federal Review Panel: Prosperity Gold-Copper Mine Project, Taseko Mines Ltd. British Columbia.* July 2, 2010. CEAA reference no. 09-05-44811. www.ceaa-acee.gc.ca/050/documents/46911/46911E.pdf.

Changing Vancouver. "1201 Pendrell Street" (archive for the "A J Buttimer" tag). Posted by user ChangingCity. January 18, 2018. changingvancouver.wordpress.com/tag/a-j-buttimer/.

Cheslatta Carrier Nation and British Columbia. "Interim Reconciliation Agreement." 2019. www2.gov
.bc.ca/assets/gov/environment/natural-resource-stewardship/consulting-with/firstnations
/agreements/cheslatta_interim_reconciliation_agreement_-_executed_-_20190328.pdf.

Churchill, Ward. *Kill the Indian, Save the Man: The Genocidal Impact of American Indian Residential Schools*. San Francisco: CityLights Publishers, 2004.

Cook, Eung-Do. *A Tsilhqút'ín Grammar*. First Nations Languages series. Vancouver: UBC Press, 2013.

Cruikshank, Julie, with Angela Sidney, Kitty Smith, and Annie Ned. *Life Lived like a Story: Life Stories of Three Yukon Native Elders*. Vancouver: UBC Press, 1990.

de Bruin, Tabitha, Michael Posluns, Anthony J. Hall, and David Gallant. "Assembly of First Nations." *Canadian Encyclopedia*. Historica Canada. Published February 07, 2006; last edited August 06, 2019. www.thecanadianencyclopedia.ca/en/article/assembly-of-first-nations.

Dickason, Olive Patricia, and William Newbigging. *Indigenous Peoples within Canada: A Concise History*, 4th ed. Toronto: Oxford University Press, 2018.

Dinwoodie, David W. *Reserve Memories: The Power of the Past in a Chilcotin Community*. Studies in the Anthropology of North American Indians series. Albuquerque: University of Nebraska Press with the American Indian Studies Research Institute at Indiana University, Bloomington, 2002.

Dufour, Lorne. *Jacob's Prayer: Loss and Resilience at Alkali Lake*. Halfmoon Bay [xwilkway]: Caitlin Press, 2009.

Dunbar-Ortiz, Roxanne. *An Indigenous People's History of the United States*. ReVisioning American History series. Boston: Beacon Press, 2015.

Duran, Eduardo, Tiospaye Ta Woapiye Wicasa. *Healing the Soul Wound: Trauma-Informed Counselling for Indigenous Communities*, 2nd ed. Multicultural Foundations of Psychology and Counseling series. New York: Teachers College Press, 2019.

Ehrhart-English, Cindy L. *The Heritage Significance of the Fish Lake Study Area: Ethnography*. Harmony Human and Environmental Studies, 1993–1994. www.ceaa-acee.gc.ca/050 /documents/p63928/87008E.pdf.

Farrand, Livingston. *Traditions of the Chilcotin Indians* (1900). In *Publications of the Jesup North Pacific Expedition*, vol. 2, part 1, *Ethnology and Archæology of Southern British Columbia and Washington*; *Memoirs of the American Museum of Natural History*, vol. 4, part 1. Edited by Franz Boas. Leiden: E.J. Brill; New York: G.E. Stechert and the American Museum of Natural History, 1900. hdl.handle.net/2246/39.

Feltes, Emma. "'We Don't Need Your Constitution': Patriation and Indigenous Self-Determination in British Columbia." Ph.D. diss., University of British Columbia, 2021. hdl.handle .net/2429/80484.

Fournier, Suzanne, and Ernie Crey. *Stolen from Our Embrace: The Abduction of First Nations Children and the Restoration of Aboriginal Communities* (Vancouver/Toronto: Douglas & McIntyre, 1998).

Furniss, Elizabeth. *Victims of Benevolence: The Dark Legacy of the Williams Lake Residential School*. Vancouver: Arsenal Pulp Press, 1992.

Gaadgas Nora Bellis with Jenny Nelson. *So You Girls Remember That: Memories of a Haida Elder.* Madeira Park, BC: Harbour Publishing, 2022.

Geddes, Gary. *Medicine Unbundled: A Journey through the Minefields of Indigenous Health Care.* Victoria: Heritage House, 2017.

George, Paul. *Big Trees Not Big Stumps: Years of Campaigning to Save Wilderness with the Wilderness Committee.* Vancouver: Western Canada Wilderness Committee, 2006.

Glavin, Terry, and the People of Nemiah Valley. *Nemiah: The Unconquered Country.* Vancouver: New Star Books, 1992.

Government of British Columbia, Department of Lands. *Water Powers: Fraser River.* Pamphlet. 1938. www.for.gov.bc.ca/hfd/library/documents/bib50649.pdf.

Government of Canada, Crown-Indigenous Relations and Northern Affairs Canada. "Common Experience Payments." Last modified April 22, 2013. www.rcaanc-cirnac.gc.ca/eng/1100100015594/1571582431348.

Greenwood, Margo, Sarah de Leeuw, Nicole Marie Lindsay, and Charlotte Reading, eds. *Determinants of Indigenous Peoples' Health*, 2nd ed. CSPI Series in Indigenous Studies. Toronto: Canadian Scholars' Press, 2018.

Haig-Brown, Helen, dir. *My Legacy.* 2014. 62 min.

Hanson, Erin, with Daniel P. Gamez and Alexa Manuel. "The Residential School System." Indigenous Foundations. 2009, updated 2020. indigenousfoundations.arts.ubc.ca/residential-school-system-2020/.

Hanna, Alan. "Going Circular: Indigenous Legal Research Methodology as Legal Practice." *McGill Law Journal / Revue de droit de McGill* 65, no. 4 (June 2020): 671–709. lawjournal.mcgill.ca/article/going-circular-indigenous-legal-research-methodology-as-legal-practice/.

———. "Dechen ts'edilhtan: Implementing Tŝilhqot'in Law for Watershed Governance." Ph.D. diss., University of Victoria, 2020. hdl.handle.net/1828/11933.

Harland, Fraser. "Taking the 'Aboriginal Perspective' Seriously: The (Mis)use of Indigenous Law in *Tsilhqot'in Nation v. British Columbia.*" *Indigenous Law Journal* 16/17, no. 1 (2018): 21–50. ilj.law.utoronto.ca/sites/ilj.law.utoronto.ca/files/users/enrightp/ILJ14_Fraser_Harland.pdf.

Henderson, William B. "The Indian Act, R.S.C. 1985, c. I-5 (Annotated)." Web page. Last modified January 15, 1996. www.bloorstreet.com/200block/sindact.htm.

Hogan, Linda. *Dwellings: A Spiritual History of the Living World.* New York: Simon & Schuster, 1995.

Hoogeveen, Dawn. "Geographies of Settler Colonial Dispossession: Rejecting Gold and Prosperity on Tsilhqot'in Territory." Ph.D. diss, University of British Columbia, 2016. hdl.handle.net/2429/57079.

Ignace, Marianne, and Ronald E. Ignace. *Secwépemc People, Land, and Laws / Yerí7 re Stsq̓ey̓s-kucw.* McGill-Queen's Indigenous and Northern Studies. Montréal and Kingston: McGill-Queen's University Press, 2017.

Indigenous Corporate Training Inc. "The Indian Act, Residential Schools and Tuberculosis Cover Up." May 17, 2016. www.ictinc.ca/blog/the-indian-act-residential-schools-and-tuberculosis-cover-up.

Jones, Esyllt. "Surviving Influenza: Lived Experiences of Health Inequity and Pandemic Disease in Canada." *Canadian Medical Association Journal (CMJA)* 192, no. 25 (June 22, 2020): E688–E689. doi.org/10.1503/cmaj.201074.

———. "Recollecting Influenza: Pandemic Disease, Health Inequity, and Social Change." With a poster by Karen Jeane Mills. Part of the Graphic History Collective's online Remember | Resist | Redraw: A Radical History Poster Project series. December 17, 2020. graphichistorycollective .com/project/poster-27-1918-1919-flu-pandemic.

Joseph, Bob. *21 Things You May Not Know about the Indian Act: Helping Canadians Make Reconciliation with Indigenous Peoples a Reality.* Vancouver: Indigenous Relations Press, 2018.

Joseph, Bob, with Cynthia E. Joseph, *Indigenous Relations: Insights, Tips & Suggestions to Make Reconciliation a Reality.* Vancouver: Indigenous Relations Press, 2019.

Kelm, Mary-Ellen. *Colonizing Bodies: Aboriginal Health and Healing in British Columbia, 1900–50.* Vancouver: UBC Press, 1998.

———. *A Wilder West: Rodeo in Western Canada.* Vancouver: UBC Press, 2011.

Kelm, Mary-Ellen, and Keith D. Smith. *Talking Back to the Indian Act: Critical Readings in Settler Colonial Histories.* Toronto: University of Toronto Press, 2018.

Kopecky, Arno. "Title Fight." *Walrus,* July 22, 2015; updated January 21, 2020. thewalrus.ca /title-fight/.

Kunkel, Titilope I. "Aboriginal Values, Sacred Landscapes and Resource Development in the Cariboo Chilcotin Region of BC." Ph.D. diss., Nizdeh Nekeyoh Hohudel'eh Baiyoh University of Northern British Columbia, 2014. core.ac.uk/download/pdf/84871589.pdf.

Lane, Robert B. "Cultural Relations of the Chilcotin Indians of West Central British Columbia." Ph.D. diss., University of Washington, 1953. search-bcarchives.royalbcmuseum.bc.ca/lane -robert-brockstedt-1923.

Lange, Greg. "Smallpox Epidemic of 1862 among Northwest Coast and Puget Sound Indians." HistoryLink.org. February 4, 2003. www.historylink.org/File/5171.

Legat, Allice. *Walking the Land, Feeding the Fire: Knowledge and Stewardship among the Tłı̨chǫ Dene.* First Peoples: New Directions in Indigenous Studies. Tucson: University of Arizona Press, 2012.

Linnitt, Carol. "A Timeline from Birth to Death of Taseko's Embattled New Prosperity Mine in B.C." *Narwhal,* May 14, 2020. thenarwhal.ca/timeline-birth-to-death-tasekos-embattled -new-prosperity-mine-bc/.

Lutz, John Sutton. *Makúk: A New History of Aboriginal-White Relations.* Vancouver: UBC Press, 2008.

Lux, Maureen K. *Separate Beds: A History of Indian Hospitals in Canada, 1920s–1980s.* Toronto: University of Toronto Press, 2016.

Mandell, Louise. "Tracking Justice: The Constitution Express to Shared Sovereignty," *BC Studies* 212 (Winter 2021/2022): 165–204. doi.org/10.14288/bcs.no212.195688.

Mandell Pinder LLP. "Tsilhqot'in Nation v. British Columbia 2014 SCC 44 – Case Summary." June 27, 2014. www.mandellpinder.com/tsilhqotin-nation-v-british-columbia-2014-scc -44-case-summary/.

Manuel, Arthur, and Grand Chief Ronald Derrickson. *The Reconciliation Manifesto: Recovering the Land, Rebuilding the Economy.* Toronto: James Lorimer & Company, 2017.

McNeil, Kent. "Has Constitutionalizing Aboriginal and Treaty Rights Made a Difference?" *BC Studies* 212 (Winter 2021/2022): 137–164. doi.org/10.14288/bcs.no212.192441.

Ministry of Environment and Climate Change, Impact Assessment Agency of Canada. "Backgrounder: Proposed New Prosperity Gold-Copper Mine Project." October 31, 2013. Document reference no. 1185. ceaa.gc.ca/050/evaluations/document/98460?culture=en-CA.

Miller, J.R. *Shingwauk's Vision: A History of Native Residential Schools.* Toronto: University of Toronto Press, 1996.

Milloy, John S. *A National Crime: The Canadian Government and the Residential School System, 1879 to 1986,* 2nd ed. Winnipeg: University of Manitoba Press, 2017.

Mosby, Ian. "Administering Colonial Science: Nutrition Research and Human Biomedical Experimentation in Aboriginal Communities and Residential Schools, 1942–1952." *Histoire sociale / Social History* 46, no. 91 (May 2013): 615–642. doi.org/10.1353/his.2013.0015.

Mosby, Ian, and Erin Millions. "Canada's Residential Schools Were a Horror." *Scientific American,* August 1, 2021. www.scientificamerican.com/article/canadas-residential-schools-were-a -horror/.

Myers, Tony, Charlie Quilt, Henry Solomon, and Eugene Williams. *Chilcotin Stories.* Williams Lake, BC: School District 27, Chilcotin Language Committee, 1982.

Napoleon, Val. "Tŝilhqot'in Law of Consent." *UBC Law Review* 48 (2015): 873. heinonline.org /HOL/LandingPage?handle=hein.journals/ubclr48&div=29&id=&page=.

National Centre for Truth and Reconciliation. "Memorial Register." nctr.ca/memorial/national -student-memorial/memorial-register/.

Neary, Kevin. "Newcombe, Charles Frederic." *Dictionary of Canadian Biography,* vol. 15, *1921–1930.* Online. Toronto: University of Toronto; Québec City: Université Laval, 2003. www.biographi .ca/en/bio/newcombe_charles_frederic_15E.html.

Penn, Briony, with Cecil Paul. *Following the Good River: The Life and Times of Wa'xaid.* Calgary: Rocky Mountain Books, 2020.

Portelli, Alessandro. "Living Voices: The Oral History Interview as Dialogue and Experience." *Oral History Review* 45, no. 2 (2018): 241–242. doi.org/10.1093/ohr/ohy030.

Ross, Russell Samuel Myers. "Deyenz Lhuy Belh Nandlagh: A Story of Transformations." M.A. thesis, Indigenous Governance, University of Victoria, 2005. docplayer.net/174903590 -Udeyenz-lhuy-belh-nandlagh-a-story-of-transformations.html.

Sarich, Anthony. *Report on the Cariboo-Chilcotin Justice Inquiry.* Victoria: Cariboo-Chilcotin Justice Inquiry, 1993.

Sarris, Greg. *Keeping Slug Woman Alive: A Holistic Approach to American Indian Texts.* Oakland: University of California Press, 1993.

School District #27 Curriculum Team with the Tsilhqot'in National Government. *The Chilcotin War: Unit Plan and Resources.* 2019. www.tsilhqotin.ca/wp-content/uploads/2021/02 /TNG-Chilcotin-War-Unit-Plan_2020.pdf.

Sellars, Bev. *They Called Me Number One: Secrets and Survival at an Indian Residential School.* Vancouver: Talonbooks, 2013.

Shandro, Janis, Mirko Winkler, Laura Jokinen, and Alison Stockwell. *Health Impact Assessment for the 2014 Mount Polley Mine Tailings Dam Breach: Screening and Scoping Phase Report.* First Nations Health Authority. January 22, 2016. www.fnha.ca/Documents/FNHA-Mount -Polley-Mine-HIA-SSP-Report.pdf.

Simard, Susanne. *Finding the Mother Tree: Discovering the Wisdom of the Forest.* Toronto: Penguin, 2021.

Smith, Linda R. "*Súwh-tŝ'éghèdúdính*: The *Tsìnlhqút'ín Nímính* Spiritual Path." M.A. thesis, University of Victoria, 2008. hdl.handle.net/1828/934.

———. *Nabaŝ Oral Literature Documentation, October 17th, 2011–September 30th, 2012.* Final Report to Terralingua, a Collaboration Research Study with the Yunesit'in Government (Stone Band) and the Xeni Gwet'in Government (Nemiah Band). 2012. terralingua.org /wp-content/uploads/2018/09/Nabas-Oral-Literature-Documentation-Report.pdf.

———. *Nabaŝ: CEAA Panel Submission 2013.* 2013. www.ceaa-acee.gc.ca/050/documents /p63928/93512E.pdf.

Smitten, Susan, dir. *Blue Gold: The Tsilhqot'in Fight for Teztan Biny (Fish Lake).* 2010. 40 min. 57 sec. vimeo.com/9679174.

Solomon, Maryann. *Xeni Gwet'in First Nations Traditional Medicines.* Nemaiah Valley, BC: Xeni Gwet'in First Nations Government, 2004.

———. *Xeni Gwet'in Ancestral Laws and Customs / Xeni Gwet'in ʔEsggidam Dechen Ts'edilhtan.* Nemaiah Valley, BC: Xeni Gwet'in First Nations Government, 2012.

Starblanket, Tamara. *Suffer the Little Children: Genocide, Indigenous Nations and the Canadian State.* Atlanta: Clarity Press, 2018.

Swanky, Tom. *The True Story of Canada's "War" of Extermination on the Pacific, Plus the Tsilhqot'in and Other First Nations Resistance.* Surrey, BC: Dragon Heart Enterprises, 2012.

———. *The Smallpox War in Nuxalk Territory.* Surrey, BC: Dragon Heart Enterprises, 2016.

———. "Puntzi Lake and the Martyrdom of 'The Chilcotin Chiefs." Shawn Swanky (website). October 16, 2013. www.shawnswanky.com/articles/canadas-war/puntzi-lake-and-the -martyrdom-of-the-chilcotin-chiefs.

Swanky, Tom, and Shawn Swanky. *The Smallpox War against the Haida.* Surrey, BC: Dragon Heart Enterprises, 2023.

Teit, James. *The Shuswap* (1909). In *Publications of the Jesup North Pacific Expedition*, vol. 2, part 7; *Memoirs of the American Museum of Natural History*, vol. 4, part 7. Edited by Franz Boas. Leiden: E.J. Brill; New York: G.E. Stechert and the American Museum of Natural History, 1909. hdl.handle.net/2246/38.

Thistle, John. *Resettling the Range: Animals, Ecologies, and Human Communities in British Columbia.* Nature | History | Society series. Vancouver: UBC Press, 2015.

Tasker, John Paul. "'We Are Truly Sorry': Trudeau Exonerates Tsilhqot'in Chiefs Hanged in 1864." CBC News, March 26, 2018. www.cbc.ca/news/politics/pm-trudeau-exonerate-tsilhqotin -chiefs-1.4593445.

Truth and Reconciliation Commission of Canada. *Honouring the Truth, Reconciling for the Future: Summary of The Final Report of the Truth and Reconciliation Commission of Canada.* 2015. irsi.ubc.ca/sites/default/files/inline-files/Executive_Summary_English_Web.pdf.

———. *What We Have Learned: Principles of Truth and Reconciliation.* 2015. publications.gc.ca/collections/collection_2015/trc/IR4-6-2015-eng.pdf.

Tŝilhqot'in National Government. *Strategic Plan for the Management of Tŝilhqot'in Cultural Heritage.* 2022. www.tsilhqotin.ca/wp-content/uploads/2022/03/TNGStrategicPlanTsilhqotin Heritage.pdf.

Turkel, William J. *The Archive of Place: Unearthing the Pasts of the Chilcotin Plateau.* Nature | History | Society series. Vancouver: UBC Press, 2007.

Turner, Nancy J. *Ancient Pathways, Ancestral Knowledge: Ethnobotany and Ecological Wisdom of Indigenous Peoples of Northwestern North America.* Vol. 1., *The History and Practice of Indigenous Plant Knowledge.* Montréal and Kingston: McGill-Queen's University Press, 2014.

Turpel-Lafond Aki-Kwe, Mary Ellen. *In Plain Sight: Addressing Indigenous-Specific Racism and Discrimination in B.C. Health Care.* Addressing Racism Review Summary Report. November 2020. engage.gov.bc.ca/app/uploads/sites/613/2020/11/In-Plain-Sight-Summary-Report. pdf. (Full report: engage.gov.bc.ca/app/uploads/sites/613/2020/11/In-Plain-Sight-Full -Report-2020.pdf.)

Union of BC Indian Chiefs (UBCIC) and the First Nations Studies Program at the University of British Columbia. *The Constitution Express: A Multimedia History,* "Interviews." constitution .ubcic.bc.ca/node/133.

Union of British Columbia Indian Chiefs. Constitution Express Digital Collection. Website. constitution.ubcic.bc.ca.

VanStone, James W. "Material Culture of the Chilcotin Athapaskans of West Central British Columbia: Collections in the Field Museum of Natural History." *Fieldiana. Anthropology* 20 (May 28, 1993): 4–5. www.jstor.org/stable/29782599.

Verhaeghe, Crystal, Emma Feltes, and Jocelyn Stacey. *Nagwediẑk'an gwaneŝ gangu ch'inidẑed ganexwilagh / The Fires Awakened Us.* Tŝilhqot'in Report on the 2017 Wildfires. Williams Lake, BC: Tŝilhqot'in National Government, 2017. www.tsilhqotin.ca/wp-content /uploads/2020/12/the-fires-awakened-us.pdf.

Vowel, Chelsea. "Indigenous Issues 101." *âpihtawikosisân* (blog). N.d. apihtawikosisan.com /aboriginal-issue-primers/.

Webstad, Phyllis. *Beyond the Orange Shirt Story.* Nanaimo, BC: Medicine Wheel Education, 2021.

Weir, Lorraine. "'Oral Tradition' as Legal Fiction: The Challenge of Dechen Ts'edilhtan in *Tsilhqot'in Nation v British Columbia.*" *International Journal for the Semiotics of Law / Revue internationale de Sémiotique juridique* 29 (2016): 159–189. doi.org/10.1007/s11196-015-9419-8.

Whitehead, Margaret. *The Cariboo Mission: A History of the Oblates.* Victoria: Sono Nis Press, 1981.

Wickwire, Wendy. *At the Bridge: James Teit and an Anthropology of Belonging.* Vancouver: UBC Press, 2019.

Wikipedia: The Free Encyclopedia. S.v. "St. Joseph's Mission, Williams Lake." en.wikipedia.org/ wiki/Saint_Joseph%27s_Mission_(Williams_Lake).

William, Chief Roger. "Title Is with Me." *Northern Public Affairs* 4, no. 2 (May 2016): 27–31. whatis .fpic.info/files/npa_right_to_fpic.pdf.

William, Chief Roger, and Jack Woodward. *Sechanalyagh: A Book of Gratitude*. Victoria: Woodward and Company, 2007.

Williams, Jeremy, dir. *Tsilhqot'in Journey for Justice*. Episodes 1 (untitled), 2 ("Reconciliation Means Title"), and 3 ("Supreme Court of Canada"). October 31, 2013, November 4, 2013, and January 30, 2014. Exhibits U of T (University of Toronto Libraries): exhibits.library .utoronto.ca/items/show/2496; YouTube: youtu.be/QbjIPGqOaMs, youtu.be/xd3u7hS4yiI, and youtu.be/i3wJ6DFJkkc.

Womack, Craig. *Red on Red: Native American Literary Separatism*. Minneapolis: University of Minnesota Press, 1999.

Index

Lha yudit'ih We Always Find a Way

Index

Lha yudit'ih We Always Find a Way

Lha yudit'ih We Always Find a Way

LORRAINE WEIR is a fifth-generation descendant of An gorta mor Irish Famine survivors. Born in Tiohtià:ke Montréal, she grew up in Québec and Newfoundland. She was educated at McGill University and Ollscoil na hÉireann (National University of Ireland) and holds a Ph.D. in Irish literature from An Coláiste Oilscoile, Baile Átha Cliath University College, Dublin. Weir is an Emeritus Professor of Indigenous Studies, Department of English Language and Literatures, University of British Columbia, Vancouver.

CHIEF ROGER WILLIAM is the Plaintiff in the Tŝilhqot'in Title and Rights case. Born at Naghataneqed in Xeni, he is from the Bulyan family and is the great-great-grandson of Warrior Qaq'ez, older brother of Warrior Chief Lhatŝ'assʔin. Currently in his sixth term as Chief, he has also served three terms as Councillor for his community, Xeni Gwet'in. He did rodeo bullriding for fifteen years, mountainraced for thirty-two years, achieved thirty-eight first-place wins and twenty-six Championship wins over one hundred six mountain races, was Overall Bull Riding Champion in 1993, and won the King of the Hill Mountain Race Championship in 2012 and 2013. In recognition of his twenty-five-year contribution to the Title case, Chief William was awarded an honorary LL.D. by University of Northern British Columbia in 2015.

ADVANCE PRAISE FOR
Lha yudit'ih We Always Find a Way

If you want to know why Tŝilhqot'in law lives today, read this book. The Tŝilhqot'in people, lands, and spirit will inspire you. The book is very engaging, with great stories and helpful context. It is so rich, so clear, so beautiful. It shows resilience in the face of trauma and tragedy. It also does not shy away from challenges. It exposes hard truths and reaches great heights of spiritual understanding. It is deeply connective. It is inspiring. It is a treasure.
—**JOHN BORROWS**, Loveland Chair in Indigenous Law, Faculty of Law, University of Toronto

Like all Indigenous people across what is now called Canada, the Tŝilhqot'in survived atrocities and oppression in an uncompromising struggle for their territory, a territory that has generously enabled people and their culture to flourish for thousands of years. In return, they felt a sacred duty to protect that land. Despite systemic racism and an alien language and legal system imposed by colonizing powers, the Tŝilhqot'in people fought for and won the right to carry out their sacred responsibilities. It has been an honour and privilege to be a small part of this important story.
—**DAVID SUZUKI**, environmental activist and science broadcaster

A rich and compelling compilation of stories, experiences, teachings, and perspectives from members of the Xeni Gwet'in community of the Tŝilhqot'in Nation of British Columbia, *Lha yudit'ih* comprises the words of the people themselves: Elders, leaders, healers, residential school Survivors, grandparents and grandchildren, as well as some non-Indigenous allies. Filled with history and emotion, the contributors' words – some in the original Tŝilhqot'in language – all reflect a deep and abiding knowledge and love of the land and the people it has embraced. Some stories will make you weep, others will make you smile. Always, they bring a clearer understanding of a group of strong, independent, resourceful people who, despite immense obstacles, make their home in the mountainous, breathtakingly beautiful Tŝilhqot'in Territory.
—**NANCY J. TURNER**, ethnobotanist, author of *Ancient Pathways, Ancestral Knowledge*

This is a book about how an Indigenous community succeeded in gaining recognition of their Aboriginal Title through litigation in Canadian courts. For that reason alone, it is invaluable. More than that, it offers comprehensive information essential for an in-depth understanding of this case through a conversational voice that makes it accessible to everyone. It raises our awareness of the roles played by their friends in the settler community as well as the opposition they faced, and, most crucially, how they chose to work with those with whom they disagreed. Relying largely on voices from the community, it tells this story in a way that also offers invaluable insights into processes of attempted dispossession and resistance in British Columbia from first colonization. It is an excellent book all of us can learn from.
—**MICHAEL ASCH**, political anthropologist, author of *On Being Here to Stay: Treaties and Aboriginal Rights in Canada*

ALSO BY LORRAINE WEIR

Jay Macpherson and Her Works

Margaret Atwood: Language, Text, and System
(co-edited with Sherrill Grace)

Writing Joyce: A Semiotics of the Joyce System